Contents

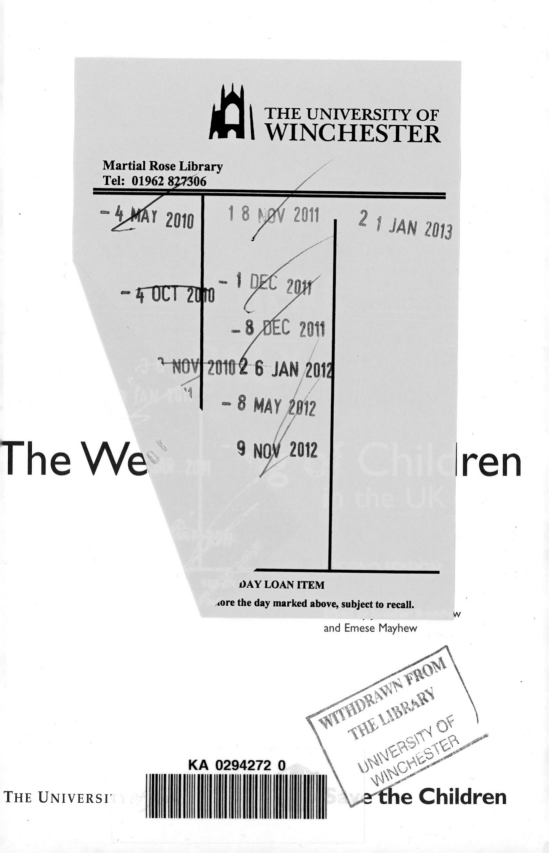

THE UNIVERSITY OF
WINCHESTER

Martial Rose Library
Tel: 01962 827306

The We...   ...lren

and Emese Mayhew

THE UNIVERSI...   ...e the Children

Save the Children fights for children in the UK and around the world who suffer from poverty, disease, injustice and violence. We work with them to find lifelong answers to the problems they face.

Save the Children UK is a member of the International Save the Children Alliance, the world's leading independent children's rights organisation, with members in 27 countries and operational programmes in more than 100.

Published by
Save the Children
1 St John's Lane
London EC1M 4AR
UK

First published 2005

© The Save the Children Fund 2005

Registered Company No. 178159

ISBN 1 84187 101 X

Typeset by Avon DataSet Ltd, Bidford on Avon, Warwickshire

Printed by Page Brothers, Norwich, Norfolk

List of contributors

Dr Bryony Beresford	Senior Research Fellow, Social Policy Research Unit, University of York
Professor Jonathan Bradshaw	Professor of Social Policy and Co-Director, Centre for Research on the Development and Well-being of Children, University of York
Bob Coles	Senior Lecturer in Social Policy, University of York
Naomi Finch	Research Fellow, Social Policy Research Unit, University of York
Dr Ian Gibbs	Senior Research Fellow, Social Work Research and Development Unit, University of York
Dr Carol-Ann Hooper	Lecturer in Social Policy, University of York
Deborah Quilgars	Senior Research Fellow, Centre for Housing Policy, University of York
Antonia Keung	Doctoral student, Department of Social Policy and Social Work, University of York
Emese Mayhew	Research Fellow, Social Policy Research Unit, University of York
Dr Joanne Neale	Senior Lecturer in Social Policy, University of York
Dominic Richardson	Doctoral student, Department of Social Policy and Social Work, University of York
Beverley Searle	Research Fellow, Centre for Research on the Development and Well-being of Children, University of York
Professor Ian Sinclair	Co-Director, Social Work Research and Development Unit, University of York
Dr Christine Skinner	Lecturer in Social Policy, University of York
Professor Patricia Sloper	Professor of Children's Health Care, Social Policy Research Unit, University of York

Professor Mike Stein   Co-Director, Social Work Research and
                                   Development Unit, University of York

Abbreviations

BCS	British Crime Survey
BMI	Body mass index
CAB	Citizens Advice Bureau
CASE	Centre for the Analysis of Social Exclusion
CEC	Commission of the European Community
CiN	Children in Need
CIS	Children's Information System
CLL AOL	Communication Language and Literacy Areas of Learning
COM	Commission Paper
CSIW	Care Standards Inspectorate for Wales
CtC	Communities that Care
CYPS	Children and Young People Survey
CYPU	Children and Young People's Unit
DfES	Department for Education and Skills
DHSSPS	Department of Health, Social Services and Public Safety (Northern Ireland)
DWP	Department for Work and Pensions
EAR	Estimated Average Requirement
ECHP	European Community Household Panel
ELR	Exceptional leave to remain
EPPE	Effective Provision of Pre-School Education
ESRC	Economic and Social Research Council
EU	European Union
FaCS	Family and Child Survey
FES	Family Expenditure Survey
FRS	Family Resources Survey
GCSE	General Certificate of Secondary Education
GDP	Gross Domestic Product
GHQ	General Health Questionnaire
GHS	General Household Survey

GOR	Government Office Region
HBAI	Households Below Average Income
HBSC	Health Behaviour in School-aged Children
HiB	Haemophilus influenza
HRBQ	Health Related Behaviour Questionnaire
HSE	Health Survey for England
IMD	Index of multiple deprivation
IS/JSA	Income Support/Income-Based Jobseeker's Allowance
JSA	Jobseeker's Allowance
LGA	Local Government Association
MMR	Mumps, measles, rubella
NACRO	National Association for the Care and Resettlement of Offenders
NAO	National Audit Office
NAPs	National Action Plans
NCB	National Children's Bureau
NESS	National Evaluation of Sure Start local programmes in England
NHS	National Health Service
NICHD	National Institute of Child Health and Human Development Study of Early Child Care
NICS	Northern Ireland Crime Survey
NIFRS	Northern Ireland Family Resource Survey
NISRA	Northern Ireland Statistics and Research Agency
NQ	National Qualifications
NSPCC	National Society for the Prevention of Cruelty to Children
NS-SEC	National Statistics Socio-Economic Classification
NTDS	National Travel Survey for Great Britain
NVQ	National Vocational Qualification
ODPM	Office of the Deputy Prime Minister
OECD	Organisation for Economic Co-operation and Development
Ofsted	Office for Standards in Education
ONS	Office for National Statistics
PISA	Programme for International Student Assessment
PSAs	Public Service Agreements
PSE AOL	Personal, Social and Emotional Development Areas of Learning

PSE	Poverty and Social Exclusion Survey
SALSUS	Scottish Schools Adolescent Lifestyle and Substance Use Survey
SCS	Scottish Crime Survey
SDQ	Strengths and Difficulties Questionnaire
SEN	Special educational needs
SHEU	Schools Health Education Unit
SID	Sudden infant death
SIDS	Sudden infant death syndrome
SILC	Survey of Income and Living Conditions
SOA	Income Deprivation Affecting Children Index at Super Output Area
SPSS	Statistical Package for the Social Sciences
SSU	Sure Start Unit
SWB	Subjective well-being
TFR	Total Period Fertility Rate
UASC	Unaccompanied asylum-seeking children
UNCRC	United Nations Convention on the Rights of the Child
UNICEF	United Nations Children's Fund
WFTC	Working Families Tax Credit
WHO	World Health Organization
YJB	Youth Justice Board
YLS	Youth Lifestyle Survey

Preface

Mike Aaronson

This new edition of *The Well-being of Children in the UK* contains a unique collection of evidence on children across the UK. It presents and analyses data covering 12 domains of child well-being: demography, child poverty, health, lifestyle, mental health, children's time and space, child maltreatment, children in and leaving care, childcare, children and crime, education, and housing. What it shows is that overall child well-being is getting better in line with the wider society - children are better off, surviving more births, and doing better at school. But there are some worrying trends. We have seen a downward trend in a range of health indicators: despite some decline since 1997, large numbers of children still live in workless households; children's use of public space is ever more restricted; and more are being excluded from school. The question is why are we failing children in these crucial areas of well-being?

Publication of this new edition of *The Well-being of Children in the UK* comes at a time when the question of child outcomes and child well-being is rising up the political agenda. Policy-makers are increasingly concerned about how best to measure the impact of policies and to ensure more effective implementation. Yet how can we fully understand the impact of policy inputs without knowing the effects they have on children? And how can we assess what policy interventions are required and are appropriate across the UK if we do not have a coherent picture of children's lives?

We began the last book with the observation that the UK does not produce a regular comprehensive analysis of the well-being of children. This is still true. Since the last report the United Nations Committee on the Rights of the Child has also expressed concern at the absence of a UK-wide mechanism to collect and analyse data on children. This is why, with the University of York, Save the Children decided to produce a new, expanded, UK-wide report, to highlight and fill this continuing gap. Since 2002 the Department for Education and Skills in England, the Welsh Assembly, the Northern Ireland Assembly and the Scottish Executive have each embarked on initiatives aimed at monitoring child outcomes. However, these are at various stages of development and have not been done in a co-ordinated way so that important lessons can be shared.

Of course, enhancing child well-being is not just about improving government policy. It is also about supporting families, looking at the circumstances in which children live and opening them up to different perspectives and outlooks. An understanding of children's lives is critically important for all of us working with and on behalf of children – from parents, teachers and social workers, to academics, policy-makers and government ministers. This book provides us with the information we need to ask the right questions about how to make children's lives better.

Acknowledgements

This project was steered by a Save the Children Advisory Group (Kate Bratt-Farrar, Anne Crowley, Susan Elsley, Michelle Foster, Goretti Horgan, Francis McGlone, Kath Pinnock, Margaret Thompson and Carol Sexty), and they and John Rowlands, Professor Mike Sullivan (University of Wales, Swansea) and Dr Kay Tisdall (University of Edinburgh) read drafts. We are very grateful for their comments and suggestions. Professor Eithne McLaughlin (The Queen's University, Belfast) acted as a consultant on our Northern Ireland material, for which many thanks. Finally, we are grateful to our liaison officer in Save the Children, Kath Pinnock.

1 Introduction

Jonathan Bradshaw and Emese Mayhew

About this book

This second edition of *The Well-being of Children in the UK* is an update and expansion of the previous edition published in 2002 (Bradshaw, 2002). It has been produced by a team at the University of York and is intended to be a discursive critical review of the evidence on the well-being of children, rather than merely a statistical compendium. All children, not just poor children, and children not families, are the principal focus of the analysis.[1] Although we have been pragmatic about the upper age limit of childhood, the book is not a youth study; it looks at both children and young people. Where possible we attempt to explore differentials in well-being over time, and by gender, age, ethnicity, class, and geographical area.

The book is not an evaluation of policies except in so far as an evaluation is implied by a focus on outcomes. It attempts to cover the whole of the UK and uses data available in England, Scotland, Wales and Northern Ireland, and where the data exist attempts to make comparisons between them. It is for the most part a review of the evidence – based on scholarship rather than original empirical work. However, some original secondary analysis of existing data has been undertaken and some as yet unpublished data are presented. For the most part, this volume stands alone and does not assume knowledge of the previous edition. In some chapters, where there is little new information, the data from the previous edition are not re-presented but rather referred to as a source.

The book also fills a number of gaps in the original edition – for example, on children's rights, child asylum-seekers, and children with learning disabilities and special educational needs. Moreover, there is an explicit recognition of children as economic and civil actors and more attention paid to the time and space of children. But due to lack of new data the coverage of other topics has

---

[1] We do, of course, recognise the role of others, particularly parents/carers in influencing children's well-being.

been reduced, including children as carers and teenage pregnancy and childbirth.

During and since the publication of the first edition, there have been some notable policy developments in the area of monitoring outcomes for children. In England, the Children and Young People's Unit (CYPU) was established and a strategy for children and young people published (*Tomorrow's Future: Building a strategy for children and young people*, CYPU, 2001). The CYPU has since been absorbed into the Department for Education and Skills (DfES) with the introduction of a new Minister for Children.[2] At the same time, a strategy for children and young people is under development in Northern Ireland.

At the time of the publication of the last volume, one possibility under discussion within the DfES was the regular publication by Government of a state of the nation report for children. However, it was clear that even if the Government decided to produce a state of the nation's children's report, this would be some time in the future. Furthermore, any such report produced by DfES would inevitably be on behalf of the Government and, given its remit, would be England-specific. It would also likely be a statistical summary, similar to the Government's annual poverty report, *Opportunity for All* (Department for Work and Pensions, 2001a, 2003, 2004b), which reports on a number of statistical indicators (see page 6). *The Well-being of Children in the UK*, published by Save the Children, is independent of government, is UK-wide, and offers a critical, discursive review of available data.

Likewise, while there continue to be many official sources of data on children's well-being,[3] the lack of any one study which analyses child well-being across the UK and which looks at trends over time, confirmed to Save the Children the need for a second edition of *The Well-being of Children in the UK*.

---

[2] Government bodies responsible for children's health and welfare have been centralised within the DfES: Children's Social Services, the Teenage Pregnancy Unit, the Family Policy Unit and Family Law Policy have all been transferred to the DfES. The Children and Young People's Unit, established in 2001, has merged with the Children, Young People and Families Directorate in the DfES.

[3] For example: Office for National Statistics *Social Focus on Children* (1994), *Social Focus on Young People* (2000), *Health of Children,* forthcoming; Office of the Children's Rights Commissioner for London, *The State of London's Children Report* (2001) (at the time of writing the Children and Young People's Unit of the Mayor's Office is working on a new volume); C. Horton (ed.) (2003), *Working with Children 2004-5,* NCH/Society Guardian, 2003.

The structure of the book

In the 2002 edition, we treated the topics in 23 separate chapters.[4] For this edition, we have organised the information into a fewer number of chapters in response to feedback received from readers. The Green Paper *Every Child Matters* (DfES, 2003b) was based on the outcomes framework developed by the CYPU. The outcomes framework was derived from a range of methods that aimed to find a consensus between children and young people, parents and carers and professionals working with or for children. The outcomes framework identified five domains (see Box 1.1)

Box 1.1 The Children and Young People's Outcomes Framework, DfES

- *Economic well-being*: having sufficient income and material comfort to be able to take advantage of opportunities.
- *Being healthy*: enjoying good physical and mental health and living a healthy lifestyle.
- *Staying safe*: being protected from harm and neglect and growing up able to look after themselves.
- *Enjoying and achieving*: getting the most out of life and developing broad skills for adulthood.
- *Making a positive contribution*: developing the skills and attitudes to contribute to the society in which they live.

For this edition, we considered adopting the five domains of the outcomes framework as our structure. However, we decided that collecting the material together under only five headings would lead to overlong and highly unbalanced sections. So instead, we have gone for something in between: a smaller number of longer chapters, which can be attributed to the well-being domains. Box 1.2 shows how the chapters broadly fall within the five DfES domains.

---

[4] These were: children and poor children; comparisons of child poverty and deprivation internationally; mortality; diet and nutrition; children's health; unintentional injuries; maltreatment of children; looked after children; young people leaving care and children who go missing; children as carers; childcare provision; teenage pregnancy and motherhood; the environment and children; homeless children; educational achievement; physical activity; truancy and school exclusion; children and crime; smoking, drinking and drug use; youth suicide; child labour; mental health of children; and conclusion.

Box 1.2 Distribution of chapters within the five domains

- *Economic well-being* is covered mainly in Chapter 3 on child poverty and to some extent in Chapter 13 on the environment of children.
- *Being healthy* is covered in Chapters 4 on physical health, 5 on Lifestyle and 6 on mental health and well-being.
- *Staying safe* is covered in Chapter 4 on physical health, Chapter 6 on mental health, Chapter 8 on maltreatment, Chapter 9 on substitute care and 12 on crime.
- *Enjoying and achieving* are covered in Chapter 6 on mental well-being, Chapter 7 on children's time and space, Chapter 10 on childcare and Chapter 12 on educational outcomes.
- Some elements of *Making a positive contribution* are also covered in those chapters and in Chapter 11 on crime. But there is a lack of evidence covering elements of this domain, particularly in respect of life skill, social skills, and participation in decision-making, volunteering and community service.

New to this edition are chapters on the demography of the child, and on children's time and space. The first provides necessary contextual information on the trends in child population, their spatial distribution, patterns of fertility and childbirth, children's parents and siblings, and the prevalence of family disruption. The latter provides data showing how and where children spend their time – including leisure, paid work and unpaid care.

The data in this volume are as up-to-date as possible at the time of going to press in January 2005. We continue to review the content, scope and coverage of these volumes and welcome comments, criticisms and suggestions.

What do we mean by child well-being?

At the University of York we have been engaged in research on the well-being of children since we were commissioned by UNICEF to write the UK report (Bradshaw, 1990) for its comparative study of the well-being of children in industrialised countries (Cornia and Danziger, 1997). We had originally worked on the UNICEF report as a sub-contractor of the National Children's Bureau (NCB), and the NCB funded an update of that review (Kumar,

1995). Then, as part of the Economic and Social Research Council (ESRC) Programme on Children 5–16 we were funded to undertake *Poverty: The outcomes for children* (Bradshaw, 2001a). In that book we conceptualised well-being as:

- physical well-being – including mortality, morbidity, accidents, diet, abuse and neglect
- cognitive well-being – mainly educational attainment
- behavioural well-being – crime, drugs, alcohol, tobacco
- emotional well-being – mental illness, happiness and self-esteem.

As we have seen with the DfES outcomes framework, child well-being has often been presented as a set of domains, which are informed by a variety of indicators. Some of the domains and indicators are concerned with children's well-*being* – how they are here and now, and some are concerned with their well-*becoming* – how they will do in adulthood. A balance has to be struck between well-being now and well-becoming in the future – not least because they may be in conflict. For example, society requires children to attend school in the hope that they will acquire knowledge and skills that will make them productive and successful adults. However, the stress of the exams that they have to take as part of this may have a negative impact on their current well-being.

The United Nations Convention on the Rights of the Child (UNCRC) contains 54 articles that cover every aspect of a child's life, applying without exception or discrimination to all children under 18. These articles can provide a framework for examining well-being. The articles of the UNCRC divide into the broad areas of survival rights, development rights, protection rights and participation rights. The Convention states that the primary consideration in all actions concerning children must be in their best interest and their views must be taken into account.

Given the central role of parents/carers in bringing up children, as established in law, an understanding of the influence they have on present and future child well-being cannot be ignored.[5] For example, the chapter on demography points out increasing numbers of lone mothers (due to increased rates of separation,

---

[5] A parent is responsible for the care and upbringing of their child and the Children and Young Persons Act 1933 imposes criminal liability for abandonment, neglect or ill-treatment upon any person over the age of 16 years who is responsible for a child under 16 years. The 1989 Children Act further emphasises the concept of parental responsibility, defining this as 'all the rights, duties, powers, responsibilities and authority which by law a parent of a child has in relation to the child and his property'.

e and unmarried motherhood). Is such a trend a significant contributing factor to changes in child well-being? Where possible this book highlights findings that illustrate the link between family type and child well-being.

The Government itself acknowledges the role of parents. In the *Every Child Matters* Green Paper for England, the Government expressed its intention to put supporting parents and carers at the heart of its approach to improving children's lives. To build additional capacity in this area, the Government has announced in the 2002 spending review the creation of a Parenting Fund of £25 million over three years for England (2003/04, 2004/05, 2005/06). It is also consulting on a long-term vision to improve parenting and family support through:

- universal services (such as schools, health and social services and childcare) providing information and advice and engaging parents to support their child's development
- targeted and specialist support to parents of children requiring additional support
- compulsory action through Parenting Orders as a last resort where parents are condoning a child's truancy, anti-social behaviour or offending.

Monitoring child well-being

In March 1999 in a speech at Toynbee Hall Prime Minister Tony Blair announced, "Our historic aim, that ours is the first generation to end child poverty forever . . . It's a 20-year mission, but I believe it can be done." He also said that it was the Government's intention to monitor progress towards that end.

The main vehicle for monitoring progress in England has been the *Opportunity for All* reports that have been published annually since 1999. These reports contain a set of indicators covering children, people of working age, older people and communities. The 23 indicators covering children and young people contain a mixture of Great Britain (ie, England, Scotland and Wales) and England data. The devolved administrations in Scotland, Wales and Northern Ireland have produced their own sometimes different indicators.

There has also been activity at a European level. At the Lisbon summit in 2000, the European Council agreed to adopt an 'open method of co-ordination' in order to make a decisive impact on the eradication of poverty and social exclusion by 2010. Member states adopted common objectives at the Nice

European Council and all member states drew up National Action Plans against poverty and social exclusion (NAPs/inclusion). The first UK National Action Plan on Social Inclusion 2001–2003 was published in July 2001 (DWP, 2001b). In December 2001 the Laeken European Council endorsed a set of 18 commonly agreed (Primary and Secondary[6]) statistical indicators for social inclusion that had been developed by a working party led by Atkinson (Atkinson *et al*, 2002). These indicators are useful for European Union (EU) comparison purposes because they are mainly based on the European Community Household Panel and the Eurostat Labour Force Survey and are therefore consistent between countries. They are not particularly child focused but some of the data are reviewed in Chapter 3.

In addition, member countries were encouraged to develop 'Tertiary' indicators, that is, more detailed indicators derived from national sources in order to provide more depth. The UK National Action Plan on Social Inclusion 2003–2005 (DWP, 2003c) has an annex which includes a set of tertiary indicators against which trend data from national sources are presented. These are more up-to-date than the primary and secondary indicators. Some of those that refer to children are included in the relevant chapters of this volume.

In its report, the Government also presents a list of targets, mainly those relevant to social exclusion. The targets include the UK Government's Public Service Agreements (PSAs) and local PSAs as well as targets set by the devolved administrations.[7]

There has also been an international collaborative project led by Professor Asher Ben Arieh to produce an international comparative set of indicators to monitor the well-being of children. The domains have been identified (see Box 1.3) and the indicators selected but as yet the data have only been gathered for some parts of the economic domain.

---

[6] So called by Atkinson *et al* (2002) on the grounds of their importance.
[7] Public Service Agreements are targets agreed between spending departments and HM Treasury in the process of negotiating public expenditure plans.

Box 1.3 Multinational indicators for monitoring and measuring child well-being

- Safety and physical status
- Personal life
- Civic life
- Economic resources and contribution
- Activities

Source: http://multinational-indicators.chapinhall.org

The participation of children in monitoring well-being

A recent review (Cutler, 2003) of the structures and resources for youth participation in the UK has identified some fundamental weaknesses. These included:

- the right to participate is not enforceable in terms of standards or legislation
- socially excluded young people are least likely to be heard
- there is a lack of clarity in objectives and parameters for decision-making, which results in tokenism
- funding is short-term or one-off
- projects are organised on adults' terms rather than young people's agendas
- there is little support and training for adults supporting young people.

In England the publication of the 2003 Green Paper *Every Child Matters* and the recent restructuring of child- and family-focused government structures have gone some way towards beginning to tackle some of these weaknesses, but clearly much more remains to be done.

In line with Article 12 of the UNCRC, many of the key organisations throughout the UK working with and for young people have policies to support their involvement in public decision-making. However, in practice, implementation is often patchy and the quality highly variable. We have, therefore, seen the introduction of a number of national standards frameworks, such as *Hear by Right* for English local authorities and *Charter Mark Save the Children* for public and voluntary sector services (Wade and Badham, 2004; Fajerman and Treseder, 2004). Others still are being developed, including the *National Service Framework for Children for the NHS* (DfES/Department of Health, 2004). In England the *Children and Young People's Participation Fund* was set up in the Department for Education and Skills to strengthen the existing participation infrastructure.

Another new and important development has been the establishment of Children's Commissioners in Wales, Scotland and Northern Ireland – with England soon to follow. Children's Commissioners are broadly defined as independent bodies set up to ensure that the rights of children and young people are upheld and that existing systems which work with and for children operate to the highest possible standard. Wales was the first to establish an office of a Children's Commissioner (in 2001). The first Northern Ireland Children's Commissioner took up his post in 2003. The Scottish Parliament passed its Commissioner for Children and Young People Bill in 2003 and the Scottish Commissioner took up her post in April 2004. In England, the Government's decision to appoint a Children's Commissioner was announced in September 2003 in the Green Paper *Every Child Matters* and was established under the Children Act 2004.

In addition to these broad developments, a raft of new initiatives across the UK signal the increasing importance afforded to children and young people's participation. With devolution, these have been developed and implemented separately in each of the four regions and countries.

England

In England the Children and Young People's Unit launched the *Learning to Listen: Core Principles for the Involvement of Children and Young People* (Children and Young People's Unit, 2001a) guidelines which affect all central Government departments in England that sign up to them. Currently 11 Government departments and the Youth Justice Board follow these standards. The National Youth Agency and the Local Government Association developed *Hear by Right*, which provides standards for the facilitation of youth participation for local authorities in England. *Hear by Right* is currently being piloted in nine local authorities and some have ascribed to it informally. The *Charter Mark Save the Children* was developed by Save the Children in collaboration with the Cabinet Office in 1999. It aims to set the standards for public sector organisations (including the voluntary sector) serving young people. The Connexions service in England was designed with young people's participation in the delivery and the evaluation of its services as fundamental. Each Connexions service has a Youth Charter developed locally with the involvement of young people, which is about the relationship between the service and young people (Cutler, 2003).

The DfES has published the *Children and Young People Survey* (CYPS) relating to children's schooling, teachers, aspirations for the future, subjects, bullying and participation in decision-making. The CYPS presently contains information taken at three stages: November 2002, February 2003 and June 2003. At each stage the survey included a representative sample of 7–16-year-olds in England – equating to 1,000 children, with about 100 students in each school year (Year 3 to Year 11). In the last wave of the survey, 80 per cent of children aged 11–16 agreed with the statement that 'There are opportunities for pupils to be involved in making decisions in how the school is run – for example through pupil councils'; 76 per cent of 11–16-year-olds agreed that 'When pupils are involved in making decisions on how the school is run, the views given by pupils are taken seriously by the school' (*Children and Young People Survey*).

Wales

Wales has set up arrangements at national, local, and school levels to enable children to participate in decisions. The national mechanism of child/youth participation is Funky Dragon – the Children and Young People's Assembly. Based on a network of local groups, the Funky Dragon Council meets regularly with the Welsh Assembly ministers of health and education. Every local authority in Wales has set up a Children and Young People's Forum which also provides the national representatives for Funky Dragon. There are plans to set up school councils in all maintained primary, secondary and special schools by July 2005. These will involve pupils in consideration of the day-to-day running of schools and of school policies (Welsh Assembly Government 2004a).

Scotland

Debates in the Scottish Parliament regularly refer to the need to consult with children and young people over national policy issues, while legislation has increasingly given children and young people rights to participate in decision-making and the planning of services. With nearly 200 elected young people aged between 14 and 25, the Scottish Youth Parliament aims to be the collective national youth voice for all young people in Scotland. While children had the right to have their views heard in certain areas before 1995, the Children (Scotland) Act 1995 incorporated the principles of the UNCRC in giving children the right to express their views in a far wider range of decisions. These include: court decisions on parental responsibilities; local authority decisions for looked-after (ie, children in the care of the local authority) children; and certain decisions made by courts and children's hearings. The Standards in Scotland's Schools Act of 2000 is a wide-ranging Act which has a significant impact on pupils' right to have a say in their education, both collectively and on some matters of individual choice. Education authorities need to have due regard to the views of pupils in decisions that will significantly affect them. The Education (Disability Strategies and Pupils' Educational Records) (Scotland) Act 2002 requires local authorities, among others, to produce accessibility strategies aimed at improving access to education for pupils with disabilities. The guidance which accompanies this legislation places an obligation on local authorities to consult with children and young people in the development of these strategies.

Northern Ireland

As part of the development of a ten-year strategy for children and young people in Northern Ireland, the Children and Young People's Unit of the Office of First and Deputy First Minister have set up an email facility to gather the opinions and suggestions of children on a better future for children and young people in Northern Ireland. The Statutory Duty for Equality in Northern Ireland introduced in 1998 requires participative policy-making processes involving consultation with those at risk of experiencing inequality or discrimination. More designated public authorities have implemented their age consultation duty in relation to older rather than younger people and children, pleading the difficulty of the latter.

The DfES outcomes framework (see page 3) was informed by a consultation exercise with children and young people. The choice of topics covered in this book has not been similarly informed. If it had been, the focus would inevitably have been rather different. There would have been less emphasis on children as victims, threats, apprentice adults, citizens in the making, and more on children as citizens now and actors with voices. At a recent seminar organised by Investing in Children, Durham County Council and Research in Practice, young people identified three issues that had an impact on their well-being:

- **Education**: *"UK law states that parents have the right to have their children educated, meaning the child has not rights themselves. This means it is easy for schools to treat children how they want with poor school meals, appalling toilets*

and intimidating behaviour by teachers. And if young people are unhappy with the way they are treated, apart from bringing a parent in there is often little that they can do about it. The use of uniforms and general atmosphere of schools means that young people can lose their sense of individuality and when they try to express this individuality they are named 'rebellious' or 'rowdy'. The only two places where workers are allowed to shout at the users are prisons and schools."
Jenny Cooke

- **Anti-social behaviour:** *"A bad example (of young people not being treated as citizens) is the introduction of a 9 o'clock curfew in Seaham, County Durham, aiming to keep groups of young people off the streets. The main reason that young people hang around on streets is because they have nowhere to go, but this was not considered when the curfew was introduced – young people were not consulted, neither were the police who have to enforce the curfew and experience increased taunting from unhappy young people. This has backfired, as young people now hang around on a street opposite the curfew boundary because they have nowhere else to go to socialise with their friends."* Emily Card

- **Transport and leisure:** *"The Investing in Children card allows young people to get half-price bus fares until they reach the age of 16 – after that they pay the full adult fare . . . the card can only be used after 6pm on a week night and all day on weekends – not during school hours. For people that are not entitled to free bus passes – they need to ride on public transport and pay full fares for the over-14s (during school time). Swimming baths and leisure centres are so expensive – nearly £5 to get into a gym and under-16s have to be out by 6pm. Connexions issues the card to all young people but this does not include discounted entry to leisure centres – it allows you to get a free burger at McDonald's – and they wonder why there is a problem with obesity?"* Ashleigh Greathead

Chapter 7 on children's time and space highlights some of the factors that curtail children's liberty in the UK. From this chapter it can be seen how easily the 'well-meaning' adult-led world loses sight of children as full citizens with human rights guaranteed by international convention.

Children who fall outside of child-well-being monitoring

There are particular groups of children who fall outside the well-being discourse, children who are likely to be most in need. We tend to know the least about their needs because they are small minorities and/or because they are not picked up in surveys or administrative statistics. They include children seeking asylum and refugee children, Gypsy/Traveller children and children with disabilities.

The UK has a reservation against UNCRC Article 22, which provides that special protection is to be granted to children who are refugees or seeking refugee status. Children over the age of criminal responsibility (ten years) could be arrested for entering the UK without documentation. Unaccompanied child asylum-seekers are too often left to fend for themselves in bed and breakfast accommodation and then face the prospect of being dispersed to a different part of the UK once they reach 18 (4 Nations Child Policy Network, 2003). At the same time, there are increasing numbers of child asylum-seekers in the UK. In 2002, 6,200 unaccompanied children aged 17 or under applied for asylum in the UK. Of those, 8 per cent (540) were granted asylum, 66 per cent (4,640) were granted exceptional leave to remain (ELR), and 15 per cent (1,040) were refused both asylum and ELR, in 2002 (Health et al, 2003).

The status of children in public policy

While the role of the family is key to securing a child's well-being, the impact of public policy is also important. Trends in public spending on children are a telling indicator of the priority accorded to children in public policy. Yet, there is no official index of overall public expenditure on children.

Save the Children has been making a contribution towards filling the gap. As part of a wider project exploring the impact of devolution on children living in Wales, Save the Children (Wales) commissioned Tom Sefton (2003) to undertake an analysis of spending on children in Wales, and also to make comparisons on spending in England and Scotland. Spending per capita in 2000/01 on all services (not just children's services) was £5,558 in Scotland, £5,302 in Wales and £4,529 in England. Table 1.1 compares spending on children in Wales and England. Spending per child is higher in Wales for all services and for each service except social services.

Table 1.1: Total estimated spending on public services on children £ per child, 2000/01

	Wales	England
Health	680	610
Education	2,180	2,000
Social services	240	260
Housing	220	200
Total	3,320	3,070

Source: Sefton (2003) Table 25

Between 1996/97 and 2000/01 spending per capita increased by 12 per cent in England and 8 per cent in Wales.

Save the Children (England) then, again, commissioned Tom Sefton (2004) to undertake an analysis of public expenditure on children in England and the extent to which it was concentrated on poor children. His findings included:

Health

- Between 1996/97 and 2000/01 health spending per capita on pre-school children rose by 40 per cent in real terms – well above average, while spending on school age children fell by 8 per cent in real terms (according to the Department of Health's own published estimates).
- The NHS priorities tend to be concerned with conditions that affect older people – eg, mental health, heart disease and cancers.
- It is probable that healthcare spending has become more skewed towards deprived areas since 1997. However, higher levels of funding for poorer areas does not necessarily mean that proportionately more is spent on poor children.
- Children from poor households are more likely to report general health problems, and so they may be using fewer health resources in comparison with their needs than children from better-off families.

Education

- Spending on school and pre-school education increased by 38 per cent in real terms between 1996/97 and 2002/03. This is greater than the rise in overall government spending over the same period.
- Spending has increased fastest for the under-fives.
- As a result of being more responsive to social needs, and because an

increasing share of the budget has been channelled through special initiatives, education spending has become more skewed towards the poorer areas since 1997/98.

Social care

- Spending on social services increased by 27 per cent in real terms between 1996/97 and 2000/01, and spending on children's services increased slightly more than this. This is despite the fact that central Government's allocation to local authorities for children's services fell by 3 per cent in real terms during the period.
- Spending per looked-after child gives an indication of local authorities' decisions. There is considerable variation in expenditure between local authorities and only a small part of this variation appears to be explained by need.

Housing

- Housing subsidies, both direct and indirect, were a very targeted form of help to low-income families.

Overall

- Families with children received much more subsidy than other households in 2000/01.
- Poor households with children received much higher subsidies.
- Targeted initiatives have grown since 1997 but make up only about 5 per cent of the total welfare spend on children.

The Sefton analysis:
- shows that overall spending on children has grown by 17–19 per cent in real terms between 1996/97 and 2001/02, and this is more than the growth in expenditure on pensioners and working adults
- estimates spending on poor children (those in families receiving either Income Support or income-based Jobseeker's Allowance) is, on average, twice as high as on non-poor children. For individual services, spending on poor children is between 1.06 and 1.35 times greater than for non-poor children in education, 1.03 to 1.43 more in health, 1.22 to 4.10 more in social care and 6.8 to 7.03 more in housing (and 3.66 to 3.75 more in social security)
- concludes that overall spending has become more pro-poor. For example, 'On

average, the difference in spending per child on education between the 10 per cent most deprived authorities and the 10 per cent least deprived authorities has increased from 16 per cent in 1997/98 to 24 per cent in 2003/04.'

Most of the Sefton analysis covers a period before the three-year phase 2003/04 to 2005/06 covered by the spending review (HM Treasury, 2002a; see also for Scotland: Scottish Executive, 2002d). In the period up to 2001, spending on health and education grew in real terms but fell as a proportion of Gross Domestic Product (GDP). New spending plans envisage an overall increase of 3.3 per cent per year in real terms between 2003/04 and 2005/06, and public expenditure as a proportion of GDP will rise from 39.9 per cent in 2002/03 to 41.9 per cent in 2005/06. This increase in spending is concentrated on education (7.7 per cent growth), health (7.3 per cent growth) and transport (12.1 per cent growth). Between 2000/01 and 2005/06, educational spending will rise from 4.6 to 5.6 per cent of GDP. By 2007/08, it is envisaged that UK health spending will reach 9.4 per cent of GDP – above the current EU average of 8 per cent. While this increase in spending is likely to benefit children, it may not necessarily do so. For example, the priorities identified for the increased spending on health are mainly concerned with adult health and could result in a relative shift in the gearing of health expenditure away from children.

Spending on children compared internationally

The other main source of data on children's spending is provided by the Organisation for Economic Co-operation and Development (OECD), which collects national accounts data and classifies them in various ways, including spending on family (with children) benefits and services. This does not include education and health expenditure, which is classified separately. There is also a note of caution with the data in terms of the inconsistent classification that is used between countries and over time. Nevertheless, an analysis (Bradshaw and Mayhew 2003) comparing spending on families and pensioners using these data does provide some interesting results.

Chart 1.1 compares overall expenditure per child. The UK comes in the middle of the distribution with expenditure considerably lower than the Nordic countries and Austria but considerably higher than the southern European countries and Japan. A lower proportion of UK family expenditure is spent on services than the high-spending countries.

Chart 1.1: Expenditure on family cash benefits and services in 1998 per child, US$ purchasing power parities

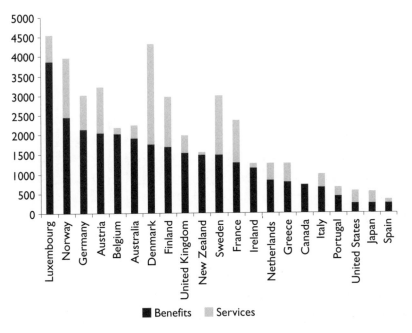

Source: OECD (2003) *Health Data 2003*

Chart 1.2 shows how expenditure per child has varied over time. In the UK it has been a comparatively constant proportion of GDP. In most other countries, expenditure on children has actually increased. The Netherlands is the only country with a consistently decreasing share of GDP spent on children over this period.

Anxiety has been expressed in the literature (Esping-Anderson and Sarasa, 2003) that with an ageing population in industrialised countries there may be a tendency for children to lose out in competition for public resources. Chart 1.3 shows spending per child as a percentage of spending per elderly person. All countries spend more on the elderly than they do on children, although the ratio varies considerably between countries. In the UK, spending per child fell as a proportion of spending per elderly person between 1985 and 1990 but has remained stable since then. In other countries there is a mixed picture with, for example, Sweden and the Netherlands reducing spending on children compared with the elderly and most other countries either steady or with increased expenditure on children compared to the elderly. Certainly there is as yet no consistent evidence of children losing out in the face of an ageing population.

Chart 1.2: Expenditure on family cash benefits and services per capita child as % of per capita GDP

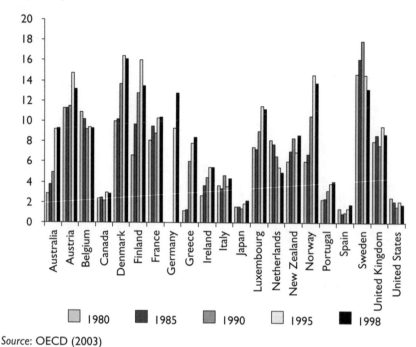

Source: OECD (2003)

Chart 1.3: Expenditure per child as percentage of expenditure per capita elderly, 1998

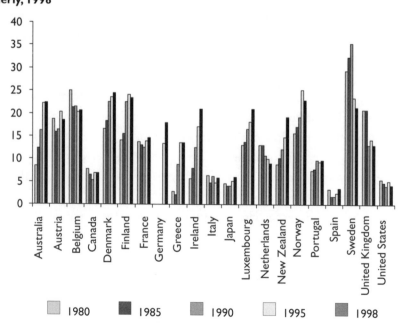

Conclusion

Children are our future. Their well-being matters to us all. As a nation we pay enormous attention to the well-being of our economy, the state of the weather, sporting league tables, the City and the Stock Market. Indicators of the performance of these have pages of the media devoted to them.

We need to begin to think more about the well-being of our children and we need to devote more public resources to understanding how they are doing. This book is a small contribution to that end.

2 Demography of childhood

Emese Mayhew

Key statistics:
- In 2002, there were 6,025,000 boys and 5,755,000 girls under 16 in the UK.
- The majority of British children are white (88 per cent), 4 per cent are black, 3 per cent are of Pakistani/Bangladeshi ethnic origin and 2 per cent are of Indian ethnic origin.
- In 2001, nearly one in four dependent children under 16 had experienced the divorce of their parents.
- In 2001, stepfamilies accounted for 8 per cent of families with dependent children in Great Britain.

Key trends:
- The proportion of children in the UK population has decreased from 25 per cent in 1976 to 20 per cent in 2002.
- Rates of childlessness among women increased: 9 per cent of the 1945 cohort was childless as opposed to 20 per cent of those born in 1965.
- In 1972, 7 per cent of children lived in lone-parent families; in 2003, 23 per cent did.

Key sources:
- Office for National Statistics
- Family Resources Survey
- Census 2001
- Millennium Cohort Study
- Eurostat Demography 2003

Introduction

This chapter summarises recent developments in the demography of children in the UK as well as their changing social relationships within the family. It uses new data to update the demography section of the previous volume and broadens the discussion to include the impact of demography on children's well-being. The chapter describes the demographic characteristics of children (ie, their numbers, gender, age, ethnicity and geographical location), their family composition and the consequences of modern family formation for children's lives.

Data sources

The main data source used is the Office for National Statistics (ONS), complemented by information from the 2001 Census and the Family Resources Survey. National Statistics supply some data in an aggregate form for England and Wales only. In order to gain more insight into inter-country and regional differences in the UK, data from the Millennium Cohort Study was used wherever appropriate. The Millennium Cohort Study is a new national birth cohort study that contains information about almost 19,000 babies born in the new millennium and their families. The sample was designed to over-represent areas of high child poverty, the smaller countries and regions of the UK (ie, Scotland, Wales and Northern Ireland), and areas with a high concentration of minority ethnic populations in England. The first sweep of data were collected during 2001/02 when the babies were aged nine months (Shepherd *et al*, 2003). The second sweep of data collection at age three is currently being done, while surveys of the children at age five and seven are being planned.

Demographic characteristics of children

Numbers of children

In 2002 the total UK population of children under 16 amounted to just under 12 million. There were 6,025,000 boys and 5,755,000 girls in all. Table 2.1 shows how the numbers and proportions of children under 16 have changed from 1971 to 2002, in each constituent country and region and the UK as a whole. Overall, the proportion of children in the UK has decreased by 5.6 per cent (from 25.5 to 19.9 per cent) over the 30-year period. The largest decreases in the proportion of children have been in Scotland and Northern Ireland, by 8.6 and 8.2 per cent respectively. At the same time the distribution of children among the four constituent countries and regions has shifted. An increasing proportion of UK children live in England: almost 84 per cent in 2002, compared to 82 per cent in 1971; and a decreasing percentage of children live in Scotland: 8 per cent in 2002 compared to 10 per cent in 1971. Children living in Wales and Northern Ireland are also making up a slightly lower proportion of UK children than they used to.

Table 2.1: Dynamics of the UK Child population 1971–2002

	England	Wales	Scotland	N. Ireland	UK
1971					
Thousands	11,648	686	1,440	483	14,257
% children in population	25.1	25.0	27.5	31.4	25.5
% children in UK	81.7	4.8	10.1	3.4	100
1981					
Thousands	10,285	626	1,188	444	12,543
% children in population	21.9	22.3	22.9	28.7	22.3
% children in UK	82.0	5.0	9.5	3.5	100
1991					
Thousands	9,658	589	1,021	417	11,685
% children in population	20.2	20.5	20.1	25.9	20.3
% children in UK	82.7	5.0	8.7	3.6	100
1999					
Thousands	10,010	594	995	408	12,006
% children in population	20.4	20.5	19.6	24.3	20.5
% children in UK	83.4	4.9	8.3	3.4	100
2002					
Thousands	9,830	582	955	393	11,759
% children in population	19.8	19.9	18.9	23.2	19.9
% children in UK	83.6	4.9	8.1	3.3	100

Source: ONS 2003g, 2004d

Age composition of the child population

Table 2.2 shows how the age composition of children in the UK has changed from 1971 up to 2002. The number of preschool-age children has been steadily decreasing since 1971, interrupted by a brief recuperation in numbers during the late 1980s to early 1990s. There has been slightly more fluctuation in the numbers of school-age children, but the overall picture is still that of decline.

Table 2.2: Number of children by age, UK, thousands

	1971	1976	1981	1986	1991	1999	2002
Under 1	899	677	730	748	790	704	660
1–4	3,654	3,043	2,726	2,886	3,077	2,896	2,747
5–14	8,916	9,176	8,147	7,143	7,141	7,688	7,586

Chart 2.1 shows the projected numbers of children in different age groups in the UK, based on 2002 estimates. Projections estimate the numbers of preschool-age children to remain more or less level over the next decade, followed by a small increase from 2011 onwards. Sustained low fertility rates (see Chart 2.2) are reflected in the parallel delayed drops in the numbers of each consecutive age group. The numbers of 5–9-year-olds and 10–14-year-olds will decrease until about 2010 and 2014 respectively, and following an initial increase, the numbers of 15–19-year-olds will be decreasing until 2019. After these periods of decrease, the numbers of children will recover slightly and level out in all age groups.

Chart 2.1: Projected numbers of children in different age groups (UK), thousands

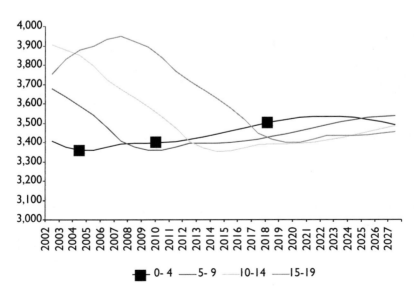

Source: Government Actuary Projections 2004

Fertility rates

The numbers and age composition of children reflect changes in fertility and birth rates. The total period fertility rate (TFR) (ie, the number of children a woman is predicted to have if current trends continue) has been low and relatively stable in the UK for over 30 years, dropping from 1.82 in 1991 to 1.65 in 2002 (provisional estimate). During this period, Northern Ireland experienced the largest drop in fertility among the UK constituent countries and regions, from 2.7 children per woman in 1976, to 2.16 in 1991 and a further fall to 1.75 (below replacement level) by 2000. Scotland has exhibited the lowest fertility rates since the late 1980s and has reached and maintained a record low fertility rate of 1.48 children per woman since 2000 (see Chart 2.2).

Period fertility rates are affected by changes in the number of children women have as well as by changes in the timing of having children. Late childbearing therefore can have a lowering effect on overall cohort fertility rates. The average age of mothers at first birth has been rising, from 23.9 years in 1971 to 29.7 in 2002 (provisional estimate) (England and Wales, ONS 2003g). This trend is reflected in the first wave of the Millennium Cohort Study: 35 per cent

Chart 2.2: Trends in (TFR) fertility rates, UK constituent countries and regions

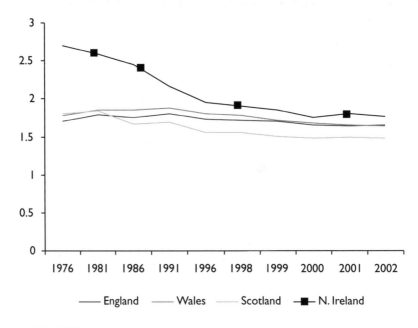

Source: ONS 2003g

of first-time mothers were at least 28 years old in Wales and Northern Ireland, and over 40 per cent of first-time mothers were aged 28 or over in England and Scotland (Table 2.3).

Table 2.3: Mother's age at first ever live birth, percentages (2001)

	England	Wales	Scotland	N. Ireland	UK
Less than 21	23	28	24	23	23
21 to 27	37	37	33	42	37
28 or over	40	35	43	36	40
Total	100	100	100	100	100
Numbers	14,661	949	1,695	631	17,936

Numbers = unweighted sample size
Source: Millennium Cohort Study 2001

Chart 2.3 shows the fertility recuperation rates for women born in various birth cohorts compared to the TFR of women born between 1945 and 1949. Due to delayed childbearing, the fertility rates of younger women are well below that of

Chart 2.3: Cohort fertility recuperation rates compared to the fertility rates of women born in 1945–49 (with a cohort TFR of 2.13 children) UK

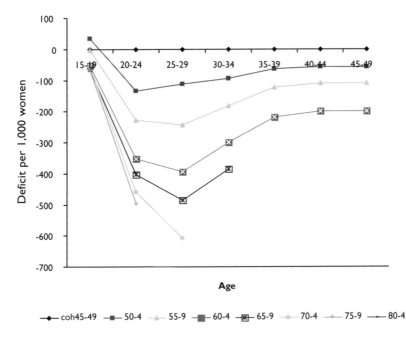

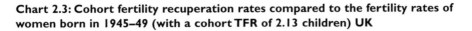

Source: Private communication from Professor Ron Lesthaeghe

the 1945–49 generation, but from the age of 25–29 onwards partial recuperation of fertility rates does occur, although they never reach the level of that of the 1945–49 cohort. Consecutive cohorts have similar patterns but increasingly lower rates of fertility.

Average family size

Rates of childlessness among women increased dramatically towards the end of the twentieth century. Only 9 per cent of the 1945 cohort of women was childless as opposed to 20 per cent of those born in 1965. While some women are voluntarily childless, others may be unable to have children due to fertility problems. The postponement of motherhood to later in life can lead to difficulties in conceiving (ONS 2003b). An increased rate of childlessness is complemented by a decrease in multiple birth orders (ie, the number of children a woman has), especially those of three and above. As a result, the average completed family size is getting smaller.

Table 2.4: Number of children and average completed family size by women's year of birth (projections in italics), England and Wales

Cohort born	1945	1950	1955	1960	1965	1970	1975	1980	1985	1990
Number of children (%)										
Childless	9	14	15	19	20	20	21	22	22	22
I child	14	13	13	12	13	14	15	15	15	15
2 children	43	44	41	40	39	40	39	40	40	40
3 children	21	20	20	20	18	17	16	16	16	16
4+ children	12	11	10	10	10	9	8	8	7	7
Average family size	2.19	2.07	2.02	1.98	1.90	1.87	1.80	1.78	1.76	1.75

Source: ONS 2003g

Children's ethnicity and geographical location

The vast majority of children living in the UK are of white ethnic origin. Table 2.5 shows the distribution of ethnicities among the four countries and regions of the UK. England and Wales are the richest in ethnic variation, while in Scotland and Northern Ireland children from non-white ethnic backgrounds constitute a very small proportion of the child population. In England and Wales, Asian/Asian British children represent the largest minority ethnic group.

Table 2.5: Ethnicity of Dependent Children* (% of all within countries) 2001

	England and Wales	Scotland	N. Ireland**
White			
English/Welsh	84.7	3.9	
Irish	0.36	0.3	99
Scottish	–	91.5	
Other white	1.7	1.1	
Mixed	2.4	0.5	0.4
Asian/Asian British			
Indian	2.4	0.4	
Pakistani	2.4	1.1	0.2
Bangladeshi	1.0	0.06	
Black			
Black Caribbean	1.1	0.03	
Black African	1.4	0.1	0.06
Other black	0.3	0.03	
Other	0.8	0.8	0.3
Total	100	100	100
Numbers	11,665,266	1,072,669	453,392

*Dependent children: aged 0–15.
**The Northern Ireland Census only provides ethnicity data in the main categories of:
White, Mixed, Asian, Black and Chinese or Other.
– No data available.
Sources: Census 2001: National report for England and Wales (ONS, 2004a); Scotland's Census 2001; Northern Ireland Census 2001.

Although the minority ethnic population only makes up 2 per cent of the total population of Scotland, a high percentage (20 per cent) of the minority ethnic groups (apart from Caribbean) are under 16 (Scottish Executive, 2004b). At the same time, the concentration of minority ethnic groups in Scotland is much higher in Glasgow, Edinburgh and Dundee.

Trends in family formation and composition

Marriage, cohabitation and lone parenthood

One of the main precursors of late childbearing is the postponement of marriage. The mean age of first marriage for women has risen from 23.1 years in 1981 to 28.4 years in 2001 (in England and Wales). The majority of births (59 per cent) still occur within marriage, so the postponement of marriage leads to later fertility (ONS, 2003g).

Marriage rates are continuing to fall. In England and Wales, the first-marriage rate of men in 2001 was 26 per thousand single adults as opposed to 75 per thousand in 1961. The first-marriage rate of women was 31 per thousand single adults in 2001 compared to 83 per thousand in 1961. Chart 2.4 shows the proportions of all live births to unmarried mothers of all ages and within selected age groups (ONS, 2003g). The overall rate of births outside marriage increased by 33 percentage points from 8 per cent in 1971 to 41 per cent in 2002. In 1971, 26 per cent of all live births to women aged under 20 were outside marriage; in 2002, 90 per cent were outside marriage. Having children within marriage is most prevalent among mothers aged 30-34; 26 per cent of live births within this age-group were outside marriage, which is the lowest among all age-groups.

Chart 2.4: Live birth rates outside marriage England and Wales

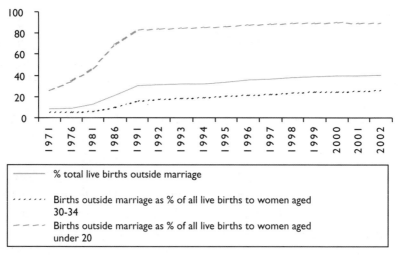

Source: ONS 2003g

The marriage rate in itself reveals increasingly little about household composition because of the significant increase in the levels of cohabitation, especially within the younger (25–34) age groups. While in the 1970s, over 50 per cent of unmarried mothers were lone parents, in 2002 this is by no means the case. These days most births outside marriage are registered by both parents living at the same address (64 per cent in 2002) and no more than 18 per cent of unmarried mothers are lone parents (Chart 2.5) (ONS, 2003g). Rates of cohabitation decrease while marriage rates increase by age, indicating that most cohabitation is a transitional period preceding marriage.

Chart 2.5: Registration rates of live births outside marriage UK

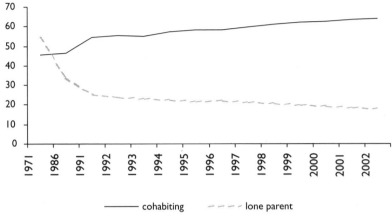

Source: ONS 2003g

The relationship between mothers' age and their partnership context is confirmed by findings from the Millennium Cohort Study (Kiernan and Smith, 2003). Marriage rates increase and cohabitation rates decrease with mothers' age (Table 2.6).

Table 2.6: Mothers' age and partnership context at birth of child (UK)

	14 to 19	*20 to 29*	*30 to 39*	*40 plus*
Married natural parents	9.4	53.5	75.5	72.5
Cohabiting parents	43.5	30.5	17.7	19.5
Lone mother	47.1	16.0	6.8	8.0
Sample size	1579	8667	7861	39

Source: Millennium Cohort Study 2001

Divorce and remarriage

In 2002 the divorce rate in the UK (per 1,000 adult population) was 4.8, which equals the EU average (Eurostat Demography 2003). Two-thirds of those divorcing have children under 16 (Maclean, 2004). Nearly one in four children are affected by divorce before their 16th birthday (ONS, 2001a). In 2002 almost one in four children affected by divorce was under five years, and just over two in three were aged ten or under (ONS 2004b). The divorce rate does not provide the full picture about children affected by the separation of their parents. It is more difficult to be precise about the numbers of separating cohabitants as the end of their relationship is not recorded in any public document. In 2001 the remarriage rate (per 1,000 divorced persons aged 16 and over in England and Wales) was 46 for men and 34 for women, which is about a third of what it was in 1981 and a quarter of the remarriage rate of the 1970s. There is a gap in official statistics that concerns re-partnering outside marriage.

Changes in the timing and ways of family formation, and increased rates of family dissolution and reformation, have increased the complexity of family forms. Children can become part of large networks of relationships including natural parents, grandparents, siblings, step-parents, and other step-relations, half-siblings and visiting children from parents' previous relationships. In England and Wales, in 2001, 65 per cent of children lived with both their natural parents, 11 per cent lived in a stepfamily and 23 per cent in a lone-parent family (ONS, 2004a). In Great Britain, in 2001/02, 8 per cent of all families with dependent children were stepfamilies, of which 83 per cent were headed by a stepfather and natural mother (ONS, 2003b). In Scotland, in 2001, 25 per cent of children lived in a lone-parent family and of these 92 per cent lived with the mother. At the same time, two-thirds of Scottish children lived in a married couple family and 10 per cent in a cohabiting couple family (Morrison *et al*, 2004). Table 2.7 shows the change in the composition of family types containing children in Great Britain. The percentage of children sharing a household with two parents and with no other or only one sibling has remained relatively stable

Table 2.7: Percentage of children living in different family types (Great Britain)

	1972	1981	1992	2001	2003
Couple families					
1 child	16	18	18	17	17
2 children	35	41	39	38	37
3+ children	41	29	27	25	24
Lone mother families					
1 child	2	3	4	6	6
2 children	2	4	5	7	8
3+ children	2	3	4	5	6
Lone father families					
1 child	–	1	1	1	2
2+ children	1	1	1	1	1
All children	100	100	100	100	100

Source: General Household Survey, Census, Labour Force Survey

between 1972 and 2003. The proportion of children living with two or more siblings has almost halved in couple families and tripled in lone mother families over the 30-year period.

The 2001 Census provides less-detailed information on family composition that is nevertheless available for all four constituent countries and regions of the UK, presented in Table 2.8. Over a quarter (26 per cent) of Scottish families are married couples without children, while a quarter (24 per cent) of Northern Irish families consist of married couples with dependent children. Cohabitation without children is highest in England, at 4.8 per cent. Northern Ireland has the lowest rate of cohabitation with children (1.6 per cent) and highest proportion of lone-parent families with dependent children (8.1 per cent).

Table 2.8: Percentage of families by type, Census 2001

	England	Wales	Scotland	Northern Ireland
Married couple family				
No dependent children	130.0	13.1	26.0	10.6
Dependent children*	17.6	17.5	16.0	24.3
Non-dependent children	6.0	6.6	–	8.0
Cohabiting couple family				
No dependent children	4.8	3.8	1.0	2.1
Dependent children*	3.2	3.4	3.0	1.6
Non-dependent children	0.3	0.3	–	0.2
Lone-parent family				
Dependent children*	6.4	7.3	7.0	8.1
Non-dependent children	3.0	3.4	6.0	4.6

*A dependent child is a person in a household aged 0–15 or a person aged 16–18 who is a full-time student.
– data missing
Source: Census 2001

Table 2.9 shows the proportions of babies born in different family types in the UK constituent countries and regions, within the sample of the Millennium Cohort Study. The results reflect the Census data in Table 2.8. In England, Wales and Scotland, about 60 per cent of babies were born in married couple families and a quarter of babies were born to cohabiting parents. Northern Ireland had the highest proportion of babies born to married parents (68 per cent) and the lowest proportion of babies born to cohabiting couples (15 per cent). Wales and Northern Ireland had the highest proportion of babies born to lone mothers, 18 per cent and 17 per cent respectively.

Table 2.9: Proportion of babies born in various family types, 2001 (percentages)

	England	Wales	Scotland	N Ireland	UK
Married parents	61	57	60	68	61
Cohabiting parents	26	25	26	15	25
Lone mother	13	18	14	17	14
Total	100	100	100	100	100
N	11,502	2,754	2,329	1,920	18,505

Source: Millennium Cohort Study 2001
N = sample size

Living in modern families: the outcomes for children

The outcomes of parental separation

All children experience some transition in their lives, and the separation of parents can be one of these. Parental separation is not an isolated event, but a process that starts long before a parent departs and continues throughout childhood (Maclean, 2004). Following parental separation most children undergo a period of unhappiness; many experience low self-esteem, behaviour problems and loss of contact with part of the extended family. Children of separated families tend to grow up in households with lower incomes, poorer housing and greater financial hardship than intact families. They tend to perform less well in school and gain fewer educational qualifications. They are more likely to leave school and home early and achieve less in socio-economic terms in adulthood. They tend to become sexually active, form a cohabiting partnership, and become a parent at an early age. Children of separated parents report more depressive symptoms and higher levels of smoking, drinking and other drug use during adolescence and adulthood (Rodgers and Pryor, 1998).

Although the differences in outcomes between children from intact and separated households are apparent, it cannot be assumed that parental separation itself is their underlying cause. There is a complexity of factors preceding and following divorce that make a crucial impact on children's experience of, and response to, the separation process. Financial hardship and other socio-economic circumstances play an influential role in limiting children's educational achievements (Kiernan, 1997; Joshi, 2000; Maclean, 2004). Parental conflict before, during and after separation is stressful for children and appears to be an important influence in a number of adverse outcomes, including behavioural problems (Maclean, 2004). Parenting problems after separation are often related to the circumstances that led to the ending of the relationship – eg, poverty, domestic violence (Wade and Smart, 2002). Parental divorce is often followed by a number of other changes that can be difficult for children, such as the arrival of new partners and possibly children in the household. Multiple changes in family structure appear to have an especially detrimental impact on children either in themselves or because of associated adversity (Rodgers and Pryor, 1998; Maclean, 2004).

The negative impacts of divorce on children can be minimised by effective communication and by sensitively listening to children's opinions about decisions that affect them. Wider kin networks such as siblings and grandparents can play an important part in supporting children and grandchildren through the time of separation (Perry *et al*, 2000; Dunn and Deater-Deckard, 2001). Continuing contact with the non-resident parent may benefit children's adjustment following separation (Rodgers and Pryor, 1998). The quality of relationships between parents and children, and between parents themselves, is important in helping children adjust to life after separation (Hawthorne *et al*, 2003).

Stepfamilies

Consecutive separations and re-partnerings result in 'aggregated families' containing a complex web of 'new kin'. For children with aggregated families, the separation of their parents is often only one major event in a life already full of fluctuations and change (Wade and Smart, 2002). Re-partnering often results in the improvement of household finances but creates new sources of tensions between children and their stepfamilies. Many children find it difficult to take discipline from a step-parent and feel insecure about their position in the family with regard to their step- and/or half-siblings (Dunn and Deater-Deckard, 2001). Becoming part of a stepfamily seems to be helpful for younger children but harder for older children to adapt to (Hawthorne *et al*, 2003). Older children have a higher risk of adverse outcomes, especially in areas of educational achievement, family relationships, sexual activity, early partnership formation and young parenthood (Rodgers and Pryor, 1998).

Only children

The reduction in the number of siblings and especially the growth in the proportion of only children raises the question whether 'only childhood' affects children's social development. The positive aspects of growing up in a small family are associated with reduced risks of experiencing poverty and increased parental attention devoted to the only child. There are, however, some possible drawbacks. Siblings can play a critical role in child socialisation (Parke and Buriel, 1998). Research shows that children with siblings have better conflict resolution skills (Patterson, 1986) and form closer friendships with peers (Stocker and Dunn, 1990) than only children. Children with siblings can learn through observing parent–sibling interactions and are exposed to experiences that provide the opportunity to learn to deal with differential treatment, rivalry and jealousy (Dunn *et al*, 1994). Also, inter-sibling interactions provide important practice for similar exchanges with peers and help children gain practice with affective perspective-taking and consideration of others' feelings (Youngblade and Dunn, 1995). Having a sibling can also be a source of support in periods of stress (such as parental divorce) (Caya and Liem, 1998). The social benefits of being a sibling have a bigger role in childhood than in adulthood. Self-report studies of adults have not found differences between adults with or without siblings in terms of social skills and social competence (Riggio, 1999).

Conclusion

Delayed fertility, falling birth rates and the relative instability of new family forms is giving rise to very different experiences of childhood both within and between peer groups. Children of the twenty-first century have a higher probability of experiencing parental separation, lone parenting, stepfamilies, visiting families, half-siblings and being an only child than children of any previous period of time. In 2003, a quarter of all dependent children lived in a household without other siblings. One in four children experience parental separation, one in ten live in stepfamilies, and almost one in four in a lone-parent family. Family disruption and its correlates are associated with increased risks of poverty, academic underachievement, behavioural problems, and early partnership formation and parenthood. Recent demographic changes challenge the well-being of UK children, and the outcomes depend on children's and their families' ability to develop strategies that help them to successfully adapt to changing circumstances.

3 Child poverty and deprivation

Jonathan Bradshaw

Key statistics:
- In 2002/03 28 per cent of children were living in poverty in Great Britain.
- In 2001, the UK had the fifth highest child poverty rate in the EU.
- Of the regions and countries in the UK, Wales has the highest child poverty rate before housing costs. However, after housing costs London has by far the highest child poverty rate.

Key trends:
- The child poverty rate has been falling since 1999/2000 and the Government should meet its target to reduce child poverty by a quarter by 2004/05.
- Only two of the *Opportunity for All* (DWP, 2004d) indicators for children and young people were moving in the wrong direction, although seven others showed no improvement in 2004.
- The UK continues to have the highest proportion of its children living in workless families in the EU.

Key sources:
- Households Below Average Income (HBAI)
- Family and Child Survey (FaCS)
- British Household Panel Survey (BHPS)
- European Community Household Panel (ECHP)
- Luxembourg Income Study

Introduction

This book is about all children in the UK not just poor children. However, the well-being of children is affected if children are poor, and, as we will see, most domains of current well-being are affected by poverty. Poor children are deprived of material assets, they experience higher morbidity and mortality, their activities and opportunities are constrained, they are more likely to be mentally ill and they are more likely to live in poor housing in poor neighbourhoods. Poverty in childhood has very strong associations with well-becoming. Child poverty is thus a very powerful indicator of the well-being of children.

The best measure of public concern for children is the extent to which children are protected from poverty. In 1999 the Prime Minister made the historic commitment to end child poverty in 20 years, and since then child poverty has been a cause at the heart of the domestic agenda. In this chapter we shall examine the progress that has been made towards that objective. In 1999 the first five-year target was set, but even if it is met, child poverty will remain a huge problem. The proportion of children living in relative poverty will still be more than double what it was 25 years ago and Britain will still have one of the highest child poverty rates in the industrial world.

Child poverty

Chart 3.1 shows that at the start of the 1980s the UK had a child poverty rate (using the now conventional definition of 60 per cent of equivalent median income before housing costs) of only 12 per cent. That rate more than doubled during the 1980s, continued to rise slowly during the 1990s and only since 1998/99 has it shown real evidence of a decline.

The Government's target is:

'To reduce the number of children in low-income households by at least a quarter by 2004 as a contribution towards the broader target of halving child poverty by 2010 and eradicating it by 2020. The target for 2004 will be monitored by reference to the number of children in low-income households by 2004/05. Low-income households are defined as households with income below 60 per cent of the median as reported in the HBAI statistics [DWP, 2004a]. Progress will be measured against the 1998/99 baseline figures and methodology.' (HM Treasury, 2002b)

Chart 3.1: Child poverty rate: percentage below 60% median contemporary income[1]

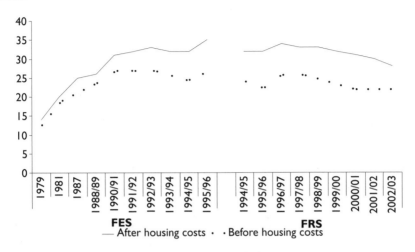

FES   **FRS**
— After housing costs · · Before housing costs

Source: Households Below Average Income (DWP, 2004a).

Because child poverty statistics are derived from survey evidence, the latest data at the time of writing is for 2002/03. Table 3.1 shows a reduction in the child poverty rate of 16 per cent before housing costs and 15 per cent after housing costs from 1998/99. However, given policies already announced and coming on stream, the general consensus (Brewer, 2004; Sutherland, 2004; House of Commons Work and Pensions Select Committee, 2004; HM Treasury, 2004a) is that the Government will certainly meet its 25 per cent reduction target by 2004/05 before housing costs and probably after housing costs as well.

Table 3.1: Percentage of children living in households with equivalent income less than 60 % of the contemporary median

	Before housing costs	After housing costs
1998/99	24	33
1999/2000	23	32
2000/01	21	31
2001/02	21	30
2002/03	21	28
% Change: 1998/99–2001/02	16%	15%

Source: DWP (2004a)

[1] The Family Expenditure Survey (FES) was replaced by the Family Resources Survey (FRS) from 1994/95 with a slightly different methodology – hence the discontinuity.

A slightly more up-to-date picture can be obtained from administrative statistics (DWP, 2004c) on the numbers of children living in families receiving Income Support (IS).[2] In November 1997, 2.314 million children under 16 were dependent on IS – that was roughly 20 per cent of all children. By May 2004 (the latest data available) that number had fallen to 1.922 million children under 16 – or roughly 16 per cent of all children. During this period, and especially after 2000, there was a substantial real increase in the IS scales for children that would have, all other things being equal, brought more families into eligibility for IS. So the fact that the numbers of children on IS has fallen is good evidence that child poverty has been falling.

The Government published its Sixth Annual Report *Opportunity for All* in September 2004 (DWP, 2004d). This is the main vehicle used by the Government to monitor its anti-poverty strategy. There are 23 indicators covering children and young people (see Table 3.2). Since the baseline year (mostly 1997), 12 indicators have moved in the right direction, four show no significant movement, for five there are insufficient data to tell, and two show data moving in the wrong direction. These are obesity for children under 16 and families in temporary accommodation – both indicators introduced for the first time in 2004. In addition to these, the latest results show that seven indicators did not improve in the latest year – children in workless households; persistent child poverty; teenage conceptions; school attendance; education gap of children in care; 16–18-year-olds in learning; and serious unintentional injuries.

Country, regional and area variations in child poverty

The Family Resources Survey[3] of 2002/03 was the first to include Northern Ireland, and so for the first time we are able to compare child poverty rates for all the countries and regions of the UK on a consistent basis (DWP, 2004a). Unexpectedly, given the survey evidence on deprivation, including the fact that wages are lower and a higher proportion of the population are dependent on benefits (Hillyard *et al*, 2003), Northern Ireland does not have the highest child

---

[2] This is not the same as 60 per cent of the median. However, 42 per cent of children living in families on IS had income less than 60 per cent of the median after housing costs and 75 per cent of children in families receiving IS were poor by this definition. So it is a useful proxy.

[3] The FRS has become the main vehicle for monitoring income poverty. It is an annual sample survey of about 25,000 households which was first launched in Britain in 1994/95.

Table 3.2: Opportunity for All indicators for children and young people

Indicator								
% children living in workless households (Great Britain (GB))	18.5 (1997)	18.5 (1998)	18.0 (1999)	16.4 (2000)	16.1 (2001)	16.7 (2002)	16.1 (2003)	15.9 (2004)
% children living in households with income below 60% of the contemporary median before housing costs (GB)	25 (1996/97)	25 (1997/98)	24 (1998/99)	23 (1999/00)	21 (2000/01)	21 (2001/02)	21 (2002/03)	
% children living in households with income below 60% of the median after housing costs (GB)	34 (1996/97)	33 (1997/98)	33 (1998/99)	32 (1999/00)	31 (2000/01)	30 (2001/02)	28 (2002/03)	
% children living in households with income below 60% of the 1996/97 median held constant in real terms before housing costs (GB)	25 (1996/97)	24 (1997/98)	22 (1998/99)	19 (1999/00)	16 (2000/01)	12 (2001/02)	12 (2002/03)	
% children living in households with income below 60% of the 1996/97 median held constant in real terms after housing costs (GB)	34 (1996/97)	32 (1997/98)	31 (1998/99)	28 (1999/00)	24 (2000/01)	20 (2001/02)	17 (2002/03)	
% of children experiencing persistent low income – below 60% median household income in at least 3 out of 4 years (GB)	20 (1991/94)	16 (1994/97)	17 (1995/98)	16 (1996/99)	16 (1997/00)	15 (1998/01)	16 (1999/02)	
% children experiencing persistent low income – below 70% median household income – in at least 3 out of 4 years (GB)	29 (1991/94)	28 (1994/97)	28 (1995/98)	27 (1996/99)	26 (1997/00)	25 (1998/01)	26 (1999/02)	
% of 5-year-old children in Sure Start areas achieving appropriate levels of development at the end of the Foundation Stage (England) CLL AOL of 24+ PSE AOL of 18+							54.6 75.1 (2003)	
% of 11-year-olds achieving Level 4 or above in Key Stage 2 tests for English (England)	63 (1997)	65 (1998)	71 (1999)	75 (2000)	75 (2001)	75 (2002)	75 (2003)	77 (2004)
% of 11-year-olds achieving Level 4 or above in Key Stage 2 tests for maths (England)	62 (1997)	59 (1998)	69 (1999)	72 (2000)	71 (2001)	73 (2002)	73 (2003)	74 (2004)
% of 16-year-olds with at least one GCSE A*-C (England)	44.5 (1996)	45.1 (1997)	46.3 (1998)	47.9 (1999)	49.2 (2000)	50.0 (2001)	51.6 (2002)	52.9 (2003)
% of 19-year-olds with at least a Level 2 qualification or equivalent (England)	79.7 (1996)	72.3 (1997)	73.9 (1998)	74.9 (1999)	75.3 (2000)	74.8 (2001)	74.8 (2002)	76.1 (2003)

Indicator	1995/96	1996/97	1997/98	1998/99	1999/00	2000/01	2001/02	2002/03
% attendances in schools (England)	92.4 (1995/96)	92.8 (1996/97)	92.7 (1997/98)	92.9 (1998/99)	93.2 (1999/00)	92.7 (2000/01)	93.0 (2001/02)	93.2 (2002/03)
% of children who live in a home which falls below the set standard of decency (England)		43 (1996)				30 (2001)		
Number of homeless families with dependent children in temporary accommodation (England) each March						39,810 (2002)	53,070 (2003)	64,340 (2004)
Admission rates (per 1,000) to hospital as a result of an unintentional injury resulting in a stay of longer than 3 days for children aged under 16 (England)		1.22 (1996/97)	1.14 (1997/98)	1.03 (1998/99)	1.04 (1999/00)	0.94 (2001/01)	0.95 (2001/02)	0.94 (2002/03)
% of 16–18-year-olds in learning (England)	76.3 (1996)	74.9 (1997)	74.8 (1998)	75.4 (1999)	75.4 (2000)	74.9[4] (2001)	74.7 (2002)	75.5 (2003)
% of young people leaving care with at least 5 GCSEs (grade A*–C) or equivalent (England)				7.3 (1999/00)		7.5 (2001/02)	8.5 (2002/03)	
Reduction in the proportion of care-leavers who are not in education, employment or training (England)						29 (2002)	32 (2003)	
Under-18 conception rates per 1,000 aged 15–17 (England)	45.9 (1996)	45.8 (1997)	47.0 (1998)	45.3 (1999)	43.8 (2000)	42.3 (2001)	42.6 (2002)	
% of teenage mothers in education, employment or training (England)			23.1 (1997/99)	28.2 (1998/00)	27.0 (1999/01)	29.4 (2000/02)	27.7 (2001/03)	29.7 (2002/04)
% under-18s re-registered on the child protection register (England)		19 (1997/98)	15 (1998/99)	14 (1999/00)	14 (2001/02)	13 (2002/03)		
Ratio of infant mortality rates per 1,000 live births in England and Wales of routine and manual groups/all (England and Wales)	1.15 (1994/96)	1.14 (1995/97)	1.12 (1996/98)	1.13 (1997/99)	1.14 (1998/00)	1.17 (1999/01)	1.16 (2000/02)	
Smoking rates: during pregnancy	23 (1995)				19 (2000)			
Among children 11–15 (England)	13 (1996)		11 (1998)	9 (1999)	10 (2000)	10 (2001)	10 (2002)	9 (2003)
Obesity trends among children 2–15 Boys	10.4 (1995)	11.6 (1996)	12.8 (1997)	13.2 (1998)	15.6 (1999/00)	14.6 (2001)	16.6 (2002)	
Girls	11.4 (1995)	12.0 (1996)	12.2 (1997)	13.5 (1998)	14.1 (1999/00)	14.0 (2001)	16.7 (2002)	

Source: DWP (2004d)

---

[4] 2001 onwards not comparable with previous years.

poverty rates. On the basis of the 60 per cent of median threshold, Table 3.3 shows that before housing costs Wales has the highest child poverty rates and after housing costs England has the highest child poverty rates. Wales has higher child poverty rates at the 70 per cent threshold both before and after housing costs. Analysis of the Millennium Cohort Survey by Mayhew and Bradshaw (2004) also found that Wales had the highest poverty[5] rate among the countries and regions of the UK.

However, there is controversy in relation to the Northern Ireland comparisons. There are some anxieties about the representativeness of the achieved NIFRS sample and work by Monteith and McLaughlin (2004) on the Poverty and Social Exclusion Survey (Northern Ireland) indicates that Northern Ireland does have a higher rate of child deprivation than the rest of the UK. We will probably need to wait until the NIFRS is bedded down before reliable comparisons can be made. In the end, comparisons using the same poverty threshold to compare Northern Ireland and the rest of the UK may be inappropriate because the cost of essentials is higher in Northern Ireland.[6]

Table 3.3: Child poverty rates by country/region

	50% median	60% median	70% median
Before housing costs			
England	10	20	32
Scotland	11	23	34
Wales	10	25	39
Northern Ireland*	11	22	33
After housing costs			
England	19	32	37
Scotland	17	27	36
Wales	20	30	42
Northern Ireland*	18	27	35

*Using GB thresholds.
Source: DWP (2004a)

---

[5] But using a rather different definition of poverty.
[6] With the exception of housing. However, families on IS get their housing costs covered. Such families in Northern Ireland are receiving less for their housing and paying more for other essentials.

Table 3.4 gives the child poverty rates before and after housing costs for the regions of England. It shows that inner London has by far the most serious child poverty problem both before and after housing costs, with over half its children living below this threshold. The North East has the next highest child poverty rate. The South East has the lowest child poverty problem both before and after housing costs.

Table 3.4: Variations in child poverty rates by English region, 2002/03. Percentage of children in households with equivalent income below 60% contemporary median

	Before housing costs	After housing costs
North East	38	37
North West and Merseyside	31	30
Yorkshire and Humber	30	30
East Midlands	29	29
West Midlands	30	29
Eastern	24	23
Inner London	56	54
Outer London	31	30
South East	21	20
South West	26	25

Source: DWP (2004a)

Administrative statistics on the number of children living in families receiving an income-tested benefit – IS or Income-based Jobseeker's Allowance (JSA) – enable us to explore the spatial distribution of child poverty by local authority and ward (DWP, 2004b). The DWP data on children in families on IS/JSA are available for England, Wales and Scotland. Noble *et al*, (2004) analysed these data for England and Wales for the Work and Pensions Inquiry on child poverty. I have reanalysed them and included Scotland. Table 3.5 lists the ten local authorities with the highest and lowest child poverty rates. Seven out of the ten highest are London boroughs. Glasgow City comes into the list at tenth highest. The highest child poverty rate in Wales is Merthyr Tydfil, ranked 22 – with 32.3 per cent of children poor. There is no local authority in the South East, the South West, the West Midlands or the East Region in the top 20 local authorities.

Table 3.6 lists the wards with the highest child poverty rates. Liverpool Granby Ward has the highest child poverty rate, with 72 per cent of children living in families receiving IS or Income-based JSA; Liverpool also has four wards in the top ten. Nine of the most deprived wards are in the North West. It

Table 3.5: Child poverty rate by local authority district

Top 10 local authorities	Child poverty rate	Bottom 10 local authorities	Child poverty rate
Tower Hamlets	57.5	Isles of Scilly	2.6
Islington	47.7	Hart	4.2
Hackney	45.4	Wokingham	4.9
Manchester	44.1	South Northamptonshire	5.0
Newham	43.1	South Cambridgeshire	5.2
Camden	41.8	Mole Valley	5.5
Haringey	41.5	Uttlesford	5.6
Liverpool	40.4	Rutland	5.8
Southwark	40.4	Surrey Heath	5.8
Glasgow City	40.3	Ribble Valley	6.0

Source: Own analysis of DWP (2004b)

is interesting that none of the top ten wards are in London. The highest London ward, Spitalfields, in Tower Hamlets, is 13th. The highest child poverty ward in Scotland is King's Park in Glasgow, with 56 per cent of children on IS/JSA. The highest child poverty ward in Wales is Townhill in Swansea, with 64 per cent of children on these benefits. No wards in the South East, the East, the West Midlands, the East Midlands, Yorkshire and Humberside or Scotland fall into the 50 most deprived wards.

Table 3.6: Child poverty rate by Ward

Local authority	Ward	Child poverty rate
Liverpool	Granby	71.9
Newcastle upon Tyne	West City	71.0
Liverpool	Everton	69.1
Knowsley	Princess	69.0
Manchester	Hulme	68.5
Liverpool	Vauxhall	68.5
Manchester	Moss Side	66.6
Knowsley	Longview	65.8
Liverpool	Smithdown	65.6
Wirral	Bidston	64.5

Source: Own analysis of DWP (2004b)

The latest iteration of the English Indices of Deprivation 2004 has published an Income Deprivation Affecting Children Index at Super Output Area (SOA) level based on children under 16 who were living in families in receipt of IS/ JSA (income-based) or in families in receipt of Working Families Tax Credit or

Disabled Persons Tax Credit whose equivalised income is below 60 per cent of the median before housing costs. The inclusion of the latter is an advance, because it means that families with children working for low pay are included. However, the index is only available for England. It is possible to use this data to plot the concentration of child poverty by SOA.

Chart 3.2 shows the child poverty rates ranked by the cumulative proportion of SOAs. Child poverty rates vary from 99.3 per cent in one SOA in Westminster, London, to 0.3 per cent in one SOA in the Chilterns. There are a large number of SOAs with few poor children: 50 per cent of SOAs have less than 14.5 per cent of their children in poverty, and 75 per cent of SOAs have less than 30 per cent of their children in poverty. There are a minority of SOAs with large proportions of their children in poverty: the top 10 per cent of SOAs have more than 45 per cent and the top 1 per cent of SOAs have more than 70 per cent.

Chart 3.2: Child poverty rates by ranked SOAs: England 2001

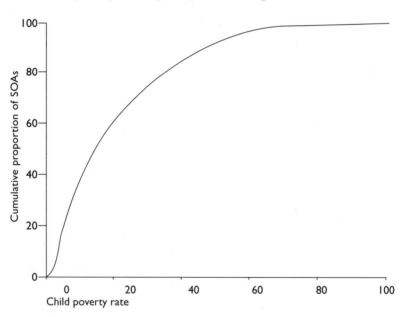

Chart 3.3 plots the cumulative proportion of child poverty against the cumulative proportion of SOAs. It is possible to use this to read off what proportion of poor children fall into what proportion of SOAs. Thus, we find that half of all poor children live in 21 per cent of SOAs, a third live in 12 per cent of SOAs and a quarter live in 8.5 per cent of SOAs.

Chart 3.3: Cumulative % of child poverty by cumulative % of SOAs: England 2001

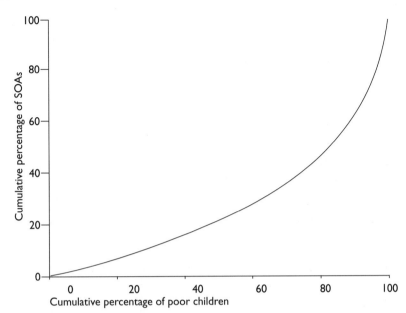

So there is no doubt that child poverty in England is concentrated in particular areas. However, there are SOAs with poverty rates in excess of 98 per cent within local authority areas which are otherwise fairly affluent – for example, there are two SOAs in Bristol with child poverty rates over 97 per cent and three SOAs in Westminster, London, with rates over 96 per cent. If a policy were concentrated on the poorest 20 per cent of SOAs (as was Sure Start), it would miss 52 per cent of all poor children in England defined in this way.

The characteristics of children in poverty

Table 3.7 provides a summary of the characteristics of children in poverty in Britain – both composition and rate:

- 45 per cent of poor children live with a lone parent, and 52 per cent of children living with a lone parent are poor. But only 15 per cent of the children of lone parents are poor if the lone parent works full time

- in couple families, children are very unlikely to be poor if both parents are in full-time employment – only 3 per cent are poor. But if neither parent is employed, 80 per cent of children are poor; 48 per cent of all poor children are living in workless households

Table 3.7: Characteristics of children in poverty (<60 median after housing costs): Great Britain data

	Composition (% of children in poverty who live in a household of this type)	Rate (% of children living in a household of this type who are poor)
Economic status and family type		
Lone parent	45	52
Of which		
In full-time work	3	15
In part-time work	8	33
Not working	35	76
Couple with children	55	21
Of which		
Self-employed	10	25
Both in full-time work	1	3
One in full-time, one in part-time work	5	6
One in full-time work, one not working	13	21
One or more in part-time work	9	58
Both not in work	17	80
Economic status of the household		
All adults in work	22	11
At least one in work but not all	29	32
Workless households	48	79
Number of children in the family		
One	20	25
Two	38	24
Three	25	32
Four or more	18	48
Disability		
Number of disabled adults	76	26
One or more disabled adults	24	39
No disabled children	88	28
One or more disabled children	12	31
Of which		
Number of disabled adults in family	6	25
One or more disabled adults in family	6	40
Ethnic group		
White	79	26
Mixed	1	34
Asian or Asian British	13	55
Of which		
Indian	2	22
Pakistani/Bangladeshi	10	75

	Composition (% of children in poverty who live in a household of this type)	Rate (% of children living in a household of this type who are poor)
Black or black British	5	46
Of which		
Black Caribbean	2	39
Black non-Caribbean	3	53
Chinese or other ethnic group	2	35
Benefit/tax credit receipt		
Disability Living Allowance	5	23
Jobseeker's Allowance	6	87
Incapacity benefit	5	42
Working Families Tax Credit	22	36
Income Support	42	75
Housing Benefit	46	74
Not in receipt of any benefit/tax credits listed above	26	12
Age of mother in the family		
Under 25	8	53
25 to 29	15	43
30 to 34	25	33
35 to 39	25	25
40 to 44	16	21
45 to 49	8	22
50 and over	4	23
Age of youngest child in the family		
Under 5	44	32
5–10	35	29
11–15	17	24
16–18	3	20
Tenure		
Local authority	35	60
Housing association	16	59
Private rented	13	53
Owned with a mortgage	29	14
Owned outright	7	23
Other	1	23
All	100	28

Source: DWP, 2004a

- 43 per cent of poor children live in large families (with three or more children) and nearly half (48 per cent) of children in families with four or more children are poor
- having a disabled adult in the household increases the risk of child poverty
- 79 per cent of all poor children live in white families. However, the risk of

poverty is much higher for children from Pakistani/Bangladeshi families (75 per cent) compared with white (26 per cent) but not higher for children in Indian families (22 per cent)

- 42 per cent of poor children are dependent on IS and a further 22 per cent are receiving Working Families Tax Credit (WFTC). 75 per cent of IS recipients are poor but only 36 per cent of WFTC recipients
- children are more likely to be poor if the mother is under 25 or under 29
- children are more likely to be poor if the youngest child in the family is under five years
- 36 per cent of all poor children are living in owner-occupied housing but the highest child poverty rates are among local authority or housing association tenants.

The first sweep of the Millennium Cohort Survey of a sample of 19,000 births in 2000/01 has become available and has been used to investigate the characteristics of children who are born poor (Mayhew and Bradshaw, 2004). The sample is very useful because, apart from its size, it is enhanced to over-sample minority ethnic births and births in poor areas. Mayhew and Bradshaw created an indicator of poverty by combining data on low income, lack of assets, a subjective measure of poverty, and dependence on means-tested benefits. They counted as poor any family who was poor on two or more of these dimensions. Overall 24 per cent of the 19,000 births were poor on this basis. Table 3.8 shows that the odds of being poor vary by the characteristics of the families. Before controlling for other factors, lone motherhood, mothers' highest qualification, paid work status during pregnancy and age are the strongest predictors of poverty after the birth. Being a lone mother increases the likelihood of experiencing poverty by 22 times, while working during pregnancy reduces the risk of poverty after childbirth by almost six times $(0.17***)$.[7] Mothers' highest educational qualification also has a significant effect on their chances of experiencing poverty. Those having an NVQ Level 5 qualification are 20 times $(0.05***)$ less likely to be poor than those who have no qualifications. Young mothers aged 14 to 19 at the time of their baby's birth are almost seven times more likely to experience poverty than older mothers.

These effects remain significant when mothers' employment during pregnancy, age, marital status, education level, number of previous children, ethnicity, type of

---

[7] */**/*** The asterisks signal the degree of significance of the results, ie, the degree to which having a characteristic, as opposed to not having it, is responsible for the change in poverty status.

Table 3.8: Odds of a child in the Millennium Cohort Survey being poor[1]

	Bivariate analysis	Controlling for all
Parents' marital status		
Married natural parents	0.11***	1.00
Cohabiting natural parents	N.S.	2.71***
Lone natural mother	22.08***	20.88***
Mother's highest qualification		
None on the list shown	6.05***	1.00
NVQ Level 1	2.51***	0.79**
NVQ Level 2	1.05***	0.54***
NVQ Level 3	0.72***	0.48***
NVQ Level 4	0.15***	0.29***
NVQ Level 5	0.05***	0.19***
Employment during pregnancy		
No	1.00	1.00
Yes	0.17***	0.29***
Mother's age at birth		
14 to 19	6.71***	1.00
20 to 29	1.59***	0.49***
30 to 39	0.28***	0.26***
40 plus	0.51***	0.26***
Mother's ethnicity		
White	0.58***	1.00
Mixed	2.75***	1.87**
Indian	0.45***	0.48***
Pakistani or Bangladeshi	1.71***	1.20
Black or black British	2.96***	1.52**
Other	0.95	1.23
Number of siblings of baby		
Only child	0.80***	1.00
1 sibling	0.74***	1.38***
2 siblings	1.35***	2.06***
3+ siblings	2.79***	3.39***
Country		
England	0.85*	1.00
Wales	1.36***	1.18*
Scotland	0.94	1.17
Northern Ireland	1.01	0.97
Type of ward		
Advantaged	1.00	1.00
Disadvantaged	3.08***	1.67***
High proportion of ethnic minorities	2.43***	1.74***

[1] The numbers in the columns indicate the extent to which the various characteristics we are looking at (eg, marital status, age, number of previous children, etc) predict the odds of being poor after childbirth. When the number is higher than 1, the presence of the characteristics increases the odds of being poor, and when the number is lower than 1, the presence of the characteristics decreases the odds of being in poverty.

*/**/*** The asterisks signal the degree of significance of the results, ie, the degree to which having a characteristic, as opposed to not having it, is responsible for the change in poverty status.

Source: Own analysis of the Millennium Cohort Study 2001.

ward they live in and country or region of residence are all controlled for. Everything else being equal, cohabiting mothers are almost three times (2.71***) and lone mothers are almost 21 times (20.88***) more likely to be poor than married mothers. Controlling for other factors, mothers gainfully employed during their pregnancy (and thus entitled to maternity benefits) are over three times (0.29***) less likely to be poor than mothers who had no paid work. Having any qualification significantly reduces the likelihood of poverty compared to having none. Being over 20 years old at the time of childbirth halves the probability of being poor and being over 30 years old quarters the likelihood of experiencing poverty. Every additional child in the household increases the risk of poverty. Mothers from a mixed minority ethnic background have the highest likelihood of experiencing poverty (1.87**), while mothers from an Indian ethnic background have the lowest likelihood of poverty (0.48***) of all ethnic groups. Compared to the other UK constituent countries and regions, mothers living in Wales are slightly more likely to be poor (1.18*); this latter finding is similar to the HBAI results which found that Wales had the highest poverty rate in the UK.

Severe poverty

In *Britain's Poorest Children* (Adelman *et al*, 2003) the authors combined three measures of poverty used in the Poverty and Social Exclusion Survey (PSE) in Great Britain (GB) – income poor, child deprivation and parent deprivation. Children were severely poor if they were poor on all three measures. The same method was replicated by Monteith and McLaughlin (2004) using the Northern Ireland PSE. Both surveys found that 8 per cent of children were poor on all three measures, but half the Northern Ireland children were poor on at least one measure compared to 45 per cent in GB.

Child poverty dynamics

It is arguable that a brief experience of living in poverty is less likely to be harmful to well-being than a long episode. There is a good deal of change over time in the population living in low-income households. While 50 per cent of individuals (not children) experienced an episode of living in the bottom two quintiles of the income distribution between 1991 and 2001, only 16 per cent spent five years in the bottom two quintiles and only 1 per cent spent all the 11 years in the bottom two quintiles (DWP, 2004a, Table 7.6). 'Children in persistent poverty' is one of the *Opportunity for All* indicators, and it can be seen in Table 3.3 (see page 41) that the proportion of children living in households with incomes below 60 or 70 per cent of the median in the last three out of four years did not fall in the latest period for which data are available. As this figure is based on a rolling four-year period derived from the British Household Panel Survey it is somewhat out of date and inevitably slow to change. Others, too, have used this source of data – eg, Hill and Jenkins (2001) traced child poverty episodes and spells over six years (1991–96) and found that 62 per cent had never been poor and only 1 per cent had been poor six times. Children 0–5 had the greatest risk of being poor more than three times. Nine per cent of children had been in poverty throughout the whole period.

Adelman and colleagues (2003) also used the British Household Panel Survey to explore severe and persistent poverty. They found that 9 per cent of children suffered severe and persistent poverty, that is, they were poor for at least three out of five years and had at least one year in severe poverty (ie, income below 27 per cent of the median). Children were more likely to be in severe and persistent poverty as a result of changes in their circumstances – eg, changes to their family's composition or changes to parental employment. Children whose family circumstances were stable but whose parents were long-term workless were also more likely to experience severe and persistent poverty. The Family and Child Survey (FaCS) (Vegeris and Perry, 2003) is becoming a more useful vehicle for studying poverty dynamics in Britain. Between 1999 and 2001 the proportion of families with children in severe hardship (using an index) fell from 26 per cent to 14 per cent, and the percentage of families in moderate hardship fell from 39 per cent to 35 per cent. Lone-parent families and large families were more likely to be in severe hardship.

The views of children

Since our last report there has been a welcome development of research that seeks the views of children living in poverty. Ridge (2002) interviewed children living in families dependent on IS. Among her findings she noted the following more striking observations:

- the extent to which children seek to protect their parents from the child's feelings of deprivation, including sometimes their hunger
- the extent to which they feel unable to have their friends round for meals or to stay

- the importance of grandparents and other relatives in providing extras that mitigate the deprivation of their lives
- the costs and inconvenience of public transport, particularly in rural areas, which restricts their lives
- the value of holiday schemes that give children the chance to get away
- the sense of shame and embarrassment when they are unable to dress like their peers
- they experience schools as exclusionary – unable to go on trips and outings, unable to contribute to school funds, ill-dressed and often identified as 'free dinner' children.

Crowley and Vulliamy (2002) also found that poor children were missing out and felt stigmatised at school.

Poverty and social exclusion

Using data collected in the PSE survey, Adelman *et al* (2003) sought to operation-alise the notion of social exclusion for children. As well as assessing income poverty they assessed the lack of assets and social activities and children's access to services. They found that children in severe poverty were much less likely to experience activities such as having friends round for tea or a snack once a fortnight because their parents could not afford it, and they were much more likely to be excluded from leisure facilities and activities which had to be paid for.

The UK National Action Plan for Social Inclusion commented especially on evidence of the very high level of financial exclusion (DWP, 2003c). The Work and Pensions Committee inquiry into child poverty was impressed by the body of evidence on the impact of debt (House of Commons Work and Pensions Select Committee, 2004). Many families with children on IS actually receive amounts of money which are well below the IS/JSA levels because of direct deductions from benefit to pay utility charges, Social Fund loans or other debts. Barnes *et al* (2004) found that a sixth of families were in arrears with bills and a quarter of workless families with children had two or more debts. The Citizens Advice Bureau (CAB) (2004) evidence to the Select Committee's inquiry found that consumer credit (including catalogue debt and doorstep collect credit with very high interest rates) formed a larger proportion of household debt than in previous years. The CAB concluded:

'It is difficult to address the issue of child poverty without addressing the issue of debt . . . initiatives must tackle irresponsible lending and borrowing, lack of access to affordable credit and access to advice.' (CAB, 2004, pp. 60–64)

International comparisons of child poverty

In our last report we presented evidence from a variety of sources which showed the following:

- Child poverty in the UK was comparatively high. The UNICEF (2000) report *A League Table of Child Poverty in Rich Nations* had found, using Luxembourg Income Study data for the mid-1990s, that the UK had the third from highest child poverty rate out of 25 countries, only less than Russia and the USA. Analysis of the European Community Household Panel (ECHP) showed that the UK had the highest child poverty rate of any country in the European Union (European Union, 2001).

- The UNICEF work and analysis by OECD (Oxley *et al*, 2001) also showed that the child poverty rate had increased faster in the UK between the mid-1980s and the mid-1990s than in almost any other industrialised country. During this period about half the countries in the analysis had experienced a reduction in their child poverty rates.

- Analysis of the ECHP and work by Bradbury *et al* (2001) indicated that the UK had comparatively high rates of persistent poverty among children.

- The UK had higher child poverty rates for three main reasons: the high proportion of lone-parent families; the high proportion of families without a parent in employment, particularly lone parents; and, probably most importantly, the tax and benefit package was comparatively less effective in reducing pre-transfer child poverty rates.

How have things changed? Chart 3.4 shows that in 2003 out of those EU countries for which there were data, the UK still had a much higher proportion of children living in workless households.

On child poverty, the Luxembourg Income Study data only take us up to 1999 for the UK, before the introduction of the increases in the real level of taxes and benefits made as a result of the Government's anti-poverty strategy. Chart 3.5 shows that in 1999 the UK still had one of the highest child poverty rates in industrialised countries.

Chart 3.4: Children under 17 living in workless householdsm 2003

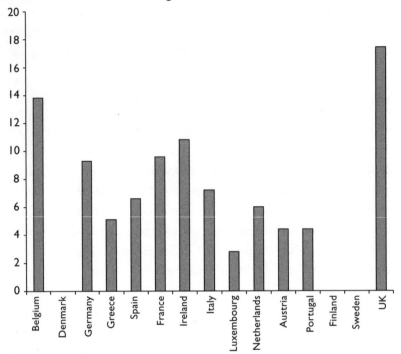

Source: http://europa.eu.int/comm/employment_social/soc-prot/soc-incl/sec_2003_1425_jir_annex_en.pdf

Chart 3.5: Comparative child poverty rates

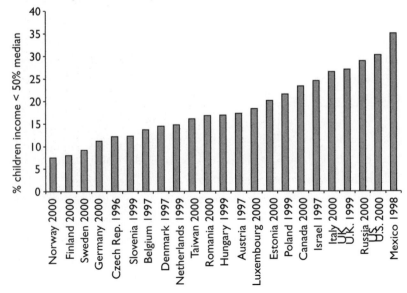

Source: Luxembourg Income Study, http://www.lisproject.org/keyfigures.htm

UNICEF (Corak, 2004) has recently updated its Report Card on child poverty. It concludes that only six out of 25 countries show a reduction in child poverty rates between the middle and the end of the 1990s and one of these is the UK, albeit from a high base.

A little more up-to-date data are available from the ECHP for 2001 (income data, 2000). Chart 3.6 is based on the EU analysis of the ECHP (Commission of the European Union, 2003). It shows that although in 2000 the child poverty rate in the UK was still the highest in the EU, by 2001 it had fallen to fifth from highest. The UK was not the only country to have seen a reduction in its child poverty rates over this period (child poverty also fell in Belgium), but the reduction in child poverty was greater in the UK.

Chart 3.6 provides a semi-official picture of child poverty in the EU in that it is based on one of the primary indicators of social inclusion endorsed by the EU in December 2001 at the Laeken European Council. These indicators had been developed by a working party led by Atkinson *et al* (2002). However, like all measures of poverty based on income, the indicators have weaknesses: they are based on a fairly arbitrary threshold; use an equivalence scale with only weak connections to science; they are before housing costs; and, are relative measures

Chart 3.6: Children aged 0–15 at risk of poverty, international comparison

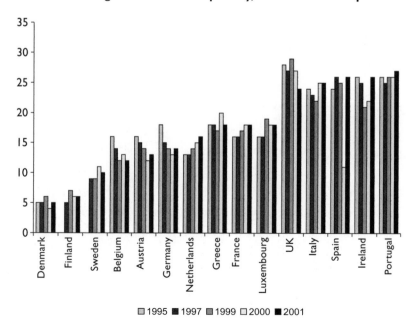

□ 1995 ■ 1997 ■ 1999 □ 2000 ■ 2001

Source: ECHP

that do not take account of the different costs of living between countries. These weaknesses have led Ritakallio and Bradshaw (2004) to investigate child poverty using other dimensions available in the ECHP. We report some of this work in the next section.

New thinking about how to measure child poverty

In Chart 3.7 we compare countries on a measure of subjective poverty: whether parents with children say that they have difficulty or great difficulty making ends meet. It can be seen that on this measure the UK comes much lower in the league table of countries.

Chart 3.7: Percentage of children in families making ends meet with difficulty or great difficulty

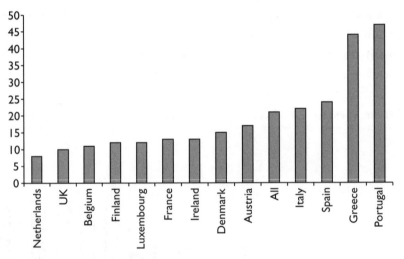

Source: Ritakallio and Bradshaw (2004), original analysis of ECHP 2001

Similarly, respondents to the ECHP were asked each of the nine questions:[8]

1. Can the household afford keeping its home adequately warm?
2. Can the household afford paying for a week's annual holiday away from home?

---

[8] There were two other questions which were not asked in the UK and have therefore been excluded in this analysis: Has the household been unable to pay scheduled utility bills, such as electricity, water and gas during the past 12 months? Has the household been unable to pay hire purchase instalments or other loan repayments during the past 12 months?

3. Can the household afford replacing any worn-out furniture?
4. Can the household afford buying new, rather than second-hand, clothes?
5. Can the household afford eating meat, chicken or fish every second day, if wanted?
6. Can the household afford having friends or family for a drink or meal at least once a month?
7. Has the household been unable to pay scheduled rent for the accommodation during the past 12 months?
8. Has the household been unable to pay scheduled mortgage payments during the past 12 months?
9. Is there normally some money left to save (considering household's income and expenses)?

By simply adding these items it is possible to establish a cumulative ordinal scale with a range 0–6. Chart 3.8 compares the proportion of children living in families lacking three or more of these deprivation items. Again, UK children do comparatively better in their relative position on this measure compared with income (although some countries have had to be excluded because of missing data).

Chart 3.8: Percentage of children lacking three or more deprivation items

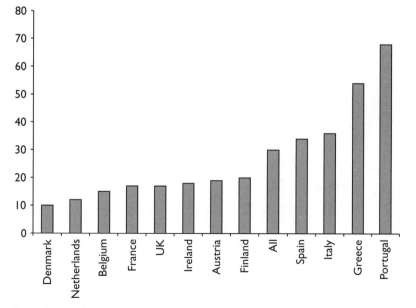

Source: Ritakallio and Bradshaw (2004), original analysis of ECHP 2001

Chart 3.9 compares the performance of countries on all three dimensions. In contrast to Denmark, for example, the UK, Ireland and France have higher child poverty rates on the relative income measure than they do on the other two measures.

Chart 3.9: Child poverty rates by dimension

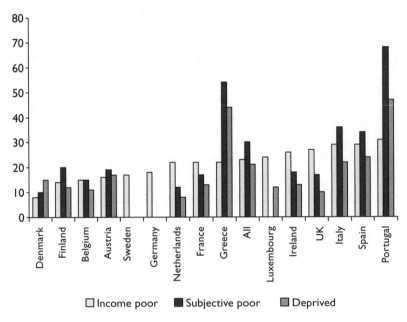

□ Income poor   ■ Subjective poor   ▨ Deprived

Source: Ritakallio and Bradshaw (2004), original analysis of ECHP 2001

We have used all three measures in developing what we call a 'true' measure of child poverty – that is, a child is only counted as poor if he or she is poor on at least two measures. The measure is true in the sense that it is arguably a more reliable and less relative indicator of poverty. This produces the distribution shown in chart 3.10.[9] Data are not available for all EU countries but there is much less variation between the poverty rates in the Nordic and northern EU countries, and there is a clear gap between them and the southern EU countries. Using this measure, it is possible to compare child poverty rates over time, compare consistent poverty between countries, and compare the characteristics of poor children.

Chart 3.11 compares the child poverty rates produced by this measure at 1996 and 2001. The child poverty rate fell in all EU countries except Denmark

[9] Sweden and Germany are missing from subsequent charts because the questions were not all asked in their surveys.

Chart 3.10: True child poverty rate: poor on two or more dimensions

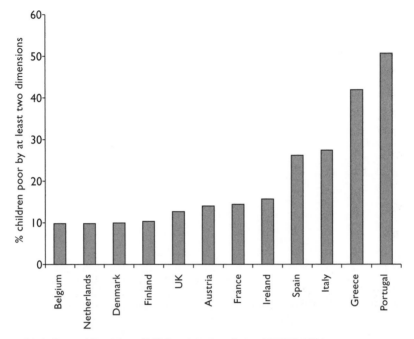

Source: Ritakallio and Bradshaw (2004), original analysis of ECHP 2001

Chart 3.11: True child poverty rates

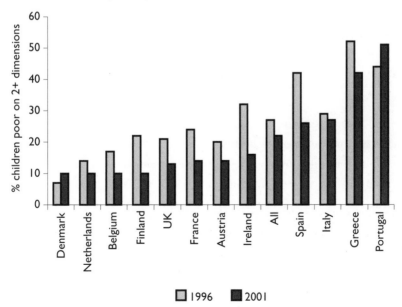

☐ 1996   ■ 2001

Source: Ritakallio and Bradshaw (2004), original analysis of ECHP 2001

and Portugal over this period. Child poverty rates have been cut in Finland and Ireland by one-half and in the UK by one-third.

Chart 3.12 presents the persistent child poverty rate using this true measure. It shows the proportion of children who were in poverty in two out of the last three years in 2001. The Netherlands has the lowest persistent child poverty rate; the UK is on a par with Belgium and France, with 6 per cent of children in persistent poverty.

Chart 3.12: Persistent true child poverty: poor in two of three years

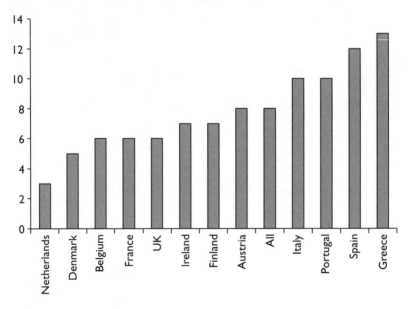

Source: Ritakallio and Bradshaw (2004), original analysis of ECHP 2001

Chart 3.13 shows the true child poverty rate by family type. The Netherlands has the lowest proportion of children who are poor in couple families but the largest gap in the child poverty rates between couples and lone parents: the child poverty rate in lone-parent families is 9.6 times that in couple families. In Denmark, the child poverty rate in lone-parent families is 4.8 times that in couple families, in Belgium it is 4.6 times, and in the UK 3.8 times. The rates are much more similar in the southern EU countries – in Portugal it is only 1.8 times.

In most countries, but not all, the child poverty rate in large families is higher than in small families. Chart 3.14 shows, curiously, that the biggest difference between the child poverty rate in large and small families is found in

Chart 3.13: True child poverty rate by family type

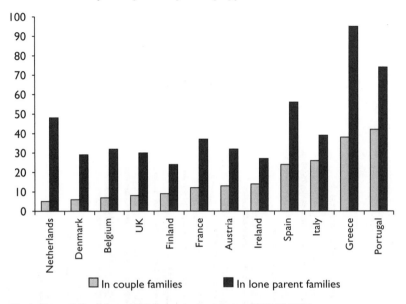

Source: Ritakallio and Bradshaw (2004), original analysis of ECHP 2001

Chart 3.14: True child poverty rate by number of siblings

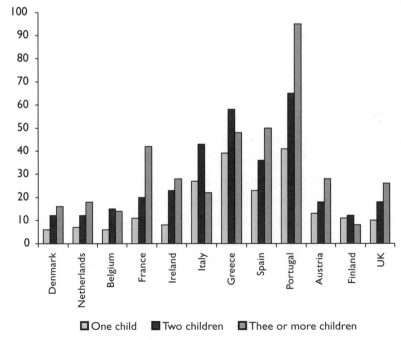

Source: Ritakallio and Bradshaw (2004), original analysis of ECHP 2001

France, a country which gears its child benefit package towards large families. Finland is the only country that maintains equity in its child poverty rate regardless of family size. Italy and Greece have rather irregular patterns.

Chart 3.15: True child poverty rate by employment

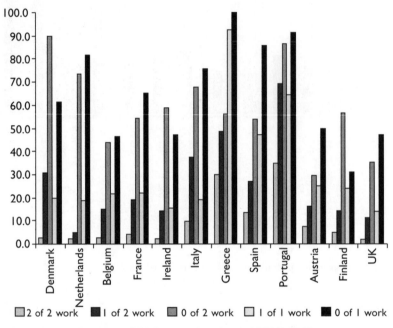

Source: Ritakallio and Bradshaw (2004), original analysis of ECHP 2001

Child poverty is much higher in all countries among children living in workless families but especially in workless lone-parent families. However, it also true that families with only one worker have appreciable proportions of children in poverty.

So, comparatively, things have got better, but it is still the case that in the UK not only is there a relatively high proportion of children living in workless families but also the tax benefit system is relatively unsuccessful in mitigating the child poverty that this generates. This is illustrated in Chart 3.16, which compares child poverty rates (equivalent income less than 60 per cent of median before housing costs) before and after income transfers.[10] It can be seen that the variation in child poverty rates before transfers is much less than after transfers, and that, for example, Sweden and the UK had identical child poverty rates before transfers

---

[10] Before-transfer income is income from the market place – mainly earnings. After-transfer income is after the impact of taxes and benefits (but not services).

Chart 3.16: Children 0–15 at risk of poverty 2001(ECHP)

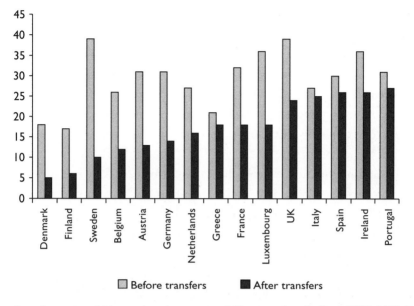

Source: http://europa.eu.int/comm/employment_social/soc-prot/soc-incl/sec_2003_1425_jir_annex_en.pdf

but after the impact of transfers Sweden had reduced theirs by about 75 per cent whereas the UK reduced theirs by only 40 per cent. This is a better poverty reduction rate than the southern EU countries but in comparison with the other countries it could be much more effective. Policy does matter.

Conclusion

The UK has moved from the EU country with the highest child poverty rates to tenth highest out of 15. There is welcome evidence that child poverty in the UK is beginning to decline. The Government should reach its target to reduce child poverty by a quarter by 2004/05. However, child poverty will still be more than double the rate it was in 1979, and will still be comparatively high given the level of our national wealth. Child poverty is also very concentrated geographically and in certain types of household. The proportion of children in workless households is still comparatively high in the UK, despite the fact that unemployment is at its lowest level for over three decades.

From 2004/05 the Government will be introducing a new, three-tiered system for headline measures of child poverty that includes a measure which will combine relative low income and deprivation (DWP, 2003a). It has been criticised by the Work and Pensions Committee (House of Commons Work and Pensions Select Committee, 2004), among others, for adopting a before-housing costs measure in line with EU practice. However, after-housing costs poverty rates will still be published, and with new questions on deprivation being added to the Family Resources Survey, as well as the Family and Child Survey becoming a more useful vehicle for monitoring child poverty over time, there is an adequate array of data sources on poverty.

The Survey of Income and Living Conditions (SILC) is to begin to replace the European Community Household Panel from 2004. It is too early to say whether it will be a better vehicle for monitoring poverty and social exclusion, but it will cover more countries. Comparative data will inevitably continue to provide a somewhat historical picture of child poverty, but comparative research is still worth doing for the insights it presents and because the Government has now set itself a comparative target.

As far as the Government is concerned, beyond 2004/05 child poverty will be said to be falling when all three of the new indicators are moving in the right direction and eradicated when no children are materially deprived and when the UK is ranked *'amongst the best in Europe on relative low incomes'* (DWP, 2004e). There is a very long way to go to achieve that objective.

4 Physical health

Bryony Beresford, Tricia Sloper and Jonathan Bradshaw

Key statistics:

- UK infant mortality rates are higher than those of most other European countries.
- In 2000, the UK had one of the highest proportions of low birth weight live births in the Organisation for Economic Co-operation and Development (OECD).
- In England and Wales in 2002, 73 per cent of babies were initially breastfed.
- In the UK, 8 per cent of boys and 6 per cent of girls are reported by their parents as having a limiting, longstanding illness.
- The UK is one of the European countries with the highest number of children being born to HIV-positive mothers. In the past three years, 374 children have become HIV positive and 28 children have died.
- Thirty per cent of men and 26 per cent of women report having first intercourse at younger than 16 years.
- The birth rate among women under 20 years in the UK was the second highest out of 28 OECD countries.

Key trends:

- The long-term downward trend in infant and child mortality has continued and the infant mortality rate for the UK is the lowest ever recorded.
- The gap between the infant mortality rate of routine and manual social groups and all social groups has been growing since 1996/98.
- There has been a recent rise in stillbirths in England, Wales and Northern Ireland.
- The number of sudden infant deaths has continued to decline.
- The number of low birth weight babies being born is increasing.
- In 1997 in England and Wales nine out of ten children had been immunised against measles, mumps and rubella (MMR); in 2003 this

figure had fallen to eight out of ten children. There have also been falls in immunisation rates in Scotland and Northern Ireland.

- There has been an increase in notifications of measles and mumps.
- Incidence rates of Type 1 diabetes and asthma (in children over seven years) continue to rise.
- Cases of genital chlamydia, gonorrhoea and syphilis have continued to rise.
- Annual figures for the number of child pedestrian deaths or serious injuries in Great Britain is declining among all age groups and for both boys and girls.

Key sources:
- Office for National Statistics
- Northern Ireland Statistics and Research Agency
- General Register for Scotland
- ISD Scotland (NHS National Services, Scotland)
- OECD
- UNICEF
- World Health Organization (WHO) Health Behaviour in School-aged Children (HBSC) Survey
- Department for Transport
- National Survey of Sexual Attitudes and Lifestyles

Introduction

The previous edition of this book explored the physical health of children and health issues in a number of different chapters covering mortality, diet and nutrition, health, unintentional injury, teenage pregnancy and teenage motherhood, and smoking, drinking alcohol and drug use. In this current edition, issues of physical health are brought together into two chapters. This chapter will report on children's physical health and ill-health, and the following chapter looks at children's lifestyle and its impact on health. Mental health and well-being is dealt with in Chapter 6.

This chapter spans birth to early adulthood and necessarily can only provide an overview of data on what are regarded as the key health outcomes and emerging health issues for children in 2004. Thus, the topics covered include child and infant mortality, birth weight, immunisations, self-reported health, longstanding illnesses and chronic conditions, non-intentional accidents and injuries, HIV/AIDS, sexual health and teenage conceptions. In the main we have restricted our report to children aged 16 years and under, although in terms of sexual health we also report data for young people aged 16 to 19 years.

The purpose of this book is to monitor and reflect on changes in indicators of child well-being for children living in the UK, and where possible to offer comparisons with what is known about children living in other countries. As in the previous edition, we also explore, where possible, the association between social, demographic and economic factors and child health. It has not always been possible to update the data reported in the previous edition as it is not always the case that new data have been collected in the interim period. In some instances, data have been updated for one UK country or region, but not for others. However, it should be said that sufficient new data have been collected and made available to ensure this chapter contains much new, and valuable, information in terms of emerging health issues and trends in existing indicators of child health.

Infant and child mortality

In the previous edition of this book, we examined in some detail infant and child mortality, and the factors associated with higher or lower mortality rates (Sloper and Quilgars, 2002). At that time the most recent mortality statistics for the four countries and regions of the UK were for 1999. Statistics are now available for years up to and including 2002. This section will provide an update on these statistics and on research concerning factors associated with mortality rates.

Definitions and sources of data

Mortality statistics are produced annually in the UK by the Northern Ireland Statistics Research Agency (NISRA), Information and Statistics Division Scotland, and Office for National Statistics (ONS) (covering England and Wales). These are based on information recorded on registration of deaths. Official publications categorise five types of infant mortality:

- *perinatal:* stillbirths plus early neonatal deaths
- *early neonatal deaths:* deaths at up to six completed days of life
- *late neonatal:* deaths at 7–27 completed days of life

- *post-neonatal:* deaths at 28 days and over but under one year
- *infant deaths:* deaths at ages under one year.

Early and late neonatal deaths are usually presented together as *neonatal deaths,* and *stillbirths* are often presented separately. *Child mortality* is commonly presented in three age groups: 1–4, 5–9 and 10–14 years.

A number of detailed analyses of factors related to mortality have been carried out, particularly by staff at the ONS, but many of these analyses only cover figures for England and Wales or the whole of the UK, without disaggregation by country or region. One of the reasons for this is that when disaggregated, the numbers for each country are small, making it difficult to conduct reliable analyses.

Age and time trends

In the whole of the UK, mortality rates are highest at and just after birth. They then fall in the post-neonatal period and during childhood, with the lowest rates between the ages of five and nine (Charts 4.1 and 4.2).

Chart 4.1: Stillbirths and infant mortality rates, England and Wales: 1982, 1992, 1999–2002

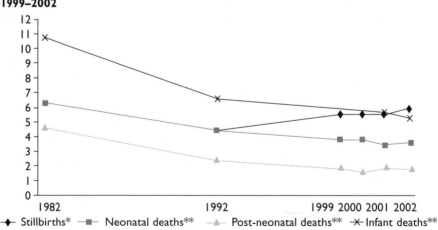

* Stillbirth rates per 1,000 total births
** Neonatal, post-neonatal and infant deaths per 1,000 live births
Note: Up to 1992, figures for stillbirths represent fetal deaths at or over 28 weeks gestation, and from 1993 at or over 24 weeks gestation.
Source: ONS (2004c)

Chart 4.2: Child mortality rates, England and Wales: 1982, 1992, 1999–2002

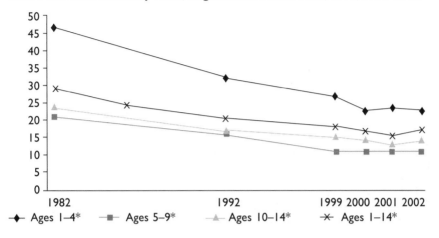

*Childhood deaths per 100,000 population of the same age
Source: ONS (2004c)

The figures indicate that the long-term downward trend in infant mortality has continued and the infant mortality rate for England and Wales in 2002 is the lowest figure ever recorded (ONS, 2003d). Figures for Scotland and Northern Ireland show similar patterns, with infant mortality at a historically low level for both (Table 4.1). Rates for child mortality have shown little change over the last few years. Due to smaller populations in Wales, Scotland and Northern Ireland, mortality rates show greater variation from year to year than for England and the UK as a whole, but no distinct pattern emerges to suggest that rates are consistently different between them.

Table 4.1: Stillbirths and infant mortality rates 1998-2002: UK, England, Wales, Scotland and Northern Ireland

Year	Stillbirths*					Infant deaths**				
	98	99	00	01	02	98	99	00	01	02
UK	**5.4**	**5.3**	**5.3**	**5.3**	**5.6**	**5.7**	**5.8**	**5.6**	**5.5**	**5.2**
England[1]	5.3	5.3	5.3	5.3	5.6	5.6	5.7	5.6	5.4	5.2
Wales[1]	5.4	4.8	4.6	5.0	5.4	5.6	6.1	5.3	5.4	4.5
Scotland[2]	6.1	5.2	5.6	5.7	5.4	5.6	5.0	5.7	5.5	5.3
Northern Ireland[3]	5.1	5.7	4.3	5.1	5.7	5.7	6.4	5.1	6.1	4.7

* Stillbirth rates per 1,000 total births; ** Infant deaths per 1,000 live births
[1] Excluding non-residents of England and Wales; [2] Including non-residents of Scotland; [3] Including non-residents of Northern Ireland
Source: ONS (2000b, 2001b, 2002c, 2003f, 2004c)

Table 4.2: Child mortality rates 1998–2002: UK, England, Wales, Scotland and Northern Ireland*

Year	Ages 1–4					Ages 5–9					Ages 10–14				
	98	99	00	01	02	98	99	00	01	02	98	99	00	01	02
UK	27	27	23	23	23	13	12	11	12	11	15	14	15	15	15
England[1]	27	26	22	23	23	12	11	11	11	11	14	14	13	13	14
Wales[1]	18	33	22	23	18	12	9	12	5	10	14	15	15	10	11
Scotland[2]	26	24	23	19	30	19	13	11	14	11	18	15	15	17	15
Northern Ireland[3]	26	33	24	15	30	13	18	18	12	12	15	14	13	17	14

*Childhood deaths per 100,000 population of the same age
[1] Excluding non-residents of England and Wales
[2] Including non-residents of Scotland
[3] Including non-residents of Northern Ireland
Source: ONS (2000b, 2001b, 2002c, 2003f, 2004c)

The figures in Table 4.1 also indicate a recent rise in stillbirths in 2002 for England, Wales and Northern Ireland, but not Scotland. An investigation into the increase for England and Wales (ONS, 2003e) showed that compared to the previous year there had been a 24 per cent increase in the stillbirth rate among sole registration births outside marriage; a 6 per cent increase in the rate of stillbirths among singleton (as opposed to multiple) births; and higher than usual rates in spring and summer 2002. The reasons for these increases are not yet known and it will be important to examine figures for the following years as they become available.

International comparisons

The latest figures available for a range of OECD countries are for 2001 and these show that the UK infant mortality rate for that year of 5.5 per 1,000 live births is higher than that of most other European countries, and considerably higher than those for Iceland, Finland, Sweden, Norway, Spain, Czech Republic, Italy, Germany, France, Austria and Denmark (see Table 4.3).

Recent research has indicated some of the factors associated with these differences. Richardus *et al* (2003) carried out an audit investigating associations between perinatal mortality rates and characteristics of care for 1,619 individual cases of perinatal death in ten countries in Europe, including seven former NHS regions in England and one region of Scotland. There was a positive association between the proportion of cases with care that was rated as less than optimal and overall mortality rates in the regions studied. The characteristics of care rated

Table 4.3: Infant mortality rates for OECD countries 2001*

Country	Infant mortality rate
Turkey	38.7
Mexico	22.4
Hungary	8.1
Poland	7.7
Slovak Republic	6.2
Greece	5.9
Luxembourg	5.9
Ireland	5.8
United Kingdom	5.5
Australia	5.3
Netherlands	5.3
Belgium	5.0
Portugal	5.0
Denmark	4.9
Austria	4.8
France	4.6
Germany	4.5
Italy	4.3
Czech Republic	4.0
Spain	3.9
Norway	3.8
Sweden	3.7
Finland	3.2
Japan	3.1
Iceland	2.7
Canada	–
Korea	–
New Zealand	–
Switzerland	–
United States	–

* Rate per 1,000 live births
Source: OECD (2003)

'less than optimal' included 'professional care delivery', 'infrastructure/service organisation' and 'maternal/social' factors. The most common areas of less than optimal care were failure to detect intrauterine growth restriction and maternal smoking. This study suggests that some of the variance in mortality rates between the UK and other countries could be due to differences in the quality of antenatal and perinatal care and in rates of smoking during pregnancy.

Another indication of both social and healthcare system effects on infant mortality was found in an international study of 19 wealthy OECD countries. Macinko *et al* (2004) found that the level of wage inequality for the country was significantly associated with infant mortality rates. Health system variables, particularly number of physicians per 1,000 population and a tax-based rather than social security or insurance-based health financing system, significantly reduced the association between wage inequality and mortality, suggesting that this can partially compensate for effects of income inequality.

Causes of infant and child mortality

There has been little change since 1999 in the pattern of causes of death. The main causes of infant mortality (under one year) differ from causes of child mortality (1–14 years). Conditions related to immaturity are the most common cause of infant deaths, followed by congenital anomalies. Sudden infant deaths (SIDs) have continued to decline, with the death rate in England and Wales falling from 0.40 in 2000 to 0.31 in 2002 (ONS, 2003i). This decline has been observed in many countries, and a review of studies from different countries indicates that the decline is largely due to interventions resulting in a reduction in babies sleeping in the prone position (ie, on their fronts) (Ponsonby *et al*, 2002). However, in England and Wales SID rates are higher for babies born to mothers under 20, mothers who were born outside the UK, and babies born outside marriage (ONS, 2003i). Ponsonby *et al*'s review also found that SID rates had not declined to the same extent in different ethnic and socio-economic groups, suggesting that further public health initiatives must address this difference.

For children aged 1–14, the most common causes of death reported in the 2002 statistics were external causes, including injury and poisoning, and cancers (ONS, 2004c). Almost half of deaths due to injury are from road traffic accidents; in figures for 1998–2000, these accounted for 61 per cent of accidental deaths in boys and 73 per cent among girls (ONS, 2003h). Deaths due to injury show a strong association with social class (Towner, 2002). The mortality rate for childhood cancer has continued to decline, due to improvements in treatment, and around 70 per cent of children are now successfully treated (Cancer Research UK, 2003).

Key factors associated with higher or lower mortality rates

Multiple births

Infant mortality is higher for multiple births. For example, rates for England and Wales in 2002 were 4.7 for singletons, 24.9 for twins, 43.8 for triplets and 150.0 for higher multiple births (ONS, 2004c).

Gender

Boys continue to show higher mortality rates than girls at all ages. In 2002, UK infant mortality rates were 5.9 per 1,000 live births for boys and 4.5 for girls; child mortality rates (ages 1–14) were 17 per 100,000 of the same age population for boys and 13 for girls (ONS, 2004c). All countries and regions of the UK showed the same pattern.

Occupational group[1]

Despite the decline in infant mortality, there is still a social class gradient. For example, in 2002 the infant mortality rate for babies with fathers in semi-routine occupations (7.5) was nearly three times the rate for babies with fathers in higher managerial occupations (2.7) (ONS, 2004f). One of the *Opportunity for All* indicators of progress for children and young people is differentials in the infant mortality rate between routine and manual and all social groups. The differential was falling up until 1996–98 but since then has been growing.

Marital status

Lone motherhood also continues to show associations with higher infant mortality. In 2002, rates for infants born outside marriage were 5.9 (5.3 joint registration/same address; 7.4 joint registration/different address; and 6.6 sole registration) compared with 4.7 for those born inside marriage (ONS, 2004c). Recent work in New Zealand provides some indication of factors underlying this difference. Blakely *et al* (2003) analysed infant and child mortality linked to census data for 1991, showing that, in New Zealand, the associations between

---

[1] The National Statistics Socio-Economic Classification (NS-SEC) is a social classification system introduced in the 2001 census that attempts to classify groups on the basis of 'employment relations', which includes factors such as: career prospects, autonomy, mode of payment and period of notice. There are a number of operational categories and the 2002 Health Survey for England used the five-category system in which occupations are classified as: a) managerial and professional; b) intermediate, small employers and own account workers; c) lower supervisory and technical; d) semi-routine; and, e) routine occupations.

lone parenthood and mortality are due to correlated socio-economic factors, especially mother's education.

Age of mother

Infant mortality rates continue to vary by mother's age and are highest for mothers aged under 20 (eight per 1,000 live births), followed by mothers aged 40 and over (7.1) and lowest in mothers aged 30 to 34 (4.3) (ONS, 2003c). A systematic review of the literature on teenage pregnancy (Cunnington, 2001) indicated that increased risks of poor outcome were mainly due to maternal social, economic and behavioural factors, particularly smoking in pregnancy. Many studies group all ages of teenager mothers together, but studies comparing younger and older teenager mothers have found increased risk of neonatal mortality for young teenagers (under 16). Risk appears to increase with decreasing age even within this group. Young teenagers are at increased risk of very premature birth and this accounts for most of the increase in neonatal mortality. As yet, it is not clear whether this is a biological factor or due to other factors associated with teenage pregnancy. Biological factors like low body mass index and physiological immaturity at the start of pregnancy are common in this group.

Mother's country of birth

There continue to be considerable differences between ethnic groups in infant mortality rates. In 2002, babies of mothers born in Pakistan had the highest mortality rate of 11.4, which was more than double the overall infant mortality rate of 5.2 (ONS, 2003c). These differences may in part be explained by social and biological factors, such as mother's age, and quality and uptake of healthcare (Soni Raleigh and Balarajan, 1995). The effect of healthcare on differential infant mortality rates among ethnic groups was explored in a recent Swedish study (Essen *et al*, 2002) which found that suboptimal factors in perinatal care services were significantly more common among perinatal deaths in babies of African immigrants than for deaths in the native Swedish population. These factors included delay in seeking healthcare, mothers refusing Caesarean sections, insufficient monitoring of intrauterine growth restriction, inadequate medication, and problems in communication. Research in the UK shows that women of Asian descent make fewer antenatal visits than indigenous white women, and that communication and language, information, choice in childbirth, and stereotyping and racism are important issues in minority ethnic women's experiences of maternity services (D'Souza and Garcia, 2004).

Geographical area

In our previous edition, we noted the variations in mortality rates by region, with higher rates in economically depressed areas. Figures continue to show such variations by geographical area (ONS, 2003d). For example, the 2002 infant mortality figures for Wales show Dyfed Powys had the lowest rate (3.9) and Gwent the highest (5.4). While rates in both areas have reduced over time, this is the same pattern as in 1997–99. In England, similar to 1998, the East and South West and South East regions had the lowest infant mortality rates (4.4, 4.4 and 4.5 respectively), and Yorkshire and Humber remained the region with the highest rate at 6.1, although this had reduced from 6.9 in 1998. Scotland and Northern Ireland show similar trends. Rates in Northern Ireland between 1997 and 2001 were higher than average for the 20 per cent most deprived wards (7.1 compared with an average of 5.7) (Northern Ireland Statistics and Research Agency, 2004b).

Parental smoking

Parental smoking is a key risk factor for infant mortality. In the USA, the rate of infant mortality for mothers who smoke prenatally has been found to be 40 per cent higher than for non-smokers, with risk increasing with the number of cigarettes smoked (Salihu *et al*, 2003). As noted in the previous edition, parental smoking shows a clear association with social deprivation, but there are indications that smoking also has significant effects on infant mortality rates after controlling for socio-economic factors (Blair *et al*, 1996).

Birth weight

Birth weight is one of the main indicators of the outcome of pregnancy and low birth weight is a well-established risk factor for immediate and long-term health problems (Macfarlane *et al*, 2004). A birth weight of less than 2,500g is defined by the World Health Organization (WHO) as low birth weight (OECD, 2003). Compared to other countries, the UK was one of the OECD countries with the highest proportion of low birth weight live births in 2000 (7.6 per cent), and with a trend for an increasing proportion of babies being born with a low birth weight. This trend is similar to most other countries (see Table 4.4)

One of the factors contributing to this trend is likely to be the increasing survival rates of pre-term infants. However, as gestational age is not recorded at

Table 4.4: Proportion of live births which are low birth weight, by country

	1990	1995	2000
Japan	6.3	7.5	8.6
Hungary	9.3	8.2	8.4
Greece	6.0	6.8	8.1
United Kingdom	6.8	7.3	7.6
United States	7.1	7.3	7.6
Portugal	5.6	6.0	7.1
Slovak Republic	5.8	6.5	6.7
Spain	4.5	5.5	6.5
New Zealand	6.2	6.0	6.4
France	5.3	5.8	6.4
Australia	6.1	5.9	6.3
Austria	5.6	5.7	6.3
Denmark	5.2	5.5	5.9
Switzerland	5.1	5.5	5.9
Canada	5.4	5.9	5.8
Czech Republic	5.5	5.5	5.8
Poland	8.1	6.7	5.7
Norway	4.6	4.6	5.0
Ireland	4.2	4.7	4.8
Finland	3.9	4.3	4.6
Sweden	4.5	4.4	4.2
Iceland	3.2	4.7	4.1

Source: OECD (2003)

birth registration it is not possible to explore this association. As Chart 4.3 shows, within the UK, Northern Ireland consistently has the lowest proportion of low birth weight live births, with England having the highest proportion.

Factors associated with low birth weight

Analysis of ONS birth weight statistics for England and Wales carried out by MacFarlane *et al* (2004) found the following factors were associated with low birth weight:

- father's occupation: the proportion of low birth weight babies born to fathers in manual occupations was higher than to fathers in non-manual occupations
- sole registrations: a greater proportion of babies registered by the mother on her own had a low birth weight compared to babies registered by the mother and father
- mother's ethnic group: the mean birth weight of babies born to white mothers

Chart 4.3: Proportion of low birth weight live births, 1995–2002, UK

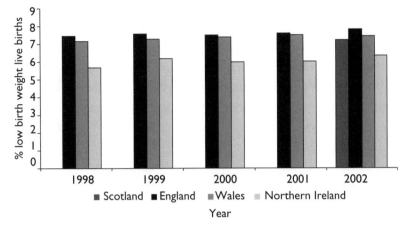

Source: 1996/2002 Child Health System, Area Health Boards; ISD Scotland National Statistics; Birth Statistics 2002. Data for 1998–2001 not available for Scotland.

was consistently higher than the mean birth weight of babies born to black women and Asian women

- mother's age: teenage mothers and mothers over 40 years were more likely to have babies with a low birth weight than mothers aged 20–39 years.

Analysis of the Millennium Cohort Survey data on birth weight are in line with these findings (Mayhew and Bradshaw, forthcoming). Mayhew and Bradshaw found that after controlling for other factors the risk of low birth weight was higher for mothers in poverty, underweight mothers, mothers who smoked in pregnancy, first births, and mothers from minority ethnic groups. However, having controlled for those factors, marital status and where you lived within the UK were not associated with low birth weight.

Infant feeding

The benefits of breastfeeding to a baby's health are well-documented and include increased immunity to infection and hence lowered susceptibility to illness. In addition, breastfeeding offers protection against chronic conditions such as asthma, inflammatory bowel disease and cancer (Department of Health, 2003b).

In the previous edition of this publication (Beresford, 2002) findings from the Infant Feeding Surveys were reported. A key finding was an increase in the incidence of initial breastfeeding (that is, breastfed at birth – even if only on one occasion) in the UK over the period 1990–2000. Compared to England and Wales, there were greater gains in incidence of initial breastfeeding for Scotland and Northern Ireland over that period, although the actual incidence of initial breastfeeding was lower than for England and Wales. Thus, in England and Wales 75 per cent of firstborn babies were breastfed initially, while in Scotland and Northern Ireland the figures were 67 per cent and 59 per cent respectively. It is important to note, however, that given the strong association between breastfeeding and the social class and age at which the mother left full-time education, these gains do not amount to more than would be expected from the changing (ie, improving) socio-economic profile of the UK population (Hamlyn *et al*, 2002). The challenge remains, therefore, of increasing breastfeeding rates among mothers in the least privileged socio-economic situations. As the Infant Feeding Survey is only repeated at five-yearly intervals there are no new UK data to report. However, data from the 2002 Health Survey for England (HSE) suggest that the incidence of initial breastfeeding remains relatively unchanged, with 73 per cent of babies being initially breastfed (Department of Health, 2003b).

Analysis (Mayhew and Bradshaw, forthcoming) of the Millennium Cohort Survey of babies at about nine months found that 71 per cent of mothers had ever tried to breastfeed their baby and that controlling for other factors the odds of breastfeeding were higher for married mothers, older mothers, home owners, only children, mothers from minority ethnic groups and mothers in England. Poor mothers were less likely to breastfeed but this association disappeared when controlling for other factors such as marital status, mother's ethnicity, paid work status, number of siblings of baby, tenure, country or region (within UK), and mother's age at birth.

The WHO and the Department of Health recommend that babies should be breastfed exclusively for up to six months, and that breastfeeding should be continued after the introduction of solid food. The 2002 HSE found that 47 per cent of babies were being breastfed for more than one month, with 15 per cent being breastfed beyond six months (Department of Health, 2003b). As with initial breastfeeding, factors affecting the duration of breastfeeding included mothers' age and socio-economic status. Older mothers and mothers from higher-income households maintained breastfeeding for longer (see Table 4.5).

Table 4.5: Incidence of breastfeeding at 1 month and 6 months by maternal age and household income (England only)

	Mother's age		Household income	
	16–24 yrs	35+ yrs	Mothers in lowest income quintile	Mothers in highest income quintile
Breastfeeding at 1 month (%)	29	60	53	91
Breastfeeding at 6 months (%)	7	17	8	28

Source: Department of Health (2003b), Volume 2: Maternal and Infant Health

Immunisations

Routine immunisation of babies and young children benefits the health of children and their communities where immunisation rates are high – so called 'herd immunity'[2] (eg, Nicoll *et al*, 1989). As reported in the previous edition of

Table 4.6: Immunisation rates by year (1997–2003) and UK country/region

	Year					
	1997/98	1998/99	1999/2000	2000/01	2001/02	2002/03
	Diphtheria, tetanus and polio[1]					
England	96	95	95	94	94	94
Scotland	97	97	98	97	97	98
Wales	96	96	96	96	96	95
N. Ireland	96	95	95	95	96	n/a[2]
	Pertussis (whooping cough)					
England	94	94	94	94	93	93
Scotland	96	96	97	97	97	97
Wales	93	93	94	95	94	94
N. Ireland	95	94	94	94	95	n/a[2]
	MMR					
England	91	88	88	87	84	82
Scotland	93	93	93	88	88	87
Wales	90	86	85	88	84	81
N. Ireland	91	91	92	90	89	n/a[2]

[1] Rates for the three immunisations diphtheria, tetanus and polio are virtually identical, as they are generally administered at the same time; for convenience only the rates for diphtheria are shown in the table.

[2] Immunisation rates for Northern Ireland for 2002/03 not available.

Sources: NHS Immunisation Statistics, England: 2002/03; 1993–2002 Child Health System, Area Health Boards; NHS Immunisation Statistics, Wales: 2002/03; Scottish Health Statistics 2004.

---

[2] If the vast majority of a population are vaccinated against a disease it is difficult for that disease to spread. This is known as herd immunity.

this book, in 2000 almost all two-year-old children in the UK had been immunised against diphtheria (95 per cent), tetanus (94 per cent), whooping cough (94 per cent), polio (95 per cent), haemophilus influenza (HiB) (95 per cent) and measles, mumps and rubella (MMR) (88 per cent) (Beresford, 2002). However, at that time, herd immunity against measles, mumps and rubella was under threat. This was due to widely reported concerns about the safety of the MMR vaccination and its purported links with autism and bowel disorders (such as Crohn's disease), which was resulting in parents deciding not to have their child vaccinated.

Table 4.6 shows immunisation rates between 1997 and 2003. For diphtheria, tetanus, polio and whooping cough the immunisation rates are fairly constant across time and between countries/regions. Historically, immunisation rates for MMR have always been lower than for other immunisations, peaking in the mid-1990s at 92 per cent. Table 4.6 shows that between 1997 and 2003 immunisation rates in England and Wales fell from nine out of ten children being immunised against MMR in 1997 to just over eight out of ten children in 2003. Declines in immunisation rates in Scotland and Northern Ireland are less marked, particularly in Northern Ireland.

Looking now at immunisation rates from an international perspective, Table 4.7 shows the proportion of children immunised against measles by two

Table 4.7: Proportion of children immunised against measles by 2 years by country: 1995 and 2001

	1995	2001
Czech Republic	96	97
Netherlands	94	96
Mexico	89	95
Denmark	88	94
Sweden	96	94
Australia	87	93
Norway	92	93
USA	90	91
Iceland	98	90
Turkey	65	90
Portugal	94	88
UK	92	85
France	83	84
Austria	60	78
Italy	50	76

Source: OECD (2003)

years in 1995 and 2001 in a selection of OECD countries (restricted to those countries where data were available for 1995 and 2001). The majority of other countries shown in the table report increases in immunisation rates for measles, with some countries, such as Italy, achieving quite substantial gains. In contrast, the UK shows a decrease of 7 per cent in immunisation rates. Thus, whereas in 1995 only five of the countries listed in the table reported higher immunisation rates than the UK, by 2001 this figure had risen to ten countries having higher measles immunisation rates.

Incidence of measles, mumps and rubella

The introduction of the MMR vaccination programme in the late 1980s resulted in a significant decrease in notifications of cases of measles, mumps and rubella among children. However, the difficulty of consistently achieving very high levels of vaccine coverage (Nicoll *et al*, 1989), in addition to specific concerns about the vaccine have, as reported above, led to a decrease in coverage, and herd immunity of children against these three infectious diseases has been threatened. For example, in Scotland the downward trend in measles, mumps and rubella notifications brought about by the introduction of vaccination programmes has reversed, with increases in notifications of all three conditions in 2002 compared to 2001 (ISD Scotland, 2003). In England and Wales there has been a rise in mumps notifications from 61 confirmed cases among children under 15 years in 1996 to 492 notifications in 2000, though this figure appears to be declining again.

The specific impact of lowered vaccine coverage due to concerns about the safety of MMR has also been demonstrated. In England, there was an outbreak of measles in south London in late 2001 and early 2002 – an area where take-up of MMR had been declining, apparently in response to concerns about the vaccine (Kirkbride and White, 2004).

Overall, the numbers of children contracting these infectious diseases are still small. However, there is continued concern at the falling vaccination rates and the implications this has for herd immunity. This is in relation not only to children's health but also to other groups of the population, where levels of immunity may be low and the consequences of contracting one of these illnesses may pose a significant health threat.

Self-assessed health

In the previous edition, data on self-assessed health collected by the 1997 HSE were reported (Beresford, 2002). As in 1997, the 2002 HSE survey took children and young people as its particular topic, and self-reported health data were collected. In both surveys informants were asked to rate their health in general on a five-point scale ('very good' to 'very bad'). While there are no comparable data available for children living in Wales or Northern Ireland, the 1998 Scottish Health Survey did ask children (over eight years) and parents of younger children to rate their health in a similar manner to the HSE.

Overall, the findings from these surveys suggest that the great majority of children (equivalent to 90 per cent) in England and Scotland rate their health as 'good' or 'very good', with children living in Scotland being more likely to report their health to be 'good' or 'very good' than are children living in England. Comparisons between the 1997 and 2003 HSE data suggest there has been a slight increase in the proportion of children reporting 'good' or 'very good' health.

Chart 4.4 shows the proportion of girls and boys reported to have 'very good' health by age in England (data from 2002) and Scotland (data from 1998).

This chart shows that over the childhood period there is a decrease in the proportion of children whose health is rated 'very good'. Around six out of ten

Chart 4.4: The proportion of children living in England and Scotland reporting 'very good health' by age

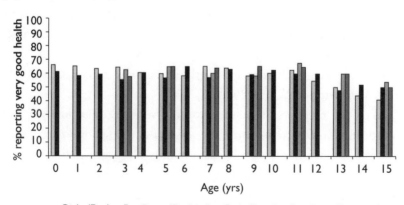

Sources: HSE 2002 Volume 1: The Health of Children and Young People; Scottish Health Survey 1998 Volume 1

preschool-aged children were rated as having very good health, but by their mid-teens, this figure falls to between four and five out of ten children. Among children living in England, a greater proportion of younger girls than boys report 'very good' health, but this pattern reverses by late childhood with a greater proportion of 15-year-old boys reporting 'very good' health (48 per cent) compared to 15-year-old girls (39 per cent). This does not happen among children living in Scotland where, apart from middle childhood, more girls report being in 'very good' health than boys. Overall, in the teenage years it is girls living in England who are least likely to report being in 'very good' health, whereas girls living in Scotland are most likely to report 'very good' health.

Factors associated with self-assessed health

In the 2002 HSE, self-assessed general health was found to be associated with other health indicators, such as socio-economic and area deprivation factors. Children with no *longstanding illness* and/or no recent *acute sickness episodes* were more likely to report having 'very good' health than boys and girls who had a longstanding illness and/or an acute sickness episode. In addition, socio-economic factors such as the *occupational group* (National Statistics Socio-Economic Classification – NS-SEC) of the household reference person and income were associated with self-reported health. Boys in the managerial and professional category were more likely to report 'very good' health compared to other boys. Similarly, among girls the NS-SEC of the household reference person was significantly associated with 'very good' general health.

In terms of *income*, boys and girls living in households with incomes in the lowest quintile were less likely than other children to report 'very good' general health. This finding differs from that of the 1997 HSE where it was only children living in households with incomes in the highest quintile who were more likely to report 'very good' general health compared to children in all other income groups.

Finally, where children lived affected self-assessed health. Children living in the two least *deprived quintiles*[3] were significantly more likely to report 'very

---

[3] The Index of Multiple Deprivation (IMD) provides a measure of area deprivation based on deprivation in six domains: income; employment; health deprivation and disability; education, skills and training; housing; and access to services. Wards are ranked on the basis of deprivation from 1 (most deprived) to 8,414 (least deprived). In the 2002 HSE, deprivation quintiles were used to generate broad categories of deprivation.

good' general health than children living in other areas. *Geographical region* also affected self-assessed health. Boys living in London were less likely to report 'very good' health than boys living in all other regions. The pattern is similar for girls, except that girls living in east England and the East Midlands, as well as in London, were also less likely to report 'very good' health compared to girls living in other regions.

Self-assessed health: international comparisons

Health Behaviour in School-aged Children (HBSC) is a WHO collaborative cross-national study. HBSC surveys are carried out every four years; the most recent

Table 4.8: Proportion of children rating their health as fair or poor by age, gender and country

		Country	
	England	Scotland	Wales
11-year-olds: boys			
Ranking[1]	7th	7th	5th
% rating their health as fair or poor	16.7	16.7	19.3
HBSC average (%)	12.1 *(min = 4.4; max = 27.2)*		
11-year-olds: girls			
Ranking	7th	15th	6th
% rating their health as fair or poor	20.0	14.9	23.4
HBSC average (%)	15.7 *(min = 4.4; max = 43.7)*		
13-year-olds: boys			
Ranking	7th	6th	2nd
% rating their health as fair or poor	18.9	19.1	24.5
HBSC average (%)	13.6 *(min = 6.3; max = 30.0)*		
13-year-olds: girls			
Ranking	8th	9th	5th
% rating their health as fair or poor	27.9	23.6	39.2
HBSC average (%)	20.8 *(min = 10.4; max = 53.9)*		
15-year-olds: boys			
Ranking	9th	14th	5th
% rating their health as fair or poor	18.7	15.9	20.7
HBSC average (%)	16.1 *(min = 7.6; max = 31.5)*		
15-year-olds: girls			
Ranking	7th	9th	5th
% rating their health as fair or poor	33.2	31.5	40.7
HBSC average (%)	27.2 *(min = 7.6; max = 63.1)*		

[1] *Data from 34 countries were collected (data unavailable for France). The ranking given indicates the position of the country in relation to the rest of the participating countries; 1st position is the country with the highest proportion rating their health as fair or poor, and so on.*

was conducted in 2001/02 and involved 35 countries and regions (WHO, 2004b). The data are collected through school-based surveys with children aged 11, 13 and 15 years taking part. One of the questions in the survey asks participants to rate their health as 'excellent', 'good', 'fair' or 'poor'.

Table 4.8 shows that in 2001/02 children living in Great Britain were more likely to rate their health as 'fair' or 'poor' than children living in many other countries around the world. Countries with more children rating their health as 'fair' or 'poor' than children living in Great Britain include Ukraine, Lithuania, Russian Federation, Greenland and Croatia. Within Great Britain, children living in Wales were more likely to rate their health as 'fair' or 'poor' than children living in England or Scotland. Consistent with the overall pattern found by this survey, girls were more likely than boys to rate their health as 'fair' or 'poor', with this effect increasing with age. A third of 15-year-old girls living in England and Scotland rated their health as 'fair' or 'poor', with this figure rising to four out of ten girls in Wales.

Longstanding illness and limiting longstanding illness

The General Household Survey (GHS) collects data annually on self-reported longstanding and limiting longstanding illness for people living in Great Britain. This provides a longitudinal picture of trends in the incidence of longstanding illness and limiting longstanding illness among children living in Great Britain. Longstanding illness is defined as an illness or disability that has troubled the child for some time. If the child has a longstanding illness, a supplementary question is asked to ascertain whether the presence of the illness or disability limits the child's activities in any way. A similar annual survey, the Continuous Household Survey, collects the same data for children living in Northern Ireland but only reports of its data on limiting longstanding illness for children could be found when compiling this report.

The 1972 GHS found that 7 per cent of boys and 4 per cent of girls were reported to have a longstanding condition. This figure has risen since; in 2002, 19 per cent of boys and 16 per cent of girls were reported to have a longstanding illness (Rickards, 2004), with older children more likely to be reported as having a longstanding illness compared to children under five years. However, data collected by the GHS also shows that, since 1998, there has been a plateauing in the number of children reported to have a longstanding condition (Rickards, 2004).

In 1975, in terms of *limiting* longstanding illness among children in Great Britain, 3 per cent of boys and girls were reported to have a limiting longstanding condition. By 2002 this figure stood at 7 per cent for boys and 6 per cent for girls: a much smaller increase than for reported longstanding illness (Rickards, 2004). In addition, comparison of data collected over the past five years suggests that rates of reporting limiting longstanding illnesses among children are levelling off. Compared to younger children, older boys and girls (5–15 years) are more likely to be reported as having a limiting longstanding illness.

Data for the prevalence of limiting long-term illness among children living in Northern Ireland are reported slightly differently to the GHS and therefore need to be reported separately. In 1997/98, 10 per cent of boys and 7 per cent of girls were reported by their parents to have limiting longstanding illness. In 2002/03 the figure had fallen slightly to 9 per cent for boys and 7 per cent for girls (NISRA, 2004a). These figures are higher than for children living in Great Britain (see Table 4.9). In addition, it would appear that, in Northern Ireland, unlike in Great Britain, the child's gender does affect reports of limiting longstanding illness.

Table 4.9: Rates of limiting longstanding illness in children by gender in the UK

	% reported as having a limiting longstanding illness	
	Boys	Girls
Children aged 0–15 years living in Great Britain	6.5	6
Children aged 0–15 years living in Northern Ireland	9	6

Sources: Rickards, 2004; NISRA, 2004a

Types of longstanding illness

Although the GHS collects information about the types of longstanding illness reported by a participant, it does not ask this about children. However, the 2002 HSE did collect those data. The most common forms of longstanding illness found among children living in Great Britain in 2002 were conditions of the respiratory system and skin complaints. Both these types of condition increase in prevalence with increasing age. A later section in this chapter looks more closely at data on respiratory health.

Factors associated with having longstanding illness

The 2002 HSE (Department of Health, 2003b) reports the outcomes of regression analysis used to identify *independent* factors associated with having longstanding illness. This means factors which, by themselves, affect prevalence of longstanding illness as opposed to factors which, though found to have an effect on prevalence rates, do not have that effect if other factors are not present. The following were identified as independent factors significantly associated with having longstanding illness:

- *age*: the odds of reporting longstanding illness increased significantly with age for boys and girls
- *self-assessed general health*: boys who rated their health as 'bad'/'very bad' were 11 times more likely to have a longstanding illness than those who rated their health as 'good'/'very good'; similarly, girls were 23 times more likely
- *income*: the probability of reporting a longstanding illness increased with decreasing income
- *Government Office Region (GOR):* boys living outside London were more likely to report a longstanding illness than boys living in London. This association was not found for girls.

It should also be noted that measures of area deprivation and socio-economic category (NS-SEC) were not found to be significantly associated with having a longstanding illness.

Ethnicity and health

Data from the 2001 Census (England and Wales) (ONS 2003a) can be used to explore the association between health status and ethnicity (see Table 4.10).

Table 4.10 shows that there are some differences between ethnic groups in terms of parental reports of general health and the presence of limiting long-term illness. The groups with the highest proportion reporting good general health were white (91 per cent) and black African (92 per cent) children, while those groups with the lowest proportion reporting good general health were black Caribbean (85 per cent), Pakistani (86 per cent) and Bangladeshi (86 per cent) children. In terms of the presence of a limiting long-term condition, 3 per cent of Chinese and Indian children were reported as having a limiting long-

Table 4.10: Health status by ethnicity for dependent children[1] in England and Wales

	White		Mixed			Asian/Asian British			Black/Black British		
	British	Irish	White & Black Caribbean	White & Black African	White & Asian	Indian	Pakistani	Bangladeshi	Black Caribbean	Black African	Chinese
General health											
Good	91	91	88	90	90	90	86	86	85	92	88
Fairly good	8	7	10	9	9	10	12	12	14	8	11
Not good	1	2	2	1	1	<1	2	2	1	<1	1
Has limiting long-term illness											
	4	4	6	4	4	3	5	5	5	4	3

[1] A dependent child is a person aged 0–15 in a household (whether or not in family) or a person aged 16–18 who is a full-time student in a family with parent(s).

Source: Census 2001

term condition compared to 6 per cent of white/black Caribbean children and 5 per cent of Pakistani, Bangladeshi and black Caribbean children.

Common chronic conditions with increasing prevalence

In our previous edition (Beresford, 2002), we reported data on the two most common chronic conditions where increases in prevalence are being reported: diabetes and asthma. We return to these two conditions now and look at current evidence on their prevalence and the possible factors underlying any changes.

Diabetes

Type (1) or insulin dependent diabetes is one of the more common chronic conditions which emerges in childhood. It is a condition which requires daily management, and poor management threatens both current and future health. The cause of Type 1 diabetes is not fully understood but is thought to be due to a genetic predisposition coupled with exposure to 'environmental risk factors' including perinatal infection and rapid growth rate in early life, though these have yet to be definitively identified. In the previous edition we reported that, across Europe, the incidence of Type 1 diabetes is rising, particularly among the under fives. In addition, incidence rates are higher in north and north-west Europe than in other areas of the continent (EURODIAB, 2000). It is important to note that the prevalence of Type 1 diabetes is not associated with disadvantage and that, indeed, some research suggests that there is a higher prevalence of Type 1 diabetes among the least deprived groups than in the most deprived groups (ONS, 1998a).

In the UK, no new prevalence data at a national level have emerged since the publication of the previous edition of this book.[4] Table 4.11 is therefore a replication of the table on prevalence of Type 1 diabetes in the mid-1990s which appeared in that volume. This table shows that the prevalence of diabetes increases with age and that, in Wales, prevalence rates for girls (5–15 years) are much higher than for boys of the same age.

---

[4] This dearth of national data is being addressed with the launch in 1999 of the National Paediatric Diabetes Audit (http://www.diabetes.org.uk/audit/npa.htm). This is a joint initiative between Diabetes UK, the Royal College of Paediatrics and Child Health, and the British Society for Paediatric Endocrinology and Diabetes. It has now established a national paediatric diabetes recording system and data collection began in July 2004.

Table 4.11: Summary of prevalence of insulin-treated diabetes per 1,000 patients,[a] by age, gender and country (1996)

	Rate per 1,000			
	0–4 years		5–15 years	
	Boys	Girls	Boys	Girls
England	0.2	0.3	1.5	1.7
Wales	0	0.3	1.2	2.5
Scotland			0.26	

[a] Patients registered in a sample of general practices
Sources: England and Wales: ONS (1998a) Table 6A8;
Scotland: Rangasami et al, (1997).

Data from local Diabetes Registers can be used to investigate more recent changes in incidence. For example, Feltbower et al (2003) looked at trends in the incidence of Type 1 diabetes in Yorkshire between 1978 and 2000. They found a steady increase in incidence, with an average annual increase of 2.9 per cent. Interestingly, they did not find an increase in incidence among young adults (15–29 years). This, they suggested, supported the idea of the influence of 'an environmental agent that is gradually affecting children at younger and younger age' (Feltbower et al, 2003, p. 437).

There is a second type of diabetes known as Type 2 diabetes, which usually occurs in adults. However, it is now beginning to be diagnosed in children. Ehtisham et al (2000) published the first case report of the incidence of Type 2 diabetes in UK children at the same time as reports of its occurrence in children in North America emerged. The onset of Type 2 diabetes in children appears to be linked to obesity and a family history of the condition, and certain minority ethnic groups are particularly at risk. It is the increase in obesity among children that is being ascribed as the cause for the emergence of Type 2 diabetes in children. The first attempt to estimate the UK prevalence of childhood Type 2 diabetes, undertaken in 2000, suggests a minimum prevalence rate of 0.21/100,000 in children under 16 years. Importantly, the estimated prevalence of Type 2 diabetes in white children is 0.10/100,000 which is significantly less than the prevalence in South Asian children (1.42/100,000) (Ehtisham et al, 2004). Prevalence figures of this sort would be regarded as indicating a condition with an extremely low prevalence, and therefore not a major public health problem. However, there are a number of reasons for concern. First, this is a new chronic condition for children. Second, it is associated with obesity – a growing health issue in the UK. Third, there is an expectation that prevalence rates will rise.

Asthma

Asthma is the most common chronic childhood illness and Britain has one of the highest prevalence rates of asthma in the world (Central Health Monitoring Unit, 1995). As in other countries its prevalence is rising in Britain, although mechanisms underlying this are unclear, with features such as the domestic and external environments being suggested as contributory factors. The 1997 and 2002 HSEs provide comparative data on the prevalence of doctor-diagnosed asthma (see Table 4.12). No equivalent datasets for Scotland, Wales and Northern Ireland were identified.

Table 4.12: Comparisons between 1995–97 and 2001–02 in prevalence of doctor-diagnosed asthma (England only)

Age	Boys (%)		Girls (%)	
	1995–97	2001/02	1995–97	2001/02
2–3	20	15	15	13
4–6	24	20	20	18
7–9	23	28	18	20
10–12	23	28	19	25
13–15	23	29	18	20

Source: Health Survey for England, 1997, 2002.

Table 4.12 shows that there has been an increase over time in the number of children aged seven or over to have had a medical diagnosis of asthma. This increase has been larger for boys than girls and, overall, more boys than girls have been diagnosed with asthma. Among children aged two to six, there has been a decrease in the number of medical diagnoses of asthma. It is not clear whether this is due to changes in medical practice with regard to diagnosing asthma and other respiratory problems, or whether other factors are at work here.

The 2002 HSE explored the association between asthma and a number of factors thought to be associated with the presence of asthma (in, for example, Belanger *et al*, 2003; Department of Health, 1998b; Rona *et al*, 1995). The findings were as follows.

- *Socio-economic classification (NS-NEC)*: the prevalence of doctor-diagnosed asthma was higher for boys and girls where the household reference person was in a semi-routine or routine occupation.
- *Income*: the prevalence of doctor-diagnosed asthma decreased as income increased.

- *Government Office Region (GOR)*: overall North East GOR was the region with the highest rates, and there was generally a higher prevalence of doctor-diagnosed asthma in the north than the south.
- *Indoor risk factors:* the prevalence of doctor-diagnosed asthma in children (0–15 years) was significantly higher in children exposed to second-hand cigarette smoke than in those not exposed (boys: 28 per cent vs. 21 per cent; girls: 22 per cent vs. 16 per cent). However, the use of domestic gas appliances and keeping household pets did not show a significant association with doctor-diagnosed asthma.
- *Degree of urbanisation:* there was no significant tendency for doctor-diagnosed asthma to be more common among children living in urban areas. In terms of measures of area deprivation, the 2002 HSE report does not contain an analysis of the association between asthma and area deprivation.

Non-intentional injuries

Injury is the leading cause of death among those aged 16 years and under in the UK (ONS 2003f). The earlier edition of this book provides a detailed account of what is known about childhood unintentional injuries in the UK and the factors which increase the risk of sustaining an unintentional injury (Croucher, 2002). Here we present current data on unintentional injuries and report trend data on child pedestrian deaths.

In 2002, 388 children (14 years and under) died due to accidental injury, poisoning or other non-intentional external causes in England, Scotland and Wales (see Table 4.13). Table 4.13 also shows that boys are more likely than girls

Table 4.13: Deaths by injury, poisoning or other consequences of external causes, 2002, England, Scotland and Wales, by age and gender

	Age band		
	< 1 year	1–4 years	5–14 years
Boys	38	60	128
Girls	39	48	75

Sources: Mortality Statistics: injury and poisoning, England and Wales, 2002; ONS 2003f; General Register Office for Scotland, 2002; Vital Events Reference Table, 2002

to die by accidental injury. Data from Northern Ireland on childhood mortality
are presented differently; there, 93 children died from non-intentional accidents
and injuries between 1998 and 2002.

While these deaths are highly unusual, it has been estimated that for *every*
death due to injury, there are numerous non-fatal accidents, including 5,000–
6,000 minor injuries as well as more serious injuries requiring a total of 45
hospital admissions and 630 doctor consultations (Conway and Morgan, 2001).
In addition, the longer-term health consequences of childhood injury represent
a significant demand on health and social care resources (Towner, 2002).

As noted in the previous edition (Croucher, 2002), road traffic accidents are
the most common cause of child deaths – just under one-half (46 per cent).
Compared to other countries, the UK has a low childhood mortality rate, but
the number of deaths due to traffic/pedestrian accidents and fires are relatively
high (UNICEF, 2001a; Towner, 2002).

It is well established that deaths due to fires and child pedestrian deaths are
both significantly more likely to occur among disadvantaged children (Licence,
forthcoming). The death rate where fire was the cause of death is 15 times higher
for children living in households in the lowest socio-economic groups than for
children in the highest socio-economic groups. In terms of child pedestrian
deaths, the most disadvantaged children are five times more likely to die in this

**Chart 4.5: Number of child pedestrian deaths or serious injuries by year and
gender, Great Britain**

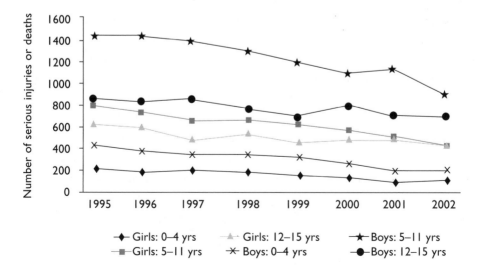

way than the most advantaged children (Towner, 2002). In addition, children in lower-income households and lone-parent households are more likely than other groups of children to sustain injuries which require a visit to a doctor or hospital (Department of Health, 2003b).

There is evidence to suggest that measures taken to modify the road environment (eg, traffic and speed restrictions, pedestrian priority areas, provision of safe crossings, and 'home zones') result in a reduction in child pedestrian deaths (Licence, forthcoming). As Chart 4.5 shows, annual figures for the number of child pedestrian deaths or serious injuries in Great Britain are declining among all age groups and for both boys and girls (Department for Transport, 2003).

HIV and AIDS

Since 1985, when recording commenced, 1,506 children have been infected with HIV; of these, 338 have died (see Table 4.14). By far the most common route of HIV infection among children is mother-to-child transmission. There have been no further infections caused by blood factor treatment since the introduction of donor screening and heat treatment of clotting-factor products in 1985 (ONS 2004g). Prior to this, 285 boys with haemophilia had been infected, of whom 123 have died.

In our previous edition (Beresford, 2002), we reported figures up to June 2001. In the three years since then a further 374 children have become infected with HIV and 28 children have died. We also reported that while the number of children being born to HIV-positive mothers was increasing, improvements in the clinical management of such cases meant there had been a decline in the proportion of children infected with the virus. As Chart 4.6 shows, this trend has continued, with over 50 per cent of children born to HIV-positive mothers in 2003 not being HIV-infected. This is in stark contrast to the late 1970s and early 1980s when all children born to an HIV-positive mother were infected with the virus (Beresford, 2002). However, it is worth noting that the UK is one of the European countries with the highest number of children being born to HIV-positive mothers, and therefore with HIV-positive children. Thus the cumulative total number of infections in Europe caused by mother-to-child transmission since 1999 is 13,603, of which 1,006 were recorded in the UK (EuroHIV, 2003).

Table 4.14: HIV infection[1] and deaths[2] in children[3] by exposure category and gender, June 2004 and June 2001[4]

	England, Wales, N. Ireland			Scotland				
	Male	Female	NS[5]	Male	Female	NS[5]	Total	Deaths
Mother to infant	558	534	3	27	24	0	1146	200
	(374)*	(364)	(2)	(21)	(19)	(0)	(780)	(172)
Blood factor (eg,	264	0	0	21	0	0	285	123
for haemophilia)	(264)	(0)	(0)	(21)	(0)	(0)	(285)	(123)
Blood tissue	22	21	3	2	2	0	50	14
transfer (eg,	(19)	(16)	(3)	(2)	(2)	(0)	(42)	(14)
transfusion)								
Other/	15	9	0	1	0	0	25	1
undetermined	(15)	(7)	(2)	(1)	(0)	(0)	(25)	(1)
Total	859	564	9	51	26	0	1506	338
	(672)	(387)	(7)	(45)	(21)	(0)	(1132)	(310)

* Note: italicised figures in brackets are figures for June 2001.
[1] Includes all children with AIDS, or with virus detected, or with HIV antibody at age 18 months or over.
[2] Death in HIV-infected children without AIDS are included.
[3] Infected with HIV aged 14 years or under.
[4] Includes 436 children who were aged 15 years or over at the end of June 2004 or at death (133 children infected through mother-to-infant transmission (three died), 268 haemophilia patients (106 died), 24 blood recipients (four died) and 11 in the other/ undetermined category.
[5] Not stated
Source: Health Protection Agency *et al*, 2004

Chart 4.6: Children born to HIV-positive mothers and number of these children who are HIV-positive in the UK, 1984–2003

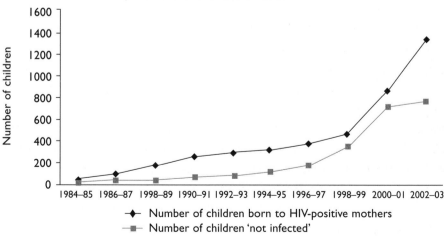

Source: Health Protection Agency *et al*, 2004

HIV/AIDS acquired through sexual intercourse or injecting drug use among 15–19-year-olds

While sexual intercourse or injecting drug use are the main ways in which adults become infected with HIV, this is virtually unheard of as a route of infection among under 15-year-olds. However, the pattern changes if one looks at 15- to 19-year-olds. While the number of recorded infections within this age band represents a very small proportion of all infections (less than 2 per cent in 2002), HIV/AIDS surveillance figures suggest that an increasing number of young people, especially young women, are becoming HIV-positive through sexual intercourse (see Chart 4.7).

Chart 4.7: HIV-positive individuals aged 15–19 years, infections probably acquired through sexual intercourse, 1989–2003.

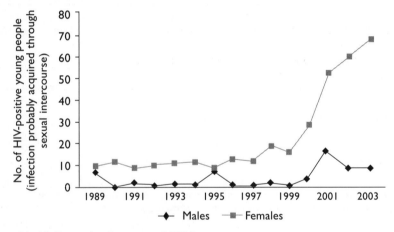

Source: Health Protection Agency *et al*, 2004

Sexual health

While adolescence is a time when physical sexual maturity is acquired, some features of adolescence, such as social immaturity, spontaneity and risk-taking, generate risks in terms of sexual and general health. For adolescents, two of the key health issues are teenage pregnancy and sexually transmitted infections (STIs). We deal with both these issues in this section. Data on adolescent sexual health are typically reported for young people under 16 years and those aged 16–19. Thus, while in much of this chapter we have restricted our data reported to children aged 15/16 years and under, in this section we have extended the upper age limit for data to 19 years so as to give as complete a picture as possible of adolescent sexual health in the UK today.

Sexual health behaviours

There are a number of ways to look at sexual health behaviours – including age at first sexual intercourse, use of condoms/contraception and number of sexual partners. Collecting such data from children and young people is ethically fraught and researchers often rely on retrospective accounts of pre-16 years sexual activity. In Great Britain, data on sexual health behaviours are collected every ten years (1990, 2000) through the National Survey of Sexual Attitudes and Lifestyles (NATSAL). Analyses of these survey data found that in the period 1999–2001, 30 per cent of men and 26 per cent of women reported first heterosexual intercourse at younger than 16 years, with the median age being 16 years. In addition, the proportion of women reporting first intercourse before 16 years increased from 1990 until the mid-1990s but then stabilised. Finally, factors associated with early age at first intercourse are well understood and include early school-leaving age, family disruption and disadvantage, and poor educational attainment (Wellings *et al*, 2001).

Wellings *et al* (2001) also generated a measure of 'sexual competence' based on four variables relating to the circumstances of first sexual intercourse: regret (ie, wished waited longer), willingness (respondent vs. partner more willing), autonomy, and use of contraception at first intercourse. Lack of 'sexual competence' was found to increase with younger age at first intercourse, as shown in Table 4.15. This table also shows that young women under 16 years who have had sexual intercourse are less 'sexually competent' than young men of the same age who have had sexual intercourse.

There have been gains, however, in levels of sexual competence. Wellings *et al* (2001) found that, despite decreasing age at intercourse, sexual competence has increased during the past three decades. Education level, source of information about sex (school-based lessons were found to be positively associated with sexual competence) and age at menarche were significantly associated with sexual competence. Wellings *et al* (2001) conclude that 'there is much that is positive in this data' (p. 1849), and argue that key factors contributing to sexual competence, such as school-based information provision, are amenable to intervention. They also note the indication that there is possible stabilisation of the trend towards early intercourse, and cite evidence from the United States where a reduction in teenage pregnancy rate followed the occurrence of a similar trend.

Table 4.15: 'Sexual competence' by age at first intercourse, Great Britain, 2000

	Age at first intercourse			
	Men		Women	
	13/14 years	*15 years*	*13/14 years*	*15 years*
Regret				
Wish waited longer	41.8	26.3	84.3	49.1
Willingness				
Respondent more willing	5.7	2.5	0.7	1.5
Partner more willing	9.0	6.8	32.9	26.0
Contraception				
No condom	31.2	19.4	33.6	16.5
No contraception	17.9	9.8	21.7	10.0
Status of partner				
Met for first time	2.5	0.9	5.3	3.1
Main reason				
Peer pressure	9.2	9.9	13.0	13.79
Drunk	11.8	6.7	6.9	7.4
Not sexually competent	66.7	46.4	91.1	62.4

All data are % respondents
Source: Wellings *et al*, 2001, p. 1846

Data from the HBSC study provide cross-country comparative data about sexual activity among 15-year-olds (WHO, 2004b). Conducted in 2001/02, this survey asked the 15-year-old cohort participating in the study if they had ever had sexual intercourse, and their age at first sexual intercourse. The findings differ from the 2000 NATSAL Survey, with over 38 per cent of 15-year-old girls and 33 per cent of boys in Great Britain reporting they have had sexual intercourse (Wellings *et al*, 2001). The difference in the figures obtained by these two surveys highlights the methodological difficulties of accessing these data, as over- and under-reporting are both possible explanations. Overall, compared to other countries participating in the HBSC study, 15-year-olds in England, Scotland and Wales were among the most likely to report having had sexual intercourse. However, compared to other countries, the mean age at first sexual intercourse was average (boys = 14.1 yrs; girls = 14.1 yrs; HBSC average = 14.0 (boys) and 14.3 (girls)).

Risky sexual behaviours

Having multiple partners and not using contraceptives and/or condoms increase the risk of early pregnancy and contracting an STI. The Contraception and Sexual Health Surveys provide longitudinal data on the number of sexual partners in the previous year reported by young people aged 16–19 (see Table 4.16).

Table 4.16: Number of sexual partners in the previous year among 16–19-year-olds by gender, 1997–2002/03

	1997	1998	1999	2000	2001/02	2002/03
Males						
0	41	50	43	31	34	45
1	31	25	29	38	26	27
2 or 3	19	19	22	22	25	19
4 and over	9	6	6	9	14	9
Females						
0	39	32	39	33	27	36
1	40	38	42	44	46	39
2 or 3	15	23	12	20	23	22
4 and over	5	8	8	4	4	4

Source: ONS: The Health of Children and Young People (1997–2001/02); Contraception and Sexual Health Survey 2002/03 ONS (2003)

Table 4.16 shows fluctuations, and certainly no increase, in the proportion of young people with multiple sexual partners between 1997 and 2002/03. Similarly, the proportion of young people not sexually active in a given year also fluctuates, and there is no clear trend of either increases or decreases in this figure.

Data on the use of contraception by young people aged 16–19 are also collected through the annual Contraception and Sexual Health Surveys. The proportion of 16–17-year-olds using at least one form of contraception has increased from 38 per cent in 1997 to 61 per cent in 2001/02. While this partly reflects an increase in the proportion of 16–17-year-olds who are sexually active, it does also represent a true rise in the use of contraception (Munro *et al*, 2004). Among 16–17-year-olds, male condoms are more likely to be used as a method of contraception than the contraceptive pill. However, among 18–19-year-olds the rates of use of these two forms of contraception are similar (pill: 40 per cent; male condom: 39 per cent). Two-thirds of 16–19-year-olds who use condoms chose this because it offered both a method as a contraceptive and a means of avoiding STIs (ONS, 2003). However, it should be noted that among sexually active young people, 28 per cent of men and 38 per cent of women reported that they did not always use a condom.

Teenage conceptions and abortions

Teenage conception is being discussed in this chapter because of evidence that teenage births are associated with poor outcomes for the teenager and her child, including health outcomes, both in the short and long term. This evidence was reviewed in *Teenage Pregnancy* (Social Exclusion Unit, 1999b) and in the previous edition of this book (Tabberer, 2002) in more detail than is included here. Teenage pregnancies are more likely to result in low birth weight babies, infant and child mortality, hospital admissions of children, postnatal depression and low rates of breastfeeding. New analysis of the Millennium Cohort Survey finds that teenage mothers were over three times more likely to be poor, the odds of a low birth weight baby were 40 per cent higher for a teenage conception, teenage mothers were 50 per cent more likely to be depressed and, as we have seen above, at least 100 per cent less likely to breastfeed (Mayhew and Bradshaw, 2005). We also know that teenage mothers are less likely to complete their education and more likely to be out of employment and to live in poverty, and their children are more likely to experience these disadvantages and twice as likely to become teenage parents in their turn (Rendall, 2003).

Chart 4.8: Percentage of all births which are teenage births

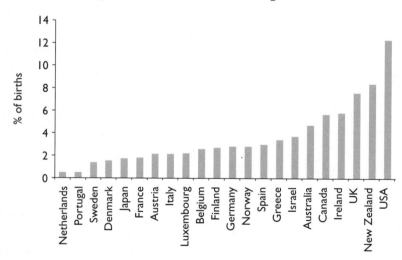

Source: Council of Europe (2004)

UNICEF (2001b) found that the under-20 birth rate in the UK was the second highest out of 28 OECD countries, only less than the USA, and even in affluent areas the teenage birth rate in the UK was higher than the average for the Netherlands or France. Chart 4.8 gives more recent data on the percentage of all births which are to a teenager and shows that the UK comes third from top only exceeded by New Zealand and the United States.

Data on teenage pregnancy in England and Wales are readily available from Health Statistics Quarterly (http://www.statistics.gov.uk/downloads/theme_health/hsq22_v1.pdf) and from the Teenage Pregnancy Unit website (http://www.info.doh.gov.uk/tpu/tpu.nsf). Data on teenage conceptions are produced by combining birth registrations and notifications of legal abortions, and so exclude miscarriages and illegal abortions. The Teenage Pregnancy Strategy Targets are to, by 2010:

- reduce by 50 per cent the 1998 England under-18 conception rate with an intermediate target of a 15 per cent reduction by 2004
- achieve a well-established downward trend in the under-16 conception rate
- reduce the inequality in rates between the fifth of wards with the highest under-18 conception rate and the average ward rate by at least 25 per cent
- increase to 60 per cent the participation of teenage parents in education, training or employment to reduce their risk of long-term social exclusion.

The first and fourth of these statistics are also being used to monitor the anti-poverty strategy in *Opportunity for All.*

At the time of writing it does not look as if these targets will be met. Table 4.17 gives the England and Wales conception rates. The under-18 conception rate did fall after 1998 but, on the basis of provisional figures, there was no reduction in 2002 and the rate of decline will have to speed up to meet the 2004 and 2010 targets. It is arguable whether the under-16 conception rate downward trend is yet well established. The percentage of teenage parents in education is currently only 37 per cent – and that proportion fell between 2002 and 2003.

The number of teenage births is a function of the proportion of conceptions that end in abortion. Table 4.18 gives the proportion of conceptions aborted by age. Nearly half of all under-18 conceptions are ended by abortion; the proportion is higher for under-16 conceptions and lower for under-20 conceptions. The proportion of conceptions that end in abortion has been increasing slowly since the mid-1990s for all groups.

Table 4.17: Conception rates per 1,000 women by age group in England and Wales

Age at conception	1991	1996	1997	1998	1999	2000	2001	2002
Under 16	8.9	9.6	9.0	9.0	8.3	8.3	8.0	–
Under 18	44.6	46.5	46.4	47.8	45.9	44.3	42.7	42.8
Under 20	64.1	63.1	62.8	65.8	63.5	62.8	60.9	–

Source: Table 4.1 *Health Statistics Quarterly:* Summer 2004

Table 4.18: Percentage of teenage conceptions terminated by abortion in England and Wales

Age at conception	1991	1996	1997	1998	1999	2000	2001	2002
Under 16	51.1	49.2	49.7	52.4	52.6	54.0	55.8	–
Under 18	39.9	40.0	40.6	42.0	43.0	44.2	45.7	45.2
Under 20	34.5	36.2	36.8	37.8	38.6	39.3	40.4	–

Source: Table 4.1 *Health Statistics Quarterly* Summer 2004

Area variations

There are unfortunate differences in the manner in which the countries and regions of the UK record teenage conceptions and abortions, but Griffiths and Kirby (2000) managed to put England, Scotland and Wales together on a consistent basis for the 1990s. They found that Wales had the highest teenage conception rate and Scotland the lowest. England had the highest proportion of conceptions leading to abortion. It can be seen in Table 4.19 that Northern Ireland has the lowest age-specific fertility rate for the under-20s and Wales the highest. The teenage conception rate is not available in Northern Ireland due to an unknown number of teenagers travelling to Britain to avail themselves of the Abortion Act (which has not been extended to Northern Ireland).

Table 4.19: Live births per 1,000 women under 20 in 2001

	England	Wales	Scotland	Northern Ireland
Live births per 1,000 women under 20	28	35	28	24

Source: ONS (2004e), Table 3.13

The ONS publishes conception rates and the proportion of conceptions ending in abortion by local authority (at least for England). There are very substantial variations. Between 1997–99 the teenage (15–17) conception rates varied between 15 per 1,000 in Uttlesford and 86 per 1,000 in Southwark. The proportion of teenage conceptions which end in abortion varied between 26 per cent in Derwentside and 68 per cent in Kensington and Chelsea. These variations have been shown to be very closely associated with the level of deprivation of an area – the conception rate is higher in deprived areas (Bradshaw and Finch, 2005) and the proportion that end in abortion is lower in deprived areas. The result is that the teenage birth rate is closely associated with deprivation (Lee *et al*, 2004).

Berthoud (2001) found that teenage motherhood was associated with ethnicity: Caribbean, Pakistani and Bangladeshi women had much higher rates than white women, but Indian women much lower rates than white women.

Sexually transmitted infections

As noted in our previous edition, young people are vulnerable to acquiring STIs as they tend to have more sexual partners and to change those partners more frequently than older age groups. The increasing incidence of STIs in the population as a whole (PHLS, 2002) only serves to increase this risk for adolescents. Table 4.20 shows the number of new episodes of five of the most commonly occurring STIs (infectious syphilis, gonorrhoea, genital chlamydia, genital herpes, and genital warts) among adolescents in England, Wales and Northern Ireland.

The most common STI occurring among adolescents is genital chlamydia, and there have been substantial increases in the number of new episodes being annually reported since 1996. Genital chlamydial infection has implications in terms of reproductive health. Among women it can result in pelvic inflammatory disease and there is increased risk of ectopic pregnancy. An increasing number of male and female adolescents are being reported as having gonorrhoea. There have been significant increases year on year in the number of new episodes of genital chlamydia and gonorrhoea being reported among adolescents under 16 years of age as well as those aged 16–19, though the actual incidence for under-16s is much lower than the 16–19 age band. Much less common, though still showing an increase in incidence, is primary and secondary syphilis. The incidence of genital herpes and genital warts is less consistent, though there are indications of an overall slowing in incidence rates.

Table 4.20: Number of new episodes of STIs by gender, age band and year

	1996	1997	1998	1999	2000	2001	2002	% change 2001/ 2002	1996– 2002
Primary and secondary syphilis									
Males									
<16 yrs	1	3	0	0	0	0	1	–	0%
16–19 yrs	4	1	5	5	7	12	29	142%	625%
Females									
<16 yrs	0	0	0	0	0	1	2	100%	–
16–19 yrs	3	3	3	12	8	11	17	55%	467%
Gonorrhoea									
Males									
<16 yrs	29	47	37	44	60	57	67	18%	131%
16–19 yrs	908	1063	1013	1387	1903	2038	2239	10%	147%
Females									
<16 yrs	134	141	156	171	218	276	281	2%	110%
16–19 yrs	1394	1442	1507	1848	2380	2605	2279	7%	99%
Genital chlamydia									
Males									
<16 yrs	43	50	52	74	69	89	98	10%	128%
16–19 yrs	1448	1886	2444	3015	3803	4260	5312	25%	267%
Females									
<16 yrs	461	524	579	713	807	959	1070	12%	132%
16–19 yrs	5876	7560	8659	10350	12190	13543	15715	16%	167%
Genital herpes (first attack)									
Males									
<16 yrs	10	12	11	5	13	9	8	–11%	–20%
16–19 yrs	273	264	326	368	408	395	404	2%	48%
Females									
<16 yrs	118	106	100	120	122	147	153	4%	30%
16–19 yrs	1685	1834	1909	1940	2013	2165	2062	–5%	22%
Genital warts									
Males									
<16 yrs	90	101	96	97	96	65	67	3%	–26%
16–19 yrs	2116	2609	2965	3262	3315	3364	3387	1%	60%
Females									
<16 yrs	506	468	462	486	448	484	515	6%	2%
16–19 yrs	7793	8487	8875	8781	8688	8847	8866	0%	14%

Source: Health Protection Agency (http://www.hpa.org.uk/infections)

Conclusion

The overall downward trend in infant mortality rates has continued, but international comparisons show there is still room for improvement across the UK – and social class differentials appear to be growing. The social and demographic factors associated with higher infant mortality are well established and these have not changed over the last three years. However, recent research, including cross-national studies, indicates some of the key factors that may underlie broad socio-demographic trends and the different rates for different countries. Characteristics of healthcare, social inequality and individual behaviour are all important.

Reductions in infant mortality are important public health priorities. In England, a Public Service Agreement (PSA) target from the Government's 2004 Spending Review is to 'reduce health inequalities by 10 per cent by 2010 as measured by infant mortality and life expectancy at birth' (HM Treasury, 2004a). The evidence indicates that interventions to reduce mortality rates need to be multi-faceted: promoting change at societal level in poverty and income inequalities; intervention at the level of the healthcare system to improve maternity care, particularly for disadvantaged groups; and public health and educational interventions, including initiatives to decrease levels of smoking and reduce SID rates in disadvantaged groups by further reducing the number of babies sleeping in the prone position. This is recognised at Government level, as health service targets set for 2003–06 in *Improvement, Expansion and Reform* (Department of Health, 2002b) include targets to 'deliver a one percentage point reduction per year in the proportion of women continuing to smoke throughout pregnancy, focusing especially on smokers from disadvantaged groups' as a contribution to the infant mortality target, and to 'improve access to services for disadvantaged groups and areas, particularly antenatal services'. Recognition of the importance of the role of education and children's social care services, as well as health, is demonstrated by the fact that the PSA target is a joint target for the Department of Health and the Department for Education and Skills. However, there is little strong research to inform the design of interventions to reach these targets. A recent review of interventions to improve maternity services for disadvantaged women (D'Souza and Garcia, 2004) highlights the scarcity of evidence on effectiveness of interventions in this area.

The evidence presented on children's physical health offers good and bad news. Overall, a key message is the association between socio-economic disadvantage and children's health, which has been shown for: increased risk for infant mortality; low birth weight; not being breastfed; poor self-assessed health; the presence of a longstanding illness; a diagnosis of asthma; non-intentional accident or injury; early age for first sexual intercourse; and teenage conception. Reducing health inequalities is a key aim of the National Service Frameworks for

England and Wales (Department of Health 2004; Welsh Assembly Government, 2004b). However, as Curtis and Roberts (in press) note: 'While the UK has a strong tradition of work on the determinants of inequalities in health, we are weaker on our understanding of what we can actually do to reduce these inequalities. Some of our actions in attempting to address inequalities are based on poor (or no) evidence, and some interventions may widen rather than narrow inequalities' (p. 1). From Curtis and Roberts' review of what works in relation to tackling health inequalities it is very apparent that a multi-faceted, multi-disciplinary, multi-agency and cross-departmental approach is required. Effective interventions identified by Curtis and Roberts include: improved housing conditions; traffic calming; drink-drive legislation; income supplementation; community-based health advice centres; parenting programmes; home-visiting support service for mothers; learning tools/programmes for preschool children, disadvantaged children, and black and minority ethnic young people; help and support with breastfeeding; and access to good, cheap food in the community and schools.

Another striking finding is that while many children in the UK rate their health as good or very good, a substantial minority report poor health and that compared to many other countries children in the UK are more likely to report poor health. This raises two issues: are UK children less healthy than their counterparts in other countries, and/or do they perceive their health to be poor for other reasons, such as low self-esteem? Both are causes of concern. Related to this is the finding that girls are more likely than boys to report poor health – and poor happiness and self-esteem (see Chapter 6). A number of possible explanations have been put forward to explain this, including maturational processes, the onset of menarche and the fact that girls may be more aware of their bodies and more able to express health concerns (Torsheim *et al*, 2004).

Other key areas for concern in terms of children's health are the continued increases in the incidence of Type 1 diabetes and asthma – and in both these cases environmental or lifestyle factors are being implicated in this upward trend. The number of cases of certain STIs has also continued to increase year on year since the publication of the first edition of this book. There is, as yet, no evidence that teenage pregnancy is on a downward trend.

In addition is the emergence of a new childhood condition – Type 2 diabetes. The first cases of this condition, formerly seen only in adults, have been recorded in the past couple of years with the rising levels of obesity being seen as the cause. (Chapter 5 looks in more detail at the issue of obesity.) Another health issue emerging since the publication of the previous edition is the drop in immunisation rates for MMR to levels where, in some localities, herd immunity has been threatened or breached and there have been outbreaks of measles and mumps. This is clearly an area which will need ongoing monitoring.

There are, however, some grounds for optimism. The decrease in the number of serious and fatal child pedestrian accidents is extremely pleasing and the effectiveness of traffic-calming schemes is seen as the primary reason behind this. In addition, levels of initial breastfeeding have been maintained. However, as noted earlier, the ability to improve breastfeeding rates now depends on helping the most disadvantaged mothers to breastfeed their babies. Arguments for the need for targeted interventions to support health improvements among the most disadvantaged families also arise from findings in the 2002 HSE, where the only difference in self-reported health lay between the children in the lowest income quintile and all other children. What is important to note here is that this differed from the findings of the 1997 HSE, where it was the children in the highest income quintile who were significantly more likely to rate their health as very good than were all other children.

Other positive signs reported in this chapter include a plateauing of the trends for increasing numbers of children reported to have a longstanding or limiting longstanding illness, and the number of young women reporting first intercourse occurring at less than 16 years. In addition, there are indications that, overall, young people are becoming more competent in terms of managing their sexuality and sexual behaviour. However, there are groups who remain vulnerable – as indicated by the rising number of young people who contract STIs.

Finally, it has been possible in this chapter to report differences in health experienced by different ethnic groups in terms of a number of indicators. We have shown that mothers' country of birth is associated with infant mortality rates, and ethnicity is associated with low birth weight, self-assessed health, presence of a limiting long-term illness, a diagnosis of Type 2 diabetes, and teenage motherhood. What is critical to emphasise here is that there were the differences *between* children from minority ethnic groups *as well as* between white children and those from minority ethnic groups. Children from minority ethnic groups living in the UK are not a homogeneous group. Children from some ethnic groups appear particularly at risk of poor health. Interventions to improve the health status of these children need to be tailored to their particular requirements and needs – a task which, to date, has proved extremely difficult to successfully achieve.

5 Children's lifestyles

Naomi Finch and Beverley Searle

Key findings:
- 31 per cent of young people aged 11–16 report drinking alcohol during the past week in England, Scotland and Wales.
- 68 per cent of young people aged 11–16 report drinking alcohol during the past 30 days in Northern Ireland.
- 20 per cent of young people smoke regularly in the UK.
- In 2001, 8.5 per cent of 6-year-olds and 15 per cent of 15-year-olds in England were obese.
- 61 per cent of young people aged 11–16 in Britain do not undertake the recommended level of physical activity each day.
- Scotland has one of the worst records out of 35 countries for both sweets and soft drink consumption.
- Wales falls in the ten countries of 35 with the worst records of both fruit and vegetable consumption.

Key trends:
- The number of units of alcohol drunk per week has risen for both girls and boys between 1988 and 2003.
- Smoking has risen, particularly in Wales among girls between 1986 and 2000.
- Between 1998 and 2001, Wales experienced a dramatic decrease in the proportion of children undertaking sport.

Key sources:
- Department of Health *Drug use, smoking and drinking among young people in England in 2003*
- *Young People in Wales: findings from the Health Behaviour in School-aged Children (HBSC) Study 1986–2000*
- *Scottish Schools Adolescent Lifestyle and Substance Use Survey (SALSUS) National Report: Smoking, Drinking and Drug use among 13 and 15-years-olds in Scotland 2002*

- Department of Health *Drinking, Smoking and Illicit Drug Use Amongst 15 and 16-year-old school students in Northern Ireland 2001*
- World Health Organization (WHO) *Health Behaviour in School-aged Children (HBSC) Study: international report from the 2001/2002 survey*
- Health Promotion Agency *Eating for health? A survey of eating habits among children and young people in Northern Ireland, undertaken in 1999*

Introduction

This chapter reviews the well-being of children in relation to their smoking and drinking behaviour, diet and physical activity. It explores trends in these lifestyle factors and compares the position of young people in different parts of the UK and with other countries. Attention is also given to gender differences, although due to limitations in data, differences between ethnic groups are not fully explored. The problems associated with poor lifestyles will be discussed, along with Government strategies which seek to tackle their negative effects on young people's health and well-being.

Sources of data

Smoking and alcohol

Department of Health biennial surveys of secondary school children have been conducted in England and Scotland since 1982 and in Wales since 1985/86. From 1999, England has conducted surveys annually. The Scottish and English surveys initially investigated the prevalence of smoking among young people, but in 1990 they also contained questions on alcohol and in 1998 questions about drug use (see Chapter 11) were added. These sources provide information updated since the first edition of *The Well-being of Children in the UK.*

- Data for England are taken from *Drug use, smoking and drinking among young people in 2003: Headline figures* (Department of Health, 2003a). This is a national survey of over 10,000 pupils aged 11–15, from 321 schools.
- Data for Scotland are taken from the *Scottish Schools Adolescent Lifestyle and Substance Use Survey* (SALSUS) (Currie *et al*, 2003), which provides information from 23,090 pupils aged 13 and 15 from 314 schools.

- Data for Wales are taken from the *Health Behaviour of School Children interim report of 2000*, on 3,485 young people aged 11–16 (Roberts *et al*, 2002).
- Data for Northern Ireland are taken from the Department of Health's *Survey on Drinking, Smoking and Illicit Drug Use in Northern Ireland* (Miller and Plant, 2001), a report on the findings of self-reported substance use among a representative sample of 723 15/16-year-old students in 71 secondary schools In Northern Ireland conducted in 1999.

Diet, obesity and physical activity

The main source of data for this section is the *Health Behaviour of School-aged Children* (HBSC) study (see below). Northern Ireland, however, was removed from the most recent HBSC study, the source used for Northern Ireland in the previous edition. Therefore, the data source for Northern Ireland is *Eating for Health? A survey of eating habits among children and young people in Northern Ireland* (Health Promotion Agency, 2001), a report on a study undertaken in autumn 1999 among a sample of 716 children aged 5–17 years in Northern Ireland. Eating habits were assessed by interviewing the parents of the children and young people about the frequency of consumption of a range of foods and about breakfast and lunchtime habits. These data are the best accessible data for children in Northern Ireland.

International comparisons

International comparisons are made using data from the HBSC, which is an international research study conducted in collaboration with the WHO. The study was established in 1982 and surveys have been conducted every four years. The most recent study was undertaken in 2001/02 and was conducted with 160,000 young people aged 11, 13 and 15, from 35 countries (WHO, 2004b). However, it did not include Northern Ireland.

Alcohol

Periodically, alcohol consumption by young people becomes the focus of public concern or mass media attention (Harrison, 1996). During the 1980s there was concern with 'lager louts' (British Medical Association, 1986), and more recently attention has turned to 'binge drinking' and its associated anti-social behaviour or potential for alcohol-related harm (Prime Minister's Strategy Unit, 2004; Scottish Executive, 2002j).[1]

Prevalence

In the UK, on average, one-third of young people report drinking during the past week. Drinking is more prevalent among boys than among girls, and young people in Scotland are more likely to drink than young people in England and Wales (Table 5.1). Due to methodological differences in the collection of available data, it is not possible to compare prevalence of drinking among all UK countries/regions, but a review of previous studies shows that alcohol consumption by teenagers in Northern Ireland generally tends to be lower than in the rest of the UK (Harrison, 1996).

Table 5.1: Prevalence of drinking in the UK

	Boys	Girls
Within last week (%)		
England[a]	26	24
Wales[b]	34	29
Scotland[c]	38	37
Within last 30 days (%)		
Northern Ireland[d]	71	64

[a] based on information for 11–15-year-olds for 2003
[b] average percentage of drinking prevalence among 11–16-year-olds for 2000
[c] based on information for 13- and 15-year-olds for 2002
[d] based on information on 15- and 16-year-olds for 1999
Source: Department of Health (2003a), Roberts *et al* (2002), Currie *et al* (2003), Miller and Plant (2001)

The HBSC survey shows that drinking alcohol at least once a week is reported by far higher proportions of teenagers in Great Britain compared to other nations, and this is particularly so in England and Wales, which had the highest proportion of young boys and girls drinking aged 13 and 15 in 2001/02 (Table 5.2).

---

[1] The WHO issued the *Declaration on Young People and Alcohol* in 2001, which complemented the European Alcohol Action Plan 2000–2005.

Table 5.2: Drinking beer, wine or spirits at least weekly by country, age and sex (%) (2001/02)

Country	Aged 11		Aged 13		Aged 15	
	Boys	Girls	Boys	Girls	Boys	Girls
England	14	8	34	25	56	49
Wales	12	7	32	24	58	54
Scotland	8	4	19	19	44	42
Northern Ireland[a]	5	1	14	6	33	20
Italy	19	9	32	16	48	28
Greece	11	3	15	8	38	18
Netherlands	9	3	23	18	56	47
France	6	2	9	5	23	11
Sweden	6	2	12	8	23	17
Czech Republic	6	3	14	6	32	26
Germany	5	2	15	11	46	33
Ireland	5	2	7	6	20	16
Canada	5	2	14	9	34	23
Spain	5	2	10	4	32	25
USA	4	3	9	7	21	11
Denmark	4	2	15	8	50	44
Switzerland	3	1	13	6	39	28
Norway	3	1	8	6	20	19
Finland	3	1	7	7	18	16
Portugal	3	0.3	13	4	21	11
HBSC Average	7	3	15	9	34	24

[a] Figures are for 1997/98
Source: Currie et al (2000, 2004)

Trends

The proportion of young people drinking increases with age, and drinking is more prevalent among boys than among girls. Chart 5.1 shows that in 2001/02 (1997/98 for Northern Ireland) the proportion of boys who drank in the last week rose from 14 per cent of 11-year-olds to 56 per cent of 15-year-olds in England, and from 12 per cent to 58 per cent in Wales, 8 per cent to 44 per cent in Scotland and 5 per cent to 33 per cent in Northern Ireland across the same age range. For girls, the proportions are lower and the same trend exists – with rates rising from 8 per cent of 11-year-olds to 49 per cent of 15-year-olds in England, from 7 per cent to 54 per cent in Wales, 4 per cent to 42 per cent in Scotland and 1 per cent to 20 per cent in Northern Ireland across the same age range.

Although generally the same proportion of young people within each age-group has consumed alcohol over time, what is of concern is the amount of

Chart 5.1: Weekly drinking among young people by age (%) (2001/02a)

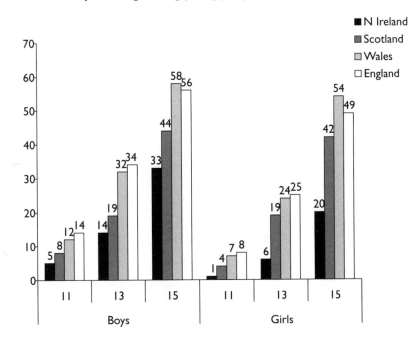

ᵃ Data for Northern Ireland are from 1997/98
Source: Currie *et al* (2000, 2004)

alcohol being consumed particularly in one session – referred to as 'binge drinking'. The proportion of young people reporting drinking five or more drinks during the last 30 days in Scotland was 37 per cent for both boys and girls. However, in Northern Ireland this rose to 61 per cent of boys and 46 per cent of girls. In England, the mean number of units of alcohol consumed in the last seven days rose from 6 to 11 units between 1988 and 2003 among boys, and from 5 to 9 units during the same period among girls (Chart 5.2). In Scotland, the average number of units consumed has remained constant between 1998 and 2002 at 9/10 units for those aged 13 and at 12/13 units among those aged 15.

Increased rates of alcohol consumption, particularly among older children, have been associated with a change in the environment in which alcohol is consumed. In a review of studies, Forsey, Loretto and Plant (1996) showed that higher alcohol consumption is related to drinking outside the home and in the company of peers, as opposed to drinking in the home with parents. A more recent literature review by Newburn and Shinner (2001) showed that while young people up to the age of 13 tend to drink at home under the supervision of

Chart 5.2: Mean alcohol consumption (units) in last seven days: England 1988–2003

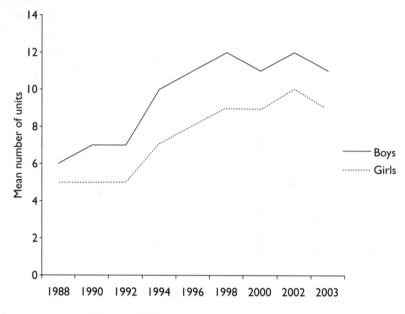

Source: Department of Health (2003a)

parents, those aged 14/15 prefer to drink outside the family environment and tend to be more secretive about their behaviour, although by the time they reach 16 or 17 young people see themselves as being more responsible drinkers: they see drinking as a sign of maturity and are more open about their drinking behaviour with their parents.

Smoking

Prevalence of smoking

Reducing the prevalence of smoking cigarettes among children in the UK is an *Opportunity for All* indicator (DWP, 2003b), and is linked to the White Paper *Smoking Kills* (UK Government, 1998) and *A Breath of Fresh Air for Scotland* (Scottish Executive, 2004a), both of which have set targets to reduce the prevalence of smoking among those aged 11–15 to 11 per cent by 2005 and to 9 per cent by 2010 in England and in Scotland to reduce smoking among young people aged 13–15 to 12 per cent in 2005 and to 11 per cent by 2010. The proportion of young people who smoke regularly (ie, weekly) is 9 per cent in

England and 13 per cent in Scotland. The proportion who smoked during the last 30 days in Northern Ireland was 32 per cent.

The prevalence of smoking regularly not only varies between countries and regions of the UK, but there are also gender differences, with girls being more likely to smoke than boys. For example, the proportion of boys smoking varies between 29 per cent in Northern Ireland to 7 per cent in England, and among girls the proportions vary between 35 per cent in Northern Ireland and 11 per cent in England. Although some of these findings may be due to methodological differences (Table 5.3).

Table 5.3: Prevalence of smoking in the UK

	Boys	Girls
Regular smokers (%)		
England[a]	7	11
Wales[b]	9	16
Scotland[c]	11	16
Northern Ireland[d]	29	35

[a] based on percentage of 11–15-year-olds who smoked weekly in 2003
[b] average percentage of 11–16-year-olds who smoked weekly in 2000
[c] based on percentage of 13- and 15-year-olds who were regular smokers in 2002
[d] based on percentage of 15- and 16-year-olds who smoked during past 30 days 1999
Source: Department of Health (2003a), Roberts *et al* (2002), Currie *et al* (2003), Miller and Plant (2001)

International comparisons show that among those aged 11, the proportion of boys who smoke every day in England is above the average for all the countries and regions included in the HBSC survey, while among girls the proportions are above average in the whole of the UK with the exception of Scotland. Among those aged 13, the proportion smoking regularly is above the average in the whole of the UK with the exception of boys in Scotland. In the oldest age group (15 years) the proportion smoking regularly is below average among boys, although among girls the proportion is higher for all UK countries and regions (Table 5.4).

Table 5.4: Young people who smoke every day by country/region, age and gender (%) (2001/02)

Country/Region	Aged 11		Aged 13		Aged 15	
	Boys	Girls	Boys	Girls	Boys	Girls
England	2	1	7	9	16	20
Wales	1	1	6	12	12	22
Scotland	1	0.4	3	6	13	19
Northern Ireland[a]	1	1	7	10	16	24
Italy	1	0	3	3	16	16
Greece	1	0	3	1	9	11
Netherlands	0	0	4	6	19	20
France	1	0.4	4	3	20	20
Sweden	0	0	3	4	6	14
Czech Republic	1	0.3	6	4	20	23
Germany	2	0.3	10	10	26	29
Ireland	1	1	3	6	15	17
Canada	1	0.3	4	5	13	11
Spain	1	1	5	4	17	23
USA	1	0.3	5	2	12	8
Denmark	0	0.2	3	3	14	16
Switzerland	1	0.3	5	3	18	17
Norway	0.2	0.4	3	4	16	20
Finland	0.3	1	7	6	22	23
Portugal	1	1	8	5	13	20
HBSC Average	1	0.4	5	4	18	17

[a] Figures are for 1997/98
Source: Currie *et al* (2000, 2004)

Trends

The proportion of young people smoking increases with age, and past the age of 11 is more prevalent among girls than boys. Chart 5.3 shows that in 2001/02 (1997/98 for Northern Ireland) the proportion of boys who smoked daily rose from 1 per cent of 11-year-olds to 12 per cent of 15-year-olds in Wales, 1 per cent to 13 per cent in Scotland, 2 per cent to 16 per cent in England, and 1 per cent to 16 per cent in Northern Ireland, across the same age range. Among girls, the proportions rose from 0.4 per cent of 11-year-olds to 19 per cent of 15-year-olds in Scotland, 1 per cent to 20 per cent in England, 1 per cent to 22 per cent in Wales and 1 per cent to 24 per cent in Northern Ireland across the same age range.

The proportion of young people smoking regularly within each age group and each UK country or region has varied over time. In England, smoking rates

Chart 5.3: Daily smoking among young people by age (%): (2001/02)[a]

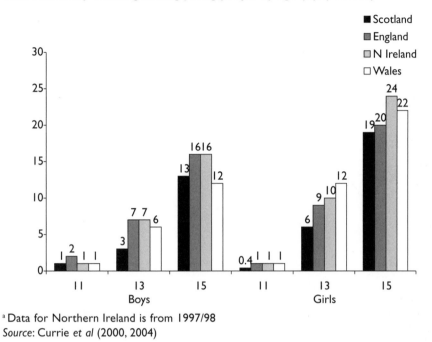

[a] Data for Northern Ireland is from 1997/98
Source: Currie *et al* (2000, 2004)

peaked during 1996, from between 8 per cent of 13-year-old boys to 33 per cent of 15-year-old girls, but have since then generally declined, to between 5 per cent of 13-year-old boys to 23 per cent of 15-year-old girls (Chart 5.4). In Scotland, among children aged 13, the proportion who smoke regularly has remained stable among girls at about 8–10 per cent, and among boys there was an initial rise from 7 per cent to a peak of 11 per cent in 1994 – but this has since fallen to 6 per cent in 2002. In Scotland among children aged 15, there was also an initial increase from 24 per cent of boys and 26 per cent of girls in 1986 to a peak of 30 per cent for both in 1996 – this has since fallen to 16 per cent of boys and 24 per cent of girls (Chart 5.5). Contrary to these trends, however, Wales on the whole has seen an increase in the proportion of young smokers, particularly among girls aged 13 and 14, where smoking rates have increased from 12–17 per cent between 1986 and 2000, and among those aged 15 and 16 the rates have risen from 16 to 20 per cent among boys and from 20 to 30 per cent among girls over the same period (Chart 5.6).

Chart 5.4: Regular smoking among young people 13–15: England 1986–2002 (%)

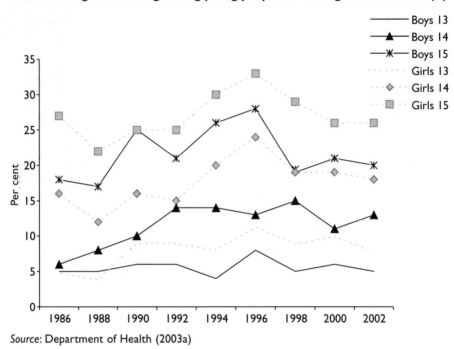

Source: Department of Health (2003a)

Chart 5.5: Regular smoking among young people aged 13 and 15: Scotland 1986–2002 (%)

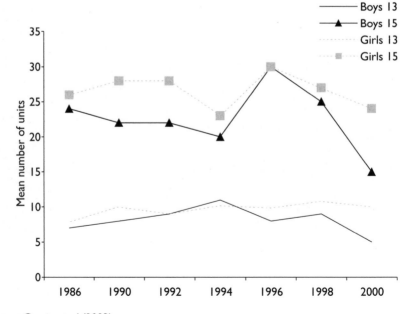

Source: Currie *et al* (2003)

Chart 5.6: Regular smoking among young people 13–16: Wales 1986–2000 (%)

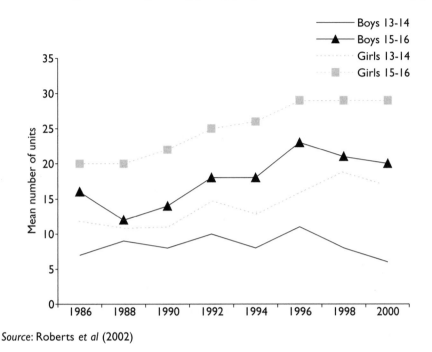

Source: Roberts *et al* (2002)

Alcohol- and smoking-related problems

Increased rates of alcohol consumption have led to concerns over binge drinking and its association with anti-social or harmful behaviour. Young people who engage in acute or periodic heavy drinking are more at risk of violence, unsafe sexual behaviour, traffic and other accidents, permanent disabilities and death (WHO, 2001). Although adolescent smoking may not immediately be associated with serious health risks, daily smoking in young people has been associated with poorer perceived health and other psychological problems, and with smoking-related illness in later life (Holeman *et al*, 2000; Bartecchi *et al*, 1994). Miller and Plant (2001) showed that in the UK at least one in three boys and nearly half of girls had ever experienced problems due to alcohol or drug use (Table 5.5). Problems were most likely to be experienced by boys in Northern Ireland (48 per cent) and by girls in Wales (50 per cent).

Table 5.5: Percentage of young people who have experienced problems due to alcohol or drugs

	England	Northern Ireland	Scotland	Wales
Boys	39%	48%	41%	39%
Girls	43%	43%	47%	50%

Source: Miller and Plant (2001)

Why young people smoke and drink

Despite the fact that the majority of young people know the harmful effects of smoking and drinking (Miller and Plant, 2001; Potter, 2002) they still engage in such behaviour, as the statistics above show. Many studies have sought to identify factors predicting, or correlated with, tobacco or alcohol use but most acknowledge the complexity of distinguishing the cause and effect of abuse of such substances. Studies have found smoking and drinking behaviour to be associated with teenage subcultures (Van der Rijt *et al*, 2002), identity and social integration (Johnson *et al*, 2003), the presence of significant others who smoke or drink (Potter, 2002; Tucker *et al*, 2003), and non-traditional family structure (Bjarnason *et al*, 2003).[2] However, national and international studies have failed to find a relationship between smoking and drinking and families' social or economic status. A survey by the Office for National Statistics (ONS) did not find any relationship between alcohol consumption and socio-economic status, and reported that the highest proportions of frequent drinkers were among those from better-off families, as well as those with lower education achievements (Goddard, 1997). The HBSC survey, despite including a different number of measures of socio-economic status, also did not find any relationship between families' socio-economic position and smoking behaviour in young people (Currie *et al*, 2000).

Smoking and alcohol reduction

Despite a growth in the popularity of educational approaches to reducing alcohol and tobacco consumption over the past few decades, such methods have proved to have limited effect, as the statistics show. Reviews of the research into why young people drink, for example, show that such behaviour is deemed part of

---

[2] For a review of previous studies, refer to Coles and Maile (2002).

the normal socialisation of becoming an adult, and that campaigns which seek to reduce such behaviour in young people are considered hypocritical when the British drinking culture normalises alcohol consumption among adults (Potter, 2002). A review of interventions in alcohol control carried out by the WHO (2004a) argues that educational approaches are less effective than more practical ones: eg, findings showed that advertising and advertising bans had a limited effect on reducing alcohol consumption, although research into smoking prevention suggests that while campaigns by themselves do not affect smoking rates, they can postpone its initiation (Reid *et al*, 1995). What such studies have shown, however, is that some of the most successful and cost-effective means of reducing alcohol and cigarette consumption include: increasing prices; stricter controls on access; and lowered blood alcohol concentration limits for young people (compared to those for adults) in respect of drink-driving offences (Emery *et al*, 2001; Sweanor and Martial, 1994; WHO, 2004a). Concerns with binge drinking and the continued trends in smoking behaviour have led to the implementation of Government strategies which now seek to tackle alcohol misuse and reduce smoking through direct as well as educational means, not only among young people but within the adult population generally (Currie *et al*, 2003; Department of Health, 2003a; Miller and Plant, 2001; Roberts *et al*, 2002).

Obesity

Widespread concern over childhood obesity has recently led to this becoming a governmental priority. The links between childhood obesity and adult health problems are not certain, but children who are overweight tend to follow obesity into adulthood. Obesity in adulthood has serious implications – increased risk of heart attack, stroke, Type 2 diabetes, bowel cancer and high blood pressure. Indeed, there have recently been cases of children diagnosed with mature onset (or Type 2) diabetes, which in the past has occurred only in middle or older age (see Chapter 4). However, children and adolescents very rarely have lifestyle-related diseases, although they do form the early phases of accumulated exposure to risk factors through the life course. Also, children and adolescents can have high levels of various risk factors for diseases, one of which is obesity. Psychologically, being an overweight child can be very distressing as a result of teasing, which affects confidence and self-esteem and can lead to isolation and depression (BUPA, 2004). There are also fears that obesity threatens to reverse gains in longevity made during the last hundred years, in which today's children will die at a younger age than their parents will. This concern has been triggered by the rising levels of overweight and obesity among children – between 1996 and 2001, the proportion of obese children aged 6–15 years rose by 3.5 per cent. The Health Survey for England (HSE) suggests that a significant number of children are either overweight or obese; in 2001, 8.5 per cent of six-year-olds and 15 per cent of 15-year-olds were obese. Around 16 per cent of children aged 2 to 15 years old are now obese. We can see from Chart 5.7 that children's (age 0–15) mean body mass index (BMI) has been gradually increasing since 1995 for both boys and girls, with girls having a consistently higher BMI than boys.

Chart 5.7: Boys and girls (aged 0–15) mean body mass index (kg/m2) 1995– 2002

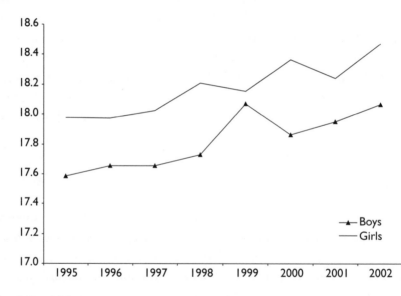

Source: HSE 2001

Childhood obesity levels in England, Wales and Scotland are also some of the highest internationally. Table 5.6 shows the ten countries with the highest overall levels of obesity for boys and girls aged 11, 13- and 15-year-olds using the HBSC (the highest average obesity level is ranked first). England, Wales and Scotland have the 4th, 5th and 6th highest obesity levels of all 35 countries in the study.

The increase in overweight and obesity is most likely due to changes in diet

Table 5.6: Obesity levels in the 10 countries with the highest levels of obesity[a]

	Boys	Girls	Rank
Malta	9.2	5.1	1
USA	9.4	4.6	2
Canada	4.5	3.4	3
England	4.5	3.0	4
Wales	5.0	2.4	5
Scotland	2.6	2.4	6
Hungary	3.1	1.6	7
Ireland	2.7	2.0	8
Finland	3.0	1.5	9
Greece	2.8	1.4	10
Average	2.4	1.3	

[a] Of the 35 countries who took part in the HBSC
Source: Currie et al (2004) and authors' own calculations

and physical activity. Britain's poor childhood obesity record compared to other countries suggests that British children perform poorly in relation to these factors. This section of this chapter serves to update information on both diet and physical activity among children, and to provide international comparisons.

Physical activity

Physical activity has a range of benefits during childhood, but the primary role of physical activity is that it helps prevent excess weight gain during childhood, or helps overweight children lose weight. It is recommended that people aged 5–18 should participate in physical activity of at least moderate intensity for one hour a day, five or more days a week. Moderate intensity is defined as being equivalent to brisk walking, which might leave the participant feeling warm and slightly out of breath (Currie et al, 2004). Physical activity can take a variety of forms. Active free play is an important aspect of physical activity for children, and is dealt with separately in Chapter 7. This chapter is concerned with more structured physical activity in the form of sport, which may take place both in school in PE lessons and out of school.

The HBSC survey provides data on the proportion of children undertaking the recommended level of physical activity. Table 5.7 shows a cross-country comparison of the proportion of young people (age 11, 13 and 15) who undertake the recommended physical activity each day. Countries are shown in descending order – ie, those with the highest proportion of children undertaking the recommended level of activity are ranked number 1 and are at the top.

- The proportion of young people undertaking the recommended amount of physical activity each day is lower than 50 per cent in all countries.
- The proportion of children *not* undertaking the recommended amount of physical activity each day in England is 58 per cent, Scotland is 62 per cent, and Wales, 64 per cent.
- Boys in all of the countries are more likely than girls to undertake the recommended amount of physical activity each day.
- England, Scotland and Wales have a relatively good record of physical activity compared to other countries, with England falling in the top ten countries with the highest proportion of children undertaking the recommended amount.

As well as lower sports participation among children, there is greater use of cars for short journeys. Increasing car use is commonly seen to be one of a number of factors explaining decreasing levels of physical activity in both children and adults. According to figures from the National Travel Survey for Great Britain, over 70 per cent of all travel by children is now by car, contrasting with a figure of 37 per cent in 1964 (Mackett *et al*, 2002). But parental reluctance to allow children to play outdoors and the increasing popularity of sedentary activities, such as watching TV, have also been associated with obesity. Table 5.7 also shows a cross-country comparison of the proportion of young people (age 11, 13 and 15) who watch TV for four or more hours a day on weekdays. Again, the country with the best record – ie, with the lowest proportion of boys and girls who watch TV for four or more hours a day – is ranked number 1. The country with the worst record is ranked number 35. Children tend to watch more TV at weekends, and thus the proportion for each country would be higher if we were investigating TV watching at weekends. We can see that:

- There is little difference between girls and boys in terms of watching television, for all countries especially in England, Wales and Scotland.
- England, Scotland and Wales have a relatively poor record in relation to television watching – both Scotland and Wales fall within the top ten countries with the highest proportion of children watching television for four or more hours a day.

Table 5.7: Cross-country comparison of young people (age 11, 13 and 15) who undertake the recommended physical activity each day and who watch four or more hours of television a day on weekdays (%)

Physical Activity[a]	Girls	Boys	Rank	Watching TV	Girls	Boys	Rank
USA	43.5	56.4	1	Switzerland	9.9	12.5	1
Canada	40.2	50	2	Austria	13.2	16.8	2
Ireland	40	49.6	3	Malta	16.3	19.4	3
Lithuania	35.6	50	4	Sweden	17	18.7	4
Czech Republic	35.7	49.7	5	Greece	14.5	21.7	5
England	32.6	51.1	6	Slovenia	16.9	20.9	6
Greenland	36.8	46.1	7	Finland	19.6	18.6	7
Austria	33.8	47.7	8	Belgium (French)	17.1	21.1	8
Slovenia	31.6	48.6	9	France	16.9	21.4	9
Netherlands	37.5	42.1	10	Ireland	17.3	21.5	10
Scotland	30.7	46.4	11	Hungary	18.8	22	11
Greece	27.6	44.2	12	Germany	18.3	22.6	12
Wales	28.1	43.6	13	Spain	21.9	22.8	13
Poland	29.7	41.1	14	Belgium (Flemish)	18.3	26.4	14
Malta	25.1	45	15	Italy	24.4	21.1	15
Ukraine	26.4	42	16	Denmark	21.1	25.5	16
Finland	30	37.6	17	Canada	20.8	26.3	17
Denmark	30.3	37	18	Netherlands	20.4	27	18
Switzerland	27.6	39.3	19	Greenland	23.8	26.2	19
Sweden	30.7	35.9	20	Czech Republic	22.9	29.3	20
Croatia	24.8	41.3	21	Norway	25.1	27.1	21
Spain	26.1	39.5	22	TFYR Macedonia	25.8	30.7	22
Russian Federation	24.9	38	23	Poland	24.4	34.2	23
Israel	22.8	38.4	24	USA	28.4	31.2	24
Latvia	23.4	37.4	25	England	29.7	31.3	25
Hungary	22.4	37.4	26	Scotland	29.7	31.6	26
TFYR Macedonia	25	32.8	27	Croatia	28.7	34.4	27
Germany	20	31.8	28	Wales	32.3	31.1	28
Norway	21.8	29.3	29	Portugal	33.9	31.5	29
Italy	20.6	30.1	30	Lithuania	29.3	38.4	30
Estonia	21.7	29	31	Russian Federation	30.8	37.7	31
Portugal	16.7	33.6	32	Estonia	33.6	43.3	32
Belgium (Flemish)	16.8	26	33	Latvia	34.5	43.1	33
France	12	26.8	34	Israel	45.6	43.7	34
				Ukraine	43.3	48.8	35
HBSC average	27.4	40		HBSC average	24.2	28.3	

[a] Data not available for Belgium (French)

Source: Currie et al (2004) and authors' own calculations

Trends

The British Household Panel Survey (BHPS) provides trend data for England, Wales and Scotland:

- In 1998, regional differences in frequency of sport playing for 11–16-year-olds were apparent: Welsh children were more likely than English and Scottish children to play sport 'most days'.
- Scottish children were most likely to play sport 'hardly ever'.
- Between 1998 and 2001 Wales experienced a decrease in the proportion of children playing sport 'most days' – from 69 per cent to 45 per cent, thus closing the regional differences.

Chart 5.8: Frequency of playing sport between 1998 and 2001 in England, Wales and Scotland

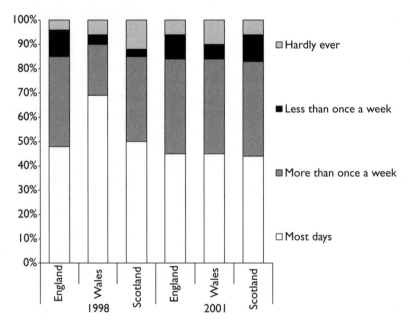

Source: BHPS

Relative to other countries, Scotland, England and Wales have a good record for children undertaking the recommended level of physical activity every day. However, 61 per cent of young people in Great Britain (GB) are not undertaking the recommended level, and this rises to 70 per cent for girls. Thus, the GB record for physical activity is actually very poor. Moreover, trend data suggest Welsh sporting activity has declined dramatically among children aged 11–16 in recent years. Also, England, Wales and Scotland's record of watching television is relatively poor – with about a third of children in each country watching four or more hours of television on weekdays.

Diet

The key for obesity levels is whether children are burning off enough energy relative to the amount consumed. Evidence suggests that energy intake in GB was below the Estimated Average Requirement (EAR) for both genders of all ages in 1997, and has actually decreased since the early 1980s. However, the main sources of energy in diets in 1997 were broadly similar to those identified in the early 1980s (Searle, 2002). Thus, while energy intake is important for young people for growth and development, diet and nutrition play a vital part in obesity. The next section investigates dietary behaviour.

Dietary behaviours that emerge in childhood may set the pattern for later in life. Good nutrition is important from day one, and studies show that breastfeeding a baby, even if only for a short period of time, may reduce the risk of obesity in later life (BUPA, 2004) (see 'Infant feeding' in Chapter 4). As children mature, their nutritional requirements change, as do dietary recommendations. The UK Government's recommended consumption of fruit and vegetables is five portions a day, and research has indicated that higher intakes of fruit and vegetables are associated with a lower risk of cancer and coronary heart disease (Department of Health, 1994, 1998c). The HBSC provides an international comparison of young people's consumption of vegetables and fruit (in separate questions). Unfortunately, Northern Ireland was not included in this survey year, and the data produced for 1997/98 are not comparable with the 2001/02 data. Northern Ireland is therefore excluded from this analysis, and will be discussed separately below. Table 5.8 gives a cross-country comparison of young people (age 11, 13 and 15) who eat vegetables or fruit every day. The country with the best record, ie, with the highest proportion of boys and girls consuming vegetables or fruit every day, is ranked number 1. The country with the worst record is ranked number 35.

- In nearly all countries and regions, girls have a better record than boys for both vegetable and fruit consumption.
- Scotland has a relatively good record for consumption of fruit and vegetables compared to England and Wales.

Table 5.8: Cross-country comparison of young people (age 11, 13 and 15) who eat vegetables and fruit every day

Vegetables	Girls	Boys	Rank	Fruit	Girls	Boys	Rank
Belgium (Flemish)	57.8	46.9	1	Israel	53.7	48.7	1
Israel	51.2	46.1	2	Portugal	52.1	43.5	2
Ukraine	48.7	43.7	3	Malta	50.9	43.2	3
Belgium (French)	48.5	41.4	4	Poland	51.2	41	4
France	45.9	41	5	TFYR Macedonia	46.8	39.4	5
Netherlands	43.6	37.6	6	Germany	46.9	37.9	6
Canada	44.1	35.7	7	Czech Republic	48.8	35.6	7
Ireland	42.2	36.3	8	Slovenia	44.4	32.7	8
Poland	40.4	32.3	9	Italy	38.5	38.4	9
Russian Federation	38	33.7	10	Belgium (French)	40	36.4	10
Switzerland	37.4	30.1	11	Greece	41.2	35	11
Scotland	35.9	30.5	12	Austria	42.9	31.9	12
TFYR Macedonia	35.5	29.6	13	Canada	40.7	34	13
Germany	37.9	26.2	14	Spain	37.6	35.7	14
Lithuania	31	29.3	15	Switzerland	40	30.9	15
Sweden	32.1	27.7	16	Croatia	38.2	31.8	16
USA	32.6	26.9	17	France	34.4	34	17
Greenland	30.1	27.7	18	Scotland	35.8	31.0	18
Latvia	30.8	26.4	19	Ireland	36.2	28.9	19
England	31	25.9	20	Denmark	38.4	25.4	20
Denmark	31.4	25.3	21	Hungary	33.4	29.3	21
Czech Republic	31.6	23.7	22	Norway	34.7	23.4	22
Portugal	29.5	22.6	23	Netherlands	29.7	26.4	23
Croatia	25.7	25.5	24	USA	27.5	27.9	24
Slovenia	29.6	21.6	25	Russian Federation	29.1	24.8	25
Norway	24.7	19.4	26	Sweden	27.9	25.5	26
Finland	27.3	16.4	27	England	28.9	24.5	27
Italy	25.8	17.7	28	Belgium (Flemish)	30.3	22.1	28
Greece	23.4	19.5	29	Ukraine	25.7	23.4	29
Wales	23.1	19.5	30	Latvia	25.8	21.8	30
Austria	17	15.3	31	Wales	26.1	20	31
Malta	18.1	13.8	32	Lithuania	24.2	20.3	32
Estonia	16.5	14.3	33	Finland	26.6	16.4	33
Hungary	16	13.8	34	Greenland	19.9	22.1	34
Spain	11.3	10.3	35	Estonia	22.9	17.3	35
HBSC average	33.8	28		HBSC average	36.4	30.2	

Source: Currie et al (2004) and authors' own calculations

- England and Wales have a significantly worse ranking for the everyday consumption of fruit compared to vegetables.
- Wales has one of the worst records of vegetable consumption of all countries – falling in the ten countries with the lowest proportion of children consuming vegetables every day.
- Both Wales and England have one of the worst records of fruit consumption of all countries – falling in the ten countries with the lowest proportion of children consuming fruit every day.

The survey of eating habits among children and young people in Northern Ireland asked questions about consumption of fruit and vegetables. Chart 5.9 shows the number of portions of fruit and vegetables eaten a day by children aged 5–17.

- Boys are less likely than girls to eat any portions of fruit or vegetables a day.
- Older children are slightly less likely than younger children to eat no portions of fruit and vegetables a day.

Chart 5.9: The number of portions of fruit and vegetables eaten a day by children in Northern Ireland

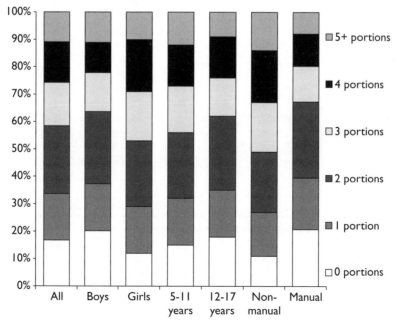

Source: Health Promotion Agency (2001)

Table 5.9: Cross-country comparison of young people (age 11, 13 and 15) who eat sweets and soft drinks every day

Sweets	Girls	Boys	Rank	Soft drinks	Girls	Boys	Rank
Finland	8.6	9.3	1	Finland	8.6	9.3	1
Denmark	11.3	11.8	2	Denmark	11.3	11.8	2
Sweden	12.2	14.9	3	Sweden	12.2	14.9	3
Greece	15.4	15.5	4	Greece	15.4	15.5	4
Norway	15.3	16.2	5	Norway	15.3	16.2	5
Lithuania	20.7	17.2	6	Latvia	13.2	18.5	6
Austria	22.5	20.2	7	Ukraine	15.3	18.9	7
Canada	21.5	23.3	8	Lithuania	20.1	17.2	8
Portugal	21.3	24	9	Austria	22.5	20.2	9
Spain	23.3	23.4	10	Russian Federation	19.6	24.1	10
Russian Federation	26.6	23.1	11	Canada	21.5	23.3	11
Czech Republic	24.8	25.6	12	Czech Republic	26.4	22	12
Slovenia	27.1	25.7	13	Italy	20.6	28.5	13
Wales	27.4	26.3	14	Poland	20.2	30.6	14
Germany	28.3	26.6	15	France	25.6	32.4	15
Switzerland	27.1	27.8	16	Spain	25.8	34.3	16
Latvia	29.1	25.9	17	Germany	25.3	34.9	17
Estonia	30	26.4	18	Croatia	31.3	33.5	18
France	26.7	30.2	19	Hungary	31.7	33.4	19
Belgium (Flemish)	25.4	32.2	20	Switzerland	27.1	38.1	20
England	31.5	31.7	21	Portugal	29.6	36.9	21
USA	34.3	31.5	22	Estonia	30	37.7	22
Hungary	36	31.4	23	TFYR Macedonia	31.3	37.3	23
Croatia	35.6	32.7	24	Greenland	30.2	40.7	24
Ukraine	37.9	32.8	25	Wales	35.4	37.6	25
Poland	37	35.8	26	Netherlands	24.7	49.3	26
Greenland	41.7	31.9	27	Ireland	34.3	40.3	27
Italy	38.5	37.9	28	Belgium (French)	33.4	42.5	28
Israel	41.8	39.5	29	England	36.4	40.6	29
TFYR Macedonia	44	39.9	30	Belgium (Flemish)	31.9	47.7	30
Belgium (French)	42.8	42.9	31	Slovenia	37.3	42.7	31
Netherlands	41.3	44.7	32	Malta	38	42.4	32
Scotland	42.9	46.8	33	USA	39.4	45.4	33
Ireland	49.4	48.1	34	Scotland	43.5	50.9	34
Malta	55	52.6	35	Israel	51	56.1	35
HBSC average	29.2	28.5		HBSC average	29.2	28.5	

Source: Currie *et al* (2004) and authors' own calculations

- Children from manual social groups are less likely than children from non-manual groups to eat any fruit and vegetables a day, and less likely to eat five portions a day.

There is evidence that eating a lot of energy-dense foods is a risk factor for obesity (WHO, 2002a). The HBSC provides an international comparison of young people's consumption of sweets and soft drinks (asked about in separate questions). Table 5.9 gives a cross-country comparison of young people (age 11, 13 and 15) who eat sweets and soft drinks every day. The country with the best record, ie, with the lowest proportion of boys and girls consuming sweets or soft drinks every day, is ranked number 1. The country with the worst record is ranked number 35.

- In Scotland, boys were more likely than girls to consume sweets every day, whereas there was little difference between the sexes in most other countries.
- In Wales, England and Scotland, as in most other countries, boys were more likely than girls to consume soft drinks every day.
- Scotland has one of the worst records for both sweets and soft drink consumption – only Ireland and Malta have a higher proportion of children consuming sweets every day, and only Israel has a higher proportion consuming soft drinks every day.
- Wales, England and Scotland rank among the worst ten countries for consumption of soft drinks every day.

Northern Ireland

The survey of eating habits among children and young people in Northern Ireland undertaken in 1999 asked about consumption of confectionery and sugary fizzy drinks by children in Northern Ireland. Chart 5.10 shows consumption of confectionery:

- There is no difference between consumption of confectionery between boys and girls.
- Older children are more likely than younger children to consume confectionery more than once a day, regardless of gender.
- Children in manual social class groups are more likely to consume confectionery every day compared to children in non-manual social class groups.

Chart 5.11 shows consumption of fizzy sugary drinks for Northern Ireland:

- Boys were more likely than girls to consume sugary fizzy drinks more than once a day.
- Younger children were slightly more likely than older children to consume sugary fizzy drinks every day.

Chart 5.10: Frequency of confectionery consumption by children in Northern Ireland

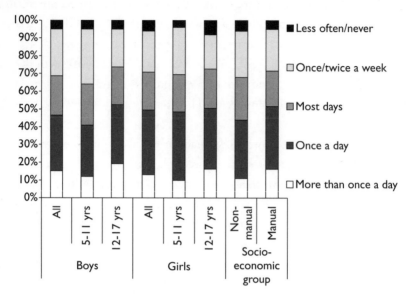

Source: Health Promotion Agency (2001)

Chart 5.11: Frequency of sugary fizzy drink consumption by children in Northern Ireland

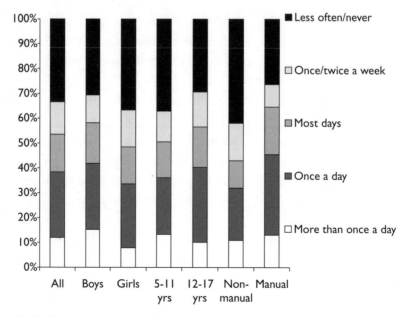

Source: Health Promotion Agency (2001)

- Children from non-manual socio-economic groups were more likely to consume sugary fizzy drinks less often than once a week compared to children in manual socio-economic groups.

Conclusion

This chapter has reviewed the well-being of children in respect of different lifestyle factors. It has shown that drinking is more prevalent among boys and smoking is more prevalent among girls. Among girls in the UK, smoking rates are above average in comparison to other European countries, and in Wales smoking rates are increasing compared to a general decrease in other UK countries and regions. Concerns about the negative effects of binge drinking and the health effects of smoking have led to the implementation of strategies which seek to reduce both activities among young people and within the population generally. However, research shows that health promotion may be more effectively achieved through direct measures (such as increased prices) than through educational campaigns.

In terms of physical activity, cross-country comparative evidence shows that levels for England, Wales and Scotland are relatively good. However, this masks the fact that the majority of young people are not undertaking the recommended amount of physical activity. Indeed, much of children's time is spent on more sedentary activities such as watching television. Low physical activity levels can be explained by the low energy levels of some British children, indicated by the failure to reach estimated average requirements for energy intake. Moreover, while energy intake is low, the diet of UK children is relatively poor – specifically, low consumption of vegetables (especially in Wales), low consumption of fruit (especially in England and Wales), but high consumption of sweets (especially in Scotland) and high consumption of fizzy drinks in England, Scotland and Wales. Likewise, among Northern Irish children, the consumption of fruit and vegetables is low, but consumption of sweets and sugary fizzy drinks is high. Thus, low physical activity and high levels of sedentary activity, coupled with a diet of high fat/high energy-dense food, goes some way to explain the high, and increasing, levels of obesity among UK children.

6 Mental health and well-being

Deborah Quilgars, Beverley Searle and Antonia Keung

Key statistics:

Mental health

- UK-wide, older children experience more mental health problems than younger children; boys are more likely to experience conduct disorders and girls are more likely to worry and suffer from depression.
- Family relationships, parenting style and parental mental health are linked to children's mental health.
- Income levels and social class are associated with only some forms of mental disorders and do not tend to predict well-being.

Suicide

- Suicide in the UK is more prevalent among boys than girls and increases with age.
- Substance abuse accounts for 43 per cent of suicides and 62 per cent of undetermined deaths of females aged 10–19 in England and Wales.
- Hanging and suffocation account for 43 per cent of suicides and 32 per cent of undetermined deaths in males aged 10–19 in England and Wales.

Key trends:

Mental health

- Conduct disorders are more persistent over time than emotional disorders (England, Wales and Scotland).
- There is some evidence that young people are worrying more about certain issues, and that conduct and emotional problems have increased over the last 25 years.

Suicide

- Between 1990 and 2002 there was a 27 per cent reduction in the number of suicides among 0–24-year-olds in the UK.
- Suicide rates remain higher in Scotland and Northern Ireland than in England and Wales.

Key sources:

Mental health

- Office for National Statistics (ONS) Survey of Children's Mental Health in England, Scotland and Wales
- The annual Health Surveys for England and Scotland
- The British Household Panel Survey (BHPS)
- International World Health Organization Health Behaviour in School-age Children (HBSC) studies
- School Health Education Unit (SHEU) Health-Related Behaviour Questionnaire (HRBQ)

Suicide

- Mortality Statistics for England and Wales, Scotland and Northern Ireland
- World Health Organization (WHO) Mortality database
- Population Trends

Introduction

This chapter critically reviews the evidence on the prevalence and nature of the mental well-being of children and young people in Britain. The recent *Child Poverty Review* (HM Treasury, 2004a) reaffirmed the importance of promoting child and adolescent mental health, and this is reflected in the development of the *Children's National Service Framework* (Department of Health, 2004) in England and Wales. Similarly, the Scottish *National Programme for Improving Mental Health and Well-Being* (Scottish Executive, 2003e) has identified the improvement of mental health of children and young people as a priority area for 2003–06. At the same time, a *Review of Mental Health and Learning Disability* (www.rmhldni. gov.uk) is currently being conducted in Northern Ireland; it includes a Child and Adolescent Mental Health Expert Working Committee.

The chapter takes a broad definition of mental health. The first sections consider children's overall emotional well-being, including the extent to which young people report that they feel happy and/or experience worry in their lives, alongside studies that examine clinically measured mental 'disorders' where a specific problem may be associated with considerable distress and interference with the child's everyday life (Meltzer *et al*, 2000). Results of original secondary analysis of the youth questionnaire of the British Household Panel Survey (BHPS), conducted for this report, are also presented. The last section considers suicide and self-harm, the most negative manifestations of poor mental health among young people. Within the UK, reducing the suicide rate is used as a proxy to cover the whole of the mental health priority area, and a national target was set in 1999 to reduce suicides by 20 per cent by 2010 (Department of Health 1998d, 1999a), reinforced in the new *National Suicide Prevention Strategy for England* (Department of Health, 2002c). Similarly, with the publication in Scotland of *Choose Life: A National Strategy and Action Plan to Prevent Suicide in Scotland* a target has been set to reduce the suicide rate by 20 per cent by 2013 (Scottish Executive, 2002c). Although such targets cover the wider population, within the *National Suicide Prevention Strategy for England*, the objectives include the promotion of mental health among children and young people under 18, particularly young men who have been identified as an 'at risk' group. The Scottish strategy also identifies young people, looked-after children and young offenders as 'at risk' groups.

Key data sources

Mental health

Available data sources on the mental health of children and young people have begun to improve in recent years. The Office of National Statistics (ONS) has undertaken a specially commissioned survey of the mental health of children in the UK, including a recent follow-up study and additional surveys of young offenders and looked-after children. Also, in the 1990s a number of general population studies introduced questions on children's mental health, and as subsequent waves of such studies are commissioned, or repeat studies conducted, time-series data are slowly becoming available. However, a key gap remains in terms of studies that systematically measure children's more general levels of emotional well-being and happiness, where studies tend to be one-off and/or non-representative surveys.

The key studies reviewed on mental health for this chapter, most of which have been updated since Quilgars (2002), include:

- *ONS Survey of the Mental Health of Children and Young People* (Meltzer *et al*, 2000): Survey of 10,438 children (aged 5–15), covering England, Scotland and Wales in 1999, with a follow-up survey in 2002.

- The *British Household Panel Survey (BHPS)*: Covering England, Scotland, Wales and Northern Ireland, includes interviews with young people aged 11–15 since 1993, with the same cohort being interviewed annually.

- The annual *Health Surveys for England* (Prescott-Clarke and Primatesta, 1998; Sproston and Primatesta, 2003) and for *Scotland* (Shaw *et al*, 2000): The English survey has included questions about children's mental health since 1995; the Scottish survey since 1998. The English survey included over 8,000 interviews, and the Scottish survey nearly 4,000 interviews with children under 16.

- International World Health Organization (WHO) *Health Behaviour Survey of School-aged Children* (HBSC) (two recent reports: Currie *et al*, 2000; Currie *et al*, 2004): Carried out every four years since 1982. The 2001/02 survey included over 17,000 young people aged 11–15 across England, Scotland, Wales and Ireland (Eire) (alongside 31 other countries).

- The School Health Education Unit *Health-Related Behaviour Questionnaire* (HRBQ): Non-representative, large-scale (between 10,000–20,000 a year) survey conducted since 1980, with annual reports[1] and trend data produced.

- Other national or regional studies: One-off community studies, usually of specific age groups and populations.

In order to assess the extent of mental health problems among children and young people, it is important to be clear about what measure of mental health is used in each study. The key measures of mental health used by the above studies include:

- General Health Questionnaire (GHQ12), a self-completion questionnaire asking about general levels of happiness, depressive feelings, anxiety and sleep disturbance in the last month (ONS studies; BHPS (measures based on GHQ); annual Health Surveys for England and Scotland; one-off community studies)

---

[1] Most recent report being *Young People in 2002,* Schools Health Education Unit (2003).

- Strengths and Difficulties Questionnaire (SDQ), filled out by parents, focusing on emotional and behavioural problems (ONS studies; annual Health Survey for England)
- other clinical measures used to diagnose mental illness, including the International Classification of Diseases (ONS study)
- self-reported feelings of life satisfaction, happiness, stress and worry (WHO study; HRBQ; one-off community studies).

Suicide

Since publication of the last edition, key statistical sources for suicide provide updated information, and include:

- annual national mortality statistics by age, cause and gender (ONS in England and Wales, the General Register Office in Scotland and the Northern Ireland Statistics and Research Agency)
- international statistics on mortality by cause, age and gender (WHO online statistics database).

Mental health and well-being

Personal characteristics: age, gender and ethnicity

One of the most consistent findings is that older children are more likely to experience mental health problems than younger children. The ONS study reported 8 per cent of children aged 5–10 suffered from a mental disorder, compared to 11 per cent of children aged 11–15 (Table 6.1). The odds of having a disorder were 50 per cent higher for older children (Table 6.2). The most recent Health Survey for England (HSE) for 2001/02 reported that 7 per cent of boys aged 13–15 had a high score on the GHQ12, compared to 12 per cent of young men aged 16–24. This compared to 13 per cent of girls aged 13–15 and 20 per cent of young women aged 16–24. The Scottish Health Survey 1998 showed a similar pattern, although slightly better scores were observed (5 per cent and 9 per cent for males, and 9 per cent and 17 per cent for females in the 13–15 and 16–24 age groups respectively). A recent Northern Ireland study (Northern Ireland Statistics and Research Agency, 2002) also found differentials by gender, with 25 per cent of young women and 15 per cent of young men assessed as being 'depressed' using the GHQ, and 41 per cent of

Table 6.1: Prevalence of mental disorders, by age and gender, England, Wales and Scotland

	5–10-year-olds (%)			11–15-year-olds (%)			All children (%)		
	Boys	Girls	All	Boys	Girls	All	Boys	Girls	All
Emotional disorders	3	3	3	5	6	7	4	5	4
Conduct disorders	7	3	5	9	4	6	7	3	5
Hyperkinetic disorders	3	*	2	2	1	1	2	*	1
Less common disorders	1	*	1	*	1	1	1	*	1
Any disorder	10	6	8	13	10	11	11	8	10
Base	2,909	2,921	5,830	2,310	2,299	4,609	5,219	5,219	10,438

Source: Meltzer *et al* (2000), Table 4.1, p. 33

Table 6.2: Odds ratios for correlates (age and gender) of mental disorders, England, Wales and Scotland

Variable	Conduct disorders Adjusted odds ratio	Emotional disorders Adjusted odds ratio	Hyperkinetic disorders Adjusted odds ratio	Any disorder Adjusted odds ratio
Age				
5–10	1.00	1.00	1.00	1.00
11–15	***1.45	***1.84	0.96	***1.48
Gender				
Female	1.00	1.00	1.00	1.00
Male	***2.42	0.89	***5.56	***1.58

Note: Odds ratios are calculated using logistic regression to produce an estimate of the probability of an event occurring when someone is in a particular category compared to a reference category (having controlled for possible confounding effects of other variables). The differences can be statistically significant at three different levels *** $p<0.001$; ** **$p<0.01$; * $p<0.05$ (in the case of the latter, the likelihood of the difference occurring simply by chance is less than 5 per cent).
Source: Meltzer *et al* (2000), Table 4.15, p. 60

women and 25 per cent of men saying they had experienced 'quite a lot' or 'a great deal' of stress over the previous 12 months. Using broader measures of mental health, the HRBQ and WHO HBSC studies also found that older pupils worried more, or were less happy, than younger ones. Analysis of the BHPS for this report (see Box 1, p. 150) also found this relationship, although 'self-esteem' was not associated with age.

Most studies also found significant differences in mental health by gender. The ONS study of mental disorders found that 11 per cent of boys suffered from mental disorders compared to 8 per cent of girls (Table 6.1), with the odds of having a mental disorder increasing by 50 per cent for boys (Table 6.2). Boys were particularly more likely than girls to have higher rates of conduct and hyperkinetic disorders. While the ONS study found few differences for emotional disorders between genders, the annual Health Surveys for England and Scotland (see above) found that girls had significantly higher GHQ12 scores than boys. Bergham and Scott's (2001) analysis of the BHPS found that boys reported higher positive self-esteem, lower negative self-image, less unhappiness and fewer past worries than girls; however, current analysis (Box 1) suggests that happiness was not associated with gender. Studies using wider measures of well-being (eg, WHO and the HRBQ) also consistently found that boys had better well-being scores than girls at all ages.

Only two studies provide any data on mental health problems among children from different ethnic groups. The ONS study found some differences between ethnic groups for clinically measured mental disorders, suggesting higher rates for black children in particular; however, ethnicity was not significant in logistic regression analysis. The 1999 HSE (Erens *et al*, 2001) found slightly higher rates of SDQ scores for black children, but Pakistani boys and girls and Indian and Irish girls were significantly more likely to have scored high than white children in the general population (Table 6.3). No significant differences, however, were found using the GHQ12.

Table 6.3: The mental health of minority ethnic groups and white majority population, 1999

Proportion with high SDQ score	Black Caribbean	Indian	Pakistani	Bangladeshi	Chinese	Irish	White pop (1997)
	%	%	%	%	%	%	%
Males	14	15	22	13	11	8	12
Females	12	16	17	12	8	14	8
Bases (weighted):							
Males	121	173	128	45	30	588	–
Females	129	136	135	41	29	630	–

Source: Erens *et al* (2001) Table 13.6

A recent study (Fazel and Stein, 2003) examined the rates of psychological disturbance, also using the SDQ, in a sample of schoolchildren who were refugees (n=101), matched for age and sex to a group of children with a minority ethnic background and white children (n = 303). Over a quarter (27 per cent) of refugee children, compared to 9 per cent of children from minority ethnic backgrounds and 15 per cent of white children, met 'case criteria' in the study, indicating that refugees might experience three times the national average scores in the ONS study (Meltzer *et al*, 2000). Interestingly, however, this study found a lower proportion of mental health problems among children from minority ethnic groups.

Family and related associations

In the ONS study, mental health problems were twice as common in children in lone-parent families, families with step-parents and larger households. While the 2001/02 HSE data did not examine household type, 1997/98 data indicated that children in lone-parent families were statistically more likely to have worse SDQ scores, and young men (but not young women) had significantly higher GHQ12 scores. Bergman and Scott (2001) also found that children (particularly boys) from lone-parent families were more likely to report past worries, but this did not apply to happiness or self-esteem. Analysis of the Avon Longitudinal Study of Parents and Children (O'Connor *et al*, 2001) also found that SDQ scores were higher in stepmother/complex stepfamilies and lone-parent families; family type did not explain this variability, but rather parent–child relationship, parental depression and socio-economic adversity were the significant factors.

The link between the nature of family relationships and children's mental health was more consistent. The ONS study, using the General Functioning Scale of the MacMaster Family Activity Device, found that children in families defined as 'unhealthy' (poor communication and low levels of support) were much more likely to have a mental disorder than children in other families (18 per cent compared to 7 per cent). Analysis of the West of Scotland Twenty-07 study (Sweeting and West, 1996) found that young people aged 15 who reported more conflict with parents were also more likely to have physical and mental health problems and lower self-esteem at age 18. A study of young people aged 11–16 in rural Scotland and Sweden (Glendinning *et al*, 2000) found that positive parental support together with accepting and uncritical parenting were associated with higher levels of self-esteem, and lower levels of depression and anxiety. BHPS analysis (Box 1) also found a significant association between parent–child relationship and mental health.

Poor parental mental health (particularly of the mother) was also found to be associated with poor mental health of children. For example, in the ONS study, 18 per cent of children of parents assessed as having a neurotic disorder using the GHQ12 had a mental disorder (compared to 8 per cent of those with parents with no condition). Analysis of the BHPS by Brynin and Scott (1996) also found a relationship between the happiness of children and their mother's (but not father's) GHQ scores. Current analysis (Box 1) found a weak association with mother's mental health. In addition, analysis of the Avon Longitudinal Study of Parents and Children (O'Connor *et al*, 2002) found that antenatal maternal anxiety predicted emotional/behavioural problems of children aged four.

Perhaps unsurprisingly, the ONS national study also found a relationship with stressful life events and poor mental health of children: 31 per cent of children with mental disorders had experienced three or more stressful life events (such as illness, death of a family member) compared to only 13 per cent of those with none.

Following the national ONS study of the mental health of children in private households, three studies were undertaken on looked-after children aged 5–17 years. Using the same definitions as the national survey of private households, these studies found that 45 per cent (in both England and Scotland) and 49 per cent (Wales) of young people either fostered, in residential care or in other looked-after settings had mental health disorders (Meltzer *et al*, 2003b, 2004). Conduct disorders accounted for the majority of problems (Table 6.4). An earlier study (Lader *et al*, 2000) of young offenders aged 16–20 in England

Table 6.4: Mental health disorders among looked-after children aged 5–17 years in England, 2002 and Scotland and Wales, 2003

	England (%)	Scotland (%)	Wales (%)
Emotional disorders	12	16	11
Conduct disorders	37	38	42
Hyperkinetic disorders	7	10	12
Less common disorders	4	2	3
Any disorder	45	45	49
Base	1,039	355	149

Source: Meltzer *et al* (2004), Table 4.1, p. 23

and Wales found that over 80 per cent of the young people met criteria for at least one personality disorder, with over 40 per cent of male young offenders and 68 per cent of females meeting criteria for at least one neurotic disorder. Over one-fifth of male and two-fifths of female young offenders reported an exceptionally threatening or catastrophic event at some point in their lives.

Socio-economic associations

Evidence for links between socio-economic associations is not consistent across studies. The ONS national study of private households (Meltzer *et al*, 2000) found a clear relationship between social class and mental health, with nearly three times as many children in Social Class V families having a mental disorder as children in Social Class I families (Table 6.5). In the 2001/02 HSE, 7 per cent of boys and

Table 6.5: Prevalence of mental disorders, by social class, England, Wales and Scotland

	I	II	IIIN	IIIM	IV	V	Never worked	All[a]
				Percentage of children with each disorder				
Emotional disorders	2	3	5	5	6	6	9	4
Conduct disorders	3	3	6	5	8	10	16	5
Hyperkinetic disorders	1	1	2	2	2	1	3	1
Less common disorders	1	1	1	*	1	1	1	1
Any disorder	5	7	12	9	12	15	21	10
Base	777	3,199	1,225	2,586	1,548	511	201	10,438

[a] No answers, members of the Armed Forces and full-time students are excluded from the six social class categories but included in the 'All' category.
Source: Meltzer *et al* (2000), Table 4.10, p. 51

4 per cent of girls in managerial and professional groups had high SDQ scores compared to 19 per cent of boys and 13 per cent of girls in semi-routine and routine occupations. A high GHQ score for 13–24-year-old females (but not males) was also more likely in lower supervisory and technical households.

In the ONS study (Meltzer *et al*, 2000), 16 per cent of children in families with a gross weekly household income of under £100 had a mental disorder, compared to only 6 per cent of children in families earning £500 or more a week. Similarly, a significant relationship was found between SDQ score and equivalised household income in the annual HSE – particularly for boys (Table 6.6). No clear pattern was found for GHQ and income quintiles.

Table 6.6: SDQ score, ages 4–15, by equivalised household income and gender, England, 2001/02

High deviance score of 17–40	1st (lowest) %	2nd %	3rd %	4th %	5th (highest) %	Total %
Males	21	13	9	8	3	12
Females	12	11	7	5	2	8
Bases (weighted):						
Males	734	692	636	571	451	3,461
Females	743	657	617	526	456	3,339

Source: Sproston and Primatesta (2003), Table 7.51.

Previous analysis of the BHPS also found little evidence of a link between poverty and emotional well-being at age 11–15 (Clarke *et al*, 1999) on a number of measures (social class, income, receipt of means-tested benefits and household assets), with the possible exception of an association with self-image. Current analysis (Box 1) also found few associations.

Some studies have, however, found a link between children's mental health and whether or not parents are employed. The ONS survey (Meltzer *et al*, 2000) found that the odds of a child having a mental disorder in a family where both parents were unemployed were nearly twice that of the odds of a child in a family where both adults were employed. BHPS analysis also found a link between employment status and children's well-being (Clarke *et al*, 1999; present analysis, Box 1).

International, inter- and intra-UK differences

The WHO survey on health behaviour in school-aged children (HBSC) represents the only ongoing international data source on the psychosocial health of young people. Past measures included the proportions of children aged 11–15 feeling 'happy' or 'low'; since 2001/02, a combined measure of health status has been used alongside a life satisfaction score using Cantrill's ladder (young people indicate the step on which they would place their lives).

A majority of young people at international level were satisfied with their lives in all countries and regions, with a high of 88 per cent of 11-year-old boys and low of 77 per cent of 15-year-old girls placing themselves above the middle of Cantrill's ladder. However, geographical differences were substantial; in particular, scores were consistently high in Finland and the Netherlands and low in Latvia, Lithuania and Ukraine. Table 6.7 shows that young people in England, Scotland, Wales and Ireland (Eire) tended to score towards the middle of all

Table 6.7: The WHO HBSC survey, 2001/02, young
people with scores above the middle of a life
satisfaction scale (%)

	Female %	Male %	Rank[a]	Base
11-year-olds				
England	82	87	28	2,239
Wales	85	89	19	1,351
Scotland	89	89	13	1,743
Ireland (Eire)	90	90	12	1,012
13-year-olds				
England	85	88	20	2,069
Wales	78	87	25	1,372
Scotland	81	89	17	1,512
Ireland (Eire)	85	88	12	944
15-year-olds				
England	78	85	19	1,773
Wales	74	90	16	1,164
Scotland	78	91	13	1,149
Ireland (Eire)	80	88	14	919

[a] Rank represents country position out of the 35 participating
countries and regions. The lower the score, the greater the
proportion of children who reported high levels of life
satisfaction.
Source: Currie et al (2004), Figure 3.3, p. 60

countries; however, young people in Scotland and Ireland tended to have slightly
higher life satisfaction than those in Wales, and in particular, England. The
HBSC survey of 1997/98 had found that England and Wales were consistently
in the top half of the countries with high rates of young people 'feeling low', with
Scotland having the lowest rates of young people feeling low.

The ONS study (Meltzer *et al*, 2000) found no significant differences for
prevalence of mental disorders in children between England, Scotland and Wales.
However, Scottish young people appeared to have slightly better well-being than
English young people by GHQ12 score according to the most recent comparable
Scottish and English Health Survey data: while 5 per cent of Scottish 13–15-
year-old boys had high scores, 7 per cent of English boys did; 8 per cent of
Scottish girls in the same age group had high scores compared to 13 per cent of
English girls.

Muldoon *et al* (2000) reviewed the research evidence on the effects of the
troubles in Northern Ireland on children's psychological development, finding
an inconsistent and complex picture. Early studies suggested profound effects

but were criticised for potential bias. More recent studies suggest that, overall, Northern Irish young people appear to exhibit few psychological problems as a result of 'the troubles', with similar levels of depression found among young people in different parts of Northern Ireland who experience different levels of violence and when compared to UK and US children. However, Muldoon *et al's* review did conclude that young people's experience of conflict in Northern Ireland may be related to externalising behaviour, although only measured in psychometric profiles rather than anti-social behaviour. On a more general level, an omnibus study (Health Promotion Agency for Northern Ireland, 2001) of 414 16–24-year-olds found that while only 2 per cent of young people, unprompted, mentioned the troubles as a common worry, 53 per cent, when prompted, said they worried about a 'return to the troubles'.

Differences in the psychological profile of young people in different regions of England are also inconclusive. Examining 2001/02 HSE data, differences were found across the age group 13–24 for young men, with high (ie, worse) scores being found in the South East (13 per cent) compared to a low of 8 per cent in the Midlands. However, no significant differences were found for young women by Government Office Region. Similarly, no relationship was found with region of residence in analysis of the BHPS (Box 1).

Studies do suggest, however, that the mental health of children varies according to type of area in which they live. In the ONS study (Meltzer *et al,* 2000), children living in neighbourhoods described as 'striving' using ACORN (A Classification Of Residential Neighbourhoods[2]) had nearly double the odds of having a mental disorder as those in 'thriving' areas (defined, according to a range of geo-demographic variables, as areas doing less or more well economically and socially). In addition, using the Index of Multiple Deprivation, the 2001/02 HSE found that 15 per cent and 9 per cent of boys and girls aged 4–15, respectively, had a high SDQ score in the most deprived areas compared to only 7 per cent and 4 per cent of boys and girls in the least deprived areas.

Changes in mental health over time

Time-trend data on the mental health of children are available in two forms: longitudinal work where the same young people are tracked over time; and,

---

[2] ACORN, produced by CACI (www.caci.co.uk), categorises neighbourhoods at a postcode level using a range of demographic statistics and lifestyle indicators.

linked or separate studies where subsequent cohorts of young people are interviewed and compared with previous cohorts.

Meltzer *et al* (2003a) undertook the first specific follow-up study of a national sample of children, conducting an 18-month follow-up postal survey and a three-year follow-up interview and assessment for all those children with mental health disorders in their 1999 study (Meltzer *et al*, 2000) and a third of children without any disorders (2,587 interviews). Some disorders were more persistent over time than others. At 18 months, 36 per cent of children with emotional disorders in 1999 were still experiencing these, compared to 73 per cent of children with other disorders. At three years, a quarter with an emotional disorder at first interview, and 43 per cent of those with a conduct disorder, also had the disorder three years later. Two factors were found to be associated with a continuing emotional disorder: mother's poor mental health and stressful life events; however, logistic regression analysis found that mother's mental health was the only factor significantly, independently associated with the persistence of emotional disorders (after controlling for all other factors). A number of factors were associated with persistent conduct disorders, including: special educational needs, parental marital status, rented housing, family income, mother's poor mental health, 'unhealthy' family functioning, and being frequently shouted at as a child. Three factors were found to be independently associated with persistent conduct disorder: special educational needs, mother's mental health, and being shouted at.

Lastly, 4 per cent of the group of children with no disorder had developed an emotional disorder and a conduct disorder, respectively. Three factors were independently associated with the onset of emotional disorders: older age, physical illness, and a greater number of stressful life events. Four factors were associated with the development of conduct disorders after controlling for all other factors: gender (being a boy), having special educational needs, having stepchildren in the family, and poor mental health of mother.

A couple of British studies (Champion *et al*, 1995; Fombonne *et al*, 2001a, 2001b) have followed smaller samples of children with mental health problems into adulthood, finding that emotional and behavioural difficulties in childhood are associated with a marked increase in the rate of severely negative events and difficulties in adulthood 20 years later. The Maudsley Hospital follow-up of 149 young people with depression found that 62 per cent experienced major depression as adults. Those that had also experienced a conduct disorder in childhood had much higher rates of drug misuse, alcoholism, anti-social personality disorders, suicidal behaviour, criminality and generally exhibited 'more pervasive social dysfunction' (including higher levels of unemployment, lower income, lower proportion in owner occupation, lower rates of cohabitation) than those who had experienced just depression.

Two reports have examined changes in subsequent cohorts of young people using the School Health Education Unit (SHEU) HRBQ (Balding *et al*, 1998; SHEU, 2004). Balding *et al* reviewed young people's worries between 1991 and 1997, finding that the top three worries had been fairly consistent: 'family'; 'the way you look'; and, for boys, 'drugs', and for girls, 'friends'. Increasing worries appeared to have been drugs, family, friends and possibly (to some extent) school, whereas decreasing worries were HIV/AIDS and gambling. A second report covering 1983–2003 (SHEU, 2004) identified a stronger trend for young people to worry about school and career problems, particularly for older children (and young women) – with a high of 39 per cent of females in 2001 and 29 per cent of males in 2001 reporting they worried about school. More positively, self-esteem levels also appeared to have increased over time (for example, 61 per cent of 14–15-year-old males had high self-esteem scores compared to 46 per cent in 1987). In addition, an upward trend was identified for young people feeling satisfied with their life, with males and younger ages consistently reporting higher satisfaction.

Health surveys in Scotland and England have not found any differences in the proportions of cohorts of young people experiencing poor emotional well-being (in either the 13–15 or 16–24 age groups, for either young men or women) using the GHQ since the mid-1990s. For example, 10 per cent of young men aged 16–24 had a GHQ score of 4 or more in the 1995 Scottish Health Survey, compared to 9 per cent in 1998. In the HSE, 12 per cent of young men aged 16–24 scored a high GHQ score in both 1997 and 2002. However, West and Sweeting (2003), comparing two cohorts of 15-year-olds in the west of Scotland over a longer period (in 1987 and 1999), found that while there was no significant change for young men (13 to 15 per cent), the proportion of young women with a high GHQ score had increased from 19 to 33 per cent. In addition, most 'worries' had increased for both sexes, with young women particularly worrying about school performance.

Recently, Collishaw *et al* (2004) undertook the most extensive examination of changes in adolescent mental health over time, covering a 25-year period, using three general population samples: the National Child Development study, the 1970 Birth Cohort Study and the ONS survey of the *Mental Health of*

Children and Young People (Meltzer *et al*, 2000). Comparable questionnaires (using the Rutter A scale[3] and SDQ, the latter being based on the former measure) were completed by parents of 15–16-year-olds at three points: 1974, 1986 and 1999. Both young men and women had increased odds of conduct disorders by about 1.5 in each successive cohort. Increases were found for all family types and across all social classes. Emotional problems increased between 1986 and 1999 for both males and females, although appeared to remain stable between 1974 and 1986. Hyperactivity scores for girls remained the same, decreasing for boys in the first time period and then increasing between 1986 and 1999. The authors concluded that these trends were unlikely to have been affected by changes in reporting, as longitudinal data from the first two cohorts showed that long-term outcomes for young people with conduct problems were similar (being much poorer than for those without conduct disorders). However, it was acknowledged that there may have been some reporting effects and changes in measurement. The study does, however, provide the first UK-based evidence for a worsening of children's mental health in the post-war period, a phenomenon that has been suggested throughout developed countries since the Second World War (Rutter and Smith, 1995).

Table 6.8: Proportions with conduct, hyperactive and emotional problems by gender and cohort

	1974 %	*1986* %	*1999* %
Conduct problems			
Boys	7.6	12.1	16.7
Girls	6.0	8.6	13.1
Total	6.8	10.4	14.9
Hyperactive problems			
Boys	11.1	8.3	16.9
Girls	6.6	5.7	7.1
Total	8.9	7.1	12.0
Emotional problems			
Boys	7.8	7.8	13.3
Girls	12.8	13.4	20.4
Total	10.2	10.5	16.9

Source: Collishaw *et al* (2004), Table 1, p. 1354

---

[3] The Rutter parents' scale is a 31-item questionnaire that measures psychiatric symptoms and deviant behaviour (Elander, J. and Rutter, M. (1996) 'Use and development of the Rutter parents' and teachers' scales'; *International Journal of Methods of Psychiatric Research*, 6, pp. 63–78.

Box I: Analysis of the 2002 BHPS Youth Questionnaire on the subjective well-being of young people aged 11–15[4]

The 2002 BHPS Youth Questionnaire included interviews with a sample of 1,400 young people aged 11–15. Three indicators, derived from questions covered by the Youth Questionnaire, were used to describe the subjective well-being (SWB) of young people: the positive effect (expressed by the feeling of happiness), negative effect (expressed by feeling troubled in terms of worry or sadness), and self-esteem.

Descriptive analysis of the relationship between SWB and a range of factors found:

- Girls were more likely to feel troubled and have lower self-esteem than boys, but happiness was not significantly associated with gender.
- Older age groups tended to be less happy and more troubled than younger age groups, but self-esteem was not significantly associated with age.
- There was no significant association between parental marital status and SWB.
- The household's employment status was associated with young people's happiness and their self-esteem: dual-earner households scored higher on all dimensions.
- No significant association was found between parents' social class and feelings of happiness, sadness or worry; however, young people whose fathers were in unskilled occupations had higher self-esteem scores.
- SWB and the receipt of means-tested benefits were not statistically associated, with the exception of lower self-esteem and Housing Benefit.
- Young people whose parents were not in any financial difficulty consistently obtained higher scores.
- No significant associations were found between regions of residence and SWB.
- Self-esteem was significantly higher for young people who lived in owned rather than rented accommodation.
- Mother's mental health was weakly associated with young people's

---

[4] A secondary analysis of the 2002 BHPS was undertaken especially for this report.

SWB. Young people were more likely to be sad or worried if they have a father whose mental health is poor and vice versa.

- The parent–child relationship (how often they quarrel, talk to parents, have an evening meal together, and whether they inform parents where they are going) was significantly associated with young people's SWB. However, it should be noted that parent-child relationship is not independent from the SWB of young people.

Multiple-regression modelling examined the extent to which different factors predicted well-being:

Happiness

Young people tended to have higher happiness scores, if they (in order of significance):

1. talked to their father about things that mattered
2. did not quarrel with their mother
3. were younger
4. had a father who was not in financial difficulty
5. told parents where they were going.

The proportion of variation explained by these factors was 15 per cent.

Girls were less likely to be happy (explaining 22 per cent of variation), if they:

1. quarrelled with their mother
2. did not talk to their father about things that mattered
3. were older
4. had a father who was in financial difficulty
5. both parents were earning.

Similarly, boys were less likely to be happy (explaining 13 per cent of variation), if they:

1. did not talk to their father about things that mattered
2. quarrelled with their mother
3. had parents in receipt of Housing Benefit.

Feeling troubled

Young people were more likely to feel troubled (explaining 13 per cent of variation), if they:

1. quarrelled with their father
2. were female
3. had a mother with poor mental health
4. quarrelled with their mother
5. had a father with poor mental health.

Girls tended to feel troubled (explaining 12 per cent of variation), if they:

1. were older
2. quarrelled with their mother
3. had a mother with poor mental health.

Similarly, boys were more likely to feel troubled (explaining 16 per cent of variation), if they:

1. quarrelled with their father
2. had a father with poor mental health
3. lived with either both parents working part time or a mother working full time and a father working part time
4. had a father who was not in financial difficulty
5. had a mother who was in financial difficulty.

Self-esteem

Young people are inclined to score lower on self-esteem (explaining 11 per cent of variation) if they:

1. quarrelled with their mother
2. did not talk to their father about things that mattered
3. were female
4. did not tell parents where they were going
5. were younger
6. had parents in receipt of Family Tax Credit.

Girls were more likely to have lower self-esteem (explaining 10 per cent of variation) if they:

1. did not talk to their father about things that mattered

2. quarrelled with their mother
3. had a father who was in financial difficulty
4. had a mother with poor mental health.

Boys tended to have lower self-esteem (explaining 14 per cent of variation) if they:
1. quarrelled with their mother
2. did not tell parents where they were going
3. were younger
4. had parents in receipt of Family Tax Credit
5. did not talk to their mother about things that mattered.

Conclusions
Young people's well-being significantly differs with gender. Regression analysis found that the well-being of boys and girls can be predicted by different combinations of family characteristics. Overall, the modelling of young people's well-being against their own as well as their households' characteristics explained about 10 to 22 per cent of the variation of SWB.

Suicide and self-harm

Suicide and undetermined death in the UK

Official statistics for the UK show that generally there has been a decline in the number of suicides among young people under 25. Between 1990 and 2002 there was a 27 per cent reduction in the number of youth suicides and undetermined deaths in the UK – from 895 to 654. However, suicide remains more prevalent among boys than girls and increases with age. For example, in 2002 the number of recorded suicides or undetermined deaths was 15 for boys aged under 15, compared to 491 for boys aged 15–24, while for girls this rose from 14 to 134 between the same age groups. The number of suicides among young men aged 15–24 has seen a 33 per cent reduction, from 731 in 1990 to 491 in 2002. However, the number of suicides among young women aged under 15 has seen a 250 per cent increase, from 4 to 14 over the same period (Table 6.9).[5]

[5] England and Wales: Office for National Statistics. Death registrations in England and Wales: Causes report of Health Statistics Quarterly (various years). Scotland: General Register Office for

Table 6.9: Suicide and undetermined death in the UK among 0–24-year-olds, by gender and age group

						Number of suicides and undetermined deaths							
	1990	1991	1992	1993	1994	1995	1996	1997	1998	1999	2000	2001	2002
0–14 years													
Male	18	14	19	37	24	17	22	22	18	14	21	14	15
Female	4	9	10	13	15	15	9	13	7	8	11	13	14
15–24 years													
Male	731	674	690	701	660	601	560	628	571	575	555	534	491
Female	142	160	151	142	117	139	149	138	159	140	143	126	134
Total	895	857	870	893	816	772	740	801	755	737	730	687	654

Source: Office for National Statistics, Register General for Scotland; Register General for Northern Ireland

Within England and Wales, the suicide rate among young men aged 15–24 has shown a steady decline from 16 per 100,000 population in 1993 to 11 in 2002, compared to fluctuations in Scotland from 26 per 100,000 population in 1992, peaking at 36 in 2000 before reducing to 30 in 2002, and in Northern Ireland from 16 per 100,000 in 1992, peaking at 31 in 2000 before reducing to 18 in 2002. Among young women aged 15–24, the rate of suicides per 100,000 population is lower than that found among young men. In England and Wales, the rate has remained fairly stable at around 3–4 per 100,000 population between 1993 and 2002. However, in Scotland the rate has risen from 7 per 100,000 population in 1992 to 10 in 2002, and in Northern Ireland the trends show a fluctuation from 2 per 100,000 in 1992, peaking at 8 in 1999 before reducing to 1 in 2002 (Table 6.10).[6]

Scotland (2004) *Quarterly Return for the Registrar General for Scotland*. Northern Ireland: Northern Ireland Statistics and Research Agency, Registrar General Quarterly Report (various years). Data up to and including the year 2000 are based on the ninth revision of the International Classification of Diseases (ICD9) codes. Data for 2001 onwards are based on the tenth revision (ICD10) codes. Hence, data for 2001 onwards are not directly comparable with previous years' data.
[6] England and Wales: Office for National Statistics. Death registrations in England and Wales: Causes report of Health Statistics Quarterly (various years). Scotland: General Register Office for Scotland (2004) *Quarterly Return for the Registrar General for Scotland*. Northern Ireland: Northern Ireland Statistics and Research Agency, Registrar General Quarterly Report (various years). Data up to and including the year 2000 are based on the ninth revision of the International Classification of Diseases (ICD9) codes. Data for 2001 onwards are based on the tenth revision (ICD10) codes. Hence, data for 2001 onwards are not directly comparable with previous years' data.

Table 6.10: Suicide and undetermined death in the UK among 15–24-year-olds by gender and country

Rates per 100,000 population aged 15–24

	1992	1993	1994	1995	1996	1997	1998	1999	2000	2001	2002
Males											
England and Wales	–	16	16	15	14	16	14	13	12	13	11
Scotland	26	31	28	25	25	30	25	33	36	30	30
Northern Ireland	16	26	23	23	18	20	22	25	31	26	18
UK	17	18	17	16	15	17	16	16	15	15	13
Females											
England and Wales	–	4	3	4	4	3	4	4	4	3	3
Scotland	7	6	6	6	9	8	10	6	8	9	10
Northern Ireland	2	3	1	3	2	5	4	8	5	2	1
UK	4	4	3	4	4	4	5	4	4	4	4

Source: Office for National Statistics, Register General for Scotland; Register General for Northern Ireland

Suicide and self-injury: International comparisons

International comparisons of 30 countries and regions using statistics from the WHO show that Northern Ireland and England and Wales have among the lowest rates of suicide and self-inflicted injury for 5–14-year-olds, for both girls and boys (0–0.1 per 100,000 population). Scotland, however, falls somewhere towards the middle of the group with 0.6 per 100,000 males and 0.3 per 100,000 females. Russia has the highest rate of suicide and self-inflicted injury among 5–14-year-old boys at 4 per 100,000 and also for girls in this age group, along with New Zealand at 1.1 per 100,000 population (Chart 6.1a).

Among 15–24-year-olds, England and Wales again have a relatively low rate of suicide for young men (8.8 per 100,000 population) and young women (2.2 per 100,000 population). Again, Scotland falls somewhere around the middle for young women (3.8 per 100,000 population), and is among the highest for suicide rates among young men, at 23.9 per 100,000 males. Northern Ireland also has among the highest rates of suicide for both young women (6.8 per 100,000 population) and young men (22.3 per 100,000 population). Once again Russia has the highest rate of suicide among young men aged 15–24 (57.7 per 100,000 population), while the highest rate for young women in this age group is in Belgium at 21.7 per 100,000 population (Chart 6.1b).[7]

---

[7] WHO statistics Mortality database: Table 1 – www3.who.int/whosis/mort/table1_process_cfm (accessed 12 July 2004)

Chart 6.1a: Suicide and self-inflicted injury 5–14 years

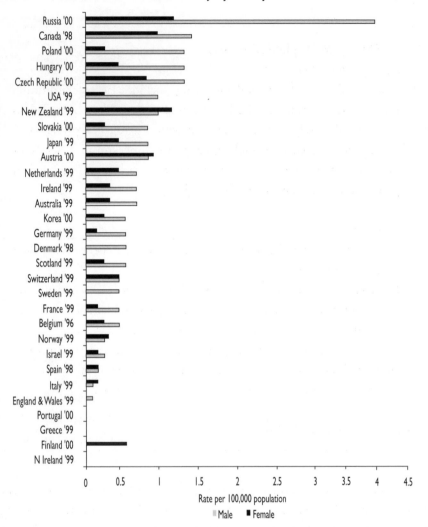

Rate per 100,000 population

■ Male   ■ Female

Explaining trends in suicide

Although data exists to show trends in suicide behaviour, finding causal explanations for those trends is a complex process. Constructing a statistical profile of youth suicide is a particularly sensitive issue and may be subject to under-recording. There are strong pressures on doctors and coroners to avoid suicide verdicts (Coleman, 1999), particularly among those under the age of 15 (Madge, 1996). Doubt is often inevitable in youth suicide and a misclassification of accidental death or open verdict is often recorded (Charlton *et al*, 1992; Hill, 1995; Madge and Harvey, 1999a), with the potential for the real rate of suicide

Chart 6.1b: Suicide and self-inflicted injury 15–24 years

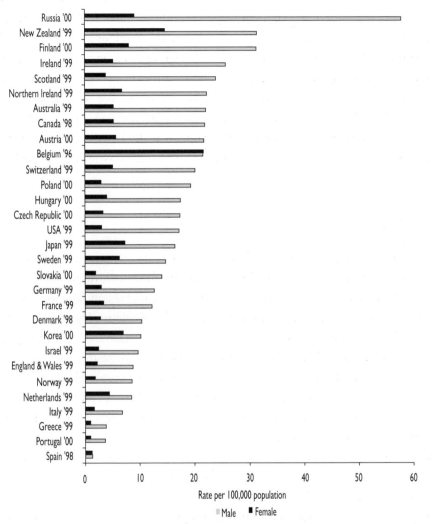

Rate per 100,000 population

■ Male   ■ Female

among young people being up to three times the officially recorded level (Madge and Harvey, 1999b). Analysis of suicide is also inhibited, since the perpetrator is inevitably unavailable, making it difficult to be completely sure of the motives leading to death. Much of the research into understanding suicide is therefore based on studies of those who engage in suicide behaviour, namely deliberate self-harm, which has been shown to be predictive of future suicide attempts (Kreitman and Foster, 1991).

Causal explanations of the key trends in suicide have previously been reported (Searle, 2002b). Mental illness continues to be the most important factor associated with youth suicide and deliberate self-harm (see, for example, Agerbo *et al*, 2002; Hawton *et al*, 2002; Fombonne *et al*, 2001b). Previous mental illness or suicide behaviour among parents or siblings (Agerbo *et al*, 2002), and recent awareness of self-harm among peers (Hawton *et al*, 2002), have also been linked to higher risk of suicide behaviour among young people. Associations have also been made between suicide behaviour and the uncertainty and anxiety associated with the transition from childhood to adulthood (Briggs, 2002). Young females are more likely to experience relationship problems (Kelly and Bunting, 1998), while suicide ideation is generally associated with a deterioration in problem-solving skills and abilities (Chang, 2002). New research also suggests that there may be wider cultural issues in explaining suicidal trends. The cultural changes of 'modern society' have long been associated with explanations of suicide (Durkheim, 1952) and in particular where there is an increasing individualisation of society, the lack of values and beliefs which hold a society together and allow individuals to make sense of their lives has been linked with the increase in the rates of psychological disorder and suicide behaviour among young people. Eckersley and Dear's (2002) international study of suicide among young people showed that measures of individualism, including personal freedom and control, were positively associated with youth suicide, particularly among males, and that the association was stronger at higher levels of individualism. They concluded that individualism creates isolation and social fragmentation, and the promotion of personal autonomy leads to expectations exceeding reality and brings about psychological dysfunction (Eckersley and Dear, 2002).

Different methods of suicide have implications for the ways in which suicide verdicts are recorded, and could account for the different levels of suicide among boys and girls. Young men more commonly use aggressive methods, such as hanging, and young women use more passive methods, such as an overdose (Marttunen *et al*, 1992; Coles, 2000). Hanging shows a degree of preparation and intent (Hill, 1995) and is more likely to be recorded as suicide (Platt *et al*, 1988; Hill, 1995) while self-poisoning is more ambiguous and less likely to be fatal or classified as suicide (Adelstein and Mardon, 1985); consequently, official statistics show that young males are more likely to commit suicide while young females are more likely to attempt suicide.

For example, statistics for the suicide and undetermined death of 10–19-year-olds in England and Wales between 1982 and 1996 show that among females 43 per cent of suicides were due to substance poisoning, while this method accounted for 62 per cent of undetermined deaths, compared to 12 per cent and 17 per cent respectively for males. Among males 43 per cent of suicides were due to hanging, and this method accounted for 32 per cent of undetermined deaths, compared to 27 per cent and 9 per cent respectively for females (Table 6.11) (Kelly and Bunting, 1998).

Table 6.11: Percentage of suicides and undetermined deaths among 10–19-year-olds by selected methods and gender: England and Wales, 1982–1996

| | Males | | Females | |
| Method | Suicides | Undetermined | Suicides | Undetermined |
	%	%	%	%
Poisoning				
By solid or liquid substances	12	17	43	62
By other gases and vapours	19	4	8	2
Hanging and suffocation	43	32	27	9
Cutting and piercing instruments	1	0	1	1
Jumping from high place	6	12	7	11

Source: Kelly and Bunting (1998)

Such findings support the view that there is a link between suicide rates and access to methods. The reduction in male suicides due to poisoning by gases and vapours (mainly motor vehicle exhaust gas) since the 1990s has been attributed to the fitting of catalytic converters to cars (Adelstein and Mardon, 1985), while the reduction of female suicides due to substance poisoning has been related to the introduction of smaller pack sizes and less toxic pharmaceutical drugs (Hawton *et al*, 2003).

Conclusion

The measurement of 'mental health' and 'mental well-being' is beset with difficulties, and variations in the mental well-being of children and young people can be observed according to different types of mental health issue and measurement used. Most obviously, boys are more likely than girls to experience some forms of mental health problems, particularly conduct disorders, while emotional health issues, including unhappiness, are more likely to be experienced by girls. However, older children experience more mental health problems than younger children, irrespective of condition. While socio-economic factors appear associated with some forms of mental health issues, this finding is not consistent, with family-related factors, particularly parent–child relationships and parental mental health, being more likely to be linked to poor mental health. Overall, similar proportions of children appear to have experienced mental health problems over the last decade but a number of studies point to young people 'worrying' more over time, and recent data suggest that conduct and emotional problems may have increased over the last 25 years.

Statistics on suicide show that youth suicide rates in the UK have fallen over the past decade, which in part has been attributed to a greater understanding of the methods available for suicide and self-harm, particularly in respect of self-poisoning, which have led to a reduction in deaths by such methods. However, variations do exist, most notably that the suicide rate has steadily risen among young girls under 15 since the late 1990s. International comparisons also show that while suicide rates are low in England and Wales, Scotland and Northern Ireland have relatively high rates among 15–24-year-olds. Reducing the suicide rate is seen as a proxy measure for improving mental health in the UK. However, youth suicide is a complex and sensitive issue and is difficult to research. As a

7 Children's time and space

Emese Mayhew, Naomi Finch, Bryony Beresford and Antonia Keung

Key statistics:

- Of an estimated population of 3.5 million 11–15-year-olds in England and Wales, around 2.3m will have worked at some time before their school-leaving age.
- Of all children aged between 5 and 15 in the UK, 114,000 (1.4 per cent – 53,000 boys and 61,000 girls) provided informal care in 2001.
- The health of 773 children under 16 in the UK, providing 20 or more hours of care, was rated as 'not good'.
- Children aged under 16 in the UK only spend 2 per cent of their time on their own.
- In England, Wales and Scotland, only 27 per cent of children report playing with their parents every day, compared to 72 per cent of parents who report playing with their child.
- In the UK, 92 per cent of pupils have access to the internet at school; 87 per cent of children have access to a computer at home and 71 per cent of children can go online from home.

Key trends:

- Because of concerns about public safety and an increased focus on academic achievement, children's play has become of a more structured variety than the more traditional definition of play, which is chosen and directed by the child.
- There is a tendency towards adult-led commercialization of play space and the treatment of children as 'consumers' of leisure activities.

Key sources:

- Office for National Statistics (ONS)
- Census 2001
- British Household Panel Study (BHPS) Youth Survey
- UK 2000 Time Use Survey
- Social and Economic Research Council

Introduction

This chapter provides a review of how and where children in the UK spend their lives. The topics encompass children's access to public and private spaces, and the extent to which they are involved in leisure activities, paid work and provision of unpaid care. The wide scope of this chapter does not allow for a detailed analysis of each issue; instead, a broad picture is given, illustrated with statistics (where available) and emerging trends. The main sources of child-centred primary data on children's use of space and time are the UK 2000 Time Use Survey, the British Household Panel Study (BHPS) Youth Questionnaire and, to a limited extent, the Census. Aside from quantitative data sources, information on children's use of time and space is also provided by qualitative studies, carried out on a smaller, local or regional scale rather than a national one.

Children's spaces

Home

Besides school, the home and family are the main physical and social spaces in which most children spend their childhood. Britain has recently witnessed significant changes to the home and family environments: specifically, there have been substantial changes in marriage and divorce patterns (see Chapter 2), which have had important ramifications in terms of children's home and family experiences. One in four children lives in a lone-parent family and one in ten in a stepfamily (see Chapter 2).

There are currently no guidelines on how much time children should spend with their non-resident parent after separation or divorce. Most parents make their own arrangements for sharing time with their children but, in England and Wales, one in ten divorced couples go to court over parental access disputes (DfES, 2004h). For children with divorced parents, 'family life no longer happens in one place but is scattered between several different locations' (Beck and Gernsheim, 2002). Indeed, the geography of divorce for these children is one of punctuated movement as the children travel from one home space to another and back again. Children often feel they are not involved in decisions about contact arrangements and become increasingly aware of the effort involved in maintaining a life across two households (Smart et al, 2001).

Private space at home: children's bedrooms

The child's bedroom began to appear in British houses during the eighteenth century, at the same time as children's nurseries and classrooms (Whitehead, 1997). From the second half of the twentieth century onwards, the ideal is still that each child has their own bedroom. Where and when children do share a bedroom, the space is usually divided such that there are clear rules as to which designated space 'belongs' to which child. Thus, the bedroom space of the child becomes symbolic of the growing child-centredness in the modern family and household arrangements (Whitehead, 1997). The quality and quantity of home space is linked to socio-economic factors. Overcrowding is endemic among low-income families (see Chapter 12), and it is these children who also perceive the greatest risks to playing out (see 'Public outdoor spaces' below). Children in families who rent their homes from their local authority or a housing association are likely to have to share a bedroom with a sibling, at least until a certain age (Mayhew et al, forthcoming).

Public outdoor spaces

Overall, public outdoor places form an important part of the lives of many UK children (see 'Children's play' below), being spaces where they can meet up with friends and be away from the 'adult gaze' (Matthews and Limb, 2000). Parental fears about safety, especially traffic, are significant influences on children's independent spatial mobility and there is an increasing tendency for parents, especially in rural areas, to escort their children to and from more structured and supervised leisure activities or to prevent their children from playing outside unsupervised (New Policy Institute, 2002; Jones et al, 2000; Mayall, 2000, Valentine and Holloway, 1997–98). As O'Brien et al (2000) note, 'increasingly, in the UK context at least, letting children roam or play out unaccompanied is becoming a marker of neglectful or irresponsible parenthood' (p. 273). Concerns about gangs and the activities associated with the illegal drugs market were greatest among children living in very deprived or troubled estates, and were a barrier to playing out – a barrier imposed both by the children themselves and their parents (Matthews, 2001). Chahal and Julienne (1999) found that racial harassment also curtailed children's use of their local neighbourhood.

Comparative data analyses suggest a rise in the age at which children tend to be allowed to play out. O'Brien et al (2000) compared data from their survey of over 1,300 children in the UK with that collected in the 1970s and 1980s

(Hillman *et al*, 1990). They found evidence of a decrease in independent use of public spaces by 10/11-year-olds, but little change among 13/14-year-olds. Other studies also reveal considerable differences between children – in terms of age, gender, location, ethnicity and income/social class – with regard to the extent to which they spend time without adults in public outdoor places, the types of public outdoor places they frequent, and what they do in these spaces (Matthews and Limb, 2000; O'Brien *et al*, 2000; Raey, 2000; Robertson and Walford, 2000). In addition, the seasons, with their associated weather and duration of daylight, affect the extent to which children play out (Matthews, 2001). Boys are more likely to use outdoor public places (see Table 7.1), and tend to use these spaces for sporting activities. For girls, outdoor public places are social venues.

Table 7.1: Playing out without an adult, by gender and location, for children aged 10–14 yrs

Inner London		Outer London		New town	
Girls	Boys	Girls	Boys	Girls	Boys
67%	84%	75%	87%	82%	93%

Source: O'Brien *et al*, 2000

Spaces for teenagers

Research with children aged 11–18 years (teenagers) and parents suggests that the lack of local, non-commercial spaces where teenagers can spend time together off the streets contributes to the reported levels of boredom and, for some, subsequent troublemaking among teenagers (NACRO, 2000; see also Chapter 11). Seventy per cent of parents and young people taking part in one survey believed that young people commit crimes because there is not enough for them to do (Nestle UK Ltd, 2002). Matthews and Limb (2000), in a study based on questionnaires from over 1,000 9–16-year-olds, found that the main reason identified for playing on the street is that children have nowhere else to go and that, certainly for less affluent children, the street may be their only social forum because a large proportion cannot afford to participate in other leisure or recreational opportunities. Older teenagers frequently use shopping malls as a place for meeting up with friends on the basis that they provide free, warm and safe places. Their use reflects the lack of appropriate venues for this age-group (New Policy Institute, 2002). The Government's campaign of 'no tolerance' of crime and anti-social behaviour contributes to the narrowing of public spaces where teenagers can congregate by imposing the threat of bans and curfews on 'troublemaking' youth. On the other hand, the Youth Green Paper currently being worked on is addressing 'places to go and things to do' for young people.

Demand for safe public spaces

A study of play by Wheway and Millward (1997) involving over 3,000 children across 12 housing estates found that the most well-used play areas were the ones that were open and visible, since these promoted a sense of security. Children also expressed a strong desire for play areas, including green open spaces such as parks. Children were on the move between a number of places, which highlights the importance for children to be able to move freely around their physical and social environment: 'going' is an important activity in itself (Wheway and Millward, 1997). A key feature of the sorts of spaces teenagers want access to is that the space is specifically for their age-group and offers the opportunity to spend unstructured time with their friends and peers. The need for access to such a facility in the evenings and not just after school has also been highlighted (Nestle UK Ltd, 2002). At the moment in the UK, access to places such as these are few and far between, though initiatives are underway to develop these sorts of services – eg, the Make Space campaign (www.makespace.org.uk), which is being led by the UK-wide organisation 4Children.

Virtual space

The nature and extent of children's access to virtual space[1] is determined by where they access it (eg, in the home or in the school) and when (eg, in the evenings or during their lunch break). The ICT in Schools Programme is the Government's key initiative to stimulate and support the use of ICT to improve standards and encourage new ways of teaching and learning. A recent research project, *UK Children Go Online* (UKCGO), investigating internet use by 1,511 9–19-year-olds in the UK (Livingstone and Bober, 2004) found that school access to the internet in the UK is near universal, with 92 per cent of pupils being able to go online at school. The majority of children also have access to a computer at home (87 per cent), and 71 per cent of children have access to the

---

[1] The terms 'virtual space', 'cyberspace' and 'Information and Communication Technologies' (ICT), are used synonymously. They refer to internet use, email, online games and general computer use, including word processing.

internet from home (Livingstone and Bober, 2004). The same study also found that, compared to childless homes, homes containing children lead in gaining internet access as well as in acquiring multiple computers and broadband access.

There are still significant inequalities in home access of the internet based on socio-economic class. Eighty-eight per cent of middle-class but only 61 per cent of working-class children have access to the internet at home (Livingstone and Bober, 2004). One-fifth of the children in the study had access to the internet in their bedroom. Having access to the internet in children's bedrooms is influenced by children's gender, social class and age. Twenty-two per cent of boys versus 15 per cent of girls, 21 per cent of middle-class versus 16 per cent of working class, and 10 per cent of 9–11-year-olds versus 26 per cent of 16–17-year-olds have internet access in their bedroom (Livingstone and Bober, 2004). Most children who are frequent users of the internet use it for homework (90 per cent), or to get information for other things (94 per cent), as well as for sending emails (72 per cent) and to play games online (70 per cent). Time spent online is still less than time spent watching television or with the family, but is similar to that spent doing homework and playing computer games (Livingstone and Bober, 2004). There is evidence to show that children often lack the skills in evaluating online content and do not receive sufficient training in how to judge the reliability of online information. The UKCGO study found that four in ten pupils trust most of the information on the internet and only 33 per cent of 9–19-year-olds who go online at least once a week say they have been told how to judge whether they can trust online information (Livingstone and Bober, 2004).

Children's play

The 1989 United Nations Convention on the Rights of the Child (UNCRC) states that children have the right to rest and leisure, to engage in play and recreational activities appropriate to their age, and to participate freely in cultural life and the arts. The UNCRC highlights three main areas which need to be addressed in terms of a child's right to play: the provision of space (ie, the basic resource needed for play), consultation with young people (ie, their participation in planning play), and integration of all children (ie, in particular those with disabilities) (New Policy Institute, 2002). The recent growth of organised out-of-school childcare provision and the focus on boosting academic attainment is influencing both the nature of recreational provision and the level of control parents exert over their children's play activities (New Policy Institute, 2002). Play is of a more structured variety than the more traditional definition of play, which is chosen and directed by the child.

Play is important for children's mental, physical and emotional development and their well-being. It provides an opportunity for them to consolidate and absorb information learned earlier, and it helps them to acquire a general mindset towards solving problems (National Playing Fields Association, 2000). The physical activity involved in most play provides exercise, encourages co-ordination and develops skills for the growing child. Active play also reduces symptoms of depression and anxiety and contributes to increased self-esteem (Mulvihill *et al*, 2000). Research by the Mental Health Foundation (1999a) highlights the importance of children being able to play, take risks and use their own initiative. During social play, children acquire the basic skills needed to become 'emotionally literate', increasing their resilience to mental health problems (Mental Health Foundation, 1999b).

There are a variety of venues where children and young people like to play, among which public outdoor places are important for meeting friends and retaining some social autonomy away from adult supervision (Matthews and Limb, 2000) (see 'Children's spaces' above). Matthews and Limb (2000) found that although there is evidence of a retreat from the street for urban children, less than one-third of young people report that they never use the street as a social venue. Nevertheless, urban geographers have raised concerns that children and young people have been conceptualised as 'problems' in urban planning and the result has been their increasing exclusion from a hostile urban environment (Woolley *et al*, 1999, Jones *et al*, 2000). At the same time, there has been a tendency towards the commercialization of play space and the commodification of childhood (McKendrick *et al*, 2000a). This is represented by the proliferation of the service and leisure industries and the growing recognition of children as consumers (McKendrick *et al*, 2000b). The growth of commercial playgrounds in the UK is, however, adult-led, reflecting a new trend in family life in which leisure is a shared family experience instead of free play directed by the child (McKendrick *et al*, 2000c). The pay-for-play leisure provision can contribute to and sustain the social exclusion of some children from disadvantaged back-grounds.

Adults themselves directly control and restrict children's free play. Outside of school, children spend more time with their friends than their parents; this is increasingly so as they get older (Morrow, 2001). But outdoor play with friends is threatened – on the one hand by adults' concerns surrounding the safety of the child in public areas as a result of 'stranger danger' and traffic – and also by intolerance of adults towards children's play in public. Adults are therefore actively discouraging children from playing outside, and thus forcing them into spending more time at home. According to a survey carried out by The Children's Society (2003), 89 per cent of children aged 7–11 and 71 per cent of children aged 11–18 reported being told off for playing outside, while half of both age groups had been shouted at for playing outside. One-quarter of the younger age group and 43 per cent of the older group had been told to go away, and a third of the younger age group and 16 per cent of the older age group were stopped from playing outside because they were told off. Children were most likely to be told off because they were making a noise or being a nuisance, and 46 per cent of the younger age group reported that it was their parents who had told them off.

Children's time use

The changing patterns of parental employment, particularly the increasing number of working mothers, has implications in terms of both where children are spending their time and how family time is spent. For much of their waking time, parents and children are apart: adults spend a large proportion of their time at work and children spend theirs at school (*UK 2000 Time Use Survey*, ONS, 2002e). Time spent together as a family is important to both parents and children (MORI, 2001; Christensen, 2002). In a survey conducted by MORI (2001), sharing time together was the single biggest factor identified by parents describing a 'successful family'. Similarly, the majority of the 489 children involved in another study (Christensen, 2002) claimed to enjoy spending time with family. A large-scale international study (including the UK) by Gershuny (2000) found that since the 1970s, despite the huge increases in working mothers and the increase in working hours, the time spent by parents with their children has increased. The reasons behind this include the fact that families are smaller, fathers are spending more time with their children, and parents are spending less time on themselves (Galinsky, 1999; Gershuny, 2000). The last reason is seen as contributing most to the observed trend. The fact that children are spending more time at home, rather than playing out, must also be contributing to this.

Children may be spending more time with parents, but how children spend this time is changing. The MORI (2001) study found only a small proportion of the families sampled (15 per cent) sat down to eat together in the evening.

Moreover, parents appear to spend, at least from the child's point of view, very little time playing with their children. This is important because, according to child development experts, children learn through playing with their parents who act as role models, and by doing so parents develop a closer relationship with their child. A recent NOP survey on behalf of The Children's Society (The Children's Society, 2004) revealed that only 27 per cent of children in Scotland, England and Wales reported playing with their parents every day, although younger children were more likely to play with their parents than older children: 28 per cent of 11–12-year-olds compared to 18 per cent of 7–8-year-olds cited *rarely* playing with their parents. Limited play with parents was considered by children to be because their parents were too busy, did not know how to play children's games, lacked imagination, were too bossy and were less fun than friends. However, there existed a discrepancy between how often parents thought they played with their children (72 per cent reported playing with their children every day), and how often children thought they played with parents (27 per cent). This discrepancy exists throughout England, Wales and Scotland, as shown in Table 7.2. Thus, parents' view of how they spent their time with their children was very different from children's.

Table 7.2: The proportion of children (aged 7–12) who said they played with their parents every day, and the proportion of parents who said they played with their children (aged 7–12) every day by ITV Region

	Children	Parents
Scotland	28	68
Wales & West	32	82
North East	20	76
North West	20	65
Yorkshire	33	68
Midlands	33	67
South	29	83
London	29	72
East Anglia	21	74
South West	48	73
All	27	72

Base: 666 parents of children aged 7–12 and 1,226 children aged 7–12 in England, Wales and Scotland.
Source: The Children's Society, 2004.

Recently published work by Christensen (2002) explored 11–13-year-olds' perspectives on 'family time' and what 'qualities of time' matter to them. Overall, the majority of children (around 63 per cent) said they enjoyed 'spending time with family', and they 'liked this time more than the time they spent with friends or on their own'. The *ordinariness and routines of domestic life* were seen as an important part of family life and featured strongly in children's descriptions of family time. *Availability of support* – to draw upon when needed – was the second valued aspect of family life, and this was not dependent on family members being physically together in the same room or being engaged in shared activities. Third, 'family time' was a time in which children felt there was the *potential to negotiate how they spent their time*. The fourth valued aspect of family time was *time to be alone in peace and quiet*, yet within reach of other family members. This was one of the aspects of family time that children often found hard to achieve.

According to the *UK 2000 Time Use Survey* (ONS, 2002e), children aged under 16 only spend 2 per cent of their time on their own. For the rest of their time, children are either in the company of their parents, siblings, friends,

Table 7.3: Time use of children and young people in the UK (average minutes per person per day spent on activity)

Main activity	8–15-year-olds	16–25-year-olds
Sleep	609	547
Eating and drinking	67	72
Personal care (eg, washing, dressing)	48	50
Employment	5	180
Study	229	84
Housework (excluding childcare)	45	74
Childcare (of own household members)	1	14
Voluntary work and meetings	9	9
Social life and resting	52	90
Entertainment and culture	9	8
Sport and outdoor activities	29	20
Hobbies and games	94	26
Reading	10	10
Watching TV and video	139	141
Listening to radio/music	8	11
Travel	76	96
Other	12	6
Total	1,440	1,440
Sample size	2,925	2,372

Source: UK 2000 Time Use Survey, ONS, 2002.

classmates and/or teachers (Mayhew *et al*, forthcoming). Table 7.3 shows children's daily time use in minutes. Younger children (aged 8–15) spend most of their time studying (229 minutes) and watching TV (139 minutes) and only spend a bit more time on hobbies and games than on travelling (94 and 76 minutes respectively). Young people (aged 16–25) spend most of their time in employment (180 minutes) followed by watching TV (141 minutes) and spend more time travelling (96 minutes) than with friends (90 minutes). The daily amount of sport and outdoor activities undertaken decreases with age from little (29 minutes) to even less (20 minutes).

Children's employment

Within the UK, combining part-time employment with full-time compulsory education is viewed as acceptable, though there is little research into the impact of child employment on well-being and achievement (Jones, 2002). Data on the employment of children are very difficult to access as Government employment surveys typically do not extend below people under 16 years of age. The results of the last survey on the employment of children (Trade Unions Congress, 2001) were presented in the previous edition of this book (Jones, 2002) and no such surveys have been done since then. Hence, in this section we explore the extent of children's employment, level of earnings and pocket money by using secondary analysis of Wave 11 of the BHPS Youth Questionnaire, as well as reviewing recent developments in child employment legislation.

The majority of school-age children have experience of part-time work. Of an estimated population of 3.5 million 11–15-year-olds (in England and Wales), around 2.3m children will have worked at some time before their school-leaving age (Better Regulation Task Force, 2004). It is estimated that at any given time, between 1.1 and 1.7 school-age children will be working (Hobbs and McKechnie, 1997). The most common types of work that children do are: newspaper delivery, shop work, waiter/waitressing, hotel and catering, agricultural work, office work and cleaning. Children work for a number of reasons, including financial independence from their parents, combating boredom, gaining work experience and earning money to buy consumer goods (Davies, 1999). Some child employment is linked to family poverty and earnings contribute towards family income (Stack and McKechnie, 2002).

We undertook a secondary analysis of the BHPS Youth Questionnaire (2002) based on a sample of over 1,000 children aged 11–15. Thirty per cent

Table 7.4: Earnings of young people: 2002 BHPS (Row percentages and Pounds)

	% with earnings	Hours spent working per week	Mean earnings £ per week
Gender			
Boys	34.1***	2.58***	5.57**
Girls	26.7	1.45	4.19
Age			
11	18.9***	0.81***	1.30***
12	23.7	1.05	2.19
13	32.3	1.93	4.17
14	38.3	2.96	7.65
15	42.9	3.54	10.76
Family type			
Couple	31.9ns	2.05ns	4.72ns
Lone parents	36.4	2.55	4.55
Parents' employment			
Two earners	32.5ns	2.13ns	4.92ns
One earner	33.6	2.07	4.45
No earners	26.2	1.55	4.17
Number of siblings			
0	34.1ns	2.4ns	5.59ns
1	33.6	2.0	4.47
2	26.5	1.27	3.92
3+	31.1	2.97	4.78
Parents receiving Income Support			
Yes	29.7ns	1.11ns	3.44ns
No	32.4	2.14	4.84
Parents receiving Jobseeker's Allowance			
Yes	0.0*	0.0ns	0.0***
No	32.5	2.09	4.79
Receiving pocket money			
Yes	30.3ns	2.02ns	4.79ns
No	29.9	1.96	5.14
All	30.4	2.01(6.51)	£4.87(11.63)

$p < 0.001$***, $p<0.01$**, $p<0.05$* where 'p' is the probability that there is no difference between the groups we are comparing (eg, between girls and boys, ages 11 to 15, etc). When 'p' is very small, there is a very high likelihood that the variation in behaviour exhibited by the groups we are comparing is not accidental. The smaller 'p' is, the higher the probability of systematic variation, this is marked by increasing numbers of asterisks */**/***.

ns = no significant variation

Source: Secondary analysis of the BHPS Youth Questionnaire (2002) by authors.

Table 7.5: Receipt of pocket money: 2002 BHPS (Row percentages and Pounds)

	% with pocket money	Mean pocket money £ per week
Gender		
Boys	89.8ns	21.31ns
Girls	90.6	20.62
Age		
11	89.3ns	22.38ns
12	92.0	21.31
13	90.0	19.13
14	89.3	19.97
15	91.7	22.21
Family type		
Couple	90.0ns	21.61ns
Lone parents	95.5	18.09
Parents' employment		
Two earners	90.1ns	21.49ns
One earner	88.3	22.03
No earners	89.5	19.88
Number of siblings		
0	94.6*	20.39ns
1	88.5	20.11
2	87.4	23.25
3+	87.8	26.88
Parents receiving Income Support		
Yes	96.9*	21.08ns
No	89.5	21.36
Parents receiving Jobseeker's Allowance		
Yes	100ns	27.88ns
No	86.9	21.29
Receiving earnings		
Yes	90.2ns	19.36ns
No	90.0	21.68
All	90.2	£23.24 (26.17)

$p < 0.001$***, $p<0.01$**, $p<0.05$* where 'p' is the probability that there is no difference between the groups we are comparing (eg, between girls and boys, ages 11 to 15, etc). When 'p' is very small, there is a very high likelihood that the variation in behaviour exhibited by the groups we are comparing is not accidental. The smaller 'p' is, the higher the probability of systematic variation, this is marked by increasing numbers of asterisks */**/***.

ns = no significant variation

Source: Secondary analysis of the BHPS Youth Questionnaire (2002) by authors.

reported that they had earnings. It can be seen in table 7.4 that boys were significantly more likely to have earnings than girls and they work significantly longer hours. As you would expect, the proportion of children who have earnings and the hours spent working increase with age, as does the wage rate. Children in lone-parent families are more likely to be earning and to work slightly longer hours. Young people living in workless families and families receiving Jobseeker's Allowance were less likely to be employed, which may be a function of local labour demand. The number of siblings does not seem to influence children's earnings and neither does whether they receive pocket money or not.

There was no significant relationship between self-esteem or happiness and whether the young person had earnings.

Over 90 per cent of young people reported receiving pocket money (see Table 7.5). There were large variations in the amounts received, with a mean of £23.24 a week. Receipt of pocket money or the amount received did not vary significantly with any of the variables we looked at, except that only-children and those with parents on Income Support were (slightly) more likely to have pocket money. Those children who received pocket money had significantly higher happiness and self-esteem scores.

Present child employment legislation

Following several amendments, the Children and Young Persons Act 1933 remains the basis of child employment law in England and Wales. It sets the minimum age at which children may be employed and allows local authorities to make bye-laws. However, a recent survey by the Children's Legal Centre (Hamilton, 2003) found that 'there is an unacceptable level of variation within local authority bye-laws in respect of child employment'. Young persons are also protected by the terms of the *European Directive on the Protection of Young People at Work*, implemented into UK legislation within the Working Time Regulations. According to present legislation, no child may be employed:

- if under the age of 12 years
- during school hours
- before 7am or after 7pm
- for more than two hours on any day on which he or she is required to attend school
- for more than two hours on a Sunday

- in any industrial undertaking or where they are likely to suffer injury from lifting carrying or moving heavy items.

A local education authority has powers to supervise the employment of school children in its area and may require particulars about a child's employment. It may prohibit or restrict employment if it feels that the employment is unsuitable, even if not unlawful. A person who wishes to employ a child must obtain a permit from the local education authority. Without a permit, children are working illegally. Yet most working children (95–97 per cent) are unlikely to hold a permit because of lack of awareness that they need one or because of the perception that it is a bureaucratic measure that is not being taken seriously (Hobbs and McKechnie, 1997).

In May 2004, the Minister for Children, Young People and Families accepted the recommendations of the Better Regulation Task Force regarding reforms to the child employment law. These recommendations include the simplification and consolidation of the child employment legislation; a move to a (child) employer registration scheme and allowing more flexibility on when children may work; and encouraging children's participation in the consultation process preceding changes to the child employment legislation.

Children as carers

The previous edition of this book devoted an entire chapter to children as carers (Baldwin and Hirst, 2002). Since then not much new research has been done on young carers, and therefore this section aims to give an up-to-date summary of the numbers and circumstances of children who are carers today in the UK and the resources available to them.

The situation of children undertaking long-term domestic care-giving has been a major child welfare concern over the last decade. In the UK, young carers are defined as those children and young people under 18 years of age whose lives are in some way restricted because of the need to take on inappropriate or excessive responsibilities for the care of a person who is ill, has a disability, is experiencing mental distress or is affected by substance misuse (Department of Health, 1999). This situation often arises because of a lack of good-quality, appropriate, affordable and accessible health and community care services and a lack of information about how to get assistance. Young carers are recognised in parliamentary legislation in the 1995 Carers (Recognition and Services) Act and they have been widely accepted as meeting the definition of children in need in the 1989 Children Act. The Government's National Strategy on Carers (Department of Health, 1999) contains a separate chapter on children providing care, and data pertaining to young carers were included in the General Household Survey (Newman, 2002).

Numbers of young carers

Young people and their parents are often silent about the extent of the support a child provides, through fear of separation, guilt, pride and a desire to 'keep it in the family'. The failure of services to recognise racial, cultural and religious differences can make the identification of young carers from black and minority ethnic groups even more difficult. For these reasons, the numbers and characteristics of young carers could, previously, only be guessed from local studies and household sample surveys. On the basis of these, the numbers of young carers were estimated to be between 10,000 and 50,000 (Banks *et al*, 2001). In 2001, for the first time, the UK census asked the entire population about their caring responsibilities and general self-rated health – with results that far exceeded expectations.

According to data from the 2001 Census, of all children aged between 5 and 15 in the UK, 114,000 (1.4 per cent – 53,000 boys and 61,000 girls) provided informal care (Doran *et al*, 2003). Of these, 18,000 provided 20 hours of care or more a week and nearly 9,000 provided at least 50 hours. The health of 773 children under 16 providing 20 or more hours of care was rated as 'not good' (Doran *et al*, 2003). Moreover, Census figures show that large proportions of young children are undertaking considerable caring responsibilities in the home (Table 7.6). Almost 0.3 per cent of all 5–7-year-olds (amounting to 5,000 children) are carers in England and Wales, and 0.45 per cent of the same age group (over 800 children) provide care in Scotland. Similarly, in Northern Ireland, in the 5–9 age group, 0.62 per cent of children were involved in unpaid care-giving. Larger proportions of young children aged 5–10 undertake very long hours of caring (50+) compared to older children (Table 7.6). Children are more likely to become carers as they get older. There were over 16,000 child carers aged 10 to 11 in England and Wales (1.18 per cent of the age group), and over 2,000 10–11-year-olds caring in Scotland in 2001 (1.6 per cent of the age group). In Northern Ireland, 4,604 children aged 10 to 15 were involved in caring tasks, which makes up almost 3 per cent (2.9 per cent) of this age group.

Table 7.6: Proportions of children and young people providing unpaid care[a] (2001) (Hours per week)

Age	England and Wales				Scotland				Northern Ireland[b]			
	None	1–19	20–49	50+	None	1–19	20–49	50+	None	1–19	20–49	50+
0–4	100.00	0.00	0	0	100	0	0	0	100.00	0.00	0.00	0.00
5–7	99.73	0.21	0.02	0.04	99.55	0.35	0.04	0.06	99.38	0.50	0.05	0.07
8–9	99.42	0.47	0.04	0.06	99.06	0.75	0.08	0.10				
10–11	98.82	0.99	0.09	0.10	98.40	1.33	0.14	0.13	97.12	2.35	0.31	0.22
12–14	97.70	1.98	0.17	0.15	97.43	2.18	0.21	0.18				
15	96.71	2.81	0.29	0.20	96.55	2.80	0.42	0.23				
16–17	95.87	3.39	0.45	0.29	95.60	3.39	0.63	0.37	94.12	4.46	0.89	0.53
18–19	95.33	3.65	0.58	0.44	95.30	3.42	0.83	0.46				
20–24	95.10	3.69	0.60	0.61	94.83	3.78	0.74	0.65	93.22	4.81	1.12	0.86
All people	89.84	6.92	1.12	2.12	90.36	6.12	1.21	2.32	89.02	6.55	1.66	2.77

[a] Row percentages.
[b] Northern Ireland uses age-groups: 5–9, 10–15,16–19.
Sources: Census 2001: National report for England and Wales; Scotland's Census 2001; Northern Ireland Census 2001.

Characteristics of young carers

A recent study of young carers living in Edinburgh (Armstrong, 2004) found that young carers:

- tend to live in more deprived areas than the general population of 5–19-year-olds living in Edinburgh
- have high rates of utilisation of health services compared to a control group of the same age, gender and deprivation category. In particular, they have high rates of admissions to casualty and hospital, and high rates of mental health outpatient appointments
- have higher rates of child protection referrals than other Scottish children in the same age groups and deprivation categories.

The finding that Scottish young carers live in more deprived circumstances is supported by previous UK-wide studies and reflects the circumstances of not only young but all carers (Holzhausen and Pearlman, 2000; Dearden and Becker, 2000; Aldridge and Becker, 1993). People who are ill or disabled are more likely to experience unemployment and poverty and to live in deprived areas. Many young carers are forced to undertake caring responsibilities due to lack of money for alternatives (Aldridge and Becker, 1993). The high rates of health service utilisation and the relatively poor mental health of young carers can be attributed to the high levels of stress and anxiety they experience, as well as to the hard physical tasks associated with caring. A study of young carers participating in the Edinburgh Young Carers Project found that 81 per cent worried about their parents' health, and over one-third of respondents had self-harmed or thought of suicide (Cree, 2002). Young carers are also exposed to a number of risk factors for child abuse and neglect, which increase their likelihood of being placed on the child protection register (Armstrong, 2004). These risk factors are: parental mental health problems (Fleming *et al*, 1997; Kotch *et al*, 1995); drug and alcohol abuse (Kotch *et al*, 1997); and a low level of social support (Kotch *et al*, 1997; Vogeltanz *et al*, 1999). A high proportion of young carers live in single-parent families, which constitutes another risk factor for child abuse (Boney-McCoy and Finkelhor, 1995).

Consequences of caring

Young people with caring responsibilities often need to cope with competing demands and obligations from those who need their care, as well as from their wider family and from formal organisations such as schools, colleges or employers who have expectations of them. Young carers are confronted with these challenges at a time when their identities, social and educational competencies and self-awareness are still at a formative stage (Grant, 2004). Having been a young carer has a lasting impact on a child's health, social network and relationships, and educational attainment. The most serious disadvantages are:

- isolation from other children of the same age and from other family members
- lack of time for play, sport or leisure activities
- conflict between the needs of the person they are helping and their own needs, leading to feelings of guilt and resentment
- feeling that there is nobody there for them and that professionals do not listen to them and are working only with the adult
- lack of recognition, praise or respect for their contribution
- feeling that they are different from other children and unable to be part of a group
- problems moving into adulthood, especially with finding work, their own home, and establishing relationships.

Source: Social Services Inspectorate (1995)

Young carers from minority ethnic groups face additional issues. Minority ethnic families may be less likely to contact social services departments for fear that their children will be taken away. Children from minority ethnic groups are also more likely to be excluded from school (Department of Health, 1999).

There are some advantages associated with caring responsibilities in childhood. In a recent study of children caring for parents with mental illness (Aldridge and Becker, 2003), young people depicted caring in positive terms, reflecting filial closeness, an increased sense of maturity, and improved empathy for other vulnerable people. It also appeared that children wanted continuity in their relationship with their parents and were keen to resist separation from them by almost any means (Aldridge and Becker, 2003). The Sample of Anonymised Records (SARs) drawn from the Census is due to be released shortly, and will provide an excellent database for exploring further the characteristics and circumstances of young carers (by ethnicity, social class, region, household characteristics, etc).

Support for young carers

As mentioned previously, children and their parents are often reluctant to seek help for a variety of reasons, including a wish for privacy, feelings of stigma and fears about community or professional responses. Others are simply unaware that they can get help (Banks *et al*, 2002). Identification of young carers is often inhibited by ignorance among professionals in contact with the families. The main external agents in the position to identify young carers and their needs are, in particular, general practitioners and other primary care staff, as well as schoolteachers, who have the most regular, direct contact with young carers and their families.

Under current legislation (Children Act 1989, Children (Northern Ireland) Order 1995, Children (Scotland) Act 1995 and Carers (Recognition and Services) Act 1995) young carers can receive support from local and health authorities. Children adversely affected by the disability of a family member are a specific category of 'children in need' under the Children (Scotland) Act 1995. This is unique in the UK. The Community Care and Health (Scotland) Act 2002 extended to informal carers, including young carers, the right to an assessment and carers must be made aware of this right. Carers' views should be taken into account when local authorities decide which services to provide.

The Carers (Equal Opportunities) Bill became an Act on 22 July 2004, marking a historic chapter in the history of carers' rights. This Act is likely to be implemented in England and Wales on 1 April 2005. When it comes into force, it will give carers more choice and opportunities to lead a more fulfilling life. The new law will:

- place a duty on local authorities to tell carers about their rights
- place a duty on local authorities when they are carrying out a carer's assessment to consider whether the carer works or wishes to work, wishes to study or have some leisure activities
- give local authorities strong powers to enlist the help of health, housing and education authorities in providing support for carers.

At present, social services departments can help young carers by considering whether their welfare or development might suffer if support is not provided. Under the Carers (Recognition and Services) Act 1995, young carers can ask for an assessment of their needs. Many are, however, not aware that this is possible. In many cases, no one outside the family is aware that the young person has caring responsibilities, and so these young people often go unnoticed and the family does not receive services and support. A study by Loughborough University found that only 11 per cent of young people with caring responsibilities have ever been assessed by their local social services department (Dearden and Becker, 2000). There is a delicate balance between the rights of a child to have support to reduce the caring burden and the reluctance of some families to accept intervention or support from social services.

Young carers' projects aim to provide relief from the isolation faced by children who are carers. They typically provide three kinds of intervention: group activities and discussions, individual counselling or befriending, and advocacy on behalf of the child or family. The majority concentrate on providing opportunities for enjoyable interaction with peers (Banks *et al*, 2002). Britain has about 110 young carers' projects across the country. Projects in England are well established; most in Scotland were set up very recently (Banks *et al*, 2002). The great majority of them are provided by the voluntary sector but some are funded by the statutory sector. Few of the projects have long-term funding. Some projects are unique, developed to meet local needs, but most are run by larger charities such as The Princess Royal Trust, National Children's Homes, Barnardo's, The Children's Society and Crossroads. Many young carers using these projects have no other support from statutory services.

Conclusions

From a very early age, the majority of children's time is taken up by structured activities, leaving very little space for individual choice. Increased perception of danger in public spaces, (adult-centred) consumerism, an achievement-orientated society, child poverty and public prejudice against children on the street are factors contributing to a narrowing of the private space, and hence the liberty, of today's children. Children's wishes often come secondary to what adults deem necessary, safe, educative or more convenient. At the same time, parents today spend more time with their children than before and children value this family time – although their perception of 'quality time' differs from that of adults.

Two-thirds of school-aged children have a part-time job, and thousands of children are undertaking unpaid domestic care. Neither the economic nor the domestic roles of children are recorded in national statistics.

The astounding lack of up-to-date, comparative data on children's use of time and space indicates a lack of policy awareness of the issues that determine how and where children spend their childhood. In these circumstances, children's rights cannot be addressed properly and represent more of a symbolic gesture than active citizenship.

8 Child maltreatment

Carol-Ann Hooper

Key statistics:

A survey of young people (Cawson *et al*, 2000) carried out for the National Society for the Prevention of Cruelty to Children (NSPCC) found the following rates of maltreatment:

- physical abuse (severe or intermediate, by parents or carers) – 21 per cent.
- physical neglect: serious or intermediate absence of care – 15 per cent, serious or intermediate absence of supervision – 17 per cent.
- sexual abuse – 16 per cent (21 per cent girls, 11 per cent boys).
- emotional maltreatment – 6 per cent (8 per cent girls, 4 per cent boys).
- witnessing domestic violence (a form of emotional abuse) – 26 per cent, constant or frequent for 5 per cent.
  [definitions given in text]

Key trends:

- Babies under one year are at the highest risk of severe physical abuse and homicide.
- Scotland has a slightly higher child homicide rate than England and Wales.
- The increased attention over the last two years to children's own views has raised important new issues for research, policy and services.

Key sources:

- Cawson *et al* (2000), *Child maltreatment in the UK* – still the best source of evidence, a survey which is to be repeated after ten years.
- There are still no Government statistics which show the extent of child maltreatment. Statistics for child protection registrations are available from National Statistics/DfES, Local Government Data Unit Wales, Scottish Executive and DHSSPS Northern Ireland. Homicide data are available from National Statistics, Scottish Executive, Police Service of Northern Ireland (PSNI) and UNICEF.

Introduction

Child maltreatment (a term which encompasses a wide range of behaviours) occurs across the world. While definitions, levels of awareness, reporting and recording practices all vary, child maltreatment is clearly a complex, multi-dimensional problem with a long history. It is unlikely that the two years since publication of the first edition of this book would see a significant shift in trends or patterns in the UK, and there are no valid data available to assess if this is the case. This chapter therefore first summarises the best available evidence on the incidence, prevalence and patterns of maltreatment. To a large extent this is still the NSPCC's prevalence study (Cawson *et al*, 2000), which was described more fully in the 2002 edition of this book and is now the accepted baseline for comparisons over time – further research evidence is added where it is available. The chapter then reviews what annual data are available to indicate any trends which can be identified – primarily in relation to fatal abuse (homicide) and child protection registrations. Finally, it considers the implications (both for the research evidence considered in relation to this topic and for policy) of a significant shift in thinking, which has gathered pace over the last two years, towards listening to children's own views.

The extent and patterns of maltreatment

There are two approaches to establishing the extent of maltreatment. Prevalence studies aim to establish the proportion of the population affected through retrospective surveys. For ethical reasons they are mostly conducted with young adults rather than children, and consequently the data relate to childhoods lived some time ago. The NSPCC study interviewed a random probability sample of 2,689 18–24-year-olds, born between 1974 and 1980. Its findings on the prevalence of the forms of child maltreatment, which are approximate to the definitions used in child protection work in the UK – ie, physical abuse, neglect, sexual abuse and emotional abuse (Department of Health, 1999b) – are summarised in boxes below; additional research findings are indicated in the text. Incidence studies establish the number of cases reported to professionals or agencies per year (for physical abuse the relevant incident is likely to be recent, though not necessarily so for other forms).

Physical punishment and abuse

The NSPCC survey: physical abuse
Definition based on experiences of: being hit with an implement or fist, kicked hard or shaken, thrown or knocked down, beaten up (hit again and again), grabbed round the neck and choked, burned or scalded on purpose, or threatened with a knife or gun.

Key findings:
- 25 per cent had experienced at least one of the behaviours above (78 per cent at home, 15 per cent at school).
- 7 per cent were judged to have experienced serious physical abuse (ie, violent treatment from parents, either regularly or which caused injury or had physical effects lasting to the next day or longer).
- a further 14 per cent were judged to have experienced intermediate physical abuse (less serious incidents which occurred regularly or serious incidents which occurred occasionally but caused no serious injury).

Source: Cawson *et al* (2000)

While a distinction is usually made between physical punishment and abuse, there is clearly an association between them. Over the past few years there has been growing pressure across the UK for legislation to ban all forms of corporal punishment. In the last two years, four more European countries (Iceland, Romania, Ukraine and, in effect, Italy) have gone down this route, making a total of at least 14 countries with such a ban so far. In the UK, smacking is now banned in all forms of daycare (including childminding) in Scotland, Wales and England, though not yet in Northern Ireland. Scotland has gone one step further, in the Criminal Justice (Scotland) Act 2003, prohibiting any physical punishment of children involving blows to the head, shaking or the use of an implement, including by parents. A complete ban on all forms of corporal punishment to include parents has so far been resisted throughout the UK, despite the recommendations of the United Nations Committee on the Rights of the Child, the European Social Rights Committee, and now the Parliamentary Assembly of the Council of Europe, a widespread professional consensus in favour, and considerable public debate including extensive consultation processes in Scotland

and Northern Ireland (Scottish Executive Justice Department, 2000; Office of Law Reform, 2001).

A useful review of evidence from countries with such a ban in place offers no support for the fears expressed in the UK of a ban resulting in over-intervention in family life and widespread criminalisation of ordinary parents (Boyson, 2002), but public attitudes in the UK are still mixed. The consultation in Northern Ireland found that while professionals and organisations were largely in favour of a ban, individuals were largely against one. A national survey (Ghate *et al*, 2003) of parents across Britain found that while only 10 per cent thought physical punishment was always acceptable, around half thought it acceptable in some circumstances. The most recent survey of adults in Great Britain, however, undertaken by Market & Opinion Research International (MORI) in May 2004 (MORI website, 19 May 2004), found 71 per cent in favour of giving children the same legal protection against being hit as adult family members, so it may be that public attitudes are changing fairly rapidly.

In practice, Ghate *et al*'s survey (involving a representative sample of 1,250 parents of 0–12-year-olds) found over half the parents interviewed had used minor physical punishment (smacking or slapping) over the past year, and 9 per cent had used severe physical punishment. Those most likely to use physical punishment were parents under 36, parents with 'unsupportive partners', parents of toddlers (aged 2–4) and/or children they see as 'difficult'. An overlap was found with emotional as well as physical abuse – parents who described their relationship in terms indicative of the 'low warmth, high criticism' environment now thought to be most damaging to children (Department of Health, 1995) were more likely to both endorse and use severe punishment (Ghate *et al*, 2003). A Scottish survey of parents found, in addition, some class effect, with parents in lower socio-economic groups more likely to both use and express support for physical punishment than parents in higher socio-economic groups (Brownlie, 2002). A similar methodology to Ghate *et al*'s has been used in a number of other countries; there are limited data available to make comparisons, but a similar level of severe violence (8 per cent) was found in Italy (WHO, 2002b).

The extent of severe physical abuse has also been explored in an incidence study based on monthly card returns from consultant paediatricians in Wales over a two-year period (1996–98) (Sibert *et al*, 2002). In this study the definition of serious physical abuse included deaths and other incidents of violence equivalent to grievous bodily harm (indicated by injuries such as fractures, burns or scalds, internal abdominal injury and subdural haemorrhage in the head).

The incidence of severe abuse was found to be 54 per 100,000 per year for babies under one year old, 9.2 per 100,000 per year for 1–4-year-olds, and 0.47 per 100,000 per year for 5–13-year-olds (ie, the risk for babies under one was 120 times higher than for 5–13-year-olds). A broader definition of physical abuse (based on professional practice) resulted in an incidence rate of 114 per 100,000 babies under one year old being physically abused per year, or 1 in 880 babies abused in their first year. These findings are broadly similar to those of Kempe *et al* in the USA in the 1970s (cited in Chadwick, 2002). The authors argue that similar rates are likely to be found across the UK.

The figures above refer mostly to physical abuse by parents. The risk of violence to children from members of their wider communities has been a recurrent concern in Northern Ireland. The table below gives statistics from the Police Service for Northern Ireland (PSNI) on what it categorises as 'paramilitary style' punishment attacks on children within the loyalist and republican communities. As with any crime statistics, these are limited to reported cases, which fit the definition of a particular offence, and the figures are therefore unlikely to be an accurate reflection of actual levels of violence. Further, the attribution of incidents to 'paramilitary organisations' is based on information available to PSNI at the time of recording. 'Punishment' beatings in particular may sometimes be carried out without organisational involvement or authorisation. While the context of political conflict is clearly unique to Northern Ireland, the exposure of children to violence within communities (whether as direct victims or witnesses) merits more attention throughout the UK.

Table 8.1: Number of shootings and assaults on children (up to and including the age of 17) by paramilitary organisations recorded in Northern Ireland

	Shootings of children by paramilitary organisations			Assaults on children by paramilitary organisations		
	Loyalist	Republican	All	Loyalist	Republican	All
1997	1	1	2	8	4	12
1998	2	1	3	7	6	13
1999	5	1	6	15	11	26
2000	5	4	9	12	9	21
2001	14	9	23	18	18	36
2002	12	7	19	9	13	22
2003	15	3	18	10	13	23
2004 (to end August)	3	3	6	11	5	16

Source: Central Statistics Unit, Police Service of Northern Ireland, cited in Kennedy (2004)

Neglect

The NSPCC survey: physical neglect

Definition on two dimensions:

- absence of physical care and nurturing: includes lack of healthcare, feeding, clean clothes, medical and dental care; children being left to look after themselves (parents away or with drug/alcohol problems).
- failure to safeguard through appropriate supervision: a series of indicators about the ages at which children are left unsupervised in particular circumstances and for how long.

Key findings:

- 18 per cent had experienced some absence of care, 20 per cent less than adequate supervision.
- 6 per cent were judged to have experienced serious absence of care, 5 per cent serious absence of supervision (exceptionally low levels of care and supervision known to carry a high risk of harm).
- a further 9 per cent were judged to have experienced intermediate absence of care, and 12 per cent intermediate absence of supervision (a range of experience with lesser and more variable risks).

Source: Cawson *et al* (2000)

There is no new research evidence on the extent of neglect. However, one trend worth noting is the increasing number of children being born to drug-using parents. In Scotland, the numbers doubled between 1996–97 and 1999–2000 (Scottish Executive, 2003d). Overall, it is estimated that between 41,000 and 59,000 children in Scotland (4–6 per cent of all children under 16), and between 200,000 and 300,000 children in England and Wales (2–3 per cent of all children under 16) may be affected by parental drug misuse (Advisory Council on the Misuse of Drugs, 2003); evidence for Northern Ireland is not available. Research evidence on the association between parental drug misuse and child maltreatment is limited and the findings mixed; one recent study found no difference between children born to drug-using and non-drug-using parents of the same social class at 18 months (Street *et al*, 2004). Clearly not all children born to or living with parents who misuse drugs suffer adverse effects, and the degree of risk depends on many factors, including the nature and extent of the drug problem, the coexistence of other problems (eg, mental illness, domestic violence) and the existence of protective factors (eg, the capacity of other carers). However, parental drug misuse does appear to increase the risk of a range of problems, probably via neglect, and the impacts of both the drug use itself (eg, loss of contact with reality) and the lifestyle associated with it, may interfere with the capacity to meet children's physical and emotional needs effectively and consistently (Cleaver *et al*, 1999).

Sexual abuse

The NSPCC survey: sexual abuse
Definition based on sexual experiences if: the other person was a parent or carer; they were against the person's wishes; or they were felt to be consensual but involved a person other than the parent who was five years older when the child was 12 or under.

Key findings:
- using the above definition, 16 per cent (21 per cent girls, 11 per cent boys) had experienced sexual abuse.
- if abuse involving no physical contact (eg, flashing or voyeurism) was excluded, the rate reduced to 11 per cent (16 per cent girls, 7 per cent boys).
- if the sexual experiences of 13–15-year-olds which they regarded as consensual but which involved someone at least five years older were included, the rate rose to 20 per cent.

Sexual abuse may be perpetrated by people in a range of relationships to the child, not only by parents. In Cawson *et al*'s survey (2000), 1 per cent had been sexually abused by a parent or step-parent, a further 3 per cent by a relative other than a parent, and 10 per cent by people known but unrelated to them. The vast majority of the perpetrators were male. Although 'stranger danger' is the primary focus of public anxiety and parental fears today, only 4 per cent of respondents reported being sexually abused by a stranger. A further survey of 2,420 school-aged children (aged 9–16) has explored the prevalence of sexual abuse by strangers more fully (Gallagher *et al*, 2002, 2003), and found a higher rate: 9 per cent were estimated to have experienced a sexual incident involving a stranger (11 per cent of girls, 5 per cent of boys). Some of the difference between the findings of the two surveys may be the result of definitions and methodology however (Gallagher *et al*, 2002). While sexual victimisation is still considerably less common than many other hazards children face, and many of these incidents are one-off and of varying seriousness, Gallagher *et al* (2003) nevertheless found that 47 per cent of children who experienced them reported being very frightened, and a further 26 per cent quite frightened by them.

Emotional maltreatment

The NSPCC survey: emotional maltreatment

Definition based on seven dimensions: psychological control and domination; psycho/physical control and domination (eg, being locked in a cupboard or room); humiliation/degradation; withdrawal (absence of affection or exclusion from family activities); antipathy; terrorising and proxy attacks (domestic violence between parents is included here, as well as attacks on pets and valued possessions).

Key findings:

- 34 per cent reported some form of 'terrorising' – the most common experience.
- 26 per cent had witnessed violence between their carers; for 5 per cent this was constant or frequent.
- using a scoring system with a cut-off point that represented adverse experiences on at least four of the dimensions listed above, 6 per cent (8 per cent girls, 4 per cent boys) were judged to have experienced emotional maltreatment, with another 6 per cent coming close to this level.

There is no further research evidence on emotional maltreatment as such. However, evidence on the prevalence of domestic violence is worth noting here. Domestic violence is both associated with an increased risk of all forms of abuse and (when witnessed by children) increasingly seen as a form of emotional abuse itself. Recent evidence continues to suggest a slight ongoing decline in domestic violence (Walby and Allen, 2004), although it remains a significant problem – it is estimated that in Scotland around 100,000 children live with domestic violence (Scottish Executive, 2000). There is also growing recognition that violence does not necessarily stop when parents separate. The recent British Crime Survey reports that where women continued to see a violent ex-partner after separating (usually in order to maintain his relationships with children), contact visits had involved threats, abuse or violence in over a third of cases (Walby and Allen, 2004).

Patterns

It is clear from these findings that child maltreatment affects a substantial minority of children. Such experiences are a significant contributor to some of the issues covered elsewhere in this book, in particular problem drug use, mental health problems, and offending and anti-social behaviour. The data are not available to make comparisons in prevalence between the four countries/regions of the UK, and there is likely anyway to be greater variation within each country/ region than between them. In Sibert *et al's* study (2002), for example, significantly higher rates of severe physical child abuse were found in urban than rural areas.

Other influences on patterns of abuse which were discussed fully in the first edition of this book include, in brief:

- *poverty and social class:* although all forms of abuse occur across class, poverty is associated with an increased risk of neglect and physical abuse, but not sexual or emotional abuse
- *gender:* girls are more vulnerable to sexual abuse than boys, and in some studies to emotional abuse; boys are commonly found to be more vulnerable to physical abuse
- *'race':* minority ethnic children are more exposed to racial abuse and harassment, both from outside and within their families
- *disability:* disabled children are at greater risk of all forms of abuse, although different disabilities affect vulnerability in different ways
- *age:* babies are most vulnerable to fatal abuse and to some forms of severe physical abuse (Sibert *et al*, 2002)
- *family structure and process:* some increased risks are associated with lone-parent families and stepfamilies, though family relationships are as important

as family structure, and domestic violence increases the risk of all forms of abuse.

A further factor which was not considered previously is *sexual orientation*. High rates of childhood abuse have been found among lesbian, gay and bisexual men and women. This may be partly because a sense of being different, felt early on in life, may increase vulnerability (Mondimore, 2000) and partly because lesbian, gay and bisexual youth are sometimes targeted because of their perceived or actual sexual orientation (YWCA, 2004).

Further evidence on patterns is offered by recent analyses of the Avon Longitudinal Study of Parents and Children (ALSPAC). The measure of abuse used in these analyses (Sidebotham *et al*, 2002, 2003) is a limited one, based on children who were placed on the child protection register during their first six years, and no distinction is made between different forms of abuse. However, a number of indicators of social deprivation were found to be associated with an increased risk of registration, suggesting that financial insecurity and material deprivation (father's and mother's unemployment, lack of car use), poor or insecure housing (council housing, overcrowding, frequent moves), and lack of social support (people to confide in/discuss decisions with/offer help when needed), all contributed (Sidebotham, 2002). While poverty is clearly associated with many sources of stress for parents (see also Ghate and Hazel, 2002), the authors suggest that the impact of unemployment may operate also via its effects on self-esteem, given the greater value attributed to paid work than caring for children – increasingly for women as well as men. Some child-related factors have also been found associated with somewhat increased risk, including low birth weight babies, unintended pregnancies, poor child health and developmental problems, all of which may themselves be influenced by social deprivation (Sidebotham *et al*, 2003). A further analysis of the same data focusing on parenting more broadly, rather than simply registration for abuse, suggests complex interactions between the parents' own experiences of childhood abuse or adversity, and their capacity to cope with parenting in deprived circumstances (Roberts *et al*, 2004). For example, mothers who had been sexually abused themselves before the age of 13 had poorer mental health (particularly when they lived in complex stepfamilies in overcrowded conditions), which in turn adversely affected their relationships with their children. It is likely that maltreatment and its impact plays a part in the passing on of disadvantage from generation to generation.

Annual trends

It is now well accepted that the annual data on child protection registrations should not be taken as a measure of maltreatment itself. Children placed on the register are those for whom there is an inter-agency protection plan and include some who are not abused but thought to be at risk (including some children not yet born) and exclude many who are known to have been abused as well as the probably far greater number whose abuse is not known to agencies. The figures are given in Table 8.1, however, as they tell us something of how known cases are being managed, which appears to be relatively stable.

Table 8.1: Number of children on child protection register, and rate per 1,000 children under 18

Date	England	Wales	Scotland[a]	Northern Ireland
31/03/1999	31,900 (2.8)	2,670 (4.0)	2,361 (2.3)	
31/03/2000	30,300 (2.7)	2,416 (3.6)	2,050 (2.0)	1,483 (3.2)
31/03/2001	26,800 (2.4)	2,126 (3.2)	2,000 (2.0)	1,414 (3.1)
31/03/2002	25,700 (2.3)	2,000 (3.0)	2,018 (2.1)	1,531 (n/a)
31/03/2003	26,600 (2.4)	2,200 (3.4)	2,289 (n/a)	1,608 (n/a)

[a] For Scotland, the rate given in brackets is per 1,000 children under 16

Sources: National Statistics/DfES, *Statistics of Education: referrals, assessments and children and young people on child protection registers: year ending 31 March 2003*; Local Government Data Unit, Wales, *Local authority child protection registers Wales 2003*; Scottish Executive, *Child Protection Statistics for the year ended 31 March 2002*; DHSSPS Northern Ireland, *Children Order Statistics 1 April 2002–31 March 2003*

While there are slight differences in rates of registration between the four countries/regions, the variation within each country/region is far greater. In all countries/regions the highest proportion of registrations are for neglect, followed by physical abuse, with some variation in relation to the two least-used categories, sexual and emotional abuse. Meaningful comparisons are difficult to make, however, as mixed categories are dealt with in different ways. Again it must be stressed that the relative use of different categories are no indicators of relative prevalence; the increase over the last decade in the use of neglect and emotional abuse categories and a decline in the use of physical and sexual abuse categories almost certainly reflects changes in professional thinking and practice rather than actual trends in maltreatment. Different levels of registration overall between countries/regions may also reflect different levels and/or forms of intervention rather than differences in the incidence of abuse itself. If a higher rate of registration reflects a higher level of intervention, whether this is a positive or negative trend depends, of course, on the outcome of the intervention.

One trend worth further comment is the considerably lower number of registrations for sexual abuse than a decade ago, at least in England and Wales where data have been available for long enough to observe trends. An international debate has developed, prompted by similarly falling rates of reported cases in the USA and Canada, about whether the incidence of child sexual abuse is actually declining (Jones and Finkelhor, 2003; Dunne *et al*, 2003). It would be unwise to draw such a conclusion in the UK, given the very limited efforts at prevention of child sexual abuse in this country, the ineffectiveness of the criminal justice system, and the nature of child protection registration decisions.

Annual data are also available on homicides (fatal abuse), although recent figures are the least reliable, as they are revised upwards or downwards later if the cause of death is reclassified. The contested nature of classifications of cause of death has become even more evident over the last two years. While a number of murder convictions involving mothers have been overturned on appeal, and many more cases where medical evidence was disputed have been reviewed as a result (so far mostly not reopened), there is still widespread agreement that maltreatment tends to be under-represented rather than over-represented in mortality statistics worldwide (May–Chahal *et al*, 2004, UNICEF, 2003; WHO, 2002b). A recent study by Levene and Bacon (2004) suggested there were around 30–40 cases a year of 'covert (ie, unrecognised) homicide' of infants in England and Wales.

Since numbers are small and annual trends often misleading in this context, the convention is to compare figures in blocks of several years. In the previous edition of this book, it was concluded that infant and child homicide rates had remained fairly stable in England and Wales through the 1980s and 1990s. Table 8.2 below suggests a slight increase over the last decade (as do the homicide rates per million population under one year), although it may be that this reflects an increased recognition of fatal abuse rather than an actual change. (The trend is also not consistently upwards; within the last six years, there have been years in which numbers have been below and above the average for the decade as a whole.)

Given the unreliability of classifications of cause of death, UNICEF (2003) takes a different approach, combining homicide figures with deaths where the cause remained 'undetermined', on the basis that many of the latter may be due to unrecognised maltreatment. On this basis, they argue that a significant decline in child maltreatment deaths has occurred, from 1.3 per 100,000 children over the period 1970–75 to 0.9 per 100,000 during a period of five years (unspecified) in the 1990s. This combined figure worsens the UK's position relative to other countries, reducing it from 6th place to 14th in a ranking of 27 countries in the Organisation for Economic Co-operation and Development (OECD). If the definition is broadened further to include deaths by injury (since the boundary here is also a difficult one to draw, eg, where a child dies in a house fire) the UK ranking improves again, however, to second place.

Table 8.2: Number of homicides involving victims under 16 in England and Wales, and average per annum

	Age under 1	1–16	0–16 total	By parent (age under 16)
1992–97	154 (26 pa)	301 (50 pa)	455 (76 pa)	313 (52 pa)
1997/98–2002/03	199 (33 pa)	284 (47 pa)	483 (80 pa)	325 (54 pa)

Source: National Statistics, *Crime in England and Wales 2002/03: Supplementary Volume 1: Homicide and Gun Crime*, January 2004

In Scotland the figures are presented differently – by age of victim and by relationship to perpetrator but not both together. Again, if there is a trend it appears slightly upwards (though again not consistently year on year), although the same cautionary notes about the validity of relying only on homicide figures apply.

Table 8.3: Number of homicides involving victims under 16 and parents as perpetrators in Scotland, and average per annum

	Age under 1	1–15	0–16 total	By parent (all ages)
1993–97	12 (2.4 pa)	43* (8.6 pa)	55* (11 pa)	27 (5.4 pa)
1998–2002	17 (3.4 pa)	22 (4.4 pa)	39 (7.8 pa)	27 (5.4 pa)

*These figures include the 17 children killed in the Dunblane shootings in 1996.
Source: Scottish Executive Statistical Bulletin (2004), *Homicide in Scotland, 2002*

Across the age range as a whole, Scotland has a significantly higher homicide rate than England and Wales. The risk of homicide is greatest for children under 1 in both contexts, but it is also slightly higher in Scotland, averaging 51 per million per year over the last 10 years, compared with 47 per million per year in England and Wales (National Statistics, 2004; Scottish Executive, 2003d).

As in the previous report, only very limited data were available for Northern Ireland. PSNI statistics indicated that 15 children under 16 were victims of homicide between April 1998 and March 2001, and six between April 2001 and March 2004.

Listening to children

Increasing attention is being paid to children's own views, both in research (see Featherstone and Evans, 2004 for an overview) and in the policy process – eg, in consultations on the Children and Young People's Unit (CYPU) *Building a Strategy for Children and Young People* (2001), on *Every Child Matters* (DfES, 2003b) and in developing the Scottish Executive's *Protecting Children and Young People: the Charter* (2004f). While in practice children's views need to be interpreted with care in the context of child maltreatment, as their ability to define their own experience as abuse may be influenced by their attachments, loyalties, reactions to abuse and knowledge of alternatives, three themes of importance can be identified from the data generated by research and consultation. First, children worry about a wider range of concerns than those which are the focus of professional child protection work – bullying by peers being prominent among these. Second, as a goal they prefer to talk of 'staying safe' rather than being protected, with 'someone to talk to' about their worries playing a significant role in achieving that goal. Third, while many children use Childline, few refer themselves to statutory services, and those who do experience statutory intervention often find it distressing.

A wider range of concerns

Children's intimate relationships feature strongly among their major concerns, but they identify relationships with peers as equally important as those with their families (Featherstone and Evans, 2004). Forms of aggression which would be labelled as child abuse in other contexts – physical, verbal, psychological or sexual – may occur in these peer relationships and may be taken less seriously under the label of 'bullying' (Cawson *et al*, 2000). Bullying (mostly from peers, mostly in school) can have serious consequences – it is a contributing factor to truancy, self-harm and suicide and may have negative impacts on self-esteem and educational attainment (Rigby, 2002). In the NSPCC survey discussed above, 43 per cent of the sample had experienced bullying, discrimination or being made to feel different by other children at some point in their childhood, and nearly a quarter of them (around 10 per cent of the sample as a whole) reported long-term effects on their lives.

High rates of bullying were found also in the WHO international survey of Health Behaviour in School-aged Children (HBSC). Findings from England, Scotland and Wales are given in Charts 8.1 and 8.2, alongside the HBSC average.

Chart 8.1: Young people aged 11 who were bullied[a] at least once in the previous couple of months (%)

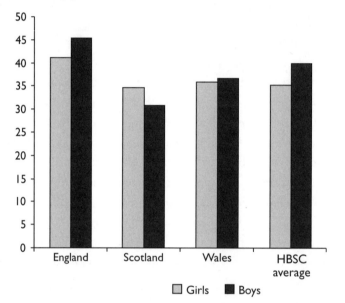

[a] The following definition was given of bullying before the survey questions: 'We say a student is being bullied when another student, or a group of students, says or does nasty and unpleasant things to him or her. It is also bullying when a student is teased repeatedly in a way he or she doesn't like, or when he or she is deliberately left out of things. But it is not bullying when two students of about the same strength quarrel or fight. It is also not bullying when the teasing is done in a friendly and playful way.'

Source: WHO (2004b)

Unsurprisingly, there is some overlap between bullying and discrimination. In some studies, minority ethnic children report higher levels of bullying than white children (Barter, 1999; Oliver and Kandappa, 2003). Findings on gender are mixed, but girls are more likely to report sexualised bullying (Oliver and Kandappa, 2003). Lesbian, gay and bisexual young people also report high rates

Chart 8.2: Young people aged 11 who were bullied[a] 2 or 3 times or more in previous couple of months (%)

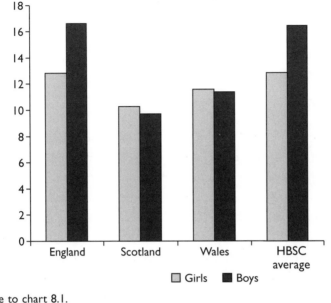

[a] See note to chart 8.1.
Source: WHO (2004b)

of verbal abuse and harassment, sometimes involving groups and persisting over years (Rivers and Duncan, 2002). Young children tend to be more vulnerable than older children, although the WHO (2004b) found 11–13 the peak age. Bullying is, however, a wider phenomenon than discrimination; in the NSPCC survey the reasons young people gave for being bullied included their size, class, intelligence, hobbies/interests, appearance and place they lived as well as disability, sexuality and 'race'. Young people from the highest socio-economic group were slightly more likely to report being bullied than others and white young people more likely in this study than young people from minority ethnic communities, though the latter group were more likely to say they had been discriminated against or made to feel different (Cawson *et al*, 2000).

Children's involvement in bullying – either as bully or victim – may be indicative of other problems at home, as well as being a problem in itself. The NSPCC survey found respondents who were maltreated at home were more likely to report being bullied, discriminated against or made to feel different (Cawson, 2002), and the WHO (2004b) found substantial overlap between those children being bullied, bullying others and involved in physical fights, though many children also fell into only one of those groups. The growth of school policies to tackle bullying may be having some effect as the BHPS Youth Questionnaire indicates some decline in the proportion of children 'worried about being bullied at school' – from 44 per cent in 1995/96, to 35 per cent in 1997/98, and to 30 per cent in 2001/02 (secondary analysis of BHPS by Antonia Keung).

'Staying safe'

The consultation conducted by the CYPU on its strategy found that children disliked the concept of 'protection', viewing it as restrictive, and talked instead of 'staying safe'. Having someone they could talk to about concerns was central to safety, and ensuring this was seen as a more realistic way forward than eradicating all bullying and abuse (CYPU, 2003b). There is a growing body of research addressing the issue of who children turn to for help, usefully summarised by Featherstone and Evans (2004). Most studies have found that the vast majority of children do have someone they can turn to, but a small minority do not (2 per cent in Cawson et al, 2000; 5 per cent in Balding et al, 1998; and 8 per cent in Gordon and Grant, 1997; all cited in Featherstone and Evans, 2004). Of those who do have someone to talk to, mothers tend to be the preferred person for young children, and both the WHO (2004b) and the BHPS (2001/02) found that young people also tend to find it easier to talk to their mothers than to their fathers. Older children increasingly turn to their friends, alongside siblings and a wider range of adults, although girls are more likely than boys to have the kind of friendships within which worries are confided. Boys are less likely to talk to anyone about their problems than girls (Gorin, 2004; Featherstone and Evans, 2004). Of adults outside the family, teachers are most commonly cited as a source of support, although children who are more familiar with a range of other professionals (eg, children with disabilities or mental health problems) are more likely to cite those professionals than other children (Featherstone and Evans, 2004). Children's decisions to tell of abuse are complex, especially where a parent is involved, and many children still tell no one. Attempts are now being made to increase the availability of people children can turn to outside the family, for example via ChildLine, and the introduction of school counsellors. It is also important to pay attention to the particular preferences children express for who they talk to – ignoring this, for example in residence arrangements when parents separate, may have significant implications for children's safety.

Access to and experience of services

Children tend to seek help initially within their informal networks (Kelly *et al*, 1991; Cawson *et al*, 2000). Their ability to access formal services is often inhibited by lack of knowledge about where to go, and also by a range of fears about the response they may receive – fears of being disbelieved or not taken seriously on the one hand, or of losing control and privacy as adults 'take over' on the other. The evidence that while many call ChildLine, very few refer themselves to statutory services reflects the preference they express for spaces in which they can talk through their problems confidentially, receive some reassurance and comfort, and think through the options and their likely consequences without being rushed into action (Scottish Executive, 2002a, f, g; Gorin, 2004; Featherstone and Evans, 2004). Those who experience statutory child protection intervention often feel anxious, confused and powerless, and distressed both by having to repeat their stories many times to different people and by the number of people who become involved. The extra fears of involving statutory agencies expressed by children in Northern Ireland were noted in the previous edition.

A striking aspect of the responses to the consultation on *Every Child Matters* is the gap between the overwhelming professional and Government consensus for information to be shared in children's interests, and the fears children and young people express about loss of confidentiality, and potential labelling on the basis of information which may not always be accurate or up-to-date (DfES, 2004). Although only a small minority of referrals come from children themselves at present (0–5 per cent according to an unpublished analysis by Wattam, cited in Featherstone and Evans, 2004), trends should be monitored to establish the impact of any changes in information-sharing systems on children's ability and willingness to access services. Cooper *et al*'s (2003) suggestion for spaces offering 'conditional confidentiality' may be a way forward for statutory services. Scotland's *Children's Charter* (Scottish Executive, 2004f) offers useful guidance for practitioners trying to improve children's experience of existing service provision.

Conclusion

There are high levels of public concern about child protection, reflected in Lord Laming's inquiry into the death of Victoria Climbié (Laming, 2003) and in the

Child Protection Audit and Review (Scottish Executive, 2002f). However, despite this concern, there remains a dearth of information which would enable the identification of trends in child maltreatment over time. The NSPCC plans to repeat its survey after ten years, but more regular surveys are needed, as is more systematic attention to maltreatment in all research considering childhood experience.

Partly as a result of the limitations of existing research, the issue of child maltreatment remains in many ways marginalised in areas of policy beyond child protection to which it is highly relevant. Many of the reports of the Social Exclusion Unit (SEU) – addressing issues such as homelessness, teenage pregnancy, re-offending, young runaways – have paid scant attention to child maltreatment as a risk factor or to its implications for policy. Such lack of attention to abuse may result in gaps in policy or indeed distort it in potentially damaging ways. For example, although girls who have been sexually abused are at increased risk of teenage pregnancy, there was no recognition of the need for better therapeutic resources for them in the SEU report (1999b). For young offenders in custody, family visits are generally assumed to be a positive influence, to be encouraged, but may not be so where the young person has been abused and may continue to be at risk. In recent research on foster care, where, similarly, contact with birth families is generally seen as beneficial, when the child had been abused outcomes were better when at least one person was forbidden contact (Sinclair *et al*, 2000).

The terms 'maltreatment' or 'abuse' cover a wide range of behaviours. It is important that distinctions between different forms are retained in measures of outcomes if trends and their implications are to be understood. The idea of a single indicator for 'maltreatment, neglect and sexual exploitation', for example, rolls together behaviours with quite different patterns and causes, and risks contributing further to the tendency effectively to address only some forms of abuse in policy (despite the emphasis on 'prevention' in *Every Child Matters*, this is interpreted as 'family support', which is of limited relevance to child sexual abuse).

Finally, interventions to protect children from maltreatment have been developed with relatively little attention so far to children's views. The increased attention to anti-bullying policies in schools, the inclusion of measures of whether children have access to a trusted person to talk to in outcomes (CYPU, 2003b), the growth of child-centred services such as ChildLine, the development of a Children's Charter in Scotland, and proposals to extend counselling services in schools, are all welcome reflections of a change of culture towards taking children's views seriously. There is some way further to go if the principle of participation for children enshrined in the UNCRC is to be integrated across policy in more than tokenistic fashion and be reconciled with a commitment to children's safety.

9 Children and young people in and leaving care

Ian Gibbs, Ian Sinclair and Mike Stein

Key statistics:

- In 2003, 78,842 children were looked after by the state in the UK.
- In 2003, Scotland had the highest rate of looked-after children and Northern Ireland the lowest.
- In 2003, a total of 8,317 young people aged 16–18 and over left care in the UK – 6,500 in England; 1,274 in Scotland; 327 in Wales; and 216 in Northern Ireland.
- Research shows that young people leave care to live independently at a much earlier age than other young people leave home.
- Looked-after children aged 11–15 are four to five times more likely to have a mental disorder than children of the same age-group living in private households.
- Looked-after young people are three times more likely to be cautioned or convicted of an offence than their peers.
- Homeless young people are ten times more likely to have been in care during childhood, and between a quarter to a third of rough sleepers were once in care.
- Care leavers are less likely to be engaged in education, employment and training than other young people aged 16–19 in the population, having between 2 to 2.5 times the unemployment rate for young people in the same age-group.

Key trends:

- Over the past ten years there has been an increase of about 23 per cent in the number of children looked after at the March year ending. The main reason for this is that children are being looked after for longer periods.
- Over the last ten years in England the proportion of children looked

after for reasons of abuse and neglect rose from 45.5 per cent in 1994 to 62.3 per cent in 2003.

- There has been a growth in adoption of looked-after children in the past five years, particularly in England and Wales.

Key sources:

- Office for National Statistics (ONS)
- Scottish Executive
- National Assembly for Wales
- Department for Education and Skills (DfES)
- Department of Health
- Department of Health, Social Services and Public Safety (DHSSPS), Northern Ireland
- Northern Ireland Statistics and Research Agency

Introduction

At the end of March 2003[1] nearly 79,000 children were looked after in 'public care' in the UK. In all four constituent countries and regions, the aims of official policy are to reduce the number of these children, lower the length of time they spend in the system, improve their well-being, and help those young people who leave the care system in their often difficult transition to adulthood.

These aims are embedded in recent policy. Support for young people leaving care is one of the Government's key objectives under the Quality Protects programme in England and the Children First programme in Wales. In addition, the Children (Leaving Care) Act 2000 placed a duty on local authorities in England and Wales to provide services to young people aged 16 and over who leave their care, including financial assistance to qualifying 16/17-year-olds in the four countries/regions of the UK.

Against that background, this chapter considers the following questions:

- How many children are looked after?
- Have the rates been increasing or decreasing?
- What are the reasons for this?
- What is known about those leaving care?

---

[1] 31 March each year marks the end of the data collection for the preceding 12 months.

- How do children and young people currently and previously in the care system fare in terms of well-being?

Much of the evidence presented in this chapter is based on statistics that are routinely produced in all four countries and regions of the UK. Where this evidence is not available we have had to rely on official information from one country or region, usually England, or data from specific research projects. In collating the evidence, we will pay particular attention to the needs of those leaving the care system.

How many children are looked after?

Over the past three years, the total number of children looked after in the UK at the end of March in any year has increased. In 2000 the number was 75,306, whereas the comparable picture in 2003 was 78,842 – a 4.7 per cent increase.

This growth in the care system has applied in England, Wales and Scotland. In England the number of children looked after has increased in recent years both in absolute terms (from 58,000 in 2000 to 60,790 in 2003) and in terms of a rate per 1,000 of all children aged under 18 (from 5.2 in 2000 to 5.5 in 2003). The picture for Wales is very similar, with absolute numbers increasing from 3,574 in 2000 to 4,219 in 2003, and the rate from 4.9 to 5.5. At first sight the picture in Scotland is rather different, where the number of children looked after in 2003 remains about the same as in 2000 – although the rate has increased from 10.1 in 2000 to 10.5 in 2003. As can be seen in Table 9.1, however, this rate of increase would be greater but for the Scottish practice of including in the statistics children who are on supervision orders but placed at home with their parents. Only in Northern Ireland have the absolute numbers and the rates remained very similar (see Tables 9.1 and 9.2).

The aggregated rates for the four countries and regions of the UK conceal considerable variation between local councils. These variations reflect differences in the needs of the children in that area and the differences in the response of councils in meeting those needs. As an example, while the rate for England as a whole in 2003 was 5.5 (see Table 9.2), in Rutland it was 1.2 and in Islington 13.5.

Table 9.1: Looked-after children (LAC) by country/region by placement, 31 March 2003

Placement	England No.	%	Wales No.	%	Scotland No.	%	Northern Ireland No.	%	UK No.	%
Residential accommodation	8,320	13.7	287	6.8	1,550	13.6	296	12.1	10,453	13.2
Foster carers	41,100	67.6	3,015	71.5	3,288	28.9	1,577	64.5	48,980	62.1
Birth parents[a]	6,400	10.5	552	13.1	4,851	42.6	494	20.2	12,297	15.6
Placed for adoption[b]	3,400	5.6	249	5.9	180	1.6	–		3,829	4.9
Other[c]	1,570	2.6	116	2.7	1,518	13.3	79	3.2	3,283	4.2
Total LAC	60,790	100.0	4,219	100.0	11,387	100.0	2,446	100.0	78,842	100.0
Total LAC as % of UK LAC	77.2		5.3		14.4		3.1		100.0	

[a] In England, Wales and Northern Ireland these figures refer to children placed on a care order with adults who have parental responsibility for them. In Scotland they include children on home supervision orders.
[b] Not included in the returns for Northern Ireland.
[c] Includes Youth Treatment Centres, Young Offenders Institutions and various other categories in England, and secure and other residential accommodation in Scotland.
Sources: Department for Education and Skills (2003a), National Assembly for Wales (2004b), Scottish Executive (2004c), Department of Health, Social Services and Public Safety, Northern Ireland (2004)

Table 9.2: Children looked after per 1,000 population aged under 18, selected years 1983–2003

Year	England	Wales	Scotland	Northern Ireland
1983	7.0	6.2	11.8	5.1
1988	5.9	5.2	–	5.8
1993	4.6	4.6	–	4.4
1998	4.9	4.9	–	5.0
2000	5.2	4.9	10.1	5.3
2003	5.5	5.5	10.5	5.4

Sources: Office for National Statistics, 2000b, 200c and 2004e (for population aged under 18 statistics)

As noted above, comparisons are distorted by the extent that Scotland counts as 'looked after' children who were at home on supervision orders,[2] who would not

---

[2] Children on home supervision orders in Scotland have the legal status of children who are looked after. The overall aim of such orders is to promote beneficial changes in the life of the child, and may include conditions covering surveillance, curfews and attendance at drug treatment programmes.

be counted as looked after in the rest of the UK. A more valid yardstick for comparison may therefore be the rate of children who are looked after and not placed with parents (see Table 9.3).

On this re-calculated measure, Table 9.3 shows that in 2000 Wales (4.9) had the highest rate and Northern Ireland (4.4) the lowest, and that in 2003 Scotland (6.0) had the highest rate and Northern Ireland (4.4) the lowest. Again the figures show that the rate has been climbing in the UK, except in Northern Ireland, with the increase in Scotland being particularly marked.

In England, at least, the increase in the number of children looked after over the past three years is part of a longer trend over the last decade. Over this period (1993–2003) there has been an increase of about 23 per cent in the number of children looked after at the end of March. A different measure for assessing the growth in the number of children in the care system is provided by the number of different children looked after at any time during the year. Over the decade this figure has also increased, but the growth is less dramatic than in the case of the March snapshot (7 per cent compared to 23 per cent).

Table 9.3: Children looked after – number and rate per 1,000 population aged under 18, 2000 and 2003 (after leaving out category 'placed with parents')

Year	England	Wales	Scotland	Northern Ireland
2000				
Number LAC	51,500	3,210	4,942	1,950
Rate	4.6	4.9	4.6	4.4
2003				
Number LAC	54,390	3,667	6,536	1,952
Rate	4.9	5.6	6.0	4.4

Sources: For 2000 figures: Department of Health, 2001a; National Assembly for Wales, 2001a; Scottish Executive, 2001a; Northern Ireland Statistics and Research Agency, 2000. For 2003 figures: Department for Education and Skills, 2003a; National Assembly for Wales, 2004b; Scottish Executive, 2004c; Department of Health, Social Services and Public Safety, Northern Ireland, 2004

Why are more children being looked after?

The increase in numbers and rates could arise because more children are entering the system. Alternatively, the length of time children stay could be increasing, or there could be a combination of these reasons. In exploring these issues we limit our discussion to England, for which there are relevant statistics. Surprisingly, the number of children who started to be looked after in any year in England over the last decade has fallen by about 26 per cent – from 31,400 in 1993/94 down to 24,100 in 2002/03. So the reason for the increase in numbers looked after at the end of March appears to be not that more children are being referred but rather that children are being looked after for longer periods. The decrease in referrals has meant that the increase in the numbers looked after has not led to a large rise in the total numbers looked after over the year.

Further evidence of lengthening stays in care is provided by a count of every day of care provided to looked-after children within the year. Table 9.4 shows that the number of care days during 2002/03 was 22.0 million, an increase of 11 per cent since 1998/99. Over the same period, the number of different children looked after at any time during the year has increased by about 4 per cent (from 80,100 in 1998/99 to 83,200 in 2002/03). As a result there has been a steady increase in the average number of care days provided for each child within the year (from 248 days in 1998/99 to 265 days in 2002/03, a rise of about 7 per cent). In short, children are staying in care for longer periods.

Table 9.4: Number of children looked after at any time during the year and the number of care days during the year

| | Year ending 31 March | | | | |
	1998/99	1999/2000	2000/01	2001/02	2002/03
Children looked after in year (thousands)	80.1	82.5	81.8	82.1	83.2
Care days provided (millions)	19.8	20.8	21.2	21.4	22.0
Average care days per child within year (days)	248	252	259	261	265

Source: Department for Education and Skills (2003a).

There are a number of different reasons why children might be looked after for longer periods of time. These include:

- changes in the reasons for which children are admitted
- increase in the number of unaccompanied asylum-seekers
- changes in the numbers adopted from care
- increase in the age at which young people leave the care system.

Changes in the reasons for which children are admitted

Over the last ten years the proportion of children looked after for reasons of abuse and neglect rose from 45.5 per cent in 1994 to 62.3 per cent in 2003 (see Table 9.5). Children looked after for these reasons tend to stay in care longer than others (Rowe *et al*, 1989). The growth in their numbers should therefore provide some of the explanation for increasing lengths of stay over the decade.

This growth in the proportion of children in the care system represents the continuation of a long-term trend. Between 1983 and 1993 the numbers and rates of children looked after fell sharply (see Table 9.2 for rates). The reasons for this fall may have been partly demographic. However, the decrease was much more marked for some groups than others. In essence, children no longer entered the care system 'simply' because they were not attending school or had fallen foul of the law. There were also drops in other groups whose problems had to do with a lack of support – eg, those who were homeless or whose mothers went to hospital to have a baby.

Those remaining must be assumed to be those whose problems were less easily dealt with at home – either because they were in danger there, or, if they were teenagers, because family relations had broken down. These children stayed longer and the numbers of them gradually built up. Table 9.5 illustrates these processes. As can be seen, the numbers looked after for reasons connected with abuse or neglect increased by 15,600 (from 22,300 in 1994 to 37,900 in 2003). The numbers in other categories have fallen by around 6,300 (from 24,700 in 1994 to 18,400 in 2003). The reasons for the rise in the number of 'abandoned' children are discussed below.

Essentially this rise comes about because of an increasing concentration on children who are difficult to look after at home. The existence of this group is emphasised by recent research (Sinclair *et al*, forthcoming) on a sample of 596 foster children in placement at a particular point in time. Those who returned home at any point over the next three years were more likely than those who remained to be re-abused, and more likely to display a variety of social problems – differences that were not apparently explained by differences in their characteristics while they were still in foster care.

Although these statistics apply to England, a similar process may be occurring in Scotland where, as seen earlier, there has recently been a drop in the number of children looked after at home. This has been accompanied by a sharp rise in

Table 9.5: Reasons for being looked after – selected years 1994–2003 (England)

Reason	1994		1996		2001		2002		2003	
	n	%	n	%	n	%	n	%	n	%
Abuse	22,300	45.5	24,700	48.2	36,200	61.5	37,100	62.1	37,900	62.3
Abandoned/ Absent parent	2,000	4.1	2,400	4.7	4,000	6.8	4,300	7.2	4,500	7.4
Other	24,700	50.4	24,100	47.1	18,700	31.7	18,300	30.7	18,400	30.3
Total looked-after children	49,000		51,200		58,900		59,700		60,800	

Sources: Department of Health, 1997 (for 1994 and 1996 figures); Department for Education and Skills, 2004a (for 2001, 2002 and 2003 figures).

the numbers looked after away from home. This suggests a concentration on children who cannot easily be looked after at home. By contrast the lack of growth in the numbers looked after in Northern Ireland indicates that this process is not occurring there. Also in Northern Ireland a surprisingly high proportion of looked-after children have been looked after for three years or more. All this suggests that the care system in Northern Ireland is used in a rather different way and one needs to appreciate the different history behind social work in this part of the UK and the impact of 'the troubles' on statutory intervention in parenting and family life (McLaughlin and Fahey, 1999).

Unaccompanied asylum-seeking children

The number of young asylum-seekers (aged under 18) has risen from 1,600 applications in 1997 to over 13,000 in 2002. Many of these young people (nearly 6,000 in 2002) enter the UK unaccompanied by a parent or responsible adult (Youth Justice Board, 2004). A significant proportion of those classified as 'unaccompanied asylum-seeking children' (UASC) are referred to local social services departments for help.

While not all UASC become looked-after children, their numbers in some authorities represent a substantial proportion of the care population. According to the Children in Need (CiN) census (Department for Education and Skills, 2004j) there were 2,100 UASC looked after during the sample week in February 2003. Nearly two-thirds (65 per cent) of these children were looked after by the Greater London boroughs, with substantial numbers in Croydon (240), Hillingdon (175) and Islington (90). Of the councils outside of London, Kent, with 175, had the largest number of looked-after UASC.

An interesting feature of these figures is that local authorities appear to deal with these minors in very different ways. For example, Croydon had 310 UASC who were deemed 'children in need', of whom 240 (77 per cent) were looked after and 70 (23 per cent) were supported in their families or independently. By contrast, Hillingdon had 710 such children, of whom 175 (25 per cent) were looked after and 535 (75 per cent) were supported in their families or independently.

While some authorities had large numbers of UASC in their care populations, it must be stressed that in England as a whole the number of these children represented only 4 per cent of all children looked after in 2003. Their relatively recent presence in the care system in England will account for some of the increase in numbers over the last few years. Because of the absence of data before 2002 (when there were 2,200 UASC looked after in England, compared to 2,400 in 2003) it is difficult to determine a pattern over time. However, some indication of it can be gained from looking at the growth in the number of 'abandoned children' since this is the code normally given to asylum-seekers. Since 1994 the numbers of children looked after under this code has risen by 2,500.

The proportion of UASC looked after in Wales and Scotland is less than in England and thus less likely to provide an explanation of the increase in the care population of those two countries.

Numbers adopted from care

The broad goal of Government is to increase the number of looked-after children who are adopted, thus removing them from the care system. Figures for England show that the percentage has risen each year since 1999 – from 4 per cent of children looked after to nearly 6 per cent in 2003 (see Table 9.1 for the number and percentage of looked-after children adopted in England, Wales and Scotland in 2003). In Wales the proportion of looked-after children placed for adoption has increased from 3.9 per cent in 2000 to 5.9 in 2003; the increase in Scotland over these dates was from 1.1 per cent to 1.6 per cent.

Over time, the effect of the growth in adoption on numbers looked after should be more marked than the statistics appear to suggest. The average age of children adopted from care in 2002/03 in England was four years two months – in fact, 62 per cent of all such adoptions were from the 1–4 age group. Only 5 per cent of adoptions from care were of children aged ten and over. Thus, those who are adopted might well have spent a long time in the care system.

The increase in adoption rates, while small, means of course that more children are leaving the care system. As such, the trend cannot explain the overall growth in the number of looked-after children. It can, however, be seen as adaptation to the problems of very young children who cannot easily return home.

Young people leaving care

According to official UK data for the year ending 31 March 2003, a total of 8,307 young people aged 16–18 and over left care – 6,500 in England; 1,274 in Scotland; 327 in Wales; and 206 in Northern Ireland (see Table 9.6). In Scotland and Wales, most of these young people left at 16 and 17. In England, just over half left at 18, and in Northern Ireland 70 per cent left at 18 or over.

Table 9.6: Number of young people aged 16–18 leaving care in the UK, year ending 31 March 2003

Country/Region	Left care at 16 & 17		Left care at 18 or over		Total
England	3,200	49%	3,300	51%	6,500
Wales	314	96%	13	4%	327
Scotland	1,146	90%	128	10%	1,274
Northern Ireland	62	30%	144	70%	206
UK	4,722	–	3,585	–	8,307

Sources: Department for Education and Skills (2003d), National Assembly for Wales (2004b), Scottish Executive (2004c), Mooney *et al* (2004)

Regional data for the year ending March 2003 show considerable variation in terms of numbers of care leavers, their final placements and their length of time in care (Department for Education and Skills, 2003d; National Assembly for Wales, 2004b; Scottish Executive, 2004c; Mooney *et al*, 2004).

Research carried out in England, Scotland and Northern Ireland shows that young people leave care to live independently at a much earlier age than other young people leave home (Biehal *et al*, 1995; Dixon and Stein, 2002; Pinkerton and McCrea, 1999; Stein, 2004). A majority of young people in the UK leave care at 16 and 17 years of age. However, in England between the years ending March 2000 and 2003 there was a drop in the percentage of young people leaving care at 16 and 17 (from 58 per cent to 49 per cent) and an increase in the percentage of those leaving at 18 and over (from 42 per cent to 51 per cent). Biehal *et al* (1995) have shown that young people who leave care in England at 18 and over tend to have better outcomes than those who leave at an earlier age.

In England there has been a fall in the absolute numbers of young people aged 16–18 and over who ceased to be looked after between 1997 and 2003. In both Wales and Scotland the numbers increased between 2000 and 2003, whereas in Northern Ireland, following a drop between 1997 and 2000, the numbers have increased in 2003 (see Table 9.7). So far, the drop in those leaving at this age in England has not led to a disproportionate increase in the numbers looked after in this age group.

Table 9.7: Young people, aged 16–18 and over, ceased to be looked after, years ending 1997, 2000, and 2003

Country/Region	1997	2000	2003
England	8,300	6,880	6,500
Wales	–	106	327
Scotland	–	1,057	1,274
Northern Ireland	248	178	206
UK	8,548	8,221	8,307

Sources: Department of Health, 1998a, 2001a; Department for Education and Skills, 2003d; National Assembly for Wales, 2001a, 2004b; Scottish Executive, 2001a, 2004c; Northern Ireland Statistics and Research Agency (2000); Mooney *et al,* 2004.

The well-being of children looked after or leaving care

There is no generally agreed measure of well-being. We look below at evidence that most would regard as relevant to it. This covers:
- mental health
- trouble with the law
- homelessness, accommodation and keeping in touch among care leavers
- the educational attainment of care leavers
- further education, employment and training among care leavers
- young parenthood
- differences between black and white young people
- young disabled people.

Young people with mental health problems

The Office for National Statistics (ONS) has carried out national surveys of the mental health of young people aged 5–17 living in private households and being looked after in England (Melzer *et al*, 2000, 2003b). In the older age-group, the 11–15-year-olds being looked after were four to five times more likely to have a mental disorder than those living in private households: 49 per cent compared with 11 per cent (there were no comparative data on 16/17-year-olds as they were not included in the private household survey).

Analysis of UK data from the National Child Development Study (not separately analysed for each UK country or region) indicates a higher risk of depression at age 23 and 33, a higher incidence of psychiatric and personality disorders, and greater levels of emotional and behavioural problems among those who had been in care, than for the same-age population who had not (Cheung and Buchanan, 1997).

Trouble with the law

In their study of children's homes, Sinclair and Gibbs (1998) found that 40 per cent of young people with no cautions or convictions had one after six months of living in a children's home. Hazel and his colleagues found that 41 per cent of young people in custody had at some time in their lives been in care (Hazel *et al*, 2002). Official data on the offending rates of looked-after children in England were collected for the first time in 2000. The figures showed that looked-after young people were three times more likely to be cautioned or convicted of an offence than their peers in the general population (Department of Health, 2003c).

Research has shown that compared with the general population, children in care and young people leaving care have relatively high levels of illicit drug use. However, there is also evidence that those young people who settle after leaving care have a reduced level of drug use (Newburn *et al*, 2002; Ward *et al*, 2003). It should not be assumed that these difficulties are necessarily the fault of the care system. Some young people are first looked after because they have fallen out with their parents and their difficulties often include problems with the law. Indeed, there is an argument that more of these young people should be looked after since some of them (around 2,586 on latest figures) are currently in prison, where there is concern that they are placed too far from their families in unsuitable, costly, regimes, too often marked by excessive use of segregation and restraint and with unacceptable levels of suicide, self-harm and assault. According to the Prison Reform Trust (2004) the number of 15–17-year-olds in prison, over half of whom have been in care, has doubled over the last ten years.

The most likely alternatives to prison are children's homes or secure provision. The latter are more costly than prisons, but not necessarily benign. One study (Sinclair and Gibbs, 1998) found that around half of a large sample of residents complained of attempted bullying or sexual harassment since arrival. Those who had experienced this were much more likely to say they had thought of suicide in the previous month (four out of ten had). In this study there were major variations between the regimes in different children's homes and, irrespective of their intake, some regimes had much more offending and much lower morale than others. It is apparent that prison is not an appropriate place for young people in trouble with the law, but the care system is not necessarily good for them either.

One promising approach that has been studied in Scotland is the use of intensive foster care (Walker *et al*, 2002). This seemed able to contain young people in considerable difficulty, some of whom might have been in secure provision. Some children's homes seem able to deal with difficult young people. Quite a lot is known about the characteristics of these successful homes but rather little about how to produce them.

Leaving home, leaving care and homelessness

Young care leavers are more likely than those of similar age in the general population to move regularly and be over-represented among the young homeless population. Comparative research drawing on data from England and Northern Ireland showed that 15 per cent of young people in England and 20 per cent in Northern Ireland experienced homelessness at some point within six months of leaving care (Stein *et al*, 2000). In a 2001 Scottish survey, 61 per cent of care leavers had moved three or more times, and 40 per cent reported having been homeless since leaving care (Dixon and Stein, 2002). Research comparing homeless with non-homeless young people found that those who were homeless were ten times more likely to have been in care during childhood, and between a quarter and a third of rough sleepers were once in care (Craig, 1996; Social Exclusion Unit, 1998a).

For the year ending March 2003, 93 per cent of care leavers in England, and 91 per cent in Wales, were in accommodation deemed 'suitable'. Again, while the information is not directly comparable, the Scottish Executive identifies 20 per cent of young people as experiencing homelessness in the year after leaving care, 10 per cent moving more than three times, and 40 per cent remaining in the same accommodation (Scottish Executive, 2004c).

For the same year ending (March 2003), local authorities remained 'in touch' with 81 per cent of care leavers in England and 75 per cent in Wales. While not comparable to the figures for England and Wales, the proportion of young people in Scotland 'with whom the social work department had lost touch increased with the length of time since leaving care – from 13 per cent of those leaving care in the previous three months, to 22 per cent of those leaving nine months ago' (Scottish Executive, 2004c).

Educational attainment

Research carried out in England, Scotland and Northern Ireland shows that young people leaving care have lower levels of educational attainment at 16 and 18, and lower post-16 participation rates than young people in the general population (Cheung and Heath, 1994; Biehal *et al*, 1995; Pinkerton and McCrea, 1999; Dixon and Stein, 2002; Jackson *et al*, 2003).

The 1998 National Priorities target in England,[3] which the Performance Assessment Framework CF/A2 indicator reflects, was that at least three-quarters of children leaving care aged 16 or over should have one or more GCSE/GNVQ by 2002/03 (Department of Health, 2003c). Table 9.8 sets out the UK figures for the years 2002 and 2003. For comparison, the figure for the general population of 16-year-olds in England stands at 95 per cent.

Table 9.8: Proportion of children leaving care aged 16 or over with 1 or more GCSE/GNVQ[a] in 2002 and 2003

Country/Region	2002	2003
England	41%	44%
Wales	30%	39%
Scotland	42%	42%
Northern Ireland	44%	42%

[a] At least one qualification at SCQF Level 3 in Scotland.
Sources: Department for Education and Skills (2004j), National Assembly for Wales (2004b), Scottish Executive (2004c), Mooney *et al* (2004).

---

[3] There is a similar target in Wales under the Children First programme.

Government performance data for England show that the percentage of care leavers with at least one qualification (one GCSE or GNVQ pass at any grade) has risen steadily from 31 per cent in 1999/2000, to 37 per cent in 2000/01 and to 44 per cent in 2002/03. Where comparable data are available in 2002/03, the 44 per cent for looked-after young people contrasts with 95 per cent for all Year 11 young people.

Also, when comparisons are made for A*-C grades, in 2001/02, just 8 per cent of young people in Year 11 who had spent at least one year in care gained five or more GCSEs, compared with half of all young people. In the same year, almost half had no qualifications at GCSE level. Of Year 11 pupils who had been in care for one year or more, 42 per cent did not sit GCSEs or GNVQs, compared to just 4 per cent of all children (Social Exclusion Unit, 2003). Recent figures for England indicate that 53 per cent of looked-after children in Year 11 achieved at least one GCSE at grade A*-G or a GNVQ, and 37 per cent of this group achieved five or more GCSEs or equivalent at these grades (Department for Education and Skills, 2004j).

There were 700 UASC in England who left care in 2002/03, 30 per cent of whom had at least one GCSE or GNVQ. This compares with the 44 per cent of all young people leaving care in England during this period (see Table 9.8 above) and to the 95 per cent of all Year 11 children. In addition, 50 per cent of former UASC who had left care were in education (10 per cent in higher education) on their 19th birthday, compared with 21 per cent of all care leavers (Department for Education and Skills, 2003d). Only 15 per cent of UASC were in training or employment, compared with 28 per cent of all care leavers.

Further education, employment and training

Research carried out in England, Scotland and Northern Ireland shows that care leavers are less likely to be engaged in education, employment and training than other young people aged 16–19 in the population, having between 2 to 2.5 times the unemployment rate for young people in the same age group (Biehal *et al*, 1995; Broad, 1998; Dixon and Stein, 2002; Pinkerton and McCrea, 1999).

A survey of care leavers carried out in England in 1998 and repeated in 2002/03 shows an increase in young people in further education, from 17.5 per cent to 31 per cent and the related proportion of young people not in any employment – a reduction from just over 50 per cent in 1998 to 29.5 per cent in 2002/03 (Broad, 1998, 2003).

In England and Wales, information on the percentage of young people looked after on 1 April aged 16 who were engaged in education, employment or training at the age of 19 (Performance Indicator CF/A4), is provided as part of the evaluation of the Performance Assessment Framework under Quality Protects and Children First programmes respectively.

Official data from England for 2001/02 shows that 46 per cent of care leavers (with whom local authorities were in touch) at age 19 were in education, employment or training compared with 86 per cent of all young people aged 19 in the population as a whole (Department of Education and Skills, 2003d). The percentage for England is 49 per cent for the year ending 31 March 2003, an increase of 3 per cent on 2001/02, and 48 per cent for Wales, the same percentage as the previous year.

The Scottish Executive (2004c) reported that '...around 60 per cent of young people receiving after-care were not in education, employment or training' (by deduction, therefore, about 40 per cent were engaged in one of these activities). Tables presented by Mooney and his colleagues (2004) for the Northern Ireland Inspectorate indicate that 44 per cent of care leavers in 2002/ 03 aged 16 and over were in education (16 per cent), employment (17 per cent) or training (11 per cent).

Young parenthood

There are no official data collected on young parents leaving care. Research carried out in England, Scotland and Northern Ireland shows that young women care leavers, aged 16–19, were more likely to be a young parent than other women of their age group (Biehal *et al*, 1995; Dixon and Stein, 2002; Pinkerton and McCrea, 1999). A study of inter-generational transmission of social exclusion estimates that young people who have been in care are 2.5 times more likely to become adolescent parents than other young people (Hobcraft, 1998).

Differences between black and white young people

Just under a quarter of young people looked after in England aged 16 and over are from minority ethnic groups (Department for Education and Skills, 2003d). Their prevalence in the care system varies greatly between different local authorities. In addition, there are differences in the ethnicities represented, language, how long their family has lived in England as well as in age, gender, exposure to disadvantage, and the other characteristics that differentiate children generally. Returns from the 2001 Census in England and Wales indicate that 13 per cent of children aged 0–18 in the general population are from minority ethnic groups. The proportion of children looked after from minority ethnic groups of the same age is 18 per cent (Department of Education and Skills, 2003a).

Much attention has been concentrated on the degree to which different ethnic groups are over- or under-represented in the care system and in the degree to which they receive matched placements.[4] In general, it seems that South East Asian groups probably make less use of the care system, along with other services. By contrast 'dual heritage' children are probably over-represented (Bebbington and Miles, 1989; Rowe *et al*, 1989). There is a lack of evidence on the effects of matching. Indeed, the most relevant study provides the paradoxical finding that long-term unmatched placements for minority ethnic boys (but not girls) are more stable than matched placements (Thoburn *et al*, 2000). The study nevertheless concluded that matched placements had advantages for the young person's identity and that where they were not possible, determined efforts should be made to overcome the disadvantages.

Very few studies have been able to make comparisons between black and white care leavers. Research in progress, based upon a quantitative sample of 261 care leavers, included 116 (45 per cent) from a minority ethnic background. Of this group just over a third (35 per cent) were of mixed heritage, just under a third Caribbean (30 per cent), a quarter African and just 10 per cent were Asian. White young people were likely to leave care earlier than mixed parentage and Caribbean young people. After leaving care black young people had similar experiences and outcomes. Most black young people had experienced direct and indirect discrimination or racist abuse and some mixed heritage young people felt they were not accepted by black or white people (Barn, 1993; Barn *et al*, 1997, forthcoming; Biehal *et al*, 1995).

Young disabled people

There is evidence that disabled children and young people are over-represented in the care system (Berridge, 1997). Estimates of prevalence vary with the definitions adopted. The most recent CiN census suggests that 10,200 (16.4 per

---

[4] Placed with carers of the same ethnicity.

cent) of the 62,300 children looked after in the February 2003 sample week were disabled (Department for Education and Skills, 2004d). Other research (Rabiee *et al*, 2001) suggests that approximately a third of young people aged under 18 with disabilities and complex health needs who are assisted by social services are looked after.

The reason disabled children and young people are over-represented in the care system is not necessarily that they are generally more difficult to look after. On the one hand, for example, Bebbington and Beecham (2003) found in their analysis of the 2001 CiN census that autistic children were over-represented and were heavy users of respite care and residential respite care. On the other hand, as yet unpublished research by Baker at the University of York suggests that disabled children who are fostered enter the system for reasons that are similar to those who are not disabled, primarily abuse. They may, however, stay longer than children who are not disabled and they are less likely to be adopted (Selwyn *et al*, 2003; Sinclair *et al*, 2004).

There are no official data on young disabled people leaving care and limited research into their experiences of leaving care (Department of Health, 2001b; Rabiee *et al*, 2001; Priestley *et al*, 2003). One of the few research studies, on 131 young disabled people in England, showed that there was a lack of planning, inadequate information and poor consultation with them. Their transitions from care could be abrupt, or delayed by restricted housing and employment options and inadequate support after leaving care (Rabiee *et al*, 2001).

Conclusion

Except for Northern Ireland, the UK has seen some growth in the numbers looked after away from home over recent years. The reason, in England at least, probably has to do with a concentration on children for whom return home is very difficult. In the main this has meant an increase in the numbers and proportion of children who were admitted for reasons of abuse. Recently, however, the rise in the number of 'abandoned children', probably unaccompanied minors seeking asylum, has also played a part. These changes have been accompanied by a fall in the numbers of children admitted for other reasons.

The evaluation of this development must depend in part on the degree to which other more satisfactory ways of dealing with the problems of those children who are no longer likely to be admitted into the care system. This chapter has provided little evidence on this, although the growth in the number of juveniles in prison is not encouraging. The changes also require a determined concentration on the problems of those children and young people who are admitted and for whom a return home is difficult or unlikely. In England and Wales, responses to this situation include a greater concern with the difficulties of care leavers, an increased emphasis on adoption, and a regime of performance indicators designed to promote a stable and high-quality upbringing.

The degree to which similar explanations apply to the growth of the looked-after populations in Scotland and Wales is unclear. If they do, it would be expected that these countries would also seek to increase the length of time that care leavers stay in the care system and increase adoption – areas of practice where England seems to differ from the others. Northern Ireland has not increased its looked-after population – possibly because the proportion of children who spend a long time looked after was already comparatively high. If this explanation is correct, it might be expected that Northern Ireland too might seek to promote adoption.

Evidence on the well-being of looked-after children suggests that some progress has been made but it has been disappointingly slow. This reflects something about the long-term damage done, sometimes by the care system itself, to children who become looked after, but more so by the accumulation of childhood experience without effective intervention. Programmes to combat the latter, such as Sure Start, are discussed in detail by Christine Skinner in Chapter 10 on childcare in the UK.

10 Childcare

Christine Skinner

Key statistics:
- Early years education and childcare have a positive impact on child development, although there is some controversy over the use of daycare by young children (aged 0–2 years).

Key trends:
- Between 1997–2003 there was an increase in daycare nursery places and out-of-school care places across the UK.
- Between 1997–2003 there was a decrease in childminder places across the UK, except in Northern Ireland, and a decrease in playgroup places across the UK.
- Policy initiatives are moving closer to integrated provision of childcare and early education.

Key sources:
- Scottish Executive
- National Assembly for Wales
- Department for Education and Skills (DfES)
- Department of Health, Social Services and Public Safety (DHSSPS), Northern Ireland
- Northern Ireland Statistics and Research Agency (NISRA)
- Office for Standards in Education (Ofsted)
- Effective Provision of Pre-School Education (EPPE) project in England and Northern Ireland

Introduction

This chapter will provide a brief update on the levels of childcare provision across the UK. It will explore the developments in policy-making in terms of planning integrated services and will report the more limited UK evidence on child well-being outcomes in the early years.

Childcare in the UK

In the previous edition of this book, the chapter on childcare focused on inputs to children's well-being rather than outcomes. It described the National Childcare Strategy and levels of provision across the four countries and regions of the UK. This was necessary as a policy commitment to improve childcare was only made in 1998 and was a new venture for the UK Government, which was, and arguably still is the 'laggard' in Europe in some areas in this policy arena (Skinner, 2002; Himmelweit and Sigala, 2004). Consequently, there was a paucity of evidence from evaluation and longitudinal studies on childcare-related outcomes.

Childcare policy-making is, therefore, only beginning to come of age. It is very dynamic, and at an exciting stage of development, with the UK heading towards more integrated provision, where childcare and early-education services are being combined. Simultaneously, however, the complexity has increased as service provision cuts across traditional health, education and social service boundaries and is replete with confusing and ill-defined terminology – within countries and regions as well as across them. For example, in England there are Early Excellence Centres, Neighbourhood Nursery Initiatives and Children's Centres, and some regions and countries have Sure Start local programmes while others have abandoned this terminology altogether.

Comparisons between countries and regions are, therefore, not straight-forward in the UK, or across Europe (Mooney *et al*, 2003). Even so, progress has been made in gathering research evidence on preschool childcare outcomes in the UK, although this remains limited – with the most comprehensive data coming from one longitudinal study, the Effective Provision of Pre-School Education (EPPE) project in England and Northern Ireland. Longitudinal evaluations of targeted intervention strategies for children in disadvantaged areas (Sure Start local programmes in England) are underway, but full results of the impact on child development will not be available until 2007 (see http://www.ness.bbk.ac.uk accessed July 2004). Currently, most of the reported evidence on childcare outcomes for the general population relies on research from the USA and the EPPE project (McQuail *et al*, 2003; Melhuish, 2004a).

To capture the changing nature of policy developments, the more holistic term of 'early-years' policy will be adopted to refer to childcare and early-education provision for the under-five age group. The distinction between child 'care' and early-education services is difficult to sustain as providers move towards more integrated services and counting these separately for statistical purposes is becoming increasingly tricky, not least because the data quality is poor.

Level of childcare and early-education provision across the UK

Table 10.1 provides statistics on the number of childcare places across the UK. But as can be seen by the extensive notes to the table, the data are problematic – most obviously in England and Wales. In England, the Office for Standards in Education (Ofsted) took over responsibility for inspection and data collection from local authorities in 2001 and the data they received were so inadequate they refused to publish figures for 2002 (Ofsted, 2003). Similarly, in Wales responsibility passed from local authorities in 2002 to a new social and health care regulator, the Care Standards Inspectorate for Wales (CSIW). The CSIW's first priority has been to inspect services; their second priority, to provide a national picture of daycare in Wales, has been left until 2004 (National Assembly for Wales, 2004, p. 26). Consequently, figures for 2002 and 2003 have not been published, and direct enquiries to CSIW have yielded figures for only the number of providers and not the number of childcare places (this is not comparable with the other data). There are also some problems with variations in definitions used across countries (see notes to table).

Making meaningful comparisons across the four countries and regions of the UK and over time is therefore difficult, although this might change in the future following improved quality control of data collection methods. With these caveats, the broad trends from 1997–2003 are:

- an increase in daycare nursery places across all countries and regions
- an increase in out-of-school care places across all countries and regions
- a decrease in childminder places across all countries and regions, except Northern Ireland
- a decrease in playgroup places across all countries and regions.

It is difficult to identify the trends in holiday scheme places within and across countries and regions. In England, holiday playschemes were reclassified as out-of-school care in 2003 and therefore figures for holiday scheme places are not available separately; this change also accounts for an apparent large increase in out-of-school places between 2001 and 2003. In Northern Ireland there appears to be a contradictory trend, with an increase in places up until 2000 followed by a decline in 2002/03; no explanation is provided for this trend in the statistical returns. In Scotland, there is a sudden rise of 110 per cent in holiday scheme places between 2002 and 2003 due to a 26 per cent increase in the number of providers (Scottish Executive, 2003h, p. 1).

These figures give an indication of the broad levels of provision but little in the way of understanding the availability of childcare services. Indeed, the National Audit Office (NAO), in its own independent review of childcare provision in England, found large variations in the extent of services regionally, ranging from 11 to 58 preschool places per 100 preschool children across local authorities (NAO, 2004b, p. 6). There was also insufficient flexible provision at evenings and weekends, for disabled children and for children living in disadvantaged areas, despite targeting services in the 20 per cent most deprived wards. The NAO argued that better information was needed in order to measure the size of the sector and assess the extent of provision. It also criticised the Government for counting the number of places simply to show whether targets for increasing the number of places in England had been reached. Moreover, just counting the number of places gives no indication of the stability of services. The NAO gauged that, due to closures, the net gain in new places was only 520,000 – way short of the target of 900,000 for 2004 (NAO, 2004b, p. 6). The latest figures show that 306,063 new childcare places were created in England in 2003/04, but simultaneously 149,246 places with childminders, out-of-school clubs and daycare disappeared (*Observer*, 25 July 2004, p. 7). Expansion in childcare places therefore appears precarious and volatile and is related both to the mixed economy of provision, which creates competition between providers, and to complex and short-term funding arrangements (NAO, 2004b). In contrast, provision of early-education places appears more stable: in all four countries and regions, the target of providing a free part-time place for all four-year-olds whose parents want one has been reached. The funding stream for this provision is more straightforward and is not time-limited. In general, inputs to early-years provision remain a key part of Government policy and relates to the commitment to eradicate child poverty.

Table 10.1: The numbers of different childcare places across the UK[a,b,c,d,e]

	1997	1998	1999	2000	2001	2002	2003
Daycare nurseries							
England	193,800	223,000	247,700	264,200	285,100	–	398,000
Wales	8,207	8,839	9,894	10,867	12,330	–	–
Scotland	25,679[aa]	–	–	–	–	118,422	122,710
N. Ireland	–	4,229	4,828	5,621	–	7,156	7,798
Out-of-school care							
England	78,700	92,300	113,800	141,100	152,800	–	293,400[dd]
Wales	4,055	5,035	5,620	7,958	8,186	–	–
Scotland	12,236	–	–	–(18,130)[bb]		30,419	41,209
N. Ireland	–	1,459	–	4,143	–	4,518	4,773
Holiday schemes							
England	209,000	256,500	435,000	490,400	594,500	–	**
Wales	–	–	–	–	–	–	–
Scotland	10,226[cc]	–	–	–	(6,586)[bb]	8,497	17,883
N. Ireland	–	3,806	–	5,038	–	1,385	1,403
Childminders							
England	365,200	370,700	336,600	320,400	304,600	–	307,500
Wales	17,284	17,484	13,923	13,039	13,351	–	–
Scotland[ee]	34,983	–	–	–	–	–	26,570[ee]
N. Ireland	–	18,795	18,807	19,151	–	20,464	21,164
Playgroups Sessional							
England	383,700	383,600	347,200	353,100	330,200	–	281,200
Wales	27,367	25,972	25,067	25,592	23,584	–	–
Scotland	41,620	–	–	–(29,892)[bb]		25,035	20,117
N. Ireland	–	15,892	16,450	16,726	–	15,032	14,648

[a] Figures for Northern Ireland (NI) not available until 1998 as compiled from Children Order (NI) 1995 returns, which was not effective until 1996.

[b] NI presents data for children under 12 years of age in relation to all categories except daycare nurseries. England, Scotland and Wales present data for children under eight.

[c] In England, figures for 2002 were not published as Ofsted felt they were inadequate. Also, improved data collection methods mean that the new 2003 figures are not comparable with earlier years, in part because playgroups are now described as 'sessional day care' and a new category of 'crèche day care' was added; it is not clear what the definitional differences are between these and earlier data (Ofsted, 2003).

[d] In Wales figures for 2003 are not published, following the transfer of responsibility for inspection and data collection from local authorities to the new Care Standards Inspectorate for Wales (CSIW) in 2002. Their first priority was to conduct inspections, leaving improvements to data collection as their next priority for 2004 (National Assembly for Wales, 2004a, p. 26).

[e] The paucity of Scottish data results from changes in data collection methods, which audited early education and childcare services together in a new Annual Integrated Census introduced in 2000/01.

– Data not available.

** Data not available separately, now added in with out-of-school care (Ofsted, 2003).

aa Statistical returns in 1997 for some daycare nursery providers were sent to both the Social Work Services Group and the Scottish Office Education and Industry Department, thus there is some double counting between daycare services and early education services.

bb ( ) = numbers of children attending and not numbers of places available.

cc This is described as the number of *term-time* places and holiday places added together; this does not make sense under this category, and it is possible that term-time means half-term holiday care.

dd The apparent large increase from 2001 to 2003 is due to holiday schemes now being included in the category of out-of-school care.

ee Scotland has conducted just two surveys of childminders, one in 1996 and the other in 2003, the figures for 2003 refer to places in term-time (http://www.scotland.gov.uk/pages/news/2003/08/SEed257.aspx).

Developments in early-years policy

Sure Start local programmes

The main childcare policy aimed specifically at dealing with child poverty and improving child and family well-being is the Sure Start Initiative. This was conceptualised following the review of children's services within the Comprehensive Spending Review published in July 1998, *Modern Public Services for Britain* (HM Treasury, 1998). It was a cross-cutting initiative, bringing together existing services and developing new ones for young children of preschool age and targeting support at deprived neighbourhoods. All four countries and regions introduced Sure Start programmes in 1999/2000 and these ran alongside pre-existing general childcare services and policy. Sure Start local programmes provided a multiple set of services which included childcare, early education, health and family support targeted at preschool children aged less than four years old living in disadvantaged areas. Delivery was through local autonomous partnerships involving providers from the voluntary, statutory and private sectors who designed and delivered services in line with local needs. The initial aim was to give young children a 'sure start in life' – by supporting and improving their health, education and well-being – to ensure they would be 'ready to flourish' when they started school. The programmes were developed to become a key strand in the fight against child poverty as they also aimed to help parents into work and/or training (DfES, 2004a, p. 4; Sure Start Scotland, 2004; DHSSPS, 2002, p. 7).

The latest available figures for Sure Start programmes are provided in Table 10.2. The data are patchy; in Wales a new childcare strategy under the Cymorth Fund means that Sure Start is no longer separately identifiable, and similarly in Scotland a new integrated childcare strategy is being developed which will subsume all Sure Start programmes. This means the effect of these programmes on outcomes is unlikely to be fully evaluated in Wales or Scotland (though they will be in England). What the changes do highlight is a major shift in early-years policy-making towards integrated provision across the UK.

Table 10.2: Sure Start local programmes across the UK

	England	Wales	Scotland	Northern Ireland
Number of local programmes 2003/04	524	Under Cymorth Fund Sure Start no longer identifiable	192	23
Age of children	0–3 years	0–10 years	0–3 years (0–5 years in future)	0–3 years
Estimated number of children receiving Sure Start services	2003/04 400,000 in deprived areas	2003/04 Under Cymorth Fund Sure Start no longer identifiable	2000/01[a] 8,864	2003/04 19,000, a third in rural areas
Funding	2001/02 £183m	2001/02 £11m	2001/02 £19m	2001/02 £6m

[a] Cunningham–Burley et al (2002)

Integrated early-years services

Policy-making in early years is undergoing a process of rationalisation in the UK. Childcare and early education are now being discussed together in planning and service delivery and are becoming subject to similar overarching objectives. These more integrated strategies are driven by a number of factors, including the UK Government's duty to meet the standards in the United Nations Convention on the Rights of the Child (UNCRC), the related appointments of Children's Commissioners, and the perceived success of integrated provision. Table 10.3 summarises policy developments across the UK.

In England, policy-making for the early years was centralised within a new interdepartmental unit – the Sure Start Unit (SSU) in 2002. Childcare, early-education and Sure Start local programmes were thus brought together under the auspices of the SSU within the Department for Education and Skills (DfES), although the SSU reports to both the DfES and the Department for Work and Pensions (DWP) – highlighting its role in the child poverty strategy (DfES,

Table 10.3: Early-years policy developments across the UK

	England	Wales	Scotland	Northern Ireland
Policy changes	2002 – Sure Start Unit (SSU) created within the DfES. New ten-year strategy to be announced (HM Treasury 2004d).	April 2003 – 'Cymorth', the Children and Youth Support Fund, introduced.	2004 – Consultation New 'Integrated Strategy for Early Years'.	2004 – Consultation 'Draft Strategy for Children and Young People'. Plus, early-education and childcare review.
Integration	SSU responsible for all childcare, early education and local Sure Start programmes.	Cymorth, unified funding subsuming Sure Start local programmes, the childcare strategy and play grant for children aged 0–10 years. (WAG, 2003a, p. 3, 2003c, p. 3).	Unified funding subsuming all health, childcare and education services for children aged 0–5 years.	Separation of 'Preschool education' and childcare in different Government departments. Sure Start local programmes still identifiable.
	Framework of distinct provision of childcare and early education with targeted support in areas of disadvantage. But expansion of integrated model through Children's Centres (HM Treasury 2004d).	Framework of universal provision with targeted support in areas of disadvantage – Cymorth Target Areas (WAG 2003c, p. 7).	Framework of universal provision with targeted support in areas of disadvantage (SE, 2003b, p. 4).	Framework of distinct provision of childcare and early education, but closer integration under consideration (DE, 2004).
Aims	'To transform education, health and family support services for children under five and their families; increase the availability of high quality childcare … ; and meet the needs of the most disadvantaged, so children can fulfil their potential and parents can find ways out of poverty' (DfES, 2004d , p. 4).	'To provide a network of support for children and young people within a framework of universal provision, in order to improve the life chances of children and young people from disadvantaged families' (WAG, 2003a, p. 3). Provide childcare to help parents work or train and tackle child poverty (WAG, 2003c).	To provide 'a framework for the effective provision of universal and targeted services for children and their families, from pre-birth to age 5' (SE, 2003: 4). To help secure the 'best start' for all children and promote their well-being (SE, 2003b, p. 4).	Aims of childcare strategy to 'ensure high quality, affordable childcare for children up to age 14' (DENI, DHSS, T&EA, 1999, p. 7). (Childcare includes preschool education).
UNCRC	Policy not explicitly based on UNCRC, but is implied.	Policy based around seven core aims related explicitly to UNCRC (WAG, 2003b, p. 5).	Policy based around five common outcomes related explicitly to UNCRC (SE, 2003b, pp. 14–15).	Draft strategy serves as NI 'Implementation Plan' of UNCRC (CYPU, 2003d, p. 6).

CYPU = Children and Young People's Unit; DE = Department of Education; DfES = Department for Education and Skills; NI = Northern Ireland; SE = Scottish Executive; UNCRC = UN Convention on the Rights of the Child; WAG = Welsh Assembly Government

2004a). Lewis (2003, p. 235) notes that despite aiming to break down barriers between early education and care this distinction remains at the level of provision. Similarly, while policy-making is combined centrally there is still a division between mainstream services and for those people living in disadvantaged areas. Mainstream services include fee-paying childcare and part-time education for three- to four-year-olds; in disadvantaged areas the services include Early Excellence Centres and Neighbourhood Nurseries with Sure Start local programmes in the 20 per cent most deprived wards in England. The structural and service differences between these latter three are not clear; all provide some combination of multiple, integrated services – mostly within areas of disadvantage. This will change slightly in the near future with policy goals set for local authorities to 'develop integrated centres in disadvantaged areas (and elsewhere where possible)', with each given targets to develop Children's Centres in the most deprived wards (DfES, 2003g: 6). Wales also has a target to develop an Integrated Centre in each local authority. Overall, 2,500 new Children's Centres are expected by March 2008, a recent increase announced in the 2004 Spending Review (up from 1,700 centres), which is seen as a step nearer to the final goal of one centre in 'every community' in England (HM Treasury, 2004d, p. 61). Children's Centres must provide five key services in a single place (but not necessarily in a single building), including full-time daycare, early education integrated with childcare for children aged 3–4 years, family support and outreach, health services, links with the Childcare Information System (CIS) and links with Jobcentre Plus (DfES, 2003g). Pre-existing daycare providers, school nurseries, Early Excellence Centres and Neighbourhood Nurseries can all be designated as Children's Centres if these five key services are provided. However, unlike existing Sure Start local programmes run by autonomous partnerships, Children's Centres are the responsibility of local authorities and are, in effect, a re-branding of existing services based on the Sure Start model. The Government is also expanding integrated provision with the introduction of 'extended schools'. It is expected there will be one in every local education authority by 2006 (DfES Press Release May 2004). Similar strategies for integrated provision in schools are planned for Wales and Scotland. These changes represent a shift in policy thinking towards more holistic, integrated services – what has been termed 'educare' (DfES, 2004d). But unlike Wales, Scotland and perhaps also Northern Ireland, the early-years strategy in England, while being built around children's needs, is not yet explicitly related to the UNCRC nor advancing the idea of the 'whole child perspective' to the same extent in policy discourse. On the one hand, Lewis (2003) argues that tensions exist in England's childcare strategy between a social investment approach in children and the aim of promoting mothers' employment. On the other hand, England has been marked out as being at the forefront of other countries in the Organisation for Economic Co-operation and Development (OECD) in offering integrated childcare and education; in that regard the quality of provision is improving, although there is still a long way to go (Bennett, 2003, p. 4242). Also, within the Green Paper *Every Child Matters,* early-years services will be drawn in to the same inspection framework for all children's services. This aims to meet five key outcomes, including: being healthy, staying safe, enjoying and achieving, making a positive contribution, and ensuring economic well-being (DfES, 2003b, p. 11). Within this broader welfare framework there is more emphasis on a social investment approach. But it remains to be seen whether specific policy developments on childcare and early years to be set out in a new ten-year childcare strategy due in December 2004 will promote fuller investment in all children, including those living outside disadvantaged areas.

In Wales, the move towards greater integration began in April 2003 with the introduction of the Cymorth Fund. This subsumed all previous services such as Sure Start, the National Childcare Strategy and the 'play grant', as well as some youth services. It places a new statutory duty on local authorities for childcare to be outlined in a Cymorth Plan alongside Early Years Development Plans for early education. Cymorth funds are to be used for providing additional services in areas of disadvantage (Cymorth Target Areas) and preferably within integrated centres supporting health, open-access play, childcare and early education provision (Welsh Assembly Government, 2003c, p. 15). In that regard Cymorth is very similar to Sure Start local programmes, but it also aims to build upon and sustain mainstream childcare places as well as provide general childcare information services (Welsh Assembly Government, 2003c, p. 17). Cymorth is explicitly related to the seven UNCRC core aims identified by the Welsh Assembly as ensuring children have a 'flying start in life' including: having access to comprehensive educational opportunities for development of social and personal skills; enjoying the best possible physical and mental health; having access to safe play, leisure, etc; being listened to; enjoying the benefit of a safe home; and being protected against disadvantage caused by poverty (Welsh Assembly Government, 2003a, p. 5, 2003b, pp. 22–29). Thus, the aim as shown in Table 10.3 'to provide a network of support for children and young people within a framework of universal provision' is operationalised, and investment in children is founded on the principles of UNCRC. In the Welsh approach, however, there is a stronger focus on children's access to play, exemplified by the incorporation of the Play Grant within Cymorth. This may be because Wales was first in the UK to give due regard to the UNCRC, in which play is seen as an important right for children. As the UN Committee on the Rights of the Child noted in 2002: 'it welcomes that the Convention has been used as a framework in the strategy for Children and Young People developed by the National Assembly for Wales, but it remains concerned that this has not been the case throughout the state party' (House of Lords, 2003, p. 84).

Scotland is currently developing its Integrated Strategy for Early Years, where all existing early-years services will be brought together and funding will be aligned across Sure Start, the childcare strategy, preschool education and some health funds. The overall aim is to align policies across departments to provide 'a co-ordinated, coherent framework for the promotion of health and well-being of children in their early years and that of their families' in order to secure the 'best start' for all children (Scottish Executive, 2003a, p. p4). This strategy is currently under consultation and a final version was expected in late 2004, now delayed until 2005. The main objective, however, is to provide fully integrated, universal services for all children under five years old, and to assist joint working with providers aiming to deliver against a common set of outcomes, but in particular to meet the Scottish Executive target of providing an integrated package of health, care and education for at least 15,000 vulnerable children (Scottish Executive, 2003a, pp. 11, 13). There are five common outcomes to be met, all explicitly based on the UNCRC: to improve children's health, their social and emotional development, and their ability to learn, to strengthen families and communities, and reduce barriers to employment (Scottish Executive, 2003a, pp. 14–15). The existing planning structure through local Childcare Partnerships is likely to undergo further changes to incorporate these outcomes. Overall, in this early-years policy discourse, there is a strong emphasis on supporting families and communities as well as children, and this is related to concerns to improve health. The rhetoric in Scotland is unique in discussing the promotion of 'resilient children' and much discussion of early-years provision focuses on improving children's health as a key element in integrating services (Scottish Executive, 2003b, p. 9). It is likely this emphasis results from both Scotland's poorer health status compared to similar countries in Europe and the ability of the Scottish Executive to focus policy attention on this area as a result of devolution (Stewart, 2004).

Northern Ireland does not appear to be so advanced in terms of planning integrated early-years services, though it is focusing on the UNCRC. Policy-makers are currently consulting on a wide-ranging Draft Strategy for Children and Young People, which, in effect, will be Northern Ireland's Implementation Plan for the UNCRC (Children and Young People's Unit (CYPU), 2003c, d). There will be ten task groups charged with the responsibility of taking forward Northern Ireland's vision of a 'whole child perspective' in service planning and delivery based on the three core themes of the UNCRC: protection, participation and provision. Childcare will come under the auspices of the Family and Community Support Task Group, and early education under the Achievement, Learning and Enjoyment Task Group: both groups are to identify high-level outcomes, measures and performance indicators for their areas of service provision (CYPU, 2003d, pp. 52–55). The strategy is not yet fully devised and is currently being considered by Ministers for approval in late 2004. Simul-taneously, two reviews are being conducted on early-years policy; one by the Inter-Departmental Group on Early Years who are responsible for overseeing the implementation of the *Children First* childcare strategy (Department of Health and Social Services, Training and Employment Agency and Department of Education Northern Ireland, 1999). This group is currently constituted of officials from the Departments of Education, Health and Social Services and Public Safety and Employment and Learning. The second review into preschool education provision is being conducted by the Department of Education (DE, 2004, p. 23). The reviews will take 'appropriate account' of the overall strategy on children and young people, but it is not clear how this will be done or how these will eventually relate to the overall strategy. Currently, there is a clear separation of responsibility for childcare and education within Government departments; however, Sure Start local programmes are still identifiable separately and do provide integrated services – though they have no contact with the education sector (DE, 2004, p. 25). The two reviews will explore further integration, and in this regard Northern Ireland views itself as lagging behind England (DE, 2004). This lag is likely to be related to the disarray in implementing devolution, culminating in the suspension of the Northern Ireland Assembly in 2002 and prior to that the focus of the Assembly on issues of equality (Mitchell and Bradbury, 2004).

Overall, despite the differences in progress towards integrated provision, there is a greater emphasis on a holistic approach to children's needs in the early years than is implied in previous policy discourses on childcare, though there are subtle differences, with play being a significant element in Wales and health in Scotland. Yet, it is not possible to tell from the policy documents whether services are truly integrated from the perspective of the end users, as arguably there is no easily identifiable universal and unified service *per se* for parents and children. Services still remain diverse and potentially precarious, operating on a mixed economy of provision involving the public, private and voluntary sectors. Nonetheless, the move towards greater integration has partly been driven by evidence on positive child well-being outcomes.

Evidence on childcare-related outcomes

In 2004 the NAO commissioned Professor Edward Melhuish, an expert on child development, to conduct a literature review of international evidence on the impact of early-years provision on children's development (Melhuish, 2004a).[1] Around the same time, the DfES also commissioned a review of cross-national evidence on childcare to address policy questions, one of which was specifically related to child outcomes (McQuail *et al*, 2003). The DfES review, however, found little systematic cross-national research on childcare outcomes. This was partly as a result of differences in concepts, purposes and values across countries and the expense involved technically and method-ologically in conducting such work (McQuail *et al*, 2003, p. 18). Melhuish, in the NAO report, makes a similar point, that 'the range, quality, quantity and age of use of childcare varies markedly between societies' and this results in different relationships between childcare and child development across countries (Melhuish, 2004a, p. 7).

Overall, the NAO and the DfES reviews cover similar studies, but the NAO's gives the most comprehensive account of the effects of preschool care and education on developmental outcomes. For that reason, the NAO review is presented here, as are the findings from the UK's main source of research evidence – the Effective Provision of Pre-School Education (EPPE) project in England and Northern Ireland. The EPPE project is the first major longitudinal study to be conducted in Europe examining the effects of preschool experiences on

---

[1] Edward C. Melhuish is the Executive Director of the National Evaluation of Sure Start local programmes in England (NESS) and is also the Principal Investigator on the Effective Provision of Pre-school Education (EPPE) projects in England and Northern Ireland.

children's social and intellectual development between the ages of three and seven years. It began in 1997 and followed 3,000 children in 141 different childcare settings across five regions in England comparing them to 200 children who had no childcare experiences outside the home (Northern Ireland covered 70 childcare settings) (Melhuish *et al*, 2001; Sammons *et al*, 2002; 2003; Siraj-Blatchford *et al*, 2003).

International evidence on effects of preschool experiences on developmental outcomes

One of the enduring and main concerns related to outcomes is the effect of pre-school care on the development of very young children (0–3 years) in the context of maternal employment. The question, which begs a definitive answer, is whether formal daycare used by working mothers is detrimental to young children.

According to Melhuish (2004a) the evidence from the first studies on child attachment behaviour in the 1950s and 1960s, through to later longitudinal studies on children's emotional and social development in the 1980s and 1990s, was generally equivocal. Positive, negative and nil effects were reported. The resultant confusion over the risk of insecure attachment from using daycare created considerable controversy. This led to the development of a major longitudinal study in the USA in 1990 – the National Institute of Child Health and Human Development Study of Early Child Care (NICHD). Results from the NICHD in 1997 finally demonstrated that there were no direct, independent effects of quantity, quality or type of care on attachment. But, attachment could be influenced by a combination of poor-quality care in the home alongside either ten or more hours a week of childcare or multiple childcare arrangements or poor-quality care (Melhuish, 2004a, p. 31). With still no definitive answer, Melhuish argued that by the end of the twentieth century the potentially negative effects of non-parental care in infancy were unresolved (Melhuish, 2004a, p. 36). However, the latest evidence from the NICHD study in the USA and in the EPPE project in the UK seems to suggest the possibility of some negative effects.

NICHD most recently reported that the more time spent in 'non-maternal' care in the first four to five years of life predicted greater aggressive or anti-social behaviour at age 4–5 years. This is also found in other US studies reported in 2001–03 (Melhuish, 2004a, p. 36; Sammons *et al*, 2003, p. 59). Similarly, the

EPPE project in the UK reports that an early start in childcare, especially below the age of two, was linked to poorer outcomes on 'anti-social-worried' behaviour. This was found both at age three on entry to the study and two years later on starting primary school (Sammons *et al*, 2003, p. 61). Moreover, this effect could not be eliminated by higher quality provision, though was ameliorated by it (Melhuish, 2004a, p. 36).

However, this evidence on the 'anti-social-worried' dimension must be balanced with the positive effects on three other measures of social behaviour[2] and on cognitive development resulting from any preschool experience (ie, in local authority day nurseries, integrated centres, playgroups, private day nurseries, nursery schools or classes). In particular, the EPPE project showed that an early start in a preschool setting produced unequivocally positive effects on cognitive development. However, starting below the age of two did not produce greater effects than starting between the age of 2–3 years (Sammons *et al*, 2002, p. 59). The EPPE authors are at pains to point out that overall the positive impact of starting early 'should not be ignored for cognitive outcomes and important aspects of social behaviour' (Sammons *et al*, 2003, p. 62). They also conclude that while they could 'not be certain' that the lower scores on cognitive and social-behavioural development found among the group that had no preschool experience outside the home was due to this lack of experience, they state that lack of preschool care in one of the group settings outlined above could put these children at a disadvantage on starting school (Sammons *et al*, 2003, p. 59, 2002, p. 61).

So the message from the UK EPPE study is clear: in general, with reasonable, quality provision, early childhood education and childcare is good for children. However, Melhuish (2004a, b) argues that the UK and USA evidence from major longitudinal studies and others provides complementary results showing that quantity of care (where children start at age two or earlier), particularly in group settings, can slightly increase the risk for anti-social behaviour – and that quality of care is important. The interaction between quantity and quality of care is also important for cognitive development and overall it appears 'that positive effects of childcare accrue from the childcare after one year of age' (Melhuish, 2004a, p. 54). But for children starting at age 2–3 years the evidence is more consistent; preschool provision is beneficial for all children behaviourally

---

[2] The three social behavioural measures are 'independence and concentration', 'peer sociability' and 'co-operation and conformity'.

and cognitively, with greater effects for higher-quality care – and disadvantaged children stand to gain the most (Melhuish, 2004a, p. 54). Cost-benefit evaluations of childcare intervention programmes in the USA and one in the UK on Early Excellence Centres also demonstrate economic advantages in providing childcare in disadvantaged communities. That is where negative outcomes, such as levels of crime and unemployment, can be reduced. What remains unclear is whether the negative effects of aggression found in the USA and in the UK were primarily related to poor-quality provision and, if so, whether changes in practice could eliminate these effects. Thus, Melhuish and others argue that quality of pre-school care is central to positive developmental outcomes (Melhuish, 2004a, b; Sammons *et al*, 2002, 2003; Siraj-Blatchford *et al*, 2003). In the EPPE project the highest-quality provision was found in integrated settings providing childcare and early education, and in nursery schools and nursery classes, all of which had support from qualified teachers (Sammons *et al*, 2002, 2003).

This work on the EPPE project and Melhuish's assessment of the international evidence for the NAO show that the key elements of quality provision include many factors. Structural factors (safe environments and high staff–child ratios) as well as process factors (a stable, trained, and supported workforce that can interact appropriately with children) are important (Melhuish, 2004b; Siraj-Blatchford *et al*, 2003). According to Melhuish, what is needed are improvements in the responsiveness of group care through maintaining high staff–child ratios and minimising staff turnover. Currently, staff turnover is said to be running as high as 30–40 per cent in England because of poor training, pay and low investment (Strategy Unit, 2002; *Guardian* 8 July 2004, p. 1); the highest turnover rates of 23 per cent and 18 per cent are occurring in out-of-school clubs and full daycare settings (DfES, 2004a, p. 7). The key concern regarding childcare-related outcomes is not necessarily the level of provision, though this remains important for encouraging maternal employment and reducing child poverty, but the quality of provision to promote children's well-being. It seems that the UK has some way to go to tackle this problem, given the high staff turnover and low level of training among workers in the sector. More evaluation studies are, however, underway.

Future evaluation studies

As discussed, England will continue to research outcomes through the National Evaluation of Sure Start local programmes (NESS) and through the EPPE project.

There are also other independent longitudinal studies, most notably the Families, Children and Childcare study of the care of 1,200 children from birth to school age being conducted by Birkbeck, University of London (www.iscfsi.bbk.ac.uk/projects/fccc.asp).

Northern Ireland is devising outcomes and indicators to monitor and evaluate progress across all children services, including childcare, which aims to meet set targets within ten years (CYPU, 2003d).

Similarly, Scotland is devising a framework to monitor and evaluate the impact of all Early Years services. An initial evaluation study was conducted in 2003 by the Centre for Research on Families and Relationships (Wasoff *et al*, 2004). A new finalised Integrated Strategy for Early Years was expected in 2004 but has been delayed until 2005 (Scottish Executive, 2003a, p. 18). Other plans for 2004 include implementing a five-year Early Years Longitudinal Survey conducted by the Scottish Centre for Social Research. It will cover children aged from birth to adolescence and will involve 10,000 interviews a year.

In Wales in 2004, consultations took place to devise an evaluation strategy to measure the impact of all services for children and young people, based on seven core aims related to the UNCRC. Evaluation of Sure Start and other childcare services for children aged 0–3 will be based on Cymorth progress reports, which is the responsibility of the local Children's Partnerships (Welsh Assembly Government, 2004a). There is a lot yet to learn on the impact of early-years provision on outcomes and children's development.

Conclusion

The general philosophy underpinning early-years policy across the UK is to develop more integrated provision bringing together early education, childcare and other health and family support services, with the overall aim of giving children – particularly those living in disadvantaged areas – a 'sure start' in life. This has found institutional expression in England with the integration of policy-making within the central Sure Start Unit, in Wales with a new Cymorth Plan, and in Scotland and Northern Ireland through the updating and developing of new strategies for the early years. The emphasis has also shifted towards a child-centred approach, with policy giving due regard to the UNCRC – most explicitly in Wales, Scotland and Northern Ireland. This has been a major change since the last edition of this book and it shows the dynamism of policy in this arena – and how it is beginning to come of age. Most recently, at the 2003 Labour Party

Conference, a commitment was made in England for universal childcare for all, though problems still remain with the level and quality of provision. Evidence on outcomes from longitudinal studies in the UK is now emerging, and preliminary indications are that early-years education and childcare have a positive impact on child development, although there is some controversy over the use of daycare for young children (aged 0–2 years) in relation to some behavioural outcomes; the relationship of this effect to quality of services is not answered. A body of evidence is, however, growing – initially with the EPPE project in England and in the future from results of the NESS – as well as from other more general evaluations on the impact of early-years provision in Wales, Scotland and Northern Ireland and longitudinal studies of general populations in Scotland and England.

11 Children, crime and illegal drug use

Joanne Neale

Key findings:

- Although a very high proportion of young people in the UK commits a crime at some point in their lives, the majority of recorded crime is committed by adults rather than by children or teenagers.
- Across the UK, the proportions of children 'ever' committing offences or 'ever' using illicit drugs are much greater than the proportions of children 'recently' offending or 'recently' using illicit drugs.
- Most crimes committed by children are of a relatively trivial nature, often offences against property.
- Illicit drug use by children and young people in the UK tends to be 'experimental' rather than 'problematic', and confined to cannabis rather than more harmful substances such as heroin or cocaine.
- Compared with England and Wales, Northern Ireland appears to have relatively low levels, and Scotland relatively high levels, of juvenile offending and illicit drug use.
- The vast majority of known offenders across the UK countries are male.
- Boys tend to commit more serious offences than their female counterparts and tend to cease their offending at a later age.
- UK children under the age of 16 are less likely to offend or to use illicit drugs than older teenagers.
- The gradual decline in crime as young people enter adulthood suggests that a significant proportion of young people grow out of their criminal behaviour.
- Across the UK, there are clear links between juvenile offending and illicit drug use, with recent drug use being a strong predictor of serious and/or persistent offending.

- Various personal, social, family, educational, community and lifestyle factors place children and young people at increased risk of committing crime and using illicit substances.
- Children and young people in the UK experience very high levels of victimisation and fear of crime, and this commonly takes the form of harassment and bullying by other children and young people.

Key trends:

- In England, Wales and Scotland, there are signs that youth crime has reached a plateau and may be beginning to decline.
- Nonetheless, a small but growing number of children are responsible for a disproportionate number of offences.
- In England and Wales, drug and violent offences have begun to constitute a larger proportion of recorded juvenile crime than in previous years.
- There are some signs from official statistics and self-report studies across the UK that the gender gap in offending behaviour is closing, with more girls offending than previously.
- Overall, patterns of crime and illicit drug use by young people have changed very little since 2002.

Key sources:

- Recorded crime statistics: Home Office; Scottish Executive; Northern Ireland Office; Youth Justice Board.
- Self-reported crime surveys: Youth Lifestyle Surveys; Annual Youth Surveys; Young Persons' Behaviour and Attitudes Survey; Understanding Offending Among Young People; Communities that Care Youth Survey.
- Crime victim surveys: The British Crime Survey; The Scottish Crime Survey; The Northern Ireland Crime Survey.

Introduction

This chapter reviews a range of key national data sources to examine the evidence on children, crime and illicit drug use. It includes both crimes committed by children and crimes committed against children, but excludes child homicides, abuse and neglect (see Chapter 8) and smoking and alcohol consumption (see Chapter 5).

Problems of definition and measurement

In order to measure any aspect of crime, it is first necessary to clarify what exactly constitutes a criminal act. Dictionary definitions generally refer to 'behaviour prohibited and punishable by law' that is 'forbidden by statute or injurious to the public welfare'. They may even refer to 'evil or injurious acts' or 'sins'. Such definitions tend to raise as many questions as they answer. While the simplest way of defining a crime might be to classify it as something that is against the law, laws are constantly changing, legality is subject to judicial interpretation, and what is illegal in one country is not necessary illegal elsewhere. At the same time, moralistic definitions that incorporate notions of being 'injurious', 'evil' or 'sinful' are problematic since beliefs founded on public acceptability inevitably vary over time as well as between individuals, groups and societies.

In brief, defining the criminal is often not straightforward. Crime is a historically and socially specific construct. Whether or not something is perceived as a criminal act will depend upon when it happens, where it happens, why it happens and who is labelling it. In examining crimes committed by children and making comparisons across countries, such definitional issues assume a particular importance. This is because the age of criminal responsibility varies widely between countries and regions. In England, Wales and Northern Ireland, a person cannot be considered responsible for a criminal act until they are at least ten years old. Such responsibility begins at eight in Scotland, 13 in France, 14 in Austria, Germany and Italy, 15 in Denmark and Sweden, 16 in Portugal and Spain, and 18 in Luxembourg and Belgium.

In the UK, three main types of national data can be used in the analysis of juvenile offending: *recorded crime statistics*; *self-reported crime surveys*; and *crime victim surveys*. These data sources do not, however, all measure the same phenomena and methods of information collection are very varied. Equally, England and Wales have different sources of statistics and different surveys from Scotland, which in turn has different systems from Northern Ireland. Finally, despite what may initially appear to be a wealth of crime data, children are often omitted or appear only at the margins. Taken together, such problems do not mean that information on children, crime and illicit drug use is not available, but simply that caution must be exercised when reviewing the evidence.

Recorded crime statistics

The recorded crime statistics provide the 'official' source of information on the involvement of young people in crime. They include information on those formally cautioned, arrested or convicted in court. However, these statistics do not measure the full extent of young people's offending. This is because they do not include crimes that do not come to the attention of the police or crimes that the police do not record or process. In 1996, less than 20 per cent of the seven million annual offences estimated to have been committed by young people were reported to the police. Furthermore, only 3 per cent of offences ended in an arrest and only 1.3 per cent resulted in a charge or summons (Audit Commission, 1996). Meanwhile, strategies designed to divert young offenders from the criminal justice system (such as informal cautioning) reduce the recorded crime statistics. In contrast, police crackdowns on youth crime or improvements in crime detection techniques tend to increase them.

Changes in police recording practices (such as the introduction of the new National Crime Recording Standards in April 2002) further confuse trends. So, statistics for England and Wales show that 1,313,100 people were arrested for notifiable offences in 2002/03, and this constituted a 3 per cent *increase* over 2001/02. However, once changes in police recording practices are taken into account, recorded crime is estimated to have *decreased* by 3 per cent over the period (Ayers *et al*, 2003). Of the 1,313,100 individuals arrested in 2002/03, 500 were under ten years of age and 299,500 were aged 10–17 years. Thus, 23 per cent (nearly a quarter) of all arrested individuals were less than 17 years of age (Ayers *et al*, 2003).

A breakdown of all arrested individuals in England and Wales (2002/03) by type of offence is shown in Table 11.1. The offence for which individuals were most commonly arrested in all age groups was theft and handling stolen goods, but this was particularly evident among those aged 17 years and under. In this age group, over one in three offences committed were in the theft and handling category. The absence of children under ten being arrested for sexual offences, robbery, burglary, fraud and forgery, or drug offences is notable, but not entirely surprising given that very young children often do not have the means to commit acts of these kinds. Equally, their actions often do not come to the attention of the police or are not formally recorded as crime – remembering that the age of criminal responsibility in England and Wales is ten.

Official statistics also show clear gender differences among arrested children

Table 11.1: Persons arrested for notifiable offences by type of offence and age group in England and Wales (2002/03)

Notifiable offence group	Aged under 10	Aged 10–17	Aged 18–20	Aged 21 and over	Age unknown	All ages
Violence against the person	100	51,600	41,900	189,800	700	284,000
Sexual offences	0	4,200	2,400	22,300	100	28,900
Robbery	0	14,800	6,500	14,500	100	35,800
Burglary	0	32,900	17,500	58,300	200	108,900
Theft & handling stolen goods	200	106,000	63,000	249,800	900	419,900
Fraud & forgery	0	2,900	5,400	30,100	100	38,600
Criminal damage	100	45,800	21,600	66,300	300	134,100
Drug offences	0	19,500	27,500	84,000	200	131,100
Other	0	21,900	21,300	88,000	500	131,800
Total	500	299,500	207,000	803,200	2,900	1,313,100

Source: Ayers et al (2003) Table AB

and young people in terms of both prevalence and types of offence committed. In 2002/03, only 100 of the 500 children arrested while under age ten were female (a female to male ratio of 1:4) and 53,800 of the 299,500 children arrested while aged 10–17 years were female (a female to male ratio of approximately 1:5) (Ayers *et al*, 2003). Offence types by sex for the 10–17-year-olds are shown in Table 11.2. This shows that females were less likely to be arrested for all offences, although the gender balance varied notably between crimes. For every female aged 10–17 years arrested for fraud and forgery there were approximately two males, but for every female of this age group arrested for a sexual offence there were 40 males. This gender difference is also evident in respect of legal proceedings. In 2002, legal action in magistrates' courts was taken against 119 females but 1,416 males aged ten and under 12 years (1:12). Among children aged 12 and under 15 years, proceedings were taken against 4,136 females and 22,412 males (1:5) and for young people aged 15 and under 18 years, proceedings were taken against 13,572 females and 104,913 males (1:8) (Research Development and Statistics Directorate, 2003).

Table 11.3 compares data on young people arrested in England and Wales in 2001/02 with those arrested in 2002/03 by type of offence and age group. The table reveals an overall decrease in the numbers of arrested young people, with stabilisation of arrests among those aged under ten and decreases in the 10–17 and 18–20 age groups. However, differences were again evident between offence

Table 11.2: Persons aged 10–17 arrested for notifiable offences by type of offence and sex in England and Wales (2002/03)

Notifiable offence group	Female	Male	All persons	Ratio of females to males
Violence against the person	11,600	40,000	51,600	1:3
Sexual offences	100	4,000	4,200	1:40
Robbery	2,100	12,700	14,800	1:6
Burglary	3,200	29,600	32,900	1:9
Theft & handling stolen goods	24,400	81,600	106,000	1:3
Fraud & forgery	900	2,000	2,900	1:2
Criminal damage	5,900	39,900	45,800	1:7
Drug offences	2,000	17,500	19,500	1:9
Other	3,500	18,400	21,900	1:5
Total	53,800	245,800	299,500	1:5

Source: Ayers et al (2003) Table AB

Table 11.3: Persons arrested for notifiable offences by type of offence and age group in England and Wales (2001/02 and 2002/03)

Notifiable offence group	2001/02			2002/03		
	Aged under 10	Aged 10–17	Aged 18–20	Aged under 10	Aged 10–17	Aged 18–20
Violence against the person	100	50,300	39,300	100	51,600	41,900
Sexual offences	0	4,200	2,000	0	4,200	2,400
Robbery	0	16,000	6,600	0	14,800	6,500
Burglary	100	34,700	18,000	0	32,900	17,500
Theft & handling stolen goods	100	120,800	71,100	200	106,000	63,000
Fraud & forgery	0	3,500	6,200	0	2,900	5,400
Criminal damage	200	47,000	20,700	100	45,800	21,600
Drug offences	0	17,600	25,000	0	19,500	27,500
Other	0	20,200	19,300	0	21,900	21,300
Total	500	314,200	208,100	500	299,500	207,000

Source: Ayers et al (2003) Table AB

types. Thus, there were increases for: theft and handling (under ten years); sexual offences (18–20 years); criminal damage (18–20 years); violence against the person (10–17 and 18–20 years); drug offences (10–17 and 18–20 years); and other crimes (10–17 and 18–20 years). As Newburn (2002) has noted, the recorded crime statistics have shown a rise in juvenile drug offences since 1985 and in violence committed by young people (largely young males) since 1987. However, the number of known juvenile offenders has actually fallen – along with a drop in overall recorded crime – since a peak in 1992. Consequently, violence and drug offences now account for a much larger proportion of recorded juvenile crime in England and Wales than was the case a decade and a half ago.

According to criminal statistics for England and Wales (Home Office, 2003), 86,000 juvenile offenders were given reprimands or final warnings in 2002. This was a fall of 12 per cent compared with 2001. Meanwhile, the peak age of known offending for males rose from 18 to 19 years (having been 18 since 1988) and the peak age of known offending for females remained at 15 years (having fluctuated over the past decade mainly between 14 and 15 but rising to 18 in 1997). Table 11.4 shows the numbers of persons found guilty at all courts or cautioned for indictable offences by age and gender for the years 1997–2002. This table clearly shows more cautions and guilty verdicts among older than younger children and among males than females, but also a slow overall decline.

In Scotland, there is a notable lack of publicly available official information

Table 11.4: Number of persons (thousands) found guilty at all courts or cautioned for indictable offences[a] by sex and age, 1997–2002 (England and Wales)

Sex & age	1997	1998	1999	2000	2001	2002
Male						
10	1.3	1.5	1.3	1.2	1.1	1.0
11	2.7	3.0	2.9	2.7	2.6	2.1
12	4.9	5.6	5.2	4.8	4.8	4.2
13	8.1	8.7	8.4	7.8	7.9	6.9
14	13.0	13.0	13.1	12.4	12.3	11.3
15	17.8	18.5	17.4	16.7	16.9	15.7
16	21.5	22.0	21.0	19.3	20.0	18.9
17	26.3	26.8	25.4	22.9	21.9	22.3
18	27.8	29.4	27.3	24.4	23.3	22.6
Female						
10	0.2	0.3	0.3	0.3	0.2	0.2
11	0.7	0.8	0.8	0.8	0.7	0.6
12	1.7	2.1	1.9	2.0	1.9	1.6
13	3.2	4.0	3.5	3.5	3.8	3.1
14	4.5	5.3	4.7	4.9	5.1	4.5
15	4.8	5.5	5.1	5.3	5.4	4.8
16	4.7	5.0	4.6	4.5	4.7	4.3
17	4.7	4.9	4.8	4.4	4.4	4.2
18	4.6	4.8	4.7	4.4	4.1	4.0

[a] For motoring offences, only persons found guilty are included
Source: Home Office (2003) Table 2.24

on children and crime. Moreover, the available data are produced as rates per 1,000 in each age group who have had a charge proved against them and there is a very distinctive legal and criminal justice system – thus making comparisons with England and Wales more difficult. One key difference is the Scottish Children's Hearing system, which deals both with children who have offended and children who are in need of care and protection. Since 1971, individuals under 16 years and some 16–18-year-olds who commit offences have mostly been dealt with by hearings rather than by the courts. Indeed, children in Scotland are only considered for prosecution in court if very serious offences have been committed. In 1991, the number of people aged less than 16 years with a charge proved against them in a Scottish court per 1,000 population was 0.4 and, by 2001, this had reduced to 0.2. For young people aged 16 years, the respective figures were 53 and 28; for those aged 17 years, 122 and 78; and for those aged 18 years, 151 and 109 (Scottish Executive, 2003g).

These statistics are consistent with the downward trend in youth crime and the lower rates of offending among under 16-year-olds found in England and Wales. Concern has, however, been expressed within Scotland that a growing number of children have become responsible for a disproportionate number of offences. Thus, in 1999/2000, 890 children had ten or more offences reported against them, an increase of approximately 20 per cent since 1998/99 (Scottish Executive, 2002i). Gender differences in juvenile recorded crime in Scotland have also been evident, with rates of male offending vastly outstripping female crime across all age groups. In 2001, the number of individuals aged less than 16 years with a charge proved against them per 1,000 population was 0.02 for females and 0.3 for males (a gender ratio of 1:15). For females and males aged 16 years, the respective figures were 5 and 51 (1:10); for those aged 17 years, 16 and 137 (1:9); and for those aged 18 years, 22 and 193 (1:9) (Scottish Executive, 2003g).

The available recorded crime statistics for all ages indicate that Northern Ireland has a relatively low level of recorded crime compared with England, Wales and Scotland. In 1997, there were 62,222 notifiable offences recorded by the police, or about 40 crimes per 1,000 of the population in Northern Ireland, and this was less than half the recorded figures in England and Wales (O'Mahony and Deazley, 2000). Lower police-recorded statistics were also evident for juvenile crime. In 2001, the average juvenile remand population in Northern Ireland was only 14 (Hague and Campbell, 2002). Nonetheless, similarities between the official crime statistics across all countries and regions of the UK are evident.

Most notably, the majority of recorded crime is committed by adults (not by children) and, where crime is committed by children, it is disproportionately committed by males.

Approximately three-quarters of all people convicted in court in Northern Ireland are aged between 18 and 39 years. In 1997, the ratio of female to male juvenile convictions was as high as 1:9, and between 1999 and 2001 at least four-fifths of those admitted onto remand in Juvenile Justice Centres were male (O'Mahony and Deazley, 2000; Hague and Campbell, 2002). Theft, violence against the person, burglary and criminal damage were the offence classifications for which most juveniles in Northern Ireland were remanded in custody. In 1999, 68 per cent of juvenile prosecutions were for indictable offences, 21 per cent for summary offences, and 11 per cent for motoring offences (National Statistics, 2003).

Collectively, these various sources of national data reinforce the conclusions of a recent Youth Crime Briefing from the National Association for the Care and Resettlement of Offenders (NACRO) based primarily on recorded crime statistics for England and Wales 2001 (NACRO, 2003). This emphasised that young people are not responsible for the majority of crime. Additionally, youth offending primarily comprises offences against property. NACRO argued that robbery by young people generates high levels of public concern and recent perceived increases in this have prompted the 'street crime initiative', launched in April 2002. Official crime statistics for 2001, however, revealed only a relatively small increase in this type of offence since the early 1990s. Furthermore, robbery continues to be rare, accounting for only 2.4 per cent of all indictable offences committed by those under 18. In respect of sex offences (another crime generating high levels of public anxiety), NACRO reports that official statistics for 2001 show that less than 1 per cent of offences committed by young people were sex crimes. Furthermore, sexual offences had fallen: both in terms of absolute numbers and as a proportion of all cautions (or reprimands and warnings) and convictions.

In England and Wales, an additional useful source of official information on young offenders is the *Youth Justice – Annual Statistics*, published by the Youth Justice Board. It includes all offences that have resulted in a disposal, with data drawn from Youth Offending Teams, the juvenile secure estate, and the courts. According to *Youth Justice – Annual Statistics 2002/03*, young people aged 10–17 committed 268,480 offences in the financial year 2002/03. Of these, 61,734 were motoring offences; 47,892 were theft and handling; 34,896 involved violence against the person; 27,516 were criminal damage; 17,790 were public order offences; and 13,414 were drugs offences (Youth Justice Board, 2003). Detailed information on the nature of drug offences committed by young people is generally not readily accessible from official crime data, but is covered more thoroughly in some of the self-reported crime studies discussed below.

Self-reported crime surveys

Since the 1950s, self-reported crime surveys have become an important source of information on offences committed, particularly in the field of youth crime. Self-report studies are able to provide information on a wide range of criminal activities, including those not detected by the police as well as those officially recorded. As such, they potentially offer a more comprehensive source of information on crime than the recorded statistics – subject, of course, to the willingness and ability of study participants to respond to questions honestly and accurately and to obtaining a good response rate. In England and Wales, the Home Office has undertaken two sweeps of a major self-report study that incorporates data on the criminal activity of young people. This is the Youth Lifestyle Survey (YLS). The first sweep was undertaken in 1992/93 and was reported by Graham and Bowling (1995). The second sweep occurred in 1998/99 and was reported by Flood-Page *et al* (2000).

Youth Lifestyle Surveys (YLS)

Using data from a random national sample of nearly 2,000 young people aged 17–25 years in England and Wales, the first YLS found that 55 per cent of males and 31 per cent of females admitted ever committing at least one of a list of 23 crimes. However, the percentages admitting offences in the year prior to interview were considerably lower (28 per cent of males and 12 per cent of females). In addition, the majority of offenders had committed only minor offences with 3 per cent responsible for a quarter of all crimes. The four most prevalent offences (bullying/selling stolen goods; fighting; shoplifting; and vandalism) were the same for both sexes, but patterns of offending varied by gender and age. The peak age of offending for males was: 14 for expressive offences (vandalism and arson) and property offences; 16 for violent offences; 17 for serious offences; and 20 for drug offences. Among females, the peak age of offending was: 15 for property, expressive and serious offences; 16 for violent offences; and 17 for drug offences (Graham and Bowling, 1995).

The second YLS study involved more participants and a wider age group than the first (4,848 people aged between 12 and 30 years). Nonetheless, the overall proportions of males and females having committed one or more offences were little changed (57 per cent of males and 37 per cent of females) and differences in the nature of the crimes committed by males and females at different ages were again found. Offending by 14–15-year-old males was largely due to their involvement in fights, buying stolen goods, other theft, and criminal damage. The most common offences committed by girls under 16 were criminal damage, shoplifting, buying stolen goods, and fighting. Similar proportions of boys and girls aged 12–13 years in the second YLS said that they had offended, but the peak age of self-reported offending was much lower for girls (at 14 years) than for boys (at 18 years) (Flood-Page *et al*, 2000).

Although unemployed young people in the second YLS were more likely to offend than those in employment or in further education, the difference was not statistically significant. That said, unemployed males were nearly twice as likely to be *serious and/or persistent* offenders as those who were either in education or work. Consistent with the results of the first YLS, respondents in the second YLS who lived with two parents had lower levels of serious or persistent criminal behaviour than those living in either lone-parent households or stepfamilies. Moreover, those with weak family attachments were more likely to be serious or persistent offenders than those with strong family bonds. The strongest predictor of serious and/or persistent offending was, however, using drugs in the last year. Males who had used drugs in the 12 months prior to their interview were nearly five times more likely to offend than those who had not.

Annual youth surveys

Additional self-report data exploring the prevalence of offending and drug use among young people in England and Wales are provided by a series of annual Youth Surveys carried out by Market & Opinion Research International (MORI) on behalf of the Youth Justice Board (YJB). As part of their 2003 research (conducted between 15 January and 14 March 2003), MORI undertook a survey of 4,963 young people aged 11–16 in mainstream education and a survey of 586 young people aged 10–16 who were excluded from mainstream schools and attending a special project. In both surveys, all questionnaires were completed in interviewer-supervised, self-completion sessions. The results of the 2003 survey were broadly consistent with those of previous surveys conducted in 1999, 2000, 2001 and 2002 (MORI, 2003).

Chart 11.1 shows the offending levels for excluded and mainstream pupils since 1999. It reveals a decrease in offending among the excluded pupils since 2000 (the date from which data for this group were first available) and relative stability among the mainstream pupils. However, differences between the two groups in respect of levels and type of offending were evident. In 2000, 72 per cent of excluded but only 22 per cent of mainstream young people said that they had committed an offence in the last 12 months. In 2003, the respective figures were 60 per cent and 26 per cent. The most common offences committed by mainstream offenders in 2003 were travelling on a bus, train or underground without paying the fare (53 per cent) and hurting someone without causing them to need medical attention (41 per cent). The most common offences committed by excluded offenders were hurting someone without causing a need for medical attention (62 per cent) and carrying a knife (62 per cent). In other words, violent or potentially violent behaviour was more widespread among those not in mainstream education.

Chart 11.1: Trends in offending levels (1999–2003)
Q. Have you committed any criminal offence in the last 12 months? This may range from something like fare-dodging (not paying for a train ticket) to stealing something.

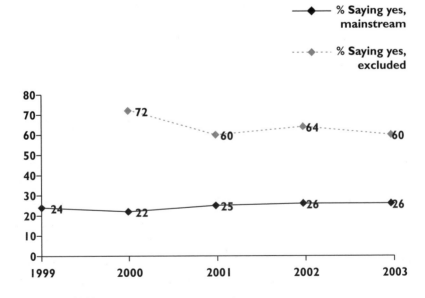

Source: MORI (2003)

Although the overall proportion of young people who had committed offences had not increased since 2002, the 2003 findings indicated that offenders (excluded and mainstream pupils) were committing *more* offences. So, the average number of offences had risen from four per mainstream offender in 2002 to five in 2003, and from ten per excluded offender in 2002 to 11 in 2003. Among young offenders in mainstream schools, the biggest increases were apparent in the two most common crimes. Travelling on a bus, train or underground without paying the fare had increased from 46 per cent in 2002 to 53 per cent in 2003 and hurting someone without causing them to need medical attention had increased from 33 per cent in 2002 to 41 per cent in 2003. The types of offence committed by excluded pupils which showed the biggest increases were: beating up someone not in their family (38 per cent in 2002 and 49 per cent in 2003); threatening or assaulting others in public (48 per cent in 2002 and 57 per cent in 2003); and stealing anything from their home (13 per cent in 2002 and 21 per cent in 2003).

As in previous Youth Surveys, males and older respondents were most likely to be offenders in 2003. Nearly a third (32 per cent) of boys in mainstream education had committed an offence, compared with 20 per cent of girls. The gender difference was less marked among excluded pupils, but the pattern was still notable: 61 per cent of excluded boys had offended, compared with 56 per cent of girls. Among mainstream pupils, only 14 per cent of 11-year-olds had offended compared with 39 per cent of 15–16-year-olds. Among excluded pupils, 43 per cent of 11-year-olds had offended compared with 61 per cent of 15–16-year-olds. The most common ages for starting to offend were between 11 and 13, with 38 per cent of mainstream and 41 per cent of excluded offenders reporting this as the age they first committed an offence.

In respect of fear of crime, 35 per cent of young people in mainstream education and 21 per cent of excluded pupils said that they felt unsafe in their local area after dark. In addition, more than half of mainstream young people said that they were worried about being physically assaulted or being a victim of theft and a third worried about bullying and racism. Excluded young people typically expressed lower levels of concern for their personal safety, but were more likely to be exposed to crime and to become a victim of crime than the mainstream school children. Fear of crime was perhaps not surprising given that 46 per cent of the young people in mainstream education and 61 per cent of excluded young people said that they had been a victim of crime in the 12 months prior to the survey. Being threatened by others was the most common offence experienced by both young people in mainstream schools (26 per cent) and excluded young people (41 per cent). Young people who had been victims of crime typically reported that another young person under the age of 18 had committed the offence.

Young Persons' Behaviour and Attitudes Survey

In Northern Ireland, a similar self-report study to the YLS was conducted during October and November 2000 by the Central Survey Unit of the Northern Ireland Statistics and Research Agency (NISRA). This was the Young Persons' Behaviour and Attitudes Survey and it involved 6,297 school children, of whom 87 per cent completed the entire questionnaire (Central Survey Unit, 2002). The research found that 15 per cent of pupils had been arrested or cautioned by the police, mostly for vandalism, under-age drinking, and disorderly behaviour. Meanwhile, 21 per cent thought that the area in which they lived was unsafe, mainly due to gangs of other people looking for trouble, vandals, and sectarian name-calling. In total, 28 per cent of pupils said they had been offered drugs (most commonly cannabis) and 17 per cent said they had used or tried drugs (again mainly cannabis). Of those who had tried drugs, 17 per cent had been in trouble with their parents or family; 14 per cent in trouble with local people; 10 per cent in trouble with school authorities; 6 per cent in trouble with the police; and 22 per cent in trouble with friends because of having used or tried drugs.

Understanding offending among young people

In Scotland, research on offending behaviour was conducted between 1996 and 1999 by Jamieson and colleagues (Jamieson *et al*, 1999). Their work consisted of a self-report survey of 1,274 third and fourth year secondary school pupils, in-depth interviews with nearly 300 young people in three age groups (14–15 years, 18–19 years, and 22–25 years), and interviews with a small sample of police officers, teachers and social workers. Findings from the self-report survey indicated that levels of crime among young people in Scotland were significantly higher than in England and Wales or Northern Ireland. Indeed, Jamieson *et al* found that 94 per cent of boys and 82 per cent of girls admitted to having ever committed one or more offences in the past, with 85 per cent of boys and 67 per cent of girls reporting offending at least once during the previous 12 months.

Although most third and fourth year pupils who were surveyed said that they had offended, the types of offences committed were generally not very serious. Vandalism, fighting in the street and shoplifting were the three most common offences for both sexes. As in other parts of the UK, boys were more likely than girls to report committing all offence types and they reported doing so more frequently. Nonetheless, rates of offending for girls were still very high (including for violent offences) and there was a striking similarity in the types of offences reportedly committed by boys and girls. In the last year, 47 per cent of boys said that they had beaten someone up and 28 per cent admitted to hurting someone with a weapon. For girls, the figures were 21 per cent for beating someone up and 11 per cent for hurting someone with a weapon.

Jamieson *et al* grouped the young people in their research into three categories: *resisters* (young people who had never offended); *desisters* (young people who had offended in the past but had not done so in the 12 months prior to their interview); and *persisters* (young people who had committed at least one serious offence or several less serious offences in the past six months). Of the three groups, persisters were most likely to identify a link between their drug use and their offending. In addition, young people's use of drugs and its contribution to their offending increased dramatically with age. Drug use, with the exception of alcohol and cannabis, was relatively uncommon among the youngest age group. In contrast, more than half of those in the oldest age group said they had used amphetamines, LSD and temazepam, and just under half had used heroin (see Table 11.5).

Table 11.5: Drug and alcohol use by age group

Substance	14–15 years (n=104)	18–19 years (n=89)	22–25 years (n=89)
Alcohol	79 (76%)	87 (98%)	75 (93%)
Amphetamines	2 (2%)	32 (36%)	49 (60%)
Cannabis	31 (30%)	61 (69%)	67 (83%)
Cocaine	0 (0%)	11 (12%)	30 (37%)
Crack	0 (0%)	4 (5%)	15 (18%)
Ecstasy	2 (2%)	31 (35%)	38 (47%)
Glue/gas	7 (7%)	11 (12%)	25 (31%)
Heroin	1 (1%)	20 (57%)	38 (47%)
LSD	6 (5%)	36 (40%)	48 (59%)
Magic mushrooms	4 (4%)	7 (8%)	31 (35%)
Methadone	1 (1%)	12 (13%)	37 (46%)
Temgesic	0 (0%)	8 (9%)	31 (35%)
Temazepam	5 (5%)	24 (27%)	44 (54%)
Tranquillisers	1 (1%)	18 (20%)	29 (36%)
Other substances	4 (4%)	6 (7%)	5 (6%)

Source: Jamieson *et al* (1999)

Communities that Care Youth Survey

One final national self-report survey that will be considered here is the Communities that Care (CtC) Youth Survey conducted in 2000/01 (Beinart *et al*, 2002). This research covered England, Scotland and Wales and involved over 14,000 participants aged 10–17 years (school years 7 to 11 or S1 to S5 in Scotland). The sample was divided fairly evenly into boys and girls and approximately 8 per cent of respondents described themselves as belonging to a minority ethnic group. Findings from the CtC research were consistent with previous self-report studies in that the proportion of those involved in ever offending was considerably larger than those involved in recent offending; boys were more likely to offend than girls; offending increased with age; the proportion of those involved in serious offending was considerably smaller than those involved in any offending; and the proportion of those using the most harmful drugs (such as heroin or cocaine) was much smaller than those who had tried any drug.

In total, 48.5 per cent of all respondents in the CtC study said that they had ever offended. Among Year 7 pupils, 13 per cent of boys and 9 per cent of girls reported vandalising property in the previous 12 months, with an increase to 30 per cent of boys and 25 per cent of girls by Year 11. Meanwhile, 8 per cent of boys and 3 per cent of girls in Year 7 reported attacking someone in the previous 12 months, and this increased to 19 per cent of boys and 9 per cent of girls by Year 11. In respect of illegal drug use, the substance that young people most often reported taking was cannabis. Cannabis had ever been used by 2 per cent of boys and by 1 per cent of girls in Year 7, but by 31 per cent of boys and by 25 per cent of girls in Year 11. In Year 11, 5 per cent of boys and 4 per cent of girls had ever used ecstasy; 4 per cent of boys and 3 per cent of girls had ever used cocaine; and 2 per cent of boys and 1 per cent of girls had ever used heroin.

Crime victim surveys

The three main crime victim surveys in the UK are: the British Crime Survey (BCS) covering England and Wales; the Scottish Crime Survey (SCS); and the Northern Ireland Crime Survey (NICS). Since 2001/02, the BCS has been conducted on an annual basis with 40,000 people. Earlier sweeps were smaller and undertaken less regularly. The 2000 SCS involved 5,059 participants, and the 2001 NICS involved 3,000 participants. Each of these surveys measures crime and its impact by questioning a representative sample of individuals aged over 16 years living in private households about any crimes that they and other members of their household have experienced in the course of the previous year. Respondents' attitudes to crime (such as how much they fear crime and what measures they take to avoid it) and their views of the criminal justice system (including the police and the courts) are also investigated.

Like self-reported crime studies, national crime victim surveys collect information on many crimes that have not been reported to the police and so potentially provide a more comprehensive source of data on the extent of crime in the UK than the recorded crime statistics. Even so, it is widely accepted that data from victim surveys tend to understate illegal activity. This may occur because individuals feel too embarrassed or ashamed to disclose crimes committed against them (especially sexual offences); victims are unaware that a crime has been committed against them (perhaps they have been overcharged in a shop); or a victim is no longer available for interview (if they have been murdered). In addition, many offences are not committed against adults in private households: so crimes against corporate bodies or public property and crimes against homeless or imprisoned people are not included.

One obvious additional problem with the national crime victim surveys is the lack of data collected on children's experiences of crime. That said, it is possible to extract some information on young people in the 16–24 age groups. For example, data from the 2003 BCS, the 2000 SCS and the 2001 NICS all revealed that males aged 16–24 years were more at risk of violent crime than other groups. In addition, adolescents aged 16–24 years were more likely than older people to have recently used drugs and the drug they most commonly used was cannabis (Scottish Executive Central Research Unit, 2002a; National Statistics, 2003; Simmons and Dodd, 2003). Table 11.6 gives the percentages of respondents in England and Wales recently using any drug (for the years 1994, 1996, 1998 and 2002) and shows that the figures have actually been very stable. In 1994, 29 per cent of respondents had used a drug in the last year compared with 28 per cent in 2002. Meanwhile, 17 per cent of respondents had used a drug in the last month in 1994 compared with 18 per cent in 2002 (Ramsay and Partridge, 1999; Condon and Smith, 2003).

Data from the 1998 BCS revealed a clear association between drug use and unemployment, with 40 per cent of 16–29-year-olds who were unemployed in the week before their interview reporting that they had used drugs in the previous

Table 11.6: Percentages of respondents aged 16–24 years in the 1994, 1996, 1998, and 2002 British Crime Surveys using any drug in the last year or month

	1994 BCS %	1996 BCS %	1998 BCS %	2002 BCS %
Any drug				
Last year	29	29	29	28
Last month	17	18	19	18

Sources: Ramsay and Partridge (1999), Condon and Smith (2003)

year – almost double the rate of those with jobs (Ramsay and Partridge, 1999). According to the 2001 BCS, 30 per cent of 16–19-year-olds with no qualifications had taken drugs within the past 12 months, compared to 26 per cent of those who had attained intermediate qualifications (Ramsay et al, 2001). The relationship between drug use and social class, however, was more complex since the highest levels of drug use were concentrated at the two extremes of household income groups, that is the most rich and the most poor. Equally, individuals who had used drugs recently were, irrespective of their age, more likely to have been living in households located in relatively affluent areas (Ramsay et al, 2001).

In recognition of the paucity of information on children generated by the main national crime victim surveys, the 1992 BCS, the 1993 SCS, the 1996 SCS, and the 2000 SCS have all included extra samples of 12–15-year-olds. The numbers of children interviewed in these supplementary studies have been relatively small (between 353 and 495 in the Scottish surveys – although more than 1,000 in the 1992 BCS). Additionally, children living in local authority homes and those who spent large periods of time away from parental supervision were excluded, and there were high levels of non-response. These limitations aside, the findings from these young persons' components still provide very valuable information.

Children in the 1992 BCS were asked about their experiences of six different types of offence over the previous six to eight months (Aye Maung, 1995). In total, 60 per cent reported that they had experienced at least one crime, with young people from minority ethnic communities (especially African-Caribbean young people) experiencing five of the six types of crime more frequently than their white peers. More than one-third of 12–15-year-olds had been assaulted, almost a quarter had had property stolen, and over one in 20 had experienced theft or attempted theft from the person. One in five reported harassment – that is, incidents in which they had been threatened, shouted at, stared at, or followed.

Sexual harassment by someone over the age of 16 was reported by 19 per cent of girls, and in six out of ten cases this involved men unknown to the victim.

In the 2000 SCS young persons' component, 50 per cent of the young people surveyed said they had been a victim of at least one unpleasant incident or crime since the beginning of the previous summer holidays (Scottish Executive Central Research Unit, 2002a). The most common offence experienced was harassment (22 per cent), followed by bullying (19 per cent), assault (19 per cent), theft of personal property (15 per cent), and sexual harassment (5 per cent). Trends in overall victimisation levels are shown in Chart 11.2 and reveal a slight decrease between 1993 and 2000.

Chart 11.2: Levels of victimisation among young people 1993–2000

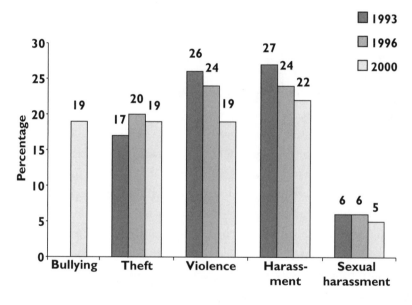

Source: Scottish Executive Central Research Unit (2002b)

In total, 34 per cent of young people in the 2002 SCS said they had personally committed an offence since the beginning of the last summer holidays, a steady increase from 22 per cent in 1993 and 28 per cent in 1996. As in many other studies, however, the offences committed tended to be relatively minor. The most common were fighting (19 per cent of respondents), travelling on public transport with an incorrect fare (15 per cent), and vandalism (8 per cent). According to the 2000 SCS data, offences were only slightly more likely to have been committed by boys (36 per cent) than by girls (32 per cent). In addition, young people who admitted that they had committed offences were more likely than the non-offenders to have been a victim of crime, played truant, or been excluded from school. They also spent more evenings away from home, were out later at night, and their parents were less likely to know where and with whom they spent their time (Scottish Executive Central Research Unit, 2002a).

Risk and protective factors

Although the official UK crime statistics provide very little information on the relationships between poverty, juvenile crime and illicit drug use, research has shown that the risks of becoming criminally involved are higher for young people raised in deprived areas (Farrington, 1996). Similarly, problematic drug use is much greater among those living in disadvantaged neighbourhoods (Parker *et al*, 1998; Foster, 2000). Despite this, the nature and causal direction of such associations are unclear (Bradshaw *et al*, 2003). The effects of poverty on crime tend to be indirect and mediated by other issues such as parental depression and family conflict. Meanwhile, these mediating factors frequently derive from family stresses brought about by prolonged economic adversity and the associated stresses on family functioning (Rutter *et al*, 1998; McGlone, 2001).

While many questions regarding causality remain unanswered, it is still the case that the various national sources of crime data presented in this chapter – along with other smaller-scale local surveys and qualitative research – have greatly enhanced our understanding of the associations between children, crime and illicit drug use. Indeed, it is now possible to identify with some confidence a number of factors that place children and young people at increased 'risk' of committing crime and consuming illicit substances. In contrast, other dynamics have been shown to 'protect' children and young people from involvement in delinquent activity. A recent report written on behalf of CtC and supported by the Joseph Rowntree Foundation (Beinart *et al*, 2002) has grouped risks for young people's involvement in crime into four broad categories: the family; the community; the school; and those that are individual, personal and related to peer group experiences.

Family risks include: poor parental supervision and discipline; family conflict; a family history of criminal activity; parental attitudes that condone anti-social and criminal behaviour; low income; poor housing; and large family size. Community risks are: living in a disadvantaged neighbourhood; community disorganisation and neglect; availability of drugs; and lack of neighbourhood attachment. School factors include: low achievement beginning in primary school; aggressive behaviour (including bullying); lack of commitment to school (including truancy); and school disorganisation. Finally, individual risks encompass: hyperactivity and impulsivity; low intelligence and cognitive impairment; alienation and lack of social commitment; attitudes that condone offending and drug misuse; early involvement in crime and drug misuse; and friendships with peers involved in crime and drug misuse.

According to CtC, factors that will help to protect children and young people from involvement in youth crime, even in the presence of the risks listed above, include: being female; having a resilient temperament; having a sense of self-efficacy; having a positive, outgoing disposition; and being of high intelligence. Other protective factors include: having strong bonds with family, friends and teachers; having parents, teachers and community leaders who promote healthy standards; having opportunities for feeling involved in families, schools and communities; having social and learning skills to take advantage of opportunities; and being recognised and praised for positive behaviour.

Although the relationships between risks and protective factors and the precise ways in which they interrelate are uncertain, it is widely agreed that risks cluster together in the lives of the most disadvantaged children. Moreover, the chances that those children will become involved in anti-social and criminal behaviour increases exponentially as the number of risk factors rises. Although differences in risk and protective factors between ethnic groups have not been well researched in the UK, US studies suggest that the various dynamics described show much consistency across different ethnic groups and cultures. However, there are undoubted differences in their prevalence and a case might consequently be made for treating experience of racial discrimination as a risk factor in its own right (Beinart *et al*, 2002).

In respect of illicit drug use, several investigations have sought to identify correlations with personality type and social circumstance. It has been found that adolescents who have tried an illicit drug tend to be similar to those who have not in terms of sociability, self-esteem, 'puritanical' outlook, and levels of trust and respect for their families (Joseph Rowntree Foundation, 1997). Furthermore, adolescents who use drugs recreationally are predominantly studious, employed and relatively affluent (European Monitoring Centre for Drugs and Drug Addiction, 2002). That said, it is also evident that while 'experimentation' with drugs and 'recreational use' cut across the social spectrum during youth, more 'problematic' patterns of drug consumption are concentrated among those who are worst-off (DrugScope and Department of Health, 2001; British Medical Association, 2003).

The 'problematic' use of illicit drugs by teenagers is clearly linked to a number of risk factors, many of which also predict other adolescent problem behaviours such as alcohol problems, smoking, and risky sexual activity (Department of Health and the National Addiction Centre, 2001). These risk factors include youth offending, truancy, school exclusion, family problems, and living in deprived communities. Such characteristics tend to be more prevalent among particular groups of young people, including: those who are in the care of social services; those with parents who misuse drugs; young offenders; those who are homeless; children who truant or have been excluded from school; those who use other substances; those with mental health problems; and those involved in prostitution. A combination of these experiences, meanwhile, increases individual vulnerability to substance misuse (Department of Health and DrugScope, 2001; British Medical Association, 2003).

Conclusion

The data reviewed within this chapter reveal that a very high proportion of young people commit a crime at some point in their lives; there have been increases in drug and violent crimes in recent years; and a small but growing number of children have become responsible for a disproportionate number of offences. Despite this, the majority of recorded crime is committed by adults rather than by children or teenagers; crime rates among all age groups – including children and young people – are plateauing and starting to fall; and illicit drug use appears to have stabilised. Furthermore, the types of offences committed by children and young people are often minor rather than serious and their drug use tends to be experimental rather than problematic.

Across the UK, boys commit considerably more crime than girls. Moreover, they tend to commit more serious offences than their female counterparts and tend to cease their offending at a later age. Nonetheless, there are some signs from official statistics and self-report studies that the gender gap in offending behaviour is closing, with more girls offending than previously. Committing crime and taking illegal drugs are less common among younger than older children in the UK, with adolescence characterised by the highest levels of both type of activity. Equally, a gradual decline in crime as young people enter adulthood suggests that a significant proportion of young people grow or mature out of their criminal behaviour (Rutherford, 1992; Newburn, 2002).

In addition to differences in criminal activity according to gender and age, patterns of crime by young people vary by geographical area. Northern Ireland has lower levels of recorded and self-reported crime and lower levels of drug use than the rest of the UK – although Higgins and McElrath (2000) provide some evidence that this may be changing. In contrast, Scotland has very high levels. Meanwhile, links between offending behaviour, illicit drug use and a wide range of other familial, social, educational, community, and lifestyle factors are evident. In particular, the increased risk of both offending and illicit drug use among young people who experience multiple personal, social and educational problems is clear. Additionally, these young people are more likely to engage in other risky behaviours, such as truanting and under-age smoking and drinking.

Finally, one important issue that is frequently omitted from discussions of youth and crime is the victimisation of young people. According to the youth component of the 1992 BCS, 12–15-year-old boys and girls are as much at risk of victimisation as adults and, for some types of crime, more at risk than adults and older teenagers (Aye Maung, 1995; Newburn, 2002). Examples of child abduction and murder, such as that of the two ten-year-old Cambridgeshire girls killed by Ian Huntley in August 2002, dramatically highlight the extreme vulnerability of young people. However, they can also distort the reality of young people's victimisation. Most children are subject to crimes of a considerably less serious nature (such as harassment and bullying) and these are often perpetrated by other children and young people rather than by adults. Furthermore, the children and young people most at risk of being a victim of crime are not very young girls but young people from minority ethnic groups and those who commit offences themselves.

Acknowledgements

This chapter builds substantially upon work done by Bob Coles and Suzanne Maile for the first edition of *The Well-being of Children in the UK* (Coles and Maile, 2002).

12 Education

Bob Coles and Dominic Richardson

Key findings:
- There are significant differences between the types of schools attended by children in the UK countries and regions: co-educational comprehensive schools are more common in Scotland and Wales; single-sex, selective, denominational schools more common in Northern Ireland; and more independent schools in England.
- Educational attainments vary with gender, social background and ethnicity.
- Girls do better in school qualifications than boys.
- All four countries and regions of the UK do much better than many of their economic competitors on standardised measures of reading, numeracy and scientific literacy which are not based on school curricula or examination performance.
- On some standardised measures Northern Ireland has a much larger ability range than other parts of the UK.
- Boys are four times more likely than girls to be excluded from school.
- Those excluded from school either permanently or for a fixed-term period are much more likely to be eligible for free school meals, have a statement (or record) of special educational need, be 'looked after' by local authorities or, where the data are available, to be classified as 'black Caribbean' or 'black other'.

Key trends:
- Educational qualifications have been improving year on year throughout the last decade.
- Whereas the 1980s showed signs of a gap between children from privileged and unprivileged backgrounds widening, since then, on some measures, those from working-class backgrounds have showed most marked improvements.
- Following the emphasis on formal measures of literacy and numeracy

at key stages there is some evidence of improvements in the proportion reaching or exceeding expected standards.

- Reductions in the number of pupils permanently excluded from school were very rapid at the end of the 1990s when ambitious targets were met. In England and Wales exclusions have started to increase since the turn of the century when the targets were dropped.

- In England, the number of 16–18-year-olds not in any form of education, employment or training has begun to decline from the high numbers at the end of the 1990s. In Scotland the figures have remained stable.

- The numbers of pupils with statements (or records) of special educational need have remained more or less the same in England, Scotland and Wales but have been increasing in Northern Ireland.

- Those with special educational needs are increasingly being educated in mainstream schools as part of the Government's social inclusion agenda. This process has been later to get off the ground in Northern Ireland than elsewhere as the Special Educational Needs and Disability Act (SENDA) has not applied there.

Key sources:
- Regional trends 1997–2004
- Research divisions of the Scottish Executive, Welsh Assembly, Department for Education in Northern Ireland, and Department for Education and Skills
- Youth Cohort Study, 5–11
- Organisation for Economic Co-operation and Development (OECD) Programme for International Student Assessment 2000 (PISA 2000)
- Academic research papers and reports

Introduction

This chapter reviews the educational attainment of children across the countries and regions of the UK and, where possible, puts this in a wider international context. It mainly uses measures similar to those used in the previous edition of this book, which concentrated on the formal qualifications attained at the end of compulsory schooling (although also reporting data on literacy and numeracy earlier in children's school careers). However, this chapter also makes use of a new set of data, the Programme for International Student Assessment (PISA). This is important in that it measures the ways in which 15-year-olds 'can use knowledge and skills to meet the challenges they are likely to meet in adult life' rather than success in formal examinations (Gill *et al*, 2002a). However, although data from this study are available for England, Scotland and Northern Ireland, they are not available for Wales. The chapter reviews data on school exclusions and truancy previously covered in a separate chapter of the earlier edition (Edwards and Coles, 2002) and also, for the first time, data and research findings on children with special educational needs.

The context of school types

All children across the UK are entitled to free, full-time education between the ages of five and 16, although there are differences between the types of schools which predominate in the different countries or regions. For instance, comprehensive schools for children over the age of 11 predominate in both Scotland and Wales. Northern Ireland still retains selective education and the vast majority of schools are associated with religious denominations. Single-sex schools are also much more widespread in Northern Ireland (33 per cent) than in England (18 per cent) and Wales (15 per cent), and are comparatively rare in Scotland (3 per cent). Independent schools are more common in England (around one in ten schools) compared to 6 per cent in Scotland and 3 per cent in Wales. These contexts may be regarded as important in relation to levels of achievement and to ameliorating or intensifying the relationship between social background and achievement. In the past, 'Home International' comparisons have pointed to both this and the likelihood of children being educated only with children of a similar social background (Croxford, 2000). In some parts of the UK there is marked religious (and associated ethnic) segregation, which is presenting a serious challenge to the community cohesion agenda (Home Office, 2001; Learning and Skills Council for West Yorkshire, 2002; Short, 2002). The impact of school type on social segregation has also been an important factor in debates about the efficacy of including children with special educational needs in mainstream schooling (Barnes *et al*, 1999).

Sources of evidence and matters of definition

Many of the educational attainment indicators are in the public domain and subject to public attention, and the reliability of qualification standards is subject to regular debate. For instance, as we report below, the formal qualifications obtained by young people between the ages 15 and 18 have been steadily rising across the UK. Some regard this as a sign that standards are declining. Since 1987 qualifications have been 'norm referenced' rather than allocated according to a distribution curve (ie, with 30 per cent failing and only 10 per cent allocated the top A grades). Norm referencing is intended to ensure that the same standards operate each year and offer some vindication to teachers and students that more and more children and young people are doing better every year. There is often debate about whether formal qualifications measure real abilities. In this chapter we report on the abilities of 15-year-olds in literacy, numeracy and science based on tests which are not directly related to the school curricula and are outside of formal examinations. The measures used in the PISA collaborative study are subject to rigorous checks for reliability across a wide range of Organisation for Economic Co-operation and Development (OECD) countries and will, in future years, provide another means of checking ability levels. Data from 32 countries are available for the 2000 survey, which focused mainly on reading literacy. Surveys conducted in 2003 and 2006 will focus, respectively, on mathematical and scientific literacy. In scrutinising these data we examine not only the average performances, but how well the top half and the bottom 10 per cent compare.

Data on truancy and school exclusions are difficult to compare across countries and regions, in part because they are subject to different legislation, regulation and even terminology (Parsons, 1999). Truancy rates are reported by all schools based upon recorded absences on each half-day on which attendance was required. England, Wales and Scotland make a distinction between authorised and unauthorised absence, with the latter reported by all schools and aggregates of these appearing in local authority league tables. In England and Wales there is a distinction between permanent and fixed-term exclusions; in Scotland the distinction is between permanent and temporary; while in Northern Ireland the terms expulsion and suspension are used.

Definitions, codes of practice and regulations covering special educational need also differ between England and Wales and Scotland and Northern Ireland. This chapter reports only on numbers with statements of educational need (called 'records of need' in Scotland), and on the numbers and proportions of children educated in special schools either within or outside the borough of their residence.

Attainments at the age of 15+

We start with the educational attainments of children at the end of compulsory schooling. Table 12.1 provides the distribution of formal qualifications in 15+ and 17+ examinations. Across the UK, girls out-perform boys, with girls in Northern Ireland and Scotland doing particularly well. Boys in Scotland do much better than their contemporaries in England and Wales and slightly better than boys in Northern Ireland. In higher qualifications, at ages 17 and 18 years

Table 12.1: Attainment level at end of Year 11, 2001–02

Country/Region	5 or more A*–C	1–4 A*–C	D–G only	No graded qualifications	2 or more A levels 3 SCE/NQ highers
England	51.6	23.6	19.4	5.4	37.6
Male	46.4	24	23.2	6.4	33.6
Female	57	23.2	15.5	4.3	41.8
Wales	50.5	23.4	18.5	7.6	30.6
Male	44.8	23.9	22	9.2	26
Female	56.4	22.8	14.9	5.9	35.3
Scotland	60.4	25.3	9.7	4.6	39.4
Male	55.2	28	11.6	5.2	33.7
Female	65.7	22.5	7.7	4	45.2
Northern Ireland	58.7	22.2	14.7	4.4	43.4
Male	51.9	23.6	18.3	6.1	34.5
Female	65.7	20.8	11	2.6	52.4
Regions of England					
North East	45.6	24.3	23.4	6.7	31.8
North West	49.7	24.7	20	5.6	35.2
Yorkshire and Humberside	45.6	23.9	24.1	6.4	32.8
East Midlands	50.8	23.2	20.8	5.2	34.8
West Midlands	49.7	24.7	20.2	5.4	35
East	55.3	22.6	17.4	4.7	40.9
London	50.6	25.4	18.6	5.5	37.6
South East	56.4	22	16.7	4.9	43.9
South West	56	22.2	17.1	4.7	40.3

England figures include GNVQ equivalents. Scottish figures include National Qualifications (NQs) from 1999/2000 onwards
Sources: ONS (2004e).

of age, girls in Northern Ireland do particularly well compared to girls in England, Scotland and Wales. Girls again do better than boys in all the UK countries and regions, with boys in Wales gaining fewest successes. Boys in Wales were also more likely than elsewhere to obtain no graded qualifications at all. There were also large differences in attainments between the different regions of England. The North East and Yorkshire and Humberside were the least successful regions, having the highest proportion of 15-year-olds gaining no qualifications and the lowest with five or more A-C grades.

Charts 12.1 and 12.2 indicate changes over time for boys and girls based on five or more A-C grades at GCSE level or equivalent. These charts show that the differences in fortunes between England, Wales, Scotland and Northern Ireland have remained the same since the mid-1990s, with year-on-year marginal increases in the percentages obtaining these grades.

Trends in the percentages of young people obtaining no graded passes in formal qualifications at 15+ show some decline, as indicated in charts 12.3 and 12.4. But this is not as consistent across all the UK or gender groups. Although in Northern Ireland the proportion of boys gaining no qualifications began to decline in the late 1990s, by 2002 it had stabilised at around 6 per cent. The

Chart 12.1: Changes in the percentage of boys obtaining 5 or more A*–C grades in the final year of compulsory schooling 1994–2002

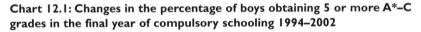

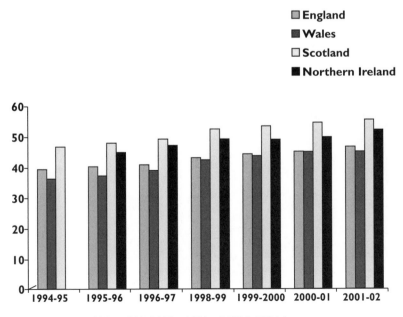

Sources: ONS (1997, 1998e, 1999, 2000c, 2001c, 2002d, 2004e)

Chart 12.2: Changes in the percentage of girls obtaining 5 or more A*-C grades in the final year of compulsory schooling 1994–2002

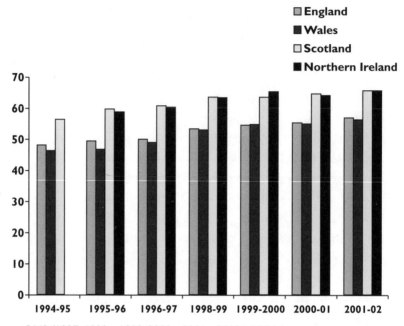

Sources: ONS (1997, 1998e, 1999, 2000c, 2001c, 2002d, 2004e)

Chart 12.3: Changes in the percentage of boys obtaining no graded pass school qualifications 1994–2002 by the end of compulsory schooling 1994–2002

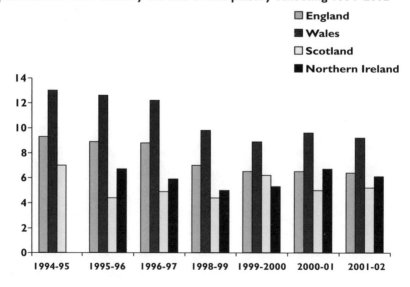

Sources: ONS (1997, 1998e, 1999, 2000c, 2001c, 2002d, 2004e)

Chart 12.4: Changes in the percentage of girls obtaining no graded pass school qualifications 1994–2002 by the end of compulsory schooling 1994–2002

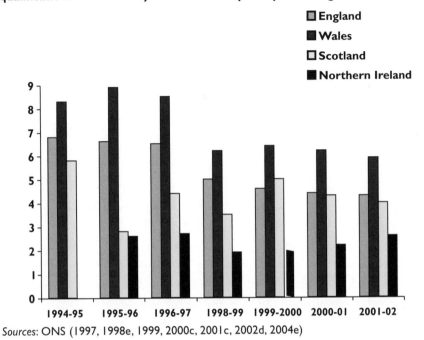

Sources: ONS (1997, 1998e, 1999, 2000c, 2001c, 2002d, 2004e)

proportion of girls in Northern Ireland gaining no qualifications also rose from the turn of the century, albeit from a low base of less than 2 per cent in 1999. Attention is also drawn to the relatively high proportion of both girls and boys in Wales who obtain no graded qualification.

Competences at the age of 15

Here we report on the Programme for International Student Assessment (PISA) and the results of the 2000 survey across 32 countries. We have already noted that the tests carried out in this survey are not based on school curricula, and in the tests of reading literacy no attempt is made to score pupils for ability in spelling or word recognition. Rather, the tests were designed to measure how young people can 'use texts to participate effectively in life'. Mathematical literacy tests 'the ability to formulate and solve mathematical problems encountered in life' and scientific literacy 'the capacity to acquire and use scientific knowledge, and to draw evidence-based conclusions' (Gill *et al*, 2002). Each of the three domains (reading, mathematics and science) are scored on a points scale constructed so as to produce an average of 500 across all students in all countries.

Scores above 500 thus indicate a better-than-average score and points below 500 a less-than-average score. The points scale is also calibrated in such a way as to give a standard deviation of 100 so that, internationally, two-thirds of students score between 400 and 600 points.

In England, the reading literacy survey involved a two-hour assessment of 4,120 pupils in a representative sample of 155 schools throughout the country. In Scotland over 2,500 students from 120 schools were tested, and in Northern Ireland 2,848 students from 115 schools took part. Smaller sub-samples were assessed for mathematical and scientific literacy (Gill *et al*, 2002a, b; Scottish Executive, 2004d).

Table 12.2 summarises a range of measures on the reading literacy of 15-year-olds across 27 countries, giving data for England, Scotland and Northern Ireland and for the UK (combining the three).

This reading literacy table shows Scotland ranked sixth, England eighth and Northern Ireland tenth, all well above the OECD average and many major competitors such as Germany (23rd), France (16th) and the United States (17th). The standard deviation (SD) indicates the spread of scores across two-thirds of the sample. Scores less than 100, therefore, indicate that the spread of scores across two-thirds of those tested is less than average. Only Northern Ireland indicates a score much higher than this, registering a SD score which is the highest of all 27 countries reported here, suggesting a much larger spread of abilities than in other countries. This may, of course, be related to the selective schooling system there, with a higher concentration on tested ability and less on key skills (Post Primary Review Body, 2001). The lowest 10 per cent on reading literacy in Northern Ireland is also much lower down the ranking position than its average score. Scotland also does better than England with this group.

Measures of mathematical literacy are given in Table 12.3. Some countries score much better on this test than on the reading literacy test; eg, Japan is top on mathematical literacy but only ninth on reading literacy. This table shows the UK again doing well, with Scotland seventh, England ninth and Northern Ireland tenth. The performance of the bottom 10 per cent in Northern Ireland indicates again some room for concern compared to the rest of the UK and others adjacent to them in the table.

The league tables for scientific literacy are reported in Table 12.4. Here, England (fourth) and Northern Ireland (eighth) do better than Scotland (ninth). The SD score for Northern Ireland is again highest of the 27 nations reported here, and the performance of the lowest 10 per cent in both Scotland and

Table 12.2: Comparison of mean reading literacy proficiency and distribution for 15-year-old population in OECD* nations (PISA 2000)

Countries in descending order (highest mean score first)	Mean score	Standard deviation	Bottom 10th	Top 50%	Points difference
			Percentiles		
Finland	546.5	89.5	428.9	552.9	124
Canada	534.3	94.7	409.9	539.6	129.7
New Zealand	528.8	108.2	381.7	537.7	156
Australia	528.6	101.8	394.1	534.1	140
Ireland	526.7	93.6	401.3	533.2	131.9
Scotland	**525.6**	**99.5**	**394.8**	**532.6**	**137.8**
Republic of Korea	524.8	69.6	432.8	530.4	97.6
United Kingdom	**523.4**	**100.5**	**390.8**	**527.3**	**136.5**
England	**523.4**	**100.4**	**391.1**	**526.7**	**135.6**
Japan	522.2	85.8	407	530.2	123.2
Northern Ireland	**519.4**	**108.5**	**376.1**	**528**	**151.9**
Sweden	516.3	92.2	391.5	523.1	131.6
Austria	507.1	93	383.1	514.7	131.6
Belgium	507.1	107.1	354.1	523.1	169
Iceland	506.9	92.4	383.4	513.4	130
Norway	505.3	103.7	363.7	514.8	151.1
France	504.7	91.8	380.9	510.7	129.8
United States	504.4	104.8	363.2	510.6	147.4
OECD Average**	**500**	**100**	**414.8**	**565.5**	**150.8**
Denmark	496.9	98.1	367.1	504.5	137.4
Switzerland	494.4	102.1	355.5	502.7	147.2
Spain	492.6	84.8	378.6	499.1	120.5
Czech Republic	491.6	96.4	367.8	497.9	130.1
Italy	487.5	91.5	367.5	492.4	124.9
Germany	484	111.3	335.4	494.4	159
Hungary	480	93.9	353.9	485.8	131.9
Poland	479.1	99.8	342.9	486.6	143.7
Greece	473.8	97.2	342.3	479.4	137.1
Portugal	470.2	97.2	337.2	475.8	138.6
Luxembourg	441.2	100.5	311.2	447.7	136.5
Mexico	422	85.9	311.3	420.2	108.9

*Does not include the Netherlands as it did not meet the sample size requirement
**OECD average artificially set, based on sample weighted contributions from the 27 OECD nations participating

Northern Ireland is much lower down the league table than the bottom 10 per cent from other nations.

Table 12.3: Comparison of mean mathematics literacy proficiency and distribution for 15-year-old population in OECD* nations (PISA 2000)

Countries in descending order (highest mean score first)	Mean score	Standard deviation	Percentiles Bottom 10th	Percentiles Top 50%	Points difference
Japan	556.6	87	440.3	563.4	123.1
Republic of Korea	546.8	84.4	438.2	552.4	114.2
New Zealand	536.9	98.8	405.2	542.7	137.5
Finland	536.2	80.4	433	538.6	105.6
Australia	533.3	90.1	418	536.4	118.4
Canada	533	84.6	422.9	535.9	113
Scotland	**532.9**	**87.9**	**419.6**	**538.3**	**118.7**
Switzerland	529.3	99.7	397.7	534.7	137
United Kingdom	**529.2**	**91.7**	**411.9**	**532.4**	**120.5**
England	**529.1**	**91.7**	**412**	**531.9**	**119.9**
Northern Ireland	**524.2**	**100.6**	**391.9**	**534**	**142.1**
Belgium	519.6	106.2	367.1	533.1	166
France	517.2	89.3	398.6	521.7	123.1
Austria	515	92.5	392	519	127
Denmark	514.5	86.6	401.4	518.5	117.1
Iceland	514.4	84.7	406.4	516.9	110.5
Sweden	509.8	93.4	386.2	514.2	128
Ireland	502.9	83.6	394.4	508.4	114
OECD Average**	**500**	**100**	**366.7**	**505.3**	**138.6**
Norway	499.4	91.6	379.1	503.4	124.3
Czech Republic	497.6	96.4	371.6	498.9	127.3
United States	493.2	98.4	360.7	497	136.3
Germany	489.8	102.6	348.7	497.2	148.5
Hungary	488	98	359.6	488	128.4
Spain	476.3	90.6	358	478.4	120.4
Poland	470.1	102.6	335.2	473.5	138.3
Italy	457.3	90.5	338.4	461.7	123.3
Portugal	453.7	91.4	331.7	458	126.3
Greece	446.9	108.4	303.3	452.9	149.6
Luxembourg	445.7	92.6	327.3	451.1	123.8
Mexico	387.3	82.7	280.6	386	105.4

*Does not include the Netherlands as it did not meet the sample size requirement
**OECD average artificially set, based on sample weighted contributions from the 27 OECD nations participating

Table 12.4: Comparison of mean science literacy proficiency and distribution for 15-year-old population in OECD* nations (PISA 2000)

Countries in descending order (highest mean score first)	Mean score	Standard deviation	Percentiles Bottom 10th	Percentiles Top 50%	Points difference
Republic of Korea	552.1	80.7	444.4	567.6	123.2
Japan	550.4	90.5	431.9	567.5	135.6
Finland	537.7	86.3	426.7	550.6	123.9
England	**533.5**	**97.5**	**405.6**	**546.7**	**141.1**
United Kingdom	**532**	**98.2**	**403.4**	**545.3**	**141.9**
Canada	529.4	88.9	413.8	542.5	128.7
New Zealand	527.7	100.8	394.4	543.9	149.5
Australia	527.5	94.3	404.3	540.7	136.4
Northern Ireland	**523.2**	**106.6**	**387.7**	**539.4**	**151.7**
Scotland	**522**	**101.6**	**390.3**	**537.5**	**147.2**
Austria	518.6	91.3	399.7	532.8	133.1
Ireland	513.4	91.8	396.3	525.1	128.8
Sweden	512.1	93.3	391.7	527.2	135.5
Czech Republic	511.4	94	391.3	522.5	131.2
France	500.5	102.4	365.3	513.2	147.9
Norway	500.3	95.6	379.2	514.8	135.6
Total	**500**	**100**	**370.5**	**513.5**	**143**
United States	499.5	101.1	369.6	512.2	142.6
Hungary	496.1	102.6	362.6	508.3	145.7
Iceland	495.9	87.8	382.6	509.7	127.1
Belgium	495.7	111	348.1	517.2	169.1
Switzerland	495.7	100.1	367.4	505.6	138.2
Spain	490.9	95.4	368.7	502.5	133.8
Germany	487.1	102	352.2	500.7	148.5
Poland	483.1	96.9	361	494	133
Denmark	481	103.3	348.5	494.2	145.7
Italy	477.6	98.1	350.6	490.1	139.5
Greece	460.6	97	335.9	472.8	136.9
Portugal	459	89.1	344.9	469	124.1
Luxembourg	443.1	96.4	321.4	456.6	135.2
Mexico	421.5	77.1	327.4	427.6	100.2

*Does not include the Netherlands as it did not meet the sample size requirement
**OECD average artificially set based on sample weighted contributions from the 27 OECD nations participating

The impact of social background

Over many years, the sociology of education has produced a wealth of evidence about the relationship between social background and educational attainments. While all studies confirm a clear relationship, different interpretations have been given as to whether inequalities are intensifying or whether the gaps are closing. Machin and Vignoles (2004) have used the longitudinal datasets based on the 1958 and 1970 birth cohorts to examine the links between higher education (degree acquisition by the age of 23 years) and family income. They conclude that the gap between richer and poorer students increased between the two cohorts. Glennester (2001), based on *Social Trend* data also indicates that, in 1998/99, children with professional parents were 5.5 times more likely to participate in higher education than those with unskilled parents, but that this was a significant improvement (from 9.2 times at the beginning of the decade).

Both the Scottish School Leavers Surveys and the Youth Cohort Studies of England and Wales allow for an examination of the relationship between social class background and attainments at 15+. Reviewing changes from 1986 to 1992, Dolton and colleagues found the biggest improvements in examination performances in boys and girls of more privileged backgrounds (Dolton *et al*, 1999). Table 12.5 shows how that relationship has changed more recently (from 1992–2000). This shows that all socio-economic groups have improved but that those from skilled manual, semi-skilled manual and unskilled manual showed particularly marked improvements.

Table 12.5: Changes in educational attainment in England and Wales by parents' occupation, 1992–2002

| | % Achieving 5 or more GCSE Grades A*–C in Year 11 | | | | | |
	1992	1994	1996	1998	2000	2002
All	37	42	44	46	49	51
Managerial/professional	60	66	68	69	69	n/a
Other non-manual	51	58	58	60	61	n/a
Skilled manual	29	36	36	40	45	n/a
Semi-skilled manual	23	26	29	32	37	n/a
Unskilled manual	16	16	24	20	30	n/a

Source: DfES (2004k) Cohorts 5–10

The classification of occupations was changed in 2000 to include a new family-based measure of socio-economic background. This takes into account the occupation and employment status of both parents rather than the father only. Table 12.6 shows the comparisons for 2000–02. This shows continued improvements in the two professional groups and occupations classified as 'routine' and 'other'.

A review of evidence across all the UK was carried out on data from the 1990s (Croxford, 2000). This found that the impact of social class was weaker in

Table 12.6: Changes in educational attainment in England and Wales

| | % Achieving 5 or more GCSE Grades A*–C in Year 11 (NS SEC) | |
	2000	2002
All	49	51
Higher professional	74	77
Lower professional	61	64
Intermediate	45	52
Lower supervisory	35	35
Routine	26	32
Other	24	32

Source: DfES (2004k) Cohorts 10–11

Scotland (and to a lesser extent in Wales) than was the case in England (Croxford, 2000). Gilbourne and Mirza (2000) used data from the Youth Cohort Studies to examine the impact of social class, gender and ethnicity throughout the 1990s. This indicates that each of the main ethnic groups increased the proportion attaining five A-C grades throughout the decade. However, African-Caribbean, Pakistani and Bangladeshi pupils were markedly less likely to obtain these upper grades than their white and Indian peers. Over the decade they conclude that 'African-Caribbean and Pakistani pupils have drawn the least benefit from rising levels of attainment', with the gap bigger at the end of the decade than at the beginning.

Education and attainments of younger children

So far we have reported only on the attainments of children and young people at the end of compulsory schooling and beyond. It is widely recognised, however, that improvements at 15+ are very dependent upon earlier secure foundations for learning (Sylva *et al*, 2003). In England, Scotland and Wales, there has been a significant increase in preschool education in recent years and there is some evidence of progress in key skills; this is much less marked in Northern Ireland, which has fewer preschool places per thousand children in comparison. Chapter 10 contains a section on childcare and early learning provision in the UK and outcomes of such provision.

The Government in England has maintained the importance of publishing tests for literacy and numeracy despite opposition from many quarters. Scotland no longer publishes Standard Assessment Tests (SATs) scores. Table 12.7

Table 12.7: Percentage of pupils reaching or exceeding expected standards at key stage teacher assessments since 2001 in England, Wales and Northern Ireland

Country/ Region		Key Stage 1			Key Stage 2			Key Stage 3		
		English	Maths	Science	English	Maths	Science	English	Maths	Science
England	2001	85	89	89	72	74	82	65	68	64
	2002	85	89	89	73	74	82	67	70	67
	2003	85	89	89	72	74	82	68	72	69
	2004	85*	89	89	74	75	83	**	74	70
Wales	2001	83	89	88	73	75	81	63	65	63
	2002	83	88	88	76	75	83	64	66	66
	2003	82	87	88	76	76	84	65	69	69
Northern	2001	95	95	–	72	75	–	73	71	71
Ireland	2002	94	95	–	73	76	–	–	–	–
	2003	95	95	–	75	77	–	74	72	72

Notes for Northern Ireland data 2003: As a result of industrial action approximately 10 per cent and 9 per cent of schools did not report KS1 and KS2 results respectively. Pupils are not assessed in science in Northern Ireland for KS1 and 2. KS1 pupils assessed aged 8. Notes for English data: Figures include schools not maintained by local education authority. 2002 figures provisional.
* This figure is the average of the speaking and listening (87), reading (84), and writing (83) results, see table 2c, DfES (2004f).
** English results have been delayed, expected announcement regarding results mid-November 2004.
Sources: ONS (2002d) and (2004e). DfES (2004e, f and g), Welsh Assembly (2002), and DENI (2004a).

summarises the scores available for England, Wales and Northern Ireland in 2001 and 2002.

This table indicates stability, some slight rises, but no dramatic improvement in the proportions of each age group attaining expected scores. For convenience, Chart 12.5 shows the changes in literacy rates for 11-year-olds over time for England and Chart 12.6 for Wales. In England the proportions of 11-year-olds achieving Level 4 rose during the late 1990s, and after levelling off from 2000, have begun to show signs of rising again in both literacy and numeracy. In Wales, literacy rates in Welsh have risen consistently throughout the last decade. The proportion of 11-year-olds reaching Key Stage 4 in English, however, dropped back between 2000 and 2001, and levels in English and numeracy have been more or less level since the turn of the century.

Chart 12.5: Trends in proportion of 11-year-olds achieving Level 4 or above in Key Stage 2 tests for literacy and numeracy (England)

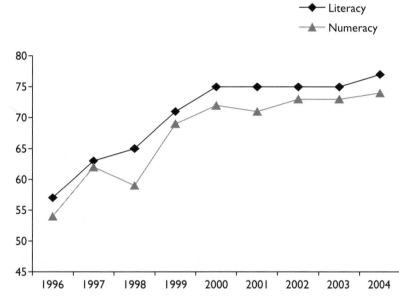

Sources: Department for Work and Pensions (2001a, 2004d) for 1996 to 2001 and 2004 data. 2002–2004 data: DfES (2004e).

Chart 12.6: Wales numeracy and literacy in English and Welsh

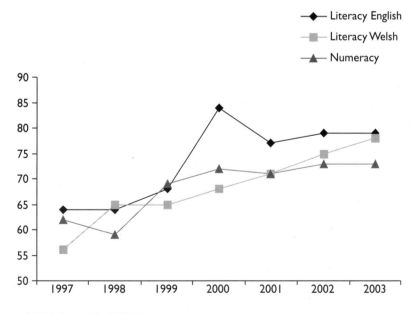

Source: Welsh Assembly (2004a).

Educational disaffection

Truancy and exclusion from school were included as a separate chapter in the last edition of this book. In the late 1990s they were seen as root causes of social exclusion and high rates of crime, and as such were one of the first areas of investigation by the Social Exclusion Unit (SEU), and its 1998 report set bold targets for both to be reduced by a third by 2002 and by a further 10 per cent by 2004 (SEU, 1998b). In England, both are taken as key *Opportunity for All* indicators used to measure progress in tackling poverty and social exclusion (DWP, 2001a). This chapter is able to review progress, but a note of caution should be made about the reliability of official statistics on both school exclusions and truancy rates. Truancy rates are reported in school league tables and are thus highly sensitive and subject to various forms of manipulation, not least as to whether absence is authorised or not (NCH, 2000; Mittler, 2000). Research also indicates that school exclusions can be manipulated by changing de facto permanent exclusion into a series of fixed-term exclusions or by agreements with parents to withdraw children under the threat of permanent exclusion should this not be done (Britton *et al*, 2002; Munn, *et al*, 2000; Osler *et al*, 2000; Vulliamy and Webb, 2000). The effect of these latter practices is to leave the child without any schooling provision.

School exclusions

As reported in the last edition, and based on estimates collected by an independent scholar, school exclusions in England rose by 450 per cent in the first half of the 1990s (Parsons, 1999). Government departments did not begin to collate figures until this time and Table 12. 8 is based on these official figures. Record-keeping on school exclusions has improved markedly in recent years with signs that, in the future, more complete records will be available on fixed-term, as well as permanent, exclusions. The SEU report was followed by a number of Government circulars to schools and local education authorities (see, for instance, DfEE, 1999a, b). Since then, the decline in permanent exclusions occurred very rapidly, as is shown in Table 12.8.

In both England and Wales the target of reducing permanent exclusions by a third was quickly reached by the turn of the century, a 35 per cent decrease in England in four years and a 38 per cent decrease in Wales. But numbers gradually rose in both countries after the turn of the century after targets were dropped, and by 2002 rates were only 26 per cent lower than in 1996/97 in England and 19 per cent in Wales. In Scotland, the figures declined dramatically for one year in 1999/2000 and again in 2002/03.

Expulsions in Northern Ireland are given in Table 12.10 and show no clear pattern over time. However, the number of pupils suspended has increased significantly since 1996, including the numbers subject to multiple suspensions since the turn of the century.

Table 12.8: Permanent exclusions from schools in England and Wales

	England Primary	England Secondary	England Special	England Total	Wales Total
DfEE/DfES figures				**Welsh Assembly**	
1995/96	1,608	10,344	524	12,476	543
1996/97	1,573	10,463	632	12,668	473
1997/98	1,539	10,187	572	12,298	503
1998/99	1,366	8, 636	436	10,438	390
1999/2000	1,266	6,713	384	8,323	337
2000/01	1,436	7,305	394	9,135	430
2001/02	1,451	7,741	343	9,535	445
2002/03	1,300	7,690	300	9,290	439

Sources: DfEE (2000), DfES (2001, 2004i) Welsh Assembly (2001, 2004b) Notes for England: 2002/03 provisional rounded to the nearest ten. Data from 2000/01 based on numbers confirmed by LEAs due to incomplete school data returns. Notes for Wales: For Wales 2003, totals include exclusions from Pupil Referral Units. This information was collected for the first time in 2002/03.

Table 12.9: Temporary exclusions, including the number of pupils temporarily excluded in 1998–2003, and permanent exclusions in Scotland

	Temporary exclusions	No. of pupils temporarily excluded	Permanent exclusions
Scottish Executive			
1999/2000	38,409	20,869	360
2000/01	38,334	21,598	322
2001/02	37,110	20,596	332
2002/03	36,204	20,180	292

Source: Scottish Executive (2001b, 2002e, 2003c, and 2004e).
Data refer to pupils removed from their schools register. Or all exclusions minus temporary exclusions.
For number of pupils excluded, each figure is taken from that year's exclusions report. Published the following year.

Different degrees of detail are collected about which pupils are most likely to be suspended or excluded. In Northern Ireland, details were left to the five area Education and Library Boards and not kept centrally until 2002/03. However, a survey in 1996/97 indicated that the vast majority of those expelled from school were male rather than female. Most were in Year 11 although 40 per cent were from Years 8, 9 and 10 (ie, pupils aged 12–15) and therefore potentially out of school for extended periods of time. Over half of those expelled were also entitled to free school meals, suggesting that they probably also came from areas of social disadvantage (DENI, 1999). In Wales in 2002/03, eight out of ten permanent exclusions were of boys, with the vast majority (90 per cent) classified as white. Those with special educational needs are over-represented among those permanently excluded, accounting for 39 per cent of the total – with more than a third of these having a formal statement of special educational need.

In Scotland, most exclusions (88 per cent) were temporary, lasting one week or less. Of all exclusions, the majority (81 per cent in 2002/03) were male. Those eligible for free school meals, pupils looked after by the local authority and those with Records of Need all had higher exclusion rates than other children. Expressed as rate per 1,000 pupils, all pupils excluded (either temporarily or permanently) in 2002/03 have a rate of 50. Those eligible for free school meals have a rate of 120, those with Records of Need a rate of 109 and those looked after a rate of 227 (4.5 times greater than other pupils). The ethnicity of those excluded is also scored by the same pupils per 1,000. Those pupils classified as 'black other' have a rate of 92, black Caribbean a rate of 74 – compared to Asian Pakistani (41), Asian Indian (15) and Chinese (6).

In England in 2002/03, the comparison of different groups is for those permanently excluded from school only and so is not directly comparable with

Table 12.10: Suspensions, including number of pupils suspended, and expulsions in Northern Ireland

	No of suspensions	No of pupils suspended	Suspended once	Suspended twice	Three or more times	No of expulsions
1996/97	3,748	2,631	...	...	...	76
1998/99	...	...	...	...	...	73
1999/2000	6,299	4,289	...	...	...	83
2000/01	...	4,740	3,517	763	460	80
2001/02	...	5,051	3,704	794	553	76
2002/03	...	5,779	4,044	921	814	70

Source: DENI (2004b).

Scotland. As in Northern Ireland, Wales and Scotland, exclusions of boys predominated, accounting for 82 per cent of permanent exclusions. The vast majority (83 per cent) were exclusions from secondary schools; 14 per cent were from primary schools and 3 per cent from special schools. A new classification of ethnicity was used in 2002/03, making comparisons with previous years difficult. The rates indicate Travellers of Irish heritage have the highest rates of exclusion (51 in every 10,000), black Caribbean (37), and mixed ethnic origin (22), which were much higher than for those classified as white British (11), Indian (3) and Chinese (2). Pupils with special educational needs (SEN) were nine times more likely to be permanently excluded than those without SEN.

Truancy

Truancy rates (the percentage of all half-days of school attendance missed) are collated by the relevant education departments, with a distinction made between explained and unexplained absences. The figures are also available for maintained primary, secondary and special schools and for city technology colleges and independent schools. Rates for unauthorised absences in primary schools are

Table 12.11: The percentage of half-days missed as a result of unauthorised absence for secondary schools in England, Wales and Scotland, including the highest and lowest rate within each (no data available for Northern Ireland) 1997–2003

		England*		Wales		Scotland
Average						
	1997/98	1.10		1.6		1.30
	1998/99	1.07		1.5		1.29
	1999/2000	1.04		1.5		1.43
	2000/01	1.07		1.6		1.54
	2001/02	1.08		1.7		1.51
	2002/03	1.08		1.6		1.4
Highest						
2002/03	Knowsley	3.1	Cardiff	3.4	Clackmannanshire	4.6
	Nottingham City	3.1				
Lowest						
2002/03	Stockton on Tees	0.5	Neath Port Talbot	0.6	Inverclyde	0.1
	Somerset	0.6	Merthyr Tydfil	0.7	Shetland Islands	0.1

Sources: DfES (2003c), Welsh Assembly (2003a), and Scottish Executive (2003a).
* Provisional data only for 2002/03, Maintained secondary schools
Note: Figures include absences due to temporary exclusion and truancy

Table 12.12: The average percentage of half-days missed as a result of unauthorised absence for special schools in England and Wales (no data available for Scotland and Northern Ireland) 1997–2003

School year	England*	Wales
1997/98	2.6	4.1
1998/99	2.45	4.2
1999/2000	2.16	3.3
2000/01	2.21	3.2
2001/02	2	3
2002/03	1.89	2.9

Sources: DfES (2003c), and Welsh Assembly (2003a).
* Provisional data only for 2002/03
Note: Includes absences due to temporary exclusion and truancy

around one-half that of secondary schools. For instance, the rate in England in 2002/03 was 0.43 for primary schools and 1.08 for secondary schools. Rates for unexplained absence from City Technology Colleges in England are even lower – 0.24 per cent half-days on average in 2002/03. Table 12.11 shows the trends for unexplained absences in secondary schools, together with the highest and lowest figures from local authorities. This indicates that unexplained absences in maintained primary and second schools, although a politically sensitive measure of social exclusion, have remained fairly static since the mid-1990s. Table 12.12, however, shows a greater degree of success in reducing unexplained absences in special schools in England and Wales.

NEET and 'status zero'

The last edition of this book reported on a third indicator of educational disaffection, initially known as 'status zero', or NEET (not in education, employment or training). Status zero referred to 16–19-year-olds not classified on careers records as being in 1 (in education), 2 (in employment), or 3 (in training). This was the subject of the fifth report of the Social Exclusion Unit (SEU, 1999a). In England this led to the launch of the Connexions Strategy and the creation of new partnership arrangements to support young people aged 13–19 in England. This has not been followed in Scotland, Wales or Northern

Ireland. The key target for the Connexions Service is the reduction in numbers of those over the age of 16 whose destinations are unknown and the reduction of those 16/17-year-olds who are NEET, by 10 per cent by the end of 2004. A recent review of the service by the National Audit Office (NAO) suggests the Connexions Service is well on the way to meeting this target (NAO, 2004a). Analysis of trends in Scotland, however, indicates little change between 1998 and 2003 (Analytical Services Division ETLLD, 2004).

Special educational needs

The definition of special educational needs (SEN) differs slightly between the different countries and regions of the UK, but there are clear similarities in the way in which identification has been 'norm referenced' since the early 1980s. What this means is that rather than identifying need according to any specific disability (physical, mental or behavioural), it will be done according to whether a pupil finds learning significantly more difficult than the majority of their age group, thus requiring special provision to be made. Conditions leading to the identification of SEN may be visual, hearing or other physical impairments, cognitive disorders, learning difficulties, or social, emotional and behavioural difficulties. Levels of need are also identified, with the most acute need being defined by a formal 'statement of special educational need' or 'record of need' in Scotland. As many as 20 per cent of children and young people are estimated to have a special educational need at some time in their lives but across the UK only around 3 per cent of the school population will have a statement or record of need at any one time.

Table 12.13 summarises the number of children with a statement or record of need since the turn of the century. This indicates broad stability of numbers in England and Scotland, some fluctuation and marginal decline of numbers in Wales, and marked increases in Northern Ireland. Most disabled children in Northern Ireland are being educated in special schools, and both deaf and blind children have to attend boarding schools outside Northern Ireland if they are to have any post-16 provision at all (Monteith *et al*, 2002). Statementing is a potentially contentious process in that it results in a legal obligation for the child to be given access to resources. Since the 1990s, codes of practice have been introduced and revised aimed at offering in-school and specialist support without recourse to the issuing of formal statements (or records) of need, to ensure that these are reviewed regularly (annually), and that they are linked to achievement targets (see, for instance, Department of Education and Science, 1994, Farrell, 2004). Scotland's record of need policy is to be replaced by a co-ordinated support plan for children with complex needs – eg, disabled or gifted children, Traveller children, and those with behavioural difficulties. The new Act of the Scottish Parliament is due to be implemented in October 2005, with a new code of practice to be published in April/May 2005. Under the new law parents will be able to request particular assessment for their children.

Table 12.13: Statemented pupils for years starting 2001–03 by registration

Total	Number			Percentage		
	2001	2002	2003	2001	2002	2003
England	258,200	248,980	250,550	3.1	3	3
Wales	17,415	17,118	17,251	3.48	3.43	3.47
Northern Ireland	...	...	...	2.9	3.1	3.4
Scotland	15,878	15,315	...	2.1	2.1	...

Sources: DENI (2003), Welsh Assembly (2003b), Scottish Executive (2003f), and DfES (2003d).
Note: Figures calculated where appropriate using ONS Regional Trends 36, 37 and 38 as a percentage of total pupil population, where pupil figures are expressed to nearest 1,000. Scottish data are for record of needs; equivalent to SEN statements. Also for Scotland, data are from September of that school year, only publicly funded schools including special schools. Welsh and English data as of January each year, data for England 2001 are estimated as data are from a year when SEN data are known to be incomplete. Northern Ireland data do not include total numbers or authority-specific data.

One of the key debates since the early 1980s concerns whether, having identified needs, provision should be made available in mainstream or special schools. The Audit Commission review of provision in England and Wales indicates that 61 per cent of pupils with SEN in special schools were not entered for any GCSE or GNVQ examination, whereas only 4 per cent were not entered for the same examinations in mainstream schools (Audit Commission, 2002). Pupils with SEN begin planning for their transition to adult life in the annual review following their 14th birthday, yet a large survey of 15-year-olds with SEN in England suggests that around 10 per cent had not undertaken that process (Polat *et al*, 2001). The study also indicates more parents and carers of pupils attending special schools (61 per cent) are satisfied with that process than those attending mainstream schools (41 per cent). However, the same study indicates that pupils attending special schools had lower aspirations and expectations for their future in terms of further education, careers and independence from their families, although this may be because of the higher severity of the difficulties they face rather than the school type they attended. Internationally there has been a clear trend towards 'mainstreaming' wherever possible, and legislation and policy in the UK has increasingly emphasised this – although with only limited success in Northern Ireland (see, for instance, Audit Scotland – HMIE, 2003; Monteith *et al*, 2002). For this reason, the data presented here not only concern numbers and educational attainment, but the degree to which SEN provision is made within mainstream schools, or if not, in other forms of provision close to home.

In England in January 2003, 60.3 per cent of pupils with SEN statements were in maintained mainstream schools, 36.9 per cent in special schools and 2.8 per cent in mainstream independent schools. In Wales, 76 per cent of children with SEN statements were educated in mainstream schools, 22 per cent in special schools and 2 per cent in independent schools. In England, the proportion of pupils with SEN statements in mainstream schools has seen very marked increases since the mid-1990s – rising from 49 per cent in 1994. A further 1,400,000 children are identified as having an SEN but do not have a formal statement (around 17 per cent of the total school population). Nearly all of these (96.5 per cent) are educated in mainstream schools (Casey *et al*, 2004).

In Scotland, around 44,000 children are estimated to have SEN, around 1 in 20 of the school population although under 16,000 children have a formal record of need (RoN). Scotland has 197 special schools attended by 8,183 pupils. Recent research, however, indicates that in special schools, around a quarter of pupils do not have a formal RoN (Riddell *et al*, 2001). Since the turn of the century, the Scottish Executive has recommended that all children in special units or special schools, and all those with RoN in mainstream schools, should have Individualised Education Programmes (IEPs). Recent research indicates that these were being used more in special schools and larger special units within mainstream schools, but that there was some confusion about the use of RoNs and IEPs (Riddell *et al*, 2001).

The Audit Commission reported in 2002 that, despite a budget of £3.6 billion in 2001/2, surprisingly little is known in England about the pattern of children's special educational needs. In England there were no common definitions used by local education authorities (LEAs) and the report (Audit Commission, 2002) recommended a consistent and standardised approach by LEAs in order to inform their inclusion strategies. By contrast, Wales and Scotland were required to report how many children had statement or records by type of need (see Table 12.14 below). A national survey for the Audit Commission reported that within LEAs there was a perception of some very significant increases in some areas of need, particularly, increases of children with autistic spectrum disorders (perceived by four-fifths of respondents), speech and communication difficulties (two-thirds of respondents), and profound and multiple learning difficulties (one-third of respondents). There was a perception of a decline of children with moderate learning difficulties by a quarter of respondents. The distribution of types of need in Scotland and Wales is given below.

Data on the full range of types of need are not available for Northern Ireland although some data on children with disabilities are available (Monteith *et al*, 2002). However, two surveys of learning difficulties at the turn of the century enable estimates and comment on patterns of provision to be made for two important groups. The first survey was of pupils with severe and profound

Table 12.14: Children with statements or records of need, by type of need in Scotland and Wales

Type of need	Wales	Scotland
Moderate learning difficulties	33%	34%
Specific learning difficulties	16%	16%
Emotional and behavioural difficulties (Wales) Social and emotional difficulties (Scotland)	11%	4%
Severe learning difficulties	11%	5%
Speech and communication difficulties (Wales) Language/communication disorder (Scotland)	8%	9%
Physical disabilities (Wales) or Physical or motor impairments (Scotland)	6%	8%
Autistic spectrum disorders	5%	9%
Profound and multiple learning difficulties	4%	1%
Hearing impairment	3%	4%
Visual impairment	1%	3%
Other	2%	6%

Source: Audit Commission, 2002 based on Welsh Assembly Government and Scottish Executive 2001

learning difficulties (SLD); it estimated that in 1998 there were 1,671 such pupils, representing around 36 per cent of those attending special schools and 18 per cent of those with SEN statements – a higher proportion than in Wales or Scotland (ETI, 2001b). The second survey (ETI, 2001a) does not indicate the number of pupils with moderate learning difficulties (MLD) but covered 23 post-primary units catering for pupils with MLD. The report calls for the

Education and Library Boards to ensure greater consistency in terms of organising, managing, staffing and resourcing MLD units, and the need for a minority of schools to review the opportunities pupils have for meaningful and successful integration.

The data from Scotland and Wales also indicate that boys are more likely to have SEN statements or RoN, across every type of need. The Audit Commission found that only a minority of LEAs collected data on SEN by ethnicity; only two-fifths did so for pupils with an SEN statement or RoN and a quarter for those without an SEN statement or RoN. Particular difficulties were reported in assessing the needs of children whose first language was not English (or English or Welsh in Wales). There were also marked differences between LEAs (and schools within LEAs) in levels of SEN identified. The proportion of children with statements varied fivefold between different authorities. The Audit Commission report comments that this 'call(s) into question how far SEN reflects the real level of need among pupils, or rather, different institutions' ability to respond' (Audit Commission, 2002)

The 11 categories of disability used in identifying special need under the 1944 Education Act were abandoned following the 1978 Warnock Report, in favour of definitions which linked needs to the type of additional provision deemed necessary. Yet both the type of need and the choices involved in linking these to patterns of provision can have profound implications for the overall welfare of the child. For instance, although children with profound hearing impairments are a tiny fraction of all those with SEN, provision for such children is sometimes highly specialised. Because of this, children in Northern Ireland often have to choose between secondary schooling in either Dublin or England, something which separates them spatially, socially and linguistically from their families (Henry and McArdle, 2002).

Conclusion

This chapter has reviewed a range of different indicators of educational attainment across England, Northern Ireland, Scotland and Wales. On many measures there are signs of a year-on-year improvement in standards and all perform well in comparison to many of our economic competitors. Some indicators also indicate a narrowing of the gap between children from privileged and under-privileged social backgrounds – a gap that had been widening during the 1980s and early 1990s. Some successes could also be claimed in reducing the numbers excluded from school and disengaged between the ages of 16 and 18. However, some of the gains in reducing permanent exclusions from school had largely been attained in the late 1990s and there had been some slipping back since then. Finally, the chapter has provided a picture, albeit incomplete, of the education of children with special educational needs, where the impact of patterns of change on the educational welfare of children is difficult to assess. Despite this, there is a clear policy agenda for greater mainstreaming of provision. Future years should be able to assess whether this trend does indeed enhance the welfare of such pupils.

13 Children, housing and neighbourhoods

Deborah Quilgars

Key findings:

- Children in minority ethnic households and those on low incomes are particularly likely to live in poor housing.
- The effects of homelessness on children are considerable, irrespective of type of temporary accommodation.
- Neighbourhood dissatisfaction is associated with social housing, social class, region, household type, ethnicity and poverty status.

Key trends:

- UK-wide, housing conditions continue to improve over time.
- Homelessness has risen in the last few years, but this is in part explained by changes in legislation.
- Children's use of public space has decreased since the 1970s.

Key sources:

- House Condition Surveys for England, Northern Ireland, Wales and Scotland
- Survey of English Housing
- Save the Children surveys of severe poverty
- Homelessness statistics
- Academic studies

Introduction

This chapter reviews the evidence of the link between the physical environment and the well-being of children and young people in the UK. Recent policy, most particularly *Sustainable Communities* (Office of the Deputy Prime Minister (ODPM), 2003b) and *Better Communities in Scotland* (Scottish Executive, 2002b), has focused attention on the importance of both the quality of housing and the impact of 'place' on people's lives, with a recognition that certain types of households and communities experience spatial disadvantage as well as income poverty. Homelessness is also recognised as a particular problem UK-wide, with a reduction in the numbers of families in temporary accommodation being a recent addition to the latest *Opportunity for All* children and young people indicators on poverty (to join the existing housing indicator to reduce the proportion of children in housing that falls below the set standard of decency). This chapter begins by reviewing the nature of poor housing; homelessness is then considered – and its impact on the lives of children and young people; finally, children's experience of poor neighbourhoods and their perspectives on space are reviewed (see also Chapter 7).

House conditions

House conditions are recognised as a key factor in ensuring that all families, irrespective of background, can enjoy a home that is in good repair, is fit for use, and has adequate facilities. In particular, the UK Government's policy is that all social rented homes should reach the 'decent homes standard'[1] by 2010. The respective governments/assemblies in England, Scotland, Wales and Northern Ireland all undertake five-yearly house condition surveys. The surveys, however, are undertaken in different years and use different measures, making comparisons problematic.[2] The most up-to-date data available are for 2001 in England and Northern Ireland, 1997/98 for Wales and 2002 for Scotland (ODPM, 2003a; Northern Ireland, Housing Executive, 2003; National Assembly for Wales, 2001b; Scottish Executive, 2004g).

Table 13.1 shows the proportions of houses in unfit condition or dwellings below tolerable housing conditions across the UK. As the figures are not directly comparable, the data should be treated with caution in making comparisons. The proportion of unfit housing varies from 1 per cent in Scotland (which uses

---

[1] *See* www.odpm.gov.uk/decenthomes. A decent home is one that: (1) meets the current statutory minimum for housing, which at present is the 'Fitness Standard'; (2) is in a reasonable state of repair – a home which fails to meet this criterion will have either one or more 'key' building components that are old and in poor condition or two or more 'other' building components that are old and in poor condition; (3) has reasonably modern facilities and services – homes which fail to meet this criterion lack three or more of a specified list of facilities; (4) provides a reasonable degree of thermal comfort, ie, it has effective insulation and efficient heating.

[2] The Joseph Rowntree Foundation funds periodic reviews of these data; the most recent undertaken by Revell and Leather (2000).

the strictest definition) to 8.5 per cent in Wales. Table 13.1 demonstrates that the private rented sector had the highest proportion of dwellings in poor condition throughout the UK, whereas owner-occupied and social housing had more similar rates, although slightly higher rates of unfitness were present in England. Over a third (37 per cent) of social housing homes were deemed not to meet the decent homes standard (utilising a much broader measure than 'unfitness') using the English House Condition Survey in 2001. Over three-quarters of private rented sector property failed to meet the decent homes standard in 2001. However, it was announced in May 2004 that the Government had reduced the number of non-decent social homes by one million since 1997 (ODPM, 2004).

Table 13.1: Housing in unfit condition or below tolerable standard, UK, by tenure

	England (%)	Scotland (%)	Wales (% of stock unfit)	Northern Ireland (% of unfit dwellings)
Owner-occupied	2.9	1.0	7.6	2.8
Private rented	10.3	2.5	18.4	8.7
Local authority	4.1	0.4	8.2 (*)	0.8
Housing association	3.0	0.4	–	2.1
Vacant dwellings	15.5	–	–	43.9
All dwellings **	4.2	0.9	8.5	4.9

* Local authority and housing association stock
** Occupied dwellings for Wales; includes vacant dwellings for Northern Ireland and England.
Sources: English House Condition Survey 2001; Northern Ireland House Condition Survey, 2001, 1997/98 Welsh Condition Survey; Scottish House Condition Survey, 2002

Average energy efficiency ratings (SAP score) are also collected as part of house condition surveys. Nine per cent of dwellings in England had scores of 30 or less, indicating an unsatisfactory energy use. The vast majority (92 per cent) of housing has central heating in Great Britain (see Wilcox, 2003), with little variation between countries and regions. Regionally, Yorkshire and Humber had the highest proportion of houses with central heating (97 per cent), with a low in the North West (88 per cent). The Scottish House Survey also collects data on dwellings with dampness; in 1996 this included 20 per cent of private rented stock, 10 per cent of public rented housing and 6 per cent of owner-occupied dwellings.

National surveys show that house conditions have improved considerably over the last two decades. Improvements recorded for England showed a reduction in unfit properties between 1986–1991 of 10 per cent, with nearly 40 per cent less unfit properties between 1996–2001. Local authority housing showed the greatest physical improvement over 1986–2001. In Wales, unfitness rates reduced from 20 per cent of stock in 1986 to 9 per cent in 1997/98. In Northern Ireland, the proportion of unfit housing reduced from 14 per cent in 1979 to 7 per cent in 1996 and 5 per cent in 2001. However, Scotland has seen less change, with 1 per cent of properties Below Tolerable Standard in 1996 and 2002.

Household characteristics

Across house condition surveys, certain types of households are more likely to live in poor housing. Table 13.2 shows the different forms of poor housing condition by type of household in England using the last House Condition Survey, 2001 (ODPM, 2003a). Considering household type, single people were more likely to live in poor housing, with families tending to have about average levels of unfitness, disrepair and so on. Couples with children tended to experience slightly better housing than lone parents (particularly levels of unfitness) although it is not known whether this is at a statistically significant level. Families with children, however, tended to have the poorest space standards, with 26–28m² per person. Other studies have also shown higher overcrowding levels for families with children (Dale *et al*, 1996). The 2001 House Condition Survey also included analysis for families with children under 11 and under five (as two of a number of potential risk groups). As with all families, these households tended to have about average or slightly better than average scores on housing conditions, with the exception of the space measure. Unsurprisingly, households with the least income and unemployed households experienced worse housing conditions than those on higher incomes and employed households. The Scottish House Condition Survey, 2002 (Scottish Executive, 2004g), Welsh House Condition Survey (National Assembly for Wales, 2001b) and Northern Ireland House Condition Survey, 2001 (Northern Ireland Housing Executive, 2003) also reported that unemployed and low-income households were more likely to be living in Below Tolerable Standard or unfit housing; single adults had the worst housing, with families less likely to live in below standard housing, although lone parents had about average scores (apart from in Northern Ireland where they had a lower rate of unfitness). The Welsh survey also found a link between unfitness and overcrowding for families with dependent children.

The 2001 English House Condition Survey also revealed that minority ethnic households tended to have worse housing conditions on all measures, with Asian households having the worst housing (Table 13.2). In particular, Pakistani and Bangladeshi households had the least space per person (averaging only 22m² per person), partly explained by the larger households and the lack of suitably sized, affordable homes (ODPM, 2003a). Numbers were too small for analysis by ethnicity in the Scottish, Welsh and Northern Ireland House Condition Surveys. Other studies have shown that Gypsies/Travellers are particularly likely to live in poor housing; for example, Travellers were found to be eight times as likely as the general population to live in overcrowded conditions and to have limited access to basic services such as water and electricity in Northern Ireland (Northern Ireland Statistics and Research Agency (NISRA), 2001).

Surveys commissioned by Save the Children on severe poverty in Great Britain and Northern Ireland (Adelman *et al*, 2003; Monteith and McLaughlin, 2004) have recently provided some up-to-date, comparable data on housing quality from the perspective of families (as opposed to surveyors, as in the house condition surveys above) highlighting how children living in poor households[3] are more likely to be living in poor housing. In the British study, three-quarters (73 per cent) of non-poor children lived in homes described as in good repair, compared to just over two-fifths (42 per cent) of severely poor children and one-half (48 per cent) of non-severely poor children. Children in severe and non-severe poverty experienced an average of 1.38 and 1.31 housing problems respectively, compared to an average of 0.49 problems for non-poor children. Children in Northern Ireland were less likely to live in accommodation where housing problems were reported, with an average of 1.19 problems being reported for those in severe poverty, 0.98 problems for non-severe poverty and 0.47 – about the same as in Britain – for non-poor children.

European comparisons

Data on house conditions are difficult to compare across Europe due to definitional and collection differences. However, the European Union (EU) collates statistics

---

[3] Child poverty was measured using a combination of three definitions: the child's own deprivation (child going without one or more 'necessities'); parents' deprivation (parents going without two or more 'necessities'); and the income poverty of the family (income below 40 per cent of median). Children were defined as being in 'severe' poverty if they were poor on all three measures, and 'non-severely poor' if poor on one or two of the three measures.

Table 13.2: Housing conditions, by households, England, 2001

Household group	% of households in the group that:					Number of households in the group (000)s	Average floor space/person of group (m²)
	Are non-decent	Fail thermal comfort	Fail disrepair	Fail fitness	Fail modernisation		
Tenure							
Owner-occupiers	29.0	22.9	7.7	2.9	1.4	14,488	46
Private tenants	48.9	39.8	16.8	10.3	4.3	2,010	40
Local authority tenants	41.9	33.4	8.6	4.1	5.8	2,684	38
RSL(a) tenants	27.1	21.8	4.7	3.0	2.4	1,328	36
Type							
Couple under 60 no dependants	27.6	21.5	8.0	3.0	1.2	4,085	41
Couple over 60, no dependants	30.8	26.0	5.8	2.1	2.7	2,925	46
Couple with dependent child(ren)	27.7	20.5	8.4	3.4	1.1	4,986	26
Lone parent with dependants	33.2	25.6	8.0	6.2	2.1	1,597	28
Other multi-person households	40.8	30.4	13.7	6.7	3.9	1,443	35
One person under 60	40.0	33.4	9.9	4.8	3.8	2,397	65
One person aged 60 or over	38.4	32.5	8.9	3.8	3.7	3,077	71
Ethnicity							
White	31.9	25.7	8.2	3.5	2.2	19,081	45
Black	35.6	22.7	14.6	8.0	7.4	497	35
Asian	44.5	32.7	14.0	9.2	3.5	644	28
Other	38.4	26.7	9.3	6.6	2.1	289	33
Income							
Lowest income quintile	42.0	34.7	10.1	6.1	4.2	4,102	52
2nd	38.0	31.0	9.3	4.1	3.2	4,103	45
3rd	33.6	27.0	9.2	4.1	1.9	4,102	43

| | | % of households in the group that: | | | | Number of households in the group (000)s | Average floor space/person of group (m²) |
Household group	Are non-decent	Fail thermal comfort	Fail disrepair	Fail fitness	Fail modernisation		
4th	25.6	19.8	6.3	2.5	1.4	4,102	38
Highest income quintile	23.5	16.9	7.9	2.2	0.9	4,101	42
Employment status							
Full time employment	28.5	22.3	8.2	3.4	1.5	10,458	39
Part-time employment	34.3	26.2	9.7	4.1	2.6	1,597	42
Retired	35.3	29.7	7.7	3.1	3.4	5,568	58
Unemployed	43.5	35.2	10.6	9.3	3.0	649	36
Full-time education	40.0	28.2	14.6	6.8	3.2	297	30
Other inactive	39.8	30.7	10.4	5.9	3.1	1,940	37
Vulnerable households [b]							
Private sector	43.2	34.4	13.2	7.5	2.7	2,687	43
Social sector	36.6	29.0	7.2	3.9	4.4	2,896	38
All vulnerable	39.8	31.6	10.1	5.6	3.6	5,583	41
Potentially at risk groups							
Children under 11	29.1	21.6	8.3	4.2	1.5	4,913	25
Children under 5	30.4	21.8	9.1	4.5	1.9	2,746	25
People over 60	35.1	29.3	7.9	3.3	3.3	6,919	56
People over 75	39.0	31.1	8.2	3.5	4.6	2,739	58
Long-term illness/disability	36.5	29.8	9.7	4.2	3.2	4,504	45
Resident 30+ years	46.5	37.3	12.5	5.9	6.5	2,465	59
All households	32.5	25.9	8.5	3.8	2.3	20,510	44

[a] Registered social landlords are not-for-profit landlords registered with the Housing Corporation, mostly housing associations, but also some trusts and cooperatives.

[b] Vulnerable households are those in receipt of income or disability related benefits.

Source: Office of the Deputy Prime Minister (2003a) Summary statistics, Table B (i), p10

on basic housing indicators on an annual basis, the most recent being for 2003 (Housing Statistics in the European Union, 2003). These statistics, however, only include England. England had a higher proportion of older houses (built before 1919) than other European countries (except Denmark and France), and one of the lowest levels of house building since 1980 (Germany and Sweden being slightly lower). England fared well on the proportion of dwelling stock having a bath/ shower (Table 13.3) but performed less well on central heating. Space standards in English housing also compared unfavourably to most European countries.

Table 13.3: Bath/shower and central heating in dwelling stock (% of total stock), Europe

	Year	Bath / shower	Year	Central heating
Belgium	1998	94	1992	60
Denmark	2001	94	2001	98
Germany[a]	1993	98	1998	88
Ex-DDR	1993	89	1998	83
Greece	1991[h]	86	1991[h]	45
Spain[c]	1998	99	1999	40[b]
France	1999	98	1999	84[b]
Ireland	1999	94	1999	83
Italy	1995	99	1995	79
Luxembourg	2001	98	2001	96
Netherlands	2000	100	2000	90
Austria[d,e]	1999	95	1999	83
Portugal	1998	95	–	nav
Finland[g]	2000	99	2000	92
Sweden	1995	99	1995	99
United Kingdom[f]	1996	99	1996	88

[a] Excluding Ex-GDR
[b] D, Ex-GDR: including district heating and storey heating; E, F: including individual and collective heating
[c] Households
[d] Principal residences
[e] Annual average in 1999
[f] England
[g] Bathing facilities (shower, bath or sauna in dwelling)
[h] Census
Source: Housing Statistics in the European Union (2003), Table 2.3.

Homelessness

In the UK, local authorities have a legal responsibility to re-house (and find temporary accommodation in the meantime) for families with children who are found to be 'statutorily homeless'. Households are considered homeless if they have no accommodation, or none they can reasonably occupy (eg, without threat of violence or abuse). Under homelessness legislation in England, Scotland, Wales and Northern Ireland, families with dependent children are accepted as being in priority need, but also have to demonstrate a local connection (unless moving due to violence) and that they are not homeless intentionally. In addition, recent legislative changes now mean that young people aged 16 and 17 and care leavers are considered to be in priority need, while other young people between 18 and 25 may be accepted as being in priority need if they can demonstrate they are 'vulnerable'.[4]

European comparisons

It is widely accepted that the number of households experiencing homelessness has increased in many European countries, but there is no precise or generally accepted measure of the size and nature of the problem and, at national level, targeted primary research on homelessness is uneven and lacks comparability (FEANTSA, 1998). Nevertheless, the European Observatory on Homelessness estimates that across the European Union, three million people have no fixed home of their own and 15 million people live in sub-standard or overcrowded accommodation. Further, FEANTSA (Edgar *et al*, 2003) publishes statistics that examine homelessness on a country-by-country basis in the EU, but due to comparability issues summary tables are not available.

Homelessness in the UK and the regions

The main statistical sources on the incidence of statutory homelessness in the UK are the returns submitted quarterly by local authorities to the ODPM, the Welsh Assembly Housing Directorate, the Northern Ireland Housing Executive (NIHE) and the Scottish Executive. These statistics, however, only measure the incidence of those presenting as homeless to a local authority, and those accepted as homeless. Much youth homelessness in particular is not captured by this data source, and there are no national statistics on 'non-statutory' homelessness.

---

[4] The Homelessness Code of Guidance for Local Authorities (ODPM, 2002) defines 'vulnerability' as whether, when homeless, 'the applicant would be less able to fend for himself than an ordinary homeless person so that he would be likely to suffer injury or detriment, in circumstances where a less vulnerable person would be able to cope without harmful effects'.

Homelessness acceptances in England, Scotland and Wales increased from the 1980s to the early 1990s, when total acceptances in the three countries peaked at 179,410 in 1992 (see Table 13.4). Homelessness acceptances then gradually declined through most of the 1990s, but started to increase again at the end of the decade, rising to a height of 169,291 in 2002. However, the recent rise, will, in part, be explained by the introduction of more generous homelessness legislation (particularly extension of priority need categories).

In Wales, the numbers of households accepted as homeless have fluctuated between a high of 11,125 in 1993 and a low of 4,171 in 1999, although rising to 6,740 in 2002 (see Table 13.4). The rate of homelessness varies between unitary authorities. In 2000, the numbers found to be unintentionally homeless and in priority need per 1,000 of the population ranged from 0.2 in Newport to 4.1 in Torfaen. At the end of 2000, some 910 homeless households were in temporary accommodation.

Homelessness acceptances in Scotland rose to 27,281 in 2002, having consistently increased throughout the 1980s and 1990s, but representing a third increase since 1999 (see Table 13.4). Of the 4,704 total households in temporary accommodation at the end of September 2002, 1,490 were families with children, including 110 families in bed and breakfast (B&B) accommodation (Scottish Executive, 2002h). Forty-six per cent of the families with children reported in temporary accommodation at the end of September 2002 were accounted for by four local authority areas: Glasgow, Edinburgh, South Lanarkshire and Fife, with Glasgow alone accounting for 24 per cent.

The number of households accepted as homeless in England since the mid-1990s has fluctuated between 113,000 and 122,000 (see Table 13.4) but increased from 112,800 in 1999 to 135,270 in 2002. In 2002, 54 per cent of priority need households were families with children, and 10 per cent included a pregnant woman. Six per cent of households were young people. At the end of 2002, 99,620 households were living in temporary accommodation in England, the highest number since the first figures were compiled in 1977. Of these, 12,670 (13 per cent) were placed in B&B accommodation; this figure, however, is likely to reduce as, since March 2004, authorities have only been able to place families in B&B accommodation in emergency situations. Table 13.5 shows homelessness by region, both for number of priority needs acceptances and the use of temporary accommodation; London accounted for 25 per cent of acceptances but 60 per cent of temporary accommodation use, reflecting the housing shortage in the capital.

Table 13.4: Homelessness acceptances, UK

Number of households

	1980	1985	1986	1987	1988	1989	1990	1991	1992	1993
Not held to be intentionally homeless										
England	60,400	91,010	100,490	109,170	113,770	122,180	140,350	144,780	142,890	132,380
+ Scotland	7,038	10,992	11,056	10,417	10,463	12,396	14,233	15,500	17,700	17,000
+ Wales	4,772	4,825	5,262	5,198	6,286	7,111	9,226	9,293	9,818	10,792
= Great Britain	72,210	106,827	116,808	124,785	130,519	141,687	163,809	169,573	170,408	160,172
Held to be intentionally homeless										
England	2,520	2,970	3,070	3,270	3,730	4,500	5,450	6,940	6,350	5,660
+ Scotland	938	980	1,144	1,030	1,128	1,271	1,580	1,800	2,200	2,000
+ Wales	674	546	703	485	532	694	737	550	452	333
= Great Britain	4,132	4,496	4,917	4,785	5,390	6,465	7,767	9,290	9,002	7,993
All homeless acceptances										
England	62,920	93,980	103,560	112,440	117,500	126,680	145,800	151,720	149,240	138,040
+ Scotland	7,976	11,972	12,200	11,447	11,591	13,667	15,813	17,300	19,900	19,000
+ Wales	5,446	5,371	5,965	5,683	6,818	7,805	9,963	9,843	10,270	11,125
= Great Britain	76,342	111,323	121,725	129,570	135,909	148,152	171,576	178,863	179,410	168,165

Table 13.4: Homelessness acceptances, UK *continued*

Number of households

	1994	1995	1996	1997	1998	1999	2000	2001	2002
Not held to be intentionally homeless									
England	122,460	117,490	113,590	102,410	104,490	105,460	111,550	118,700	125,750
+ Scotland	16,000	15,200	15,500	15,600	16,500	18,000	–	–	25,923
+ Wales	9,897	8,638	8,334	4,297	4,371	3,695	4,156	5,164	6,188
= Great Britain	148,357	141,328	137,424	122,307	125,361	127,155	–	–	157,861
Held to be intentionally homeless									
England	4,570	4,920	5,070	4,970	6,140	7,340	9,140	8,380	9,520
+ Scotland	1,800	1,700	1,700	1,800	1,900	2,300	–	–	1,358
+ Wales	396	362	815	343	380	476	510	553	552
= Great Britain	6,766	6,982	7,585	7,113	8,420	10,116	–	–	11,430
All homeless acceptances									
England	127,030	122,410	118,660	107,380	110,630	112,800	120,690	127,080	135,270
+ Scotland	17,800	16,900	17,200	17,400	18,400	20,300	–	–	27,281
+ Wales	10,293	9,001	9,149	4,640	4,751	4,171	4,666	5,717	6,740
= Great Britain	155,123	148,311	145,009	129,420	133,781	137,271	–	–	169,291

Notes: Statistics from ODPM, Scottish Executive, National Assembly for Wales. The 1990 figures for Wales include 2,000 households made homeless in Colwyn Bay by flooding in the February of that year. Scottish figures are for priority need homeless and potentially homeless cases only, for applications made during the year. The 2000 and 2001 figures were not available at the time of compilation. The 2002 figures are for the financial year 2002/03 at the time of compilation. The England and Wales figures for 1997 and later years reflect the changes in homeless legislation, and as a result no longer include 'non-priority acceptances'. In 1996 these accounted for 3,310 acceptances in England and 3,501 acceptances in Wales.

Source: Wilcox (2003) Table 90.

Table 13.5: Homelessness by region: Homeless acceptances and number of households in temporary accommodation, England 2002

Region	Homeless acceptances	Households in temporary accommodation
North East	6,460	1,780
Yorkshire and Humberside	13,980	2,220
North West	14,240	1,640
East	10,880	7,300
West Midlands	14,670	1,270
East Midlands	8,110	2,090
South West	12,290	5,930
South East	14,080	12,400
London	31,050	51,200
Total	125,750	85,770

Notes: ODPM statistics. Homeless acceptances figures are for priority need households only, and exclude households found to be intentionally homeless. Temporary accommodation figures are for the end of the year, and exclude households that are 'homeless at home'.
Source: Wilcox (2003) Tables 94a and 94b

Table 13.6: Homeless presenters and acceptances, Northern Ireland, 1999–2004

	1999/2000	2000/01	2001/02	2002/03	2003/04
Presenters	11,552	10,997	12,694	16,426	17,150
Awarded priority status	5,192	6,457	7,374	8,580	8,594
Not homeless	2,131	2,825	3,376	3,834	4,089
Homeless but not priority status	2,988	3,449	3,640	3,875	4,547

Note: Number of presenters and number of decisions do not sum exactly due to different base number for decision statistics.
Sources: Northern Ireland Housing Executive (2004), Tables 3.4 and 3.6 combined.

In Northern Ireland, the pattern of homeless presentations remained relatively constant throughout the 1980s and 1990s at around 10,000–11,000 a year and around 4,500 families – or 40 per cent of all presentations. In 2000/01, however, there was a significant increase in the numbers of presenters to 12,694, rising to 17,150 in 2003/04 (NIHE, 2004) (Table 13.6). While a slightly lower proportion of presenters were accepted as homeless, this rise is a significant one because there is already a very high homelessness rate per population rate. The highest incidences of homelessness are to be found in the urban Housing Executive Districts in Belfast and surrounding Greater Belfast; there are also pressures in the provincial cities and towns, particularly in (London) Derry, Newry and Ballymena. In Northern Ireland, around 20 per cent of families accepted as homeless are placed in temporary accommodation.

The causes of child homelessness

It is widely acknowledged that the causes of homelessness among all households are multi-faceted and complex. Homelessness statistics in England record three key reasons for loss of last home: parents, relatives or friends no longer willing or able to accommodate (35 per cent, 2002); breakdown of relationship with partner (22 per cent, 2002); and loss of private dwelling, including tied accommodation (20 per cent, 2002). These key reasons are similar across the UK. In addition, research studies have shown that violence is a significant factor in causing homelessness. For example, Vostanis *et al* (1998) in a sample of 168 homeless families, found that 89 per cent became homeless to escape violence, either in the form of direct assaults (53 per cent) or threats of violence (14 per cent), or from sustained harassment (11 per cent). In Northern Ireland, domestic violence, intimidation and neighbourhood harassment are all significant reasons for homelessness (accounting for between 7 and 10 per cent of homeless households awarded priority status respectively); bomb/fire damage/civil disturbance is also recorded, although these figures are low at present (33 cases out of 8,594 in 2003/04) (NIHE, 2004).

Other associated risk factors for homelessness include: poverty and deprivation, young parenthood and single parenthood, and poor educational achievement (Anderson and Tulloch, 2000; Motion, 2000). Parents' early experiences are also thought to be significant, and research has found that many homeless families are headed by parents who had disrupted family backgrounds (including experiencing homelessness themselves) and/or who have experienced violence and/or sexual abuse as children (Vostanis and Cumella, 1999; Bassuk and Perloff, 2001; Jones *et al*, 2002). An increasing reason for homelessness in some urban areas is where asylum-seeking families become homeless once they have been granted refugee status and National Asylum Support Service (NASS) support is withdrawn.

For older children, the evidence of family and relationship breakdown as a contributory cause of homelessness is overwhelming. In the UK as a whole, it is estimated that one in nine young people run away or are forced to leave and stay away overnight before the age of 16 (Raws, 2001). Comparative research (Bruegel and Smith, 1999) between homeless young people and young people living in deprived areas found that the homeless group were far more likely to be poor, to have experienced violence more than once, to have experienced family disruption and to have a poor relationship with their mother, than the comparison group.

The health effects of poor housing and homelessness

The relationship between health, housing and homelessness has been the subject of numerous individual studies, and national surveys are now attempting to capture some data on the health of private households, for example, the 2002 Scottish House Condition Survey (Grainger and Robinson, 2004).

A number of studies in the 1980s found links between dampness and hydrothermal growth and children's poor respiratory health in Scotland and London (Platt *et al*, 1989; Strachan, 1988). The Scottish House Condition Survey 2002 tested this association, finding that significant predictors of whether a child had symptoms of respiratory health problems included: dwelling type (house or flat); level of heating usage; presence of a smoker in the household; tenure (private or social); whether adult respondent had respiratory health problems; and satisfaction with heating. The most significant factor was whether or not the adult had respiratory problems him/herself. The predictive power of the logistic regression model was, however, very weak, only predicting whether a child had respiratory symptoms 5 per cent of the time. Overcrowding and dampness both appeared to be associated with poor respiratory health but these variables were not included in the final regression model as they had no power to predict children's respiratory health.

Research suggests that the main effects of homelessness on children result from spending long periods of time living in (often inappropriate) temporary accommodation. Much research has concentrated on the impact on families of temporary accommodation, with a proportion, particularly B&B accommodation, being below standard, overcrowded, dangerous, lacking facilities for cooking and washing, and being located outside the home borough (GLA, 2001a, 2001b). High levels of infectious illnesses, gastroenteritis infections and a range of respiratory problems are associated with such housing (eg, Royal College of Physicians, 1994; Sawtell, 2002).

Research indicates that where families are housed in self-contained accommodation in an area they know and where parents are coping well, children are largely unaffected. However, where parents are not coping well living in shared accommodation in an unknown area, then children are likely to be affected in a number of ways, including behavioural changes, bed wetting, physical health problems, reluctance to eat, a general failure to thrive and the worsening of existing conditions such as asthma and insomnia (McCrum, 2001; Hall *et al*, 2000). However, the loss of a home in itself may have significant effects due to people's loss of control over their lives, especially where this means a move of schools, and the loss of networks of friends and family (Sawtell, 2002; Shatwell, 2003). Educational impacts can include poor school attendance, lateness, difficulties in studying and fear of bullying.

As well as physical heath impacts, there is evidence that homeless children suffer higher levels of mental ill-health, psychosocial stress, behavioural problems and delayed development than children who are not homeless (Davey, 1998; Vostanis et al, 1998) with parents being more concerned about risks to their children's mental than physical health (McCrum, 2001).

The effects of homelessness on older children will, in part, depend on their circumstances. However, in particular, research has consistently shown that the health of people sleeping rough is extremely poor and that young people sleeping rough expose themselves to danger, to hunger and ill-health, to alcohol and drug abuse, and to physical and sexual abuse and prostitution (Stein et al, 1994; Palmer, 2001).

Research also indicates long-term effects of poor housing and homelessness on children. An analysis of the National Child Development Study found that three housing variables increased the odds of ill-health over the period 1958–1991: living in non-self-contained accommodation, past experience of homelessness, and dissatisfaction with area (Marsh et al, 1999). Other research has shown a weak link between childhood housing and later mortality, in particular between poor ventilation and early mortality (Dedman et al, 2001).

Poor neighbourhoods

Neighbourhood renewal is a central policy objective in the UK and much research has been undertaken to evaluate a range of policy interventions that have attempted to combat social exclusion over the last two decades (Carley et al, 2000). However, there is much less research that systematically captures the experience of families and children at a neighbourhood level.

The English Housing Condition Survey 2001 (ODPM, 2003a) is the only house condition survey in the UK that incorporates an examination of 'decent places', including both a normative perspective and households' views. Problems in the local environment were assessed by surveyors, with neighbourhoods consisting typically of between 100 and 300 dwellings. It was estimated that 11 per cent of all dwellings (2.4 million) were located in what was defined as 'poor neighbourhoods': areas where there were significant problems with the quality, condition, use or upkeep of buildings and public spaces – indicated by rundown or vacant/boarded-up buildings; areas of serious neglect or misuse in terms of graffiti, vandalism, neglected gardens; and public areas that had become disfigured by litter and dumping. Half of these 'poor neighbourhoods' were private sector housing areas and 40 per cent were predominantly local authority-built neighbourhoods. Poor neighbourhoods were also relatively concentrated in northern regions, as well as in socially and economically deprived areas – homes in the most deprived 10 per cent of wards on the 2000 Index of Multiple Deprivation were 11 times more likely to be situated in poor neighbourhoods than those within the least deprived 10 per cent of wards.

Certain types of household were more likely to be living in poor neighbourhoods. In particular, minority ethnic households were nearly three times more likely to live in poor neighbourhoods than white households (37 per cent compared to 10 per cent). Poor neighbourhoods also had higher concentrations of unemployed or economically inactive households, lone parents, and other people living alone or sharing. In addition, such neighbourhoods were found to provide residence for proportionately more households with young children than non-poor neighbourhoods (28 per cent compared to 23 per cent). Households in poor neighbourhoods were much more likely than those living elsewhere to view their area as having a wide range of environmental problems. The most common issues regarded as a 'problem' or 'serious problem' by at least one-third of households were street parking, litter and rubbish in the streets, fear of burglary and problems with dogs/dog mess. However, the most prominent differences between households in 'poor' compared to other neighbourhoods were the likelihood of the former identifying problems with a range of anti-social behaviour, including litter and rubbish, drugs, general level of crime, the state of open spaces, vandalism, troublesome teenagers/children, and fear of being burgled.

While not as up-to-date, the most robust study on neighbourhood satisfaction remains the 1994/95 Survey of English Housing and specially commissioned data from the 1991 census (Burrows and Rhodes, 1998). Table 13.7 shows that levels of dissatisfaction were highest in social housing, and that lone-parent families were significantly more likely than all other types of household to be dissatisfied. A clear social class gradient, and regional variations in area dissatisfaction, were also observed (with households in the North East, North West, Yorkshire and Humberside and London being less satisfied). There were also differences by ethnicity.

Table 13.7: Proportion of households with high levels of area dissatisfaction, England

Socio-demographic characteristics	% scoring 4 or more	Total number of households (1,000s)
All	9.7	19,198
Region		
London	14.0	2,699
South East	5.9	2,898
South West	5.8	1,995
Eastern	5.3	2,309
East Midlands	7.9	1,540
West Midlands	10.4	2,017
Yorkshire and Humberside	10.8	2,038
North East	18.1	980
North West	12.9	2,764
Social class of head of household		
I	4.5	1,351
II	7.1	5,048
IIIN	10.1	2,780
IIIM	10.9	5,295
IV	12.5	2,800
V	14.0	1,063
Other	10.3	909
Ethnicity of head of household		
White	9.7	18,319
Black	9.5	329
Indian	9.3	242
Pakistani/Bangladeshi	13.0	136
Other	10.4	216
Household structure		
Couple, no dependent children	8.5	7,002
Couple, with dependent children	9.1	4,694
Lone parent	22.2	1,101
Large adult household	8.8	1,183
Single male	11.1	2,241
Single female	8.3	3,024

Source: Burrows and Rhodes (1998), Table 2.4, p. 9

One-off community studies have also examined the issue of poor neighbourhoods. For example, Mumford (2000), focusing on low-income areas in East London, found high levels of neighbourhood dissatisfaction. Between two and three out of ten respondents were dissatisfied with their area, compared to the national Survey of English Housing average of 13 per cent. Concerns for children included safety, drugs, pollution, lack of facilities, lack of play opportunities in flats, and paedophiles. Related research by the same author in the same area has more recently highlighted the community spirit within such neighbourhoods (Mumford and Power, 2003), although worryingly found increased levels of worry about the security of the neighbourhoods.

Most recently, the Save the Children surveys on poverty in Great Britain and Northern Ireland (Adelman *et al*, 2003; Monteith and McLaughlin, 2004) have also provided information on households' experiences of their neighbourhoods. In the British study, children in severe poverty were found to be three times as likely as children in non-severe poverty to live where parents were (slightly or very) dissatisfied with the area (41 per cent compared to 13 per cent), while children in non-severe poverty were twice as likely to live in areas where parents were dissatisfied compared to non-poor children (13 compared to 8 per cent). In the Northern Ireland study, 9 per cent of severely poor children lived in an area that their parents considered 'a fairly/very bad place to live', compared to 6 per cent of children in non-severe poverty and 1 per cent of non-poor children. As with housing quality, overall, a lower proportion of families in Northern Ireland considered they were living in poor neighbourhoods compared to British families, and over half of all children (57 per cent) in Northern Ireland lived in areas where no problems with the area were reported, compared to a quarter (26 per cent) of all children in Britain. Table 13.8 shows that the mean number of problems reported by parents was also higher in Britain, and that households in severe poverty reported more problems than those in non-severe poverty, and in turn, less than those in no poverty. The most commonly reported problems (from a list of potential issues) in Britain were 'teenagers hanging around the streets' (40 per cent of all children; 76 per cent of those in severe poverty) and 'dogs and dog mess' (40 per cent of all children; 56 per cent of those in severe poverty). In Northern Ireland, the most common problems were dog mess (20 per cent and 33 per cent of all children and those in severe poverty, respectively), drunkenness (12 and 21 per cent respectively), graffiti (11 and 17 per cent) and joyriding (10 and 15 per cent). Children in severe and non-severe poverty in Northern Ireland were more likely to live in areas that experienced problems with paramilitary behaviour and sectarian harassment, than non-poor children, although these problems were relatively rare overall (3–4 per cent of all children). It is important to note that there was a greater difference between 'severely' poor and 'non-severely' poor children in terms of the likelihood of living in a poor neighbourhood compared to likelihood of living in poor housing.

Table 13.8: Number (mean) of problems with area, by poverty status, Great Britain and Northern Ireland

| | Mean number of common problems with areas experienced | |
	Northern Ireland	Great Britain
No poverty	1.12	1.59
Non-severe poverty	2.66	2.94
Severe poverty	3.29	4.83
All children	1.94	2.34

Note: Base NI = 1,195; GB = 766
Source: Monteith and McLaughlin (2004), Table 5.5

Children's perspectives on neighbourhood and space

A number of studies have demonstrated that children and young people have strong views about their localities, in part possibly because they have fewer opportunities to escape their immediate neighbourhood than adults. Children have strong spatial awareness and tend to emphasise certain types of places as being good aspects of their neighbourhood, particularly ones where they can explore, meet with friends and have an element of freedom in their environment (Speak, 2000). Children have a particular need to play and tend to highlight the importance of spaces for this activity more than their parents (O'Brien, 2003).

Robertson and Walford (2000) used children as surveyors and found a stark contrast between the views of urban and rural 'surveyors': urban surveyors had a great desire for change centring around housing developments, loss of green space, traffic, pollution and litter, recreation and aesthetics, while rural surveyors wanted things to stay the same, preserving green spaces.

A number of studies have examined how children use space in some detail. O'Brien *et al* (2000) undertook a survey of 1,378 children (aged 10–14), and their parents, on how children use their local environment in a number of inner and outer London boroughs, as well as in a New Town (Hatfield). Table 13.9 shows that boys had greater freedom to roam and play outside more independently than girls, with boys more likely to get around by bicycle and use parks. There were also gender differences in perceptions of risk of unsafe places, with the greatest difference in the New Town area. Children from different ethnic backgrounds, and gender within this, were also found to use public space very differently. For example, in London, only 37 per cent of Tower Hamlets older Asian girls were allowed to play outside unaccompanied compared to 92 per cent of older Asian boys. Reasons for this included personal preference as well as fear, racism and parental restraint.

Table 13.9: Selected children's activities and perception of risk by gender and area

	Inner London		Outer London		New Town	
	Female	Male	Female	Male	Female	Male
	(n =	(n =	(n =	(n =	(n =	(n =
	334)	344)	187)	217)	199)	80)
Activities						
Child plays out without an adult	67%	84%	75%	87%	82%	93%
Visit to park in last week	35%	56%	51%	59%	37%	51%
Child rides bicycle on main road	30%	52%	46%	67%	56%	68%
Child allowed to cross the road	68%	78%	58%	67%	87%	80%
Perceptions of risk						
Feel there are unsafe places	42%	31%	44%	32%	42%	21%
Scared of unknown adults	61%	35%	63%	36%	58%	34%
Scared of young people	51%	46%	58%	49%	54%	47%

Source: O'Brien *et al* (2000), Table 3, p. 269

These data have been compared to data collected in the 1970s and 1990s, when evidence was found of a decrease in independent use of public space for 10–11-year-olds, but little change for the older group (13–14-year-olds) (Hillman *et al*, 1990). However, some aspects of use of the environment had changed. For example, whereas in 1970, 94 per cent of children walked to school unaccompanied, in 1998 only 47 per cent did (due to both an increase in being accompanied by a parent and increased car use). An increase in parental anxiety over children's safety in public space was also evident, with fewer parents allowing children out after dark: 6 per cent in 1990 and 2 per cent in 1998.

Conclusion

Data on house conditions are generally reliable, although they are not standardised by country and region. National surveys demonstrate that certain 'types' of households, particularly minority ethnic households, although generally not households with children, experience poorer housing. Overall, house conditions have improved significantly over time. Homelessness, however, has risen in the last few years, although this can be explained in part by the introduction of more generous homelessness legislation in all countries and regions of the UK. A considerable weight of evidence suggests that the effects of poor housing and homelessness are considerable on children. Poor neighbourhoods affect a significant proportion of households with children, with lone parents and minority ethnic households in particular being over-represented in these areas.

Studies have shown that children have strong feelings and perspectives on their local neighbourhoods, tending to value outside and play space more than adults. Despite this, data suggest that young people's movements are more restricted than they were a number of decades ago.

14 Conclusion

Jonathan Bradshaw

This new edition of *The Well-being of Children in the UK* is able to provide a more up-to-date picture of children's lives. The previous edition (published in 2002) contained data only up to 2000 and many of them related either to the period before the election of the Labour Government or before the Government had released itself from the shackles of its election commitment to maintain the previous Conservative Government's spending plans. It was also before most of the new measures in pursuit of the objective to end child poverty had been implemented.

Now, in 2005, we are able to present a more modern picture. Reviewing that picture generally we can conclude that progress is being made – on the whole things are getting better for children in the UK.

- The remarkable buoyancy of the UK labour market has undoubtedly been of critical benefit to children. At the time of writing (November 2004) the unemployment (claimant count) rate is at its lowest level since July 1975, the employment rate is at record level, vacancies are up and redundancies are down and, although inactivity rates are slightly up, it is thought that this is to do with the increased number of students. Lone parents have benefited from high labour demand and the proportion in employment has been rising. Nevertheless, the proportion of children living in workless households in the UK is comparatively high and unemployment is very heavily concentrated. A recent report by the Social Exclusion Unit (2004) found that in the worst affected 1 per cent of streets in England more than half of all adults are out of work, and in some streets almost all adults are out of work.

- There have been substantial improvements since 1999 in the real level of in-work and out-of-work benefits for families with children. The income support scales for children with parents out of employment have more than doubled in real terms, child benefit has been increased and linked to the retail price index, child tax credits have been linked to the earnings index for this Parliament and, together with the minimum wage, have boosted the incomes of families with children in employment. So the safety net is more generous to children and so are the benefits of parents working outside the home.

- In the 2002 public expenditure settlement very substantial increases in public expenditure were announced and the effects of these have been coming on stream, mainly benefiting the NHS, the education budget and transport. There was some anxiety expressed by the House of Commons Work and Pensions Select Committee (2004) that these increases (especially on health and transport) were not necessarily benefiting children, and that mainstream services were not gearing their efforts sufficiently to the needs of poor children. However, the 2004 Spending Review (HM Treasury, 2004a) announced further increases in expenditure and, together with HM Treasury's Child Poverty Review (2004c) published at the same time, detailed new targets for policies for children and extra expenditure to benefit education, transport, childcare, housing and homelessness. There was also a welcome emphasis on gearing mainstream services to contribute to the child poverty strategy, and a 'child poverty accord' between central and local government has been established to that end.

- The evidence base on child well-being has been improving. New information on child well-being is emerging from the 2001 census, the Family and Child Survey (FaCS), the Millennium Cohort Study and the Scottish Household Survey. Enhancements to the British Household Panel Survey (BHPS) in Northern Ireland, Wales and Scotland will provide national-level data for the first time. The Northern Ireland Family Resources Survey and the Northern Ireland replication of the Poverty and Social Exclusion Survey provide new sources of evidence there. In addition, more use is being made of administrative statistics, especially in the context of the indices of local deprivation.

- Children's Commissioners have been appointed in Wales, Scotland and Northern Ireland, and England intends to establish one.

- A *National Service Framework for Children, Young People and Maternity Services* (Department of Health, 2004) has been published in England and this, together with the Change for Children Programme, seeks to structure policies for children with regard to their outcomes in terms of well-being and well-becoming, following the Department for Education and Skills (DfES) outcomes framework.

- In central government, through the devolved administrations and in local government, there are welcome moves to involve children and young people in the planning, provision and evaluation of services.

One impetus for this has come from the European Union (EU) which, following the Lisbon and Nice summits, set up an 'open method of co-ordination' to make a 'decisive impact on the eradication of poverty and social exclusion by 2010'. One of the objectives set was to 'mobilise all relevant bodies'. All EU countries had to write National Action Plans (NAPs) on Social Inclusion containing common primary and secondary indicators (the so-called Laeken Indicators) and although these indicators are more or less blind to children, child poverty rates are being published by the EU, child poverty has become a theme in the 2004 NAPs process, and the children's non-governmental organisations are lobbying at EU level for children to be given a much higher profile in the future of the NAPs process.

These developments have contributed to improvements in children's well-being.
- Child poverty rates have fallen and the Government will meet its objective to reduce child poverty by a quarter in five years from a 1998/99 base.
- Not all elements of child well-being have been improving but only two of the 23 *Opportunity for All* indicators for children and young people have been getting worse (obesity and child homelessness).

These achievements have been assisted by a beneficial labour market context but the demographic context has been much less benign – in two main ways.

First, most of the changes that have been taking place in the family context of children might be expected to have had a deleterious impact on their well-being. (These are discussed in more detail in Chapter 2.) Fewer children and smaller families may result in less pressure on services and resources inside and outside the family, though the increase in one-child families (together with restrictions on freedom to play) might lead to increased isolation and loneliness. However, the breakdown of parental relationships, separation, divorce, non-resident parents, shared parenting, lone parenting, increasingly complex relations with parents, step-parents, siblings, half-siblings and grandparents and other relatives, might be expected to be associated with increased poverty, disruption to education, reduced self-esteem and poorer physical and emotional health and behavioural problems.

Second, in parallel with the reduction in the number of children, there is the increase in the number of elderly people with their needs for services and benefits competing with those needed by children. Some influential commentators (eg, Esping-Andersen and Sarasa, 2003) have suggested that children may well lose out in the competition for scarce public resources, not least because unlike children, pensioners have 'grey' power through their right to vote. In Chapter 3 we found that there was little evidence so far (to 1998) that children were losing in the competition for resources with the elderly in Britain or in most other countries. However, there must be competition at the margin, given scarce resources. This demographic challenge to child well-being needs to be watched.

The evidence base

As argued above the evidence base on the well-being of children has been improving. However, there are still some important lacunae, in particular the following.

- The comparative information on child well-being leaves much to be desired. The UNICEF Innocenti Centre in its *Report Card Series* has demonstrated how valuable international comparisons can be. However, the *Luxembourg Income Study* – the main source of the UNICEF comparisons of child poverty – is dated and enables only a purely income-based analysis.

- The Laeken Primary and Secondary Indicators adopted by the EU Social Inclusion process more or less ignore children, are very economistic and reliant on the *European Community Household Panel*. The latest data available from this are for 2001, the replacement *Survey of Income and Living Conditions* enters the field over the next few years and data on all EU countries will not be available until 2007. Meanwhile there will be a hiatus in comparative data on the well-being of children.

- The international project *Monitoring and Measuring Child Well-being*[1] has established a set of domains and sub-domains on child well-being but not yet had the resources to make progress with identifying sources of data that would enable international comparisons.

In England, the DfES, as part of the development of its child outcomes framework, has come up against a lack of evidence in a number of key domains, such as bullying, violence, mental health, and access to transport. These, and

---

[1] http://multinational-indicators.chapinhall.org/

many other elements of child well-being, can only be monitored by new empirical activity – a survey of children.

We have a survey of young people in the youth survey element of the BHPS and data from that have been used in this report. But only young people aged 11–15 are interviewed in that survey – and as an adjunct to the interviews with adults. So its scope is limited. The FaCS may interview young people from 2005/06 but again only those aged 11–15. The Millennium Cohort Study is providing new data on babies and infants and we have drawn on it in this edition. There have been ad hoc surveys of child health and child mental health undertaken by the Office for National Statistics (ONS). The Children and Young People's Unit was considering launching a survey in order to provide evidence for the outcomes framework, but now, in a more limited exercise, the DfES seems to be seeking to rely on a Home Office-sponsored survey on citizenship among young people. It is extraordinary how important the WHO Health Behaviour in School-aged Children (HBSC) study is as a source of evidence on UK children.

The UK needs a full-blown national survey of children. It is quite possible to interview children aged seven or even younger with appropriate techniques. We need a survey that attempts to discover what children think about their lives, covering their attitudes, activities and aspirations, their fears, worries and concerns, their physical and social behaviour, their satisfactions and complaints, their diet, values and feelings. Ideally such a survey should have a cohort design, following the same children every two years or so over time. The most efficient way of collecting the data would be to have a split-age cohort – children aged say 7, 10, 13 and 17 with data collected on their schools, families and neighbourhoods.

There is also potential for developing the techniques employed in the 2004 English Index of Deprivation to produce an index of child well-being at small-area level. Some of the domains in the English Index already include data on children. Thus the income domain includes administrative data on children on income-tested benefits that we have used in Chapter 3. The education domain collects data on educational attainment at small-area level, and there are elements relevant to children in the other domains. However, it would be quite possible to build a child-based index for all domains. This would provide valuable information for those seeking to direct children's services at local level to those most in need, and it could also be used as a source for monitoring spatial variations in the well-being of children over time.

Variations in child well-being

Devolution in the UK provides an important context for understanding child well-being. How and why does the well-being of children differ in different parts of the UK? Comparisons between the different regions and countries of the UK have never been easy – sometimes no data are available at a national level. Sometimes the data that are there are not comparable. It may be the case that making such comparisons has become more difficult – as responsibilities for the provision of services have become devolved, so have the statistics. One of the lessons learned from the UK experience of the EU National Action Plan for Social Inclusion, was how difficult it was to collect comparable tertiary indicators for the devolved administrations. Department for Work and Pensions officials responsible for writing the report had to attempt to re-join the UK countries. Throughout this report we have sought to include the relevant data on all countries and regions on a consistent basis and make comparisons between them. Table 14.1 brings together some of the most salient comparisons to represent a summary. We are reliant for too many of these comparisons on the WHO HBSC survey of 11-, 13- and 15-year-olds with samples in England, Wales and Scotland but not Northern Ireland. There were no comparable data on children's time and space (though some could be obtained now by the secondary analysis of the BHPS), on childcare, crime and very little on child maltreatment.

There is really no consistent pattern.

- It might be possible to argue that children in **Wales** have the worst well-being of the countries of the UK. Wales has the highest child poverty rate, lone-mother birth rate, lowest proportion taking up MMR, highest proportion of girls smoking and with drug and alcohol problems, highest obesity rates for boys and the lowest physical activity rates, more TV watching among girls, lowest eating of fruit and vegetables, lowest life satisfaction, highest proportion leaving care at 16, worst educational outcomes, highest truancy rates and more unfit dwellings. However, Wales also has the lowest infant death rate in 2002.
- **Northern Ireland** has the lowest low birth weight rate, highest take-up of MMR, less teenage drinking, fewer looked-after children, fewer school leavers with no grades and more with two A Levels and the highest proportion with Key Stage 2 in maths.
- **Scotland** has the highest proportion of lone parents, high infant mortality rate, a higher proportion of young people eating fruit and vegetables but also

sweets and soft drinks, the highest level of crime and illicit drug use, the highest rate of male youth suicides, more looked-after children, more 16-year-olds achieving GCEs, and the best scores on Maths and reading.

- **England** has the lowest proportion of lone-parent families and births to single mothers, the lowest child poverty rate, the highest proportion of low birth weight, lowest rate of self-reported poor health, highest rate of girl obesity, highest rate of physical activity, highest level of bullying, lowest proportion of children in care leaving at 16, lowest Key Stage 2 achievements and the lowest truancy.

Table 14.1: Comparative summary of child well-being across the UK

Indicator	England	Wales	Scotland	Northern Ireland
% children under 16 (2002)	19.8	19.9	19.9	23.2
Total period fertility rate (2002)	1.65	1.64	1.48	1.77
% children not white (2001)	10.8 (England and Wales)		3.2	1.0
% of households with dependent children (2001)	27.2	28.2	26.0	34.0
% of households with dependent children who are lone-parent households (2001)	23.5	25.9	26.9	23.8
% births to mothers not living with a partner (2001)	13	18	14	17
% children in households with equivalent income less than 60% median before housing costs (2002/03)	20	25	23	22
% children in households with equivalent income less than 60% median after housing costs (2002/03)	32	30	27	27
Still births per 1,000 (2002)	5.6	5.4	5.4	5.7
Infant death rate per 1,000 (2002)	5.2	4.5	5.3	4.7
% low birth weight births (2002)	7.8	7.3	7.2	6.3
Live births per 100 women under 20 (2002)	28	35	28	24
MMR take-up (2002/03)	82	81	87	89 (2001/02)
% 13-year-old boys rating their health fair or poor*	18.9	24.5	19.1	–
% 13-year-old girls rating their health fair or poor*	27.9	39.2	23.6	–
Drinking beer, wine or spirits at least weekly boys aged 13*	34	32	19	14
Drinking beer, wine or spirits at least weekly girls aged 13*	25	24	19	6

Indicator	England	Wales	Scotland	Northern Ireland
Boys aged 13 smoking every day*	7	6	3	7
Girls aged 13 smoking every day*	9	12	6	10
% young boys experiencing problems due to alcohol/drug use*	39	39	41	48
% young girls experiencing problems due to alcohol/drug use *	43	50	47	43
Obesity rates boys*	4.5	5.0	2.6	–
Obesity rates girls*	3.0	2.4	2.4	–
% boys undertaking recommended physical activity each day*	51.1	43.6	46.4	–
% girls undertaking recommended physical activity each day*	32.6	28.1	30.7	–
% boys watching four or more hours TV on a weekday*	31.3	31.1	31.6	–
% girls watching four or more hours TV on a weekday*	29.7	32.3	29.7	–
% boys eating vegetables daily*	25.9	19.5	30.5	–
% girls eating vegetables daily*	31.0	23.1	35.9	–
% boys eating fruit daily*	24.5	20.0	31.0	–
% girls eating fruit daily*	28.9	26.1	35.8	–
% boys eating sweets daily*	31.7	26.3	46.8	
% girls eating sweets daily*	31.5	27.4	42.9	
% boys drinking soft drinks daily*	40.6	37.6	50.9	
% girls drinking soft drinks daily*	36.4	35.4	43.5	
% boys aged 13 with above mean life satisfaction*	88	87	89	
% girls aged 13 with above mean life satisfaction*	85	78	81	
15–24 male suicide rate (2002)		11	30	18
15–24 female suicide rate		3	10	1
Rate per 1,000 children under 18 on the child protection register (2003)	2.4	3.4	2.1** (2002)	3.1 (2001)
% boys aged 11 bullied at least once in previous couple of months*	45	37	30	
% girls aged 11 bullied at least once in previous couple of months*	41	36	35	
% children looked after per 1,000 children under 18 (2003)	4.9	5.6	6.0	4.4
% children leaving care at 16/17	49	96	90	30
% children leaving care aged 16 or over with one or more GCSE/ GNVQ or equivalent (2003)	44	39	42	42
Educational attainment (% 5+ A–C 1–4 at Year 11) (2001/02)	51.6	50.5	60.4	58.7
Educational attainment (% no graded qualifications at Year 11)	5.4	7.6	4.6	4.4
% with two or more A levels or equivalent	37.6	30.6	39.4	43.4

Indicator	England	Wales	Scotland	Northern Ireland
Mean reading literacy proficiency score for 15-year-olds (2000)	523	–	526	519
Mean Maths literacy proficiency score for 15-year-olds (2000)	529	–	533	524
Mean sciences literacy proficiency for 15-year-olds (2000)	534		522	523
Achieving expected standard in Key Stage 2 English	74(2004)	76(2003)		75(2003)
Achieving expected standard in Key Stage 2 Maths	75(2004)	76(2003)		77(2003)
Achieving expected standard in Key Stage 2 Science	83(2004)	84(2003)		–
Truancy rates (% half-days missed) 2002/03	1.1	1.6	1.4	
% statemented pupils (2003)	3	3.5	2.1(2002)	3.4
% unfit dwellings	4.2	8.5	0.9	4.9

*HBSC 2001/02
** under 16

Is the well–being of children improving or deteriorating in the UK?

This is the question that this review has sought to answer. Well-being varies by country and region, by the age of the child, by gender, family type, ethnicity and socio-economic level. These variations are reviewed in the foregoing chapters. In Table 14.2 we attempt to make an overall judgement based on what trend data are available. There are few trend data on lifestyle, time and space, mental health and child maltreatment. It is sometimes difficult to decide whether a trend is a well-being improvement or deterioration – for example, is it good that children are spending more time with their parents if this is associated with a loss of independence? Or is the decline in playgroup places a deterioration in the face of increasing nursery and childcare places? It is also a matter of judgement what the overall conclusion *should* be.

The lists of improving and deteriorating indicators are more or less equal in length. Most income/living standard indicators are improving. Most indicators of educational attainment are improving. There are a large number of health indicators moving in the wrong direction. The record level of child homelessness is a huge blot on the record. On balance, our judgement is that the UK can claim that children's lives are getting better. However, there are still far too many domains of child well-being which are getting worse or not improving.

Table 14.2: Assessment of trends in child well-being in the UK

Well-being improving	No change in well-being	Well-being deteriorating
• Absolute child poverty • Relative child poverty • Children in workless families • Infant mortality • Child accidental deaths • Breastfeeding • Reporting good health • Increased use of contraception • Smoking • 15–24 suicide rate • Time spent with parents • Domestic violence • Adoptions up • Drop in young people leaving care at 16 • Proportion leaving care with one or more GCSE • Daycare nursery places • Out-of-school places • Educational qualifications • Narrowing class differential in attainment • NEET numbers falling • SEN in mainstream schools • English, Maths and Science at Key Stages 2 and 3 • Truancy • Housing conditions • School exclusions	• Persistent child poverty • Child mortality • Whooping cough immunisation • Diphtheria, tetanus and polio immunisation • Longstanding illness • Limited longstanding illness • Risky sexual behaviour • Teenage conception rate • Playing sport • 0–14 suicide number • Youth crime • Illicit drug use • Victimisation • English, Maths and Science at Key Stage 1 • Statemented pupils	• Stillbirths • Class gap in infant mortality • Low birth weight • MMR vaccination • Measles • Mumps • Asthma • Sexually transmitted diseases • Diabetes • HIV/AIDS • Alcohol consumption • Obesity • Conduct, hyperactive and emotional problems • Playing out/liberty to play • Children born to drug users • Children looked after for longer periods • Increase in unaccompanied asylum-seeking children • Childminder places • Playgroup places • Drug and violent crime • Girls offending • Child homelessness

References and Bibliography

4 Nations Child Policy Network (2003) *Child Policy Review 2003*, London: National Children's Bureau, www.childpolicy.org.uk.

Adelman, L., Middleton, S. and Ashworth, K. (2003) *Britain's Poorest Children: Severe and persistent poverty and social exclusion*, London: Save the Children.

Adelstein, A. and Mardon, C. (1985) 'Suicides 1962–74', *Population Trends*, 2, pp. 13–18.

Advisory Council on the Misuse of Drugs (2003) *Hidden Harm: Responding to the needs of children of problem drug users*, London: Home Office.

Agerbo, E., Nordentoft, M., Mortensen, P. B. (2002) 'Familial, psychiatric and socioeconomic risk factors for suicide in young people: Nested case-control study', *BMJ*, 325, pp. 74–77.

Aldridge, J. and Becker, S. (1993) *Children who care – inside the world of young carers*, Loughborough: Department of Social Sciences.

Aldridge, J. and Becker, S. (2003) *Children Caring for Parents with Mental Illness: Perspectives of young carers, parents and professionals*, Bristol: The Policy Press.

Analytical Services Division ETLLD (2004) *Analysis of 16–19-year-olds not in employment, education or training in the 2001 Census: Summary Report*.

Anderson, I. and Tulloch, D. (2000) *Pathways through Homelessness: A review of the research evidence*, Edinburgh: Scottish Homes.

Armstrong, G. (2004) *Young Carers' Health and Well-being: A pilot study*, Edinburgh: Young Carers Project.

Atkinson, A., Cantillon, B., Marlier, E. and Nolan, B. (2002) *Social Indicators: The EU and social inclusion*, Oxford: University Press.

Audit Commission (1996) *Misspent Youth: Young people and crime*, London: Audit Commission.

Audit Commission (2002) *Special Needs: A mainstream issue*, London: Audit Commission.

Audit Scotland – HMIe (2003) *Moving to Mainstream: The inclusion of pupils with special educational need in mainstream schools*, Edinburgh: Auditor General Accounts Commission.

Aye Maung, N. (1995) *Young People, Victimisation and the Police: British Crime Survey findings on experiences and attitudes of 12–15-year-olds*, Home Office Research Study No. 140, London: Home Office.

Ayers, M., Murray, L. and Fiti, R. (2003) *Arrests for Notifiable Offences and the Operation of Certain Police Powers under PACE, England and Wales, 2002/03*, London: Home Office, Research Development and Statistics Directorate.

Balding, J., Regis, D. and Wise, A. (1998) *No Worries? Young people and mental health*, Exeter: Schools Health Education Unit.

Baldwin, S. and Hirst, M. (2002) 'Children as carers', in J. Bradshaw (ed.), *The Well-being of Children in the UK*, London: Save the Children/The University of York.

Ball, S. (2003) *Class Strategies and the Education Market*, London: Routledge Falmer.

Banks, P., Cogan, N., Deeley, S., Hill, M., Riddell, S. and Tisdall, K. (2001) 'Seeing the Invisible: Children and young people affected by disability', *Disability & Society*, Vol. 16, pp. 797–814.

Banks, P., Gallagher, E., Hill, M. and Riddell, S. (2002) *Young Carers: Assessment and services, literature review of identification, needs assessment and service provision for young carers and their families*, Scottish Executive Central Research Unit.

Barn, R. (1993) *Black Children in the Public Care System*, London: Batsford.

Barn, R., Andrew, L. and Mantovani, N. (forthcoming) *Life After Care: A study of young people from different ethnic groups*, York: Joseph Rowntree Foundation.

Barn, R., Sinclair, R. and Ferdinand, D. (1997) *Acting on Principle: An examination of race and ethnicity in social services provision to children and families*. London: British Agencies for Adoption and Fostering.

Barnes, C., Mercer, G. and Shakespeare, T. (1999) *Exploring Disability*, London: Polity.

Barnes, M. *et al* (2004) *Families and Children in Britain: Findings from the 2002 Families and Children Survey*, Leeds: Department for Work and Pensions.

Bartecchi, C. E., MacKenzie, T. D. and Schrier, R. W. (1994) 'The human costs of tobacco use (I)', *New England Journal of Medicine*, 330, pp. 907–12. Cited in T. Bjarnason, A. G. Davidaviciene, P. Miller, A. Nociar, A. Pavlakis and E. Stergar (2003) 'Family structure and adolescent cigarette smoking in eleven European countries', *Addiction*, 98, pp. 815–24.

Barter, C. (1999) *Protecting children from racism and racial abuse: A research review*, NSPCC Research Findings.

Bassuk, E. L. and Perloff, J. N. (2001) 'Multiply homeless families: the insidious impact of violence', *Housing Policy Debate*, Vol. 12, Issue 2.

Bebbington, A. and Beecham, J. (2003) *Child Care Costs: Variation and unit costs*, Discussion paper 2021, Canterbury: Personal Social Services Research Unit, University of Kent.

Bebbington, A. and Miles, J. (1989) 'The background of children who enter local authority care', *British Journal of Social Work*, 19, 5, pp. 349–86.

Beck, U. and Beck-Gernsheim, E. (2002) *Individualization*, Sage: London.

Beinart, S., Anderson, B., Lee, S. and Utting, D. (2002) *Youth at Risk? A national survey of risk factors, protective factors and problem behaviour among young people in England, Scotland and Wales*, York: Communities that Care supported by the Joseph Rowntree Foundation.

Belanger, K., Beckett, W., Triche, E., Bracken, M. B., Holford, T. and Ren, P. (2003) 'Symptoms of wheeze and persistent cough in the first year of life: Association with indoor allergens, air contaminants and maternal history of asthma', *American Journal of Epidemiology*, 158, pp. 195–202.

Bennett, J. (2003) 'Starting Strong: The persistent division between care and education', in *Journal of Early Childhood Research*, Vol. 1 (1) pp. 21–48.

Beresford, B. (2002) 'Children's health', in J. Bradshaw (ed.) *The Well-being of Children in the UK*, London: Save the Children/The University of York.

Bergman, M. M. and Scott, J. (2001) 'Young adolescents' well-being and health-risk behaviours: Gender and socio-economic differences', *Journal of Adolescence*, 24, pp. 183–97.

Berridge, D. (1997) *Foster Care: A research review*. London: The Stationery Office.

Berthoud, R. (2001) 'Teenage births to ethnic minority women', *Population Trends* 104, London: The Stationery Office.

Better Regulation Task Force (2004) *The Regulation of Child Employment*, London: Better Regulation Task Force.

Biehal, N., Clayden, J., Stein, M. and Wade, J. (1995) *Moving On: Young people and leaving care schemes*, London: HMSO.

Bjarnason, T., Davidaviciene, A. G., Miller, P., Nociar, A., Pavlakis, A., Stergar, E. (2003) 'Family structure and adolescent cigarette smoking in eleven European countries', *Addiction*, 98, pp. 815–24.

Blair, P. S., Fleming, P. J., Bensley, D., Smith, I., Bacon, C., Taylor, E., Berry, J., Golding, J. and Tripp, J. (1996) 'Smoking and sudden infant death syndrome: Results from the 1993–95 case-control study for confidential inquiry into stillbirths and deaths in infancy', *British Medical Journal*, 313, pp. 195–98.

Blakely, T., Atkinson, J., Kiro, C., Blaiklock, A. and D'Souza, A. (2003) 'Child mortality, socio-economic position, and one-parent families: Independent associations by age and cause of death', *International Journal of Epidemiology*, 32, pp. 410–18.

Boney-McCoy, S. and Finkelhor, D. (1995) 'Prior victimisation: A risk factor for child sexual abuse and for PTSD-related symptomatology among sexually abused youth', *Child Abuse & Neglect*, Volume 19, pp. 1401–21.

Boyson, R. (2002), *Equal Protection for Children*, NSPCC.

Bradbury, B., Jenkins, S. and Micklewright (2001) 'Child poverty dynamics in seven nations', in B. Bradbury, S. Jenkins and J. Micklewright (eds) *The Dynamics of Child Poverty in Industrialised Countries*, Cambridge University Press.

Bradshaw, J. (1990) *Child Poverty and Deprivation in the UK*, London: National Children's Bureau.

Bradshaw, J. (2001) *Poverty: The outcomes for children*, London: Family Policy Studies Centre/National Children's Bureau.

Bradshaw, J. (ed.) (2002) *The Well-being of Children in the UK*, London: Save the Children/The University of York.

Bradshaw, J. and Finch, N. (2005 forthcoming) 'Deprivation and area variations in teenage conceptions and abortions', *Journal of Family Planning and Reproductive Health*.

Bradshaw, J. and Mayhew, E. (2003) 'Are welfare states financing their growing elderly populations at the expense of their children?', *Family Matters*, Issue 66, pp. 20–25.

Bradshaw, J., Kemp, P., Baldwin, S. and Rowe, A. (2003) *The Drivers of Social Exclusion: A review of the literature*, London: Social Exclusion Unit.

Brewer, M. (2004) *Will the Government hit its child poverty target in 2004–05?*, Briefing Note No 47, London: The Institute for Fiscal Studies.

Briggs, S. (2002) 'Working with the risk of suicide in young people', *Journal of Social Work Practice*, 16, 2, pp. 135–48.

British Household Panel Survey (2002) Youth Questionnaire.

British Medical Association (1986) *Young People and Alcohol*, London: British Medical Association.

British Medical Association (2003) *Adolescent Health*, London: British Medical Association.

Britton, L., Chatrik, B., Coles, B., Craig, G. Hylton, C. and Mumtaz, S. (2002)

Missing Connexions: The career dynamics and welfare needs of black and minority ethnic young people at the margins, Bristol: The Policy Press.

Broad, B. (1998) *Young People Leaving Care: Life after the Children Act 1989*, London: Jessica Kingsley.

Broad, B. (2003) *After the Act: Implementing the Children (Leaving Care) Act 2000*, Leicester: Action on Aftercare Consortium/De Montfort University.

Brownlie, J. (2002) *Disciplining Children: Research with parents in Scotland*, Scottish Executive.

Bruegel, I. and, Smith, J. (1999) *Taking Risks: An analysis of the risks of homelessness for young people in London*, London: Safe in the City.

Brynin, M. and Scott, J. (1996) *Young People, Health and the Family*, London: Health Education Authority.

BUPA (2004) http://hcd2.bupa.co.uk/fact_sheets/html/child_obesity.html

Burrows, R. and Rhodes, D. (1998) *Unpopular places? Area disadvantage and the geography of misery in England*, Bristol: Policy Press/Joseph Rowntree Foundation.

Cancer Research UK (2003) *Child Cancer Factsheet December 2003.* www.cancerresearchuk.org

Carley, M., Campbell, M., Kearns, A., Wood, M. and Young, R. (2000) *Regeneration in the 21st century: Policies into practice: An overview of the Joseph Rowntree Foundation Area Regeneration Programme*, Bristol: The Policy Press.

Casey, L., Davies, P., Kalambouka, A., Nelson, N. and Boyle, N. (2004) *The influence of schooling on the aspirations of young people with special educational needs*, Stoke on Trent: University of Staffordshire.

Cawson, P. (2002) *Child maltreatment in the family: The experience of a national sample of young people*, NSPCC.

Cawson, P., Wattam, C., Brooker, S. and Kelly, C. (2000) *Child Maltreatment in the UK: A study of the prevalence of child abuse and neglect*, NSPCC.

Caya, M. L., and Liem, J. H. (1998) 'The role of sibling support in high-conflict families', *American Journal of Orthopsychiatry*, Vol. 68, pp. 327–33.

Central Health Monitoring Unit (1995) *Asthma: an epidemiological overview*, London: HMSO.

Central Survey Unit (2002) *Young Persons' Behaviour and Attitudes Survey Bulletin – October 2000–November 2000*, Belfast: Northern Ireland Statistics and Research Agency.

Chadwick, D. L. (2002) 'Letter to the Editor re 'The incidence of severe physical abuse in Wales' (Sibert *et al*, 2002)', *Child Abuse & Neglect*, 26, p. 1207.

Chahal, K. and Julienne, L. (1999) *"We can't all be white!": Racist victimisation in the UK*, York: Publishing Services/Joseph Rowntree Foundation.

Champion, L. A., Goodall, G. and Rutter, M. (1995) 'Behaviour problems in childhood and stressors in early adult life. A 20-year follow-up of London schoolchildren', *Psychol Med*, 25, 2, pp. 231–46.

Chang, E. C. (2002) 'Predicting suicide ideation in an adolescent population: Examining the role of social problem-solving as a moderator and a mediator', *Personality and Individual Differences*, 32, pp. 1279–91.

Charlton, J., Kelly, S., Dunnell, K., Evans, B., Jenkins, R. and Wallis, R. (1992) 'Trends in suicide deaths in England and Wales', in OPCS, *Population Trends*, No 69, Autumn, London: HMSO.

Cheung, S-Y and Heath, A. (1994) 'After care: The education and occupation of adults who have been in care', *Oxford Review of Education*, 20, 3, pp. 361–72.

Cheung, S-Y. and Buchanan, A. (1997) 'High malaise scores in adulthood of children and young people who have been in care', *Journal of Child Psychology and Psychiatry*, 38, pp. 575–80.

Children and Young People's Unit (CYPU) (2001) *Tomorrow's Future: Building a strategy for children and young people*, London: Children and Young People's Unit.

Children and Young People's Unit (CYPU) (2001a) *Learning to Listen: Core principles for the involvement of children and young people*, Children and Young People's Unit.

Children and Young People's Unit (2003a) *An outcomes framework for a national strategy for children and young people*.

Children and Young People's Unit (2003b) *Consultation on Building a Strategy: Children and young people's well-being: what's important* (unpublished paper).

Children and Young People's Unit (2003c) *Strategy For Children and Young People In Northern Ireland: Working paper on the emerging strategy*, Office of the First Minister and Deputy First Minister, October 2003.

Children and Young People's Unit (2003d) *The Next Step: Developing a strategy for children and young people in Northern Ireland*, Office of the First Minister and Deputy First Minister. http://www.allchildrenni.gov.uk/nextstep.pdf

Children and Young People's Unit (2004) *Part Four – Improving the lives of children and young people: A strategic framework*.

Children's Rights Alliance (2002) *State of Children's Rights in England: A report on the implementation of the Convention on the Rights of the Child in England*, Children's Rights Alliance for England.

Christensen, P. (2002) 'Why more "Quality Time" is not on the top of children's lists: The "Qualities of Time" for children', *Children and Society*, 16, 2, pp. 77–88.

Citizens Advice Bureau (2004) Evidence to the Work and Pensions Inquiry on Child Poverty, Ev 200.

Clarke, L., Bradshaw, J. and Williams, J. (1999) *Family Diversity and Poverty and the Mental Well-being of Young People*, Unpublished paper, London School of Hygiene and Tropical Medicine and University of York.

Cleaver, H. *et al* (1999) *Children's needs – parenting capacity. The impact of parental mental illness, problem alcohol and drug use, and domestic violence on children's development*, London: Department of Health.

Coffey, A. (2001) *Education and Social Change*, Buckingham: Open University Press.

Coleman, J. (1999) *Key Data on Adolescence*, Brighton: Trust for the Study of Adolescence.

Coles, B. (2000) *Joined-up Youth Research, Policy and Practice: A new agenda for change?*, Leicester: Youth Work Press.

Coles, B. and Kenwright, H. (2002) 'Educational attainment', in J. Bradshaw (ed.) *The Well-being of Children in the UK*, London: Save the Children/The University of York.

Coles, B. and Maile, S. (2002) 'Children, young people and crime', in Bradshaw, J. (ed.) *The Well-being of Children in the UK*, London: Save the Children/The University of York.

Collishaw, S., Maughan, B., Goodman, R. and Pickles, A. (2004) 'Time trends in adolescent mental health', *Journal of Child Psychology and Psychiatry*, 45, 8, pp. 1350–62.

Commission of the European Union (2003), *Joint Report on Social Inclusion: Summarising the Results of the Examination of national Action Plans for Social Inclusion (2003–2005)* {SEC (2002) 1425}COM 773. Statistical Annex.

Condon, J. and Smith, N. (2003) *Prevalence of Drug Use: Key findings from the 2002/03 British Crime Survey*, Findings 229, London: Home Office.

Conway, L. and Morgan, D. (2001) *Injury Prevention*, London: BMJ Books.

Corak, M. (2004) *Child Poverty in Rich Nations 2004*, UNICEF Innocenti Centre, Florence: UNICEF

Cornia, G. and Danziger, S. (1997) *Child Poverty and Deprivation in the Industrialised Countries 1994–1995*, Oxford: Clarendon Press.

Council of Europe (2004) *Recent Demographic Developments in Europe*, Strasbourg: Council of Europe.

Craig, C., Glendinning, C. and Clarke K. (1996) 'Policy on the hoof: The British Child Support Act in practice', in M. May, E. Brunsdon and G. Craig (eds), *Social Policy Review*, 8, London: SPA.

Craig, T. (1996) *Off to a Bad Start*, London: Mental Health Foundation.

Cree, V. E. (2002*) Under Pressure. A Study of Mental Health Needs of Young Carers*, for Edinburgh Young Carers Project, Edinburgh: University of Edinburgh, Department of Social Work.

Croucher, K. (2002) 'Unintentional injuries', in J. Bradshaw (ed.) *The Well-being of Children in the UK*, London: Save the Children/The University of York.

Crowley, A. and Vulliamy, C. (2002) *Listen up! Children and young people talk about poverty*, London: Save the Children.

Croxford, L. (2000) *Inequality in Attainment at Age 16: A 'home international' comparison*, Briefing No 19, Edinburgh: Centre for Educational Sociology, University of Edinburgh

Croxford, L. (2003) *Participation in Science, Engineering and Technology. Evidence from the Scottish School Leavers Survey*, Special CES Briefing No 30, Edinburgh: Centre for Educational Sociology, University of Edinburgh.

Cunningham-Burley, S., Jamieson, L., Morton, S., Adam., R. and McFarlane, V. (2002) *Sure Start Scotland Mapping Exercise*, Edinburgh: Scottish Executive.

Cunnington, A. (2001) 'What's so bad about teenage pregnancy?', *Journal of Family Planning and Reproductive Health Care*, 27, pp. 36–41.

Currie, C., Fairgrieve, J., Akhar, P., Currie, D. (2003) *Scottish Schools Adolescent Lifestyle and Substance Use Survey (SALSUS) National Report: Smoking, drinking and drug use among 13 and 15-year-olds in Scotland in 2002*, ISD, Scottish Executive.

Currie, C., Hurrleman, K., Settertobulte, W., Smith, R. and Todd, J. (2000) *Health and Health Behaviour among Young People: Health Behaviour in School-aged Children: A WHO Cross-National Study (HBSC) International Report*, Copenhagen: World Health Organization, Regional Office for Europe.

Currie, C., Roberts, C., Morgan, A., Smith, R., Settertobulte W., Samdal, O. and Rasmussen, V. B. (2004) *Young people's health in context. Health Behaviour in School-aged Children (HBSC) Study: International report from the 2001/02 survey*, Copenhagen: World Health Organization Regional Office for Europe.

Curtis, K. and Roberts, H. (in press) *Effective interventions to tackle inequalities in children's health*, London: London Health Commission.

Cutler, D. (2003) *Organisational Standards and Young People's Participation in Public Decision-Making*, Fife: Carnegie Young People's Initiative.

D'Souza, L. and Garcia, J. (2004) 'Improving services for disadvantaged childbearing women', *Child: Care, Health and Development*, 30: 599–611.

Dale, A., Williams, M. and Dodgeon, B. (1996) *Housing Deprivation and Social Change*, London: HMSO.

Darton, D., Hirsch, D. and Stelitz, J. (2003) *Tackling Disadvantage: A 20-year enterprise*, York: Joseph Rowntree Foundation.

Davey, T. L. (1998) 'Homeless children and stress: An empirical study', *Journal of Social Distress and the Homeless*, Vol. 7, No. 1.

Davies, P. (1999) *The Impact of Paid Employment on Young People in Full-time Education*, Further Education Development Agency.

Dearden, C. and Becker, S. (2000) *Growing up Caring: Vulnerability and transition to adulthood – young carers' experiences*, Leicester: Youth Work Press.

Dedman, D. J., Gunnell, D., Davey Smith, G. and Frankel, S. (2001) 'Childhood housing conditions and later mortality in the Boyd Orr Cohort', *Journal of Epidemiology and Community Health*, 55,1, pp. 10–15.

Department of Education, Northern Ireland (DENI) (1999) *Northern Ireland Suspension and Expulsion Study (1996/97)*. Research Briefing 1, 1999.

Department of Education, Northern Ireland (DENI) (2003) *Percentage of Statemented Pupils by Education and Library Board 2001/2002*, http://www.deni.gov.uk/facts_figures/elb/PercentofStatemented PupilsPage10.pdf, July 2004.

Department of Education, Northern Ireland (DENI) (2004a) *Education Statistics*, http://www.deni.gov.uk/facts_figures/elb/EducationAchievePages2–6.pdf, Accessed July 2004.

Department of Education, Northern Ireland (DENI) (2004b) *Suspensions and Expulsions procedures: Proposals for change*, http://www.deni.gov.uk/about/seconsultation/Proposals_for_Change.pdf, July 2004.

Department for Education and Employment (DfEE) (1999a) *Circular No 10/99 – Social Inclusion: Pupil support*, London: DfEE.

Department for Education and Employment (1999b) *Circular No 11/99 – Social Inclusion: The LEA role in pupil support*, London: DfEE.

Department for Education and Employment (2000) *Connexions: The best start in life for every young person*, Nottingham: DfEE.

Department for Education and Science (1994) *Code of Practice and the Identification of Special Educational Needs*, London: Department for Education.

Department for Education and Skills (2001) *Permanent Exclusions from Schools, England 1999/2000*, http://www.dfes.gov.uk/statistics/DB/SFR/s0275/sfr32-2001.pdf

Department for Education and Skills (2002) *Children's Day Care Facilities at 31st of March 2002: England*.

Department for Education and Skills (2003a) *Children Looked After in England: 2002-03*, London: The Stationery Office.

Department for Education and Skills (2003b) *Every Child Matters*.

Department for Education and Skills (2003c) *Pupil Absences in Schools in England, 2002/2003* (Provisional), http://www.dfes.gov.uk/rsgateway/DB/SFR/s000412/sfr24-2003.pdf, July 2004.

Department for Education and Skills (2003d) *Statistics of Education: Special educational needs in England: January 2003*.

Department for Education and Skills (2003e) *Statistics of Education: Care leavers, 2002–2003, England*. London: The Stationery Office.

Department for Education and Skills (2003f) *Statistics of Education: Public examinations GCSE/GNVQ and GCE/AGNVQ in England 2003*, London: The Stationery Office.

Department for Education and Skills (2004a) *2002-2003, Childcare and Early Years Workforce Survey, Overview Report*, http://www.surestart.gov.uk/ensuringquality/research/earlyyears/workforce/childcareandearlyyears workforcesurvey200203/

Department for Education and Skills (2004b) *Analysis of responses to the Green Paper Every Child Matters*.

Department for Education and Skills (2004c) *Children in Need in England*, London: The Stationery Office http://www.dfes.gov.uk/rsgateway/DB/VOL/

Department for Education and Skills (2004d) *Department for Education and*

Skills: Five-year strategy for children and learners, Cm 6272 Norwich: HMSO.

Department for Education and Skills (2004e) *National Curriculum Assessments of 11-yr-olds in England 2004*, Provisional. http://www.dfes.gov.uk/rsgateway/DB/SFR/s000489/SFR30-2004v2.pdf, August 2004.

Department for Education and Skills (2004f) *National Curriculum Assessments of 7-yr-olds in England 2004*, Provisional. http://www.dfes.gov.uk/rsgateway/DB/SFR/s000488/SFR29-2004v5.pdf, August 2004.

Department for Education and Skills (2004g) *National Curriculum Assessments of 14-yr-olds in England 2004*, Provisional. Part One – Mathematics and Science. http://www.dfes.gov.uk/rsgateway/DB/SFR/s000491/SFR31-2004v2.pdf, August 2004.

Department for Education and Skills (2004h) *Parental Separation: Children's needs and parents' responsibilities*, London: Department for Education and Skills, Department for Constitutional Affairs, and the Department for Trade and Industry.

Department for Education and Skills (2004i) *Permanent exclusions from schools and exclusion appeals, England 2002/2003*, http://www.dfes.gov.uk/rsgateway/DB/SFR/s000465/sfr16-2004.pdf, July 2004.

Department for Education and Skills (2004j) *Statistics of Education: Outcome indicators for looked-after children (Twelve months to 30 September 2003 England)*.

Department for Education and Skills (2004k) *Youth Cohort Studies (5–11)* .

Department for Transport (2003) *Road Casualties in Great Britain, 2002*, Annual Report, London: The Stationery Office.

Department for Work and Pensions (DWP) (2001a) *Opportunity for All – Making Progress* London: the Stationery Office.

Department for Work and Pensions (2001b) *United Kingdom National Action Plan on Social Inclusion 2001–2003*, Department for Work and Pensions.

Department for Work and Pensions (2003a) *Measuring Child Poverty*, DWP.

Department for Work and Pensions (2003b) *Opportunity for All: Fifth Annual report* Cm 5956, London: The Stationery Office.

Department for Work and Pensions (2003c) *United Kingdom National Action Plan on Social Inclusion 2003–2005*, www.dwp.gov.uk/publications/dwp/2003/nap/index.asp

Department for Work and Pensions (2004a) *Households Below Average Income: An analysis of the income distribution 1994/95–2002/03*, Leeds: Corporate Document Services.

Department for Work and Pensions (2004b) *Neighbourhood statistics* http://www.dwp.gov.uk/asd/asd1/neighbourhood/neighbourhood_2001.asp

Department for Work and Pensions (2004c) *Income Support Quarterly Statistical Inquiry – February 2004.* http://www.dwp.gov.uk/asd/isqse.asp

Department for Work and Pensions (2004d) *Opportunity for All: Sixth Annual report 2004*, Cm 6239, London: The Stationery Office.

Department for Work and Pensions (2004e) *Report on Child Poverty in the UK: Reply by the Government to the second report of the Work and Pensions Select Committee* [HC 85-1], Cm 6200, London HMSO.

Department of Education (2004) *Review of Pre-school education in Northern Ireland, http://www.deni.gov.uk/about/consultation/pre_school_review/Consultation Paper.pdf*

Department of Health (1994) *Nutritional Aspects of Cardiovascular Disease. Report of the Cardiovascular Review Group of the Committee on Medical Aspects of Food Policy*, Report on Health and Social Subjects 46. London: HMSO.

Department of Health (1995) *Child Protection: Messages from research.*

Department of Health (1997) *Children Looked After by Local Authorities: Year ending March 1996, England*, London: Government Statistical Service.

Department of Health (1998a) *Children Looked After by Local Authorities: Year ending March 1997, England*, London: Government Statistical Service.

Department of Health (1998b) *Health Survey for England 1997*, London: The Stationery Office.

Department of Health (1998c) *Nutritional Aspects of the Development of Cancer. Report of the Working Group on Diet and Cancer of the Committee on Medical Aspects of Food and Nutrition Policy*, Report on Health and Social Subjects 48, London: The Stationery Office.

Department of Health (1998d) *Our Healthier Nation*, London: The Stationery Office.

Department of Health (1999a) *Saving Lives: Our Healthier Nation*, London: The Stationery Office.

Department of Health (1999b) *Working Together to Safeguard Children: A guide to inter-agency working to safeguard and promote the welfare of children*, London: The Stationery Office.

Department of Health (1999c) *Caring about Carers: A national strategy for carers*, London: Department of Health.

Department of Health (2001a) *Children Looked After by Local Authorities: Year ending March 2000, England*, London: Government Statistical Service.

Department of Health (2001b) *Children Act Report 2000*, London: Department of Health.

Department of Health (2002a) *Children Looked After by Local Authorities: Year ending March 2001, England*, London: Government Statistical Service.

Department of Health (2002b) *Improvement, Expansion and Reform – The Next Three Years: Priorities and planning framework 2003–2006*, London: Department of Health.

Department of Health (2002c) *National Suicide Prevention Strategy for England*, London: Department of Health.

Department of Health (2003a) *Drug use, smoking and drinking among young people in England in 2003: Headline figures*, National Centre for Social Research/National Foundation for Educational Research.

Department of Health (2003b) *Health Survey for England 2002: The health of children and young people*. London: The Stationery Office.

Department of Health (2003c) *Social Services Performance Indicators 2002–03*. London: Department of Health Publications.

Department of Health (2004) *National Service Framework for Children, Young People and Maternity Services*, London: Department of Health.

Department of Health and DrugScope (2001) *Vulnerable Young People and Drugs: Opportunities to tackle inequalities*, London: Department of Health.

Department of Health and the National Addiction Centre (2001) *Consultation Draft Guidelines for Drug Prevention*, London: Department of Health.

Department of Health, Social Services and Public Safety (DHSSPS) (2002) *Equality Impact Assessment of the Sure Start Programme*, http://www.dhsspsni.gov.uk/publications/2002/surestartprogramme.pdf

Department of Health, Social Services and Public Safety (2003) *Children Order Statistics, 1st April 2002–31st March 2003*, http://www.dhsspsni.gov.uk/stats&research/childrens_order.asp

Department of Health, Social Services and Public Safety (2004) *Children Order Statistics 1 April 2002–31 March 2003* Northern Ireland, http://www.dhsspsni.gov.uk/publications/2004/Child02_03.pdf),

DHSS, T&EA, DENI (1999) *Children First: The Northern Ireland childcare strategy*, Department of Health, Social Services and Public Safety http://www.dhsspsni.gov.uk/publications/archived/cfcontents.pdf

Dixon, J. and Stein, M. (2002) *A study of throughcare and aftercare services in Scotland*, Scotland's Children, Children (Scotland) Act 1995, Research Findings No. 3, Edinburgh: Scottish Executive.

Dolton, P., Makepeace, G., Hutton, S. and Audas, R. (1999) *Making the Grade: Education, the labour market and young people* York: YPS for the Joseph Rowntree Foundation

Doran, T., Drever, F. and Whitehead, M. (2003) 'Health of Young and Elderly Informal Carers: Analysis of UK census data', *British Medical Journal*, Vol. 327, pp. 1388.

DrugScope and Department of Health (2001) *Young People, Drugs and Health Gain: What are we doing?* London: DrugScope.

Dunn, J. and Deater-Deckard, K. (2001) *Children's views of their changing families*, Joseph Rowntree Foundation, York: York Publishing Services.

Dunn, J., Slomkowski, C. and Beardsall, L. (1994) 'Sibling relationships from the preschool period through middle childhood and early adolescence', *Developmental Psychology*, Vol. 30, pp. 315–24.

Dunne, M. P., Purdie, D. M., Cook, M. D., Boyle, F. M. and Najman, J. M. (2003) 'Is child sexual abuse declining? Evidence from a population-based survey of men and women in Australia', *Child Abuse & Neglect*, 27, pp. 141–52.

Durkheim, E. (1952) *Suicide: A study in sociology*, London: Routledge and Kegan Paul.

Eckersley, R. and Dear, K. (2002) Cultural correlates of youth suicide, *Social Science and Medicine*, 55, pp, 1891–904.

Edgar, B., Doherty, J. and Meert, H. (2003) *Review of statistics on homelessness in Europe*, FEANTSA.

Edwards, E. and Coles, B. (2002) 'Truancy and school exclusions', in J. Bradshaw (ed.) *The Well-being of Children in the UK*, London: Save the Children/The University of York.

Ehtisham, S., Barrett, T. G. and Shaw, N. J. (2000) 'Type 2 diabetes mellitus in UK children – an emerging problem', *Diabetic Medicine* 17(2), pp. 867–71.

Ehtisham, S., Hattersley, A. T., Dunger, D. B. and Barrett, T. G. (2004) 'First UK survey of paediatric type 2 diabetes and MODY', *Archives of Disease in Childhood*, 89, pp. 526–29.

Emery, S., White, M. and Pierce, J. (2001) 'Does cigarette price influence adolescent experimentation?', *Journal of Health Economics*, 20, pp. 261–70. Cited in ASH (2004) *Factsheet No 3, Young people and smoking*, www.ash.org.uk/html/factsheets/html/ fact03.html

Ennew, J. (1994) *Childhood as a Social Phenomenon National Report,*

England and Wales, Eurosocial Reports Vol.36, Vienna: Austria, European Centre.

Erens, B., Primatesta, P. and Prior, G. (2001) *Health Survey for England – The Health of Minority Ethnic Groups 1999*, London: Department of Health.

Esping-Andersen, G. and Sarasa, S. (2003) 'The generational conflict reconsidered', *Journal of European Social Policy*, 12, 1, pp. 5–21.

Essen, B., Bodker, B., Sloberg, N. O., Langhoff-Roos, J., Greisen, G., Gudmundsson, S. and Ostergren, P. O. (2002) 'Are some perinatal deaths in immigrant groups linked to suboptimal perinatal care services?', *BJOG: An International Journal of Obstetrics and Gynaecology*, 109, pp. 677–82.

ETI (Education and Training Inspectorate Northern Ireland) (2001a) *A Survey of Provision for Pupils with Moderate Learning Disabilities in Units in Post-Primary Schools in Northern Ireland, 2000–2001*, Belfast: DENI.

ETI (Education and Training Inspectorate, Northern Ireland) (2001b) *A Survey of Provision for Pupils with Severe and Profound Learning Disabilities in Northern Ireland, 1998–2000*, Belfast: DENI.

EURODIAB Ace Study Group (2000) 'Variations and trends in incidence of childhood diabetes in Europe', *The Lancet*, 355, pp. 873–6.

EuroHIV (2003) *HIV/AIDS Surveillance in Europe. Mid-year report 2003. No 69*, St Maurice: European Centre for the Epidemiological Monitoring of AIDS.

European Monitoring Centre for Drugs and Drug Addiction (2002) *Drugs in Focus: Recreational use – a key EU challenge*, Luxembourg: Office for Official Publications of the European Communities.

European Union (2001) *Draft Report on Social Inclusion, Results of the European Panel Survey 1998*, Mimeo

Fajerman, L. and Treseder, P. (2004) *Children and Service Users Too: A guide to consulting children and young people*, Charter Mark and Save the Children.

Farrell, M. (2004) *Special Educational Needs: A resource for practitioners*, London: Paul Chapman.

Farrington, D. P. (1996) *Understanding and Preventing Youth Crime*, Social Policy Research 9393, York: Joseph Rowntree Foundation.

Fazel, M. and Stein, A. (2003) 'Mental Health of Refugee Children: Comparative study', *British Medical Journal*, 327, p. 134.

FEANTSA (1998) *Europe against Exclusion: Housing for All*, Brussels: European Federation of National Organisations Working with the Homeless.

Featherstone, B. and Evans, H. (2004) *Children Experiencing Maltreatment: Who do they turn to?*, NSPCC.

Feltbower, R. G., McKinney, P. A., Campbell, F. M., Stephenson, C. R. and Bodansky, H. J. (2003) 'Type 2 and other forms of diabetes in 0–30-year-olds: A hospital based study in Leeds', *Archives of Disease in Childhood*, 88, pp. 676–9.

Fleming, J., Mullen, P. and Bammer, G. (1997) 'A study of potential risk factors for sexual abuse in childhood', *Child Abuse & Neglect*, Volume 21, Issue 1, p. 10.

Flood-Page, C., Campbell, S., Harrington, V. and Miller, J. (2000) *Youth Crime: Findings from the 1998/1999 Youth Lifestyles Survey*, Home Office Research Study 209, London: Home Office.

Fombonne, E., Wostear, G., Cooper, V., Harrington, R. and Rutter, M. (2001a) 'The Maudsley long-term follow-up of child and adolescent depression: 1. Psychiatric outcomes in adulthood', *British Journal of Psychiatry*, 179, pp. 210–17.

Fombonne, E., Wostear, G., Cooper, V., Harrington, R. and Rutter, M. (2001b) 'The Maudsley long-term follow-up of child and adolescent depression: 2. Suicidality, criminality and social dysfunction in adulthood', *British Journal of Psychiatry*, 179, pp. 210–17.

Forsey, E., Loretto, W. and Plant, M. (1996) 'Alcohol and youth', in L. Harrison (ed.) *Alcohol Problems in the Community*, New York: Routledge.

Foster, J. (2000) 'Social exclusion, crime and drugs', *Drugs: Education, Prevention and Policy*, 7, 4, pp. 317–30.

Galinsky, E. (1999) *Ask the Children: What America's children really think about working parents*, New York: William Morrow and Company.

Gallagher, B., Bradford, M. and Pease, K. (2002) 'The sexual abuse of children by strangers: its extent, nature and victims' characteristics', *Children and Society*, 16, pp. 346–59.

Gallagher, B., Bradford, M. and Pease, K. (2003) 'The sexual abuse of children by strangers: Perpetrator characteristics, incident circumstances and victim responses', unpublished paper.

General Register for Scotland (2003) *Scotland's Population: the Register General's annual review of demographic trends 2002.* General Register Office for Scotland.

Gershuny, J. (2000) *Changing Times: Work and leisure in post-industrial society*, Oxford: Oxford University Press.

Ghate, D. and Hazel, N. (2002) *Parenting in poor environments: Stress, support and coping*, London: Jessica Kingsley.

Ghate, D., Hazel, N., Creighton, S., Finch, S. and Field, J. (2003) *National Study of Parents, Children and Discipline in Britain: Summary of key findings*, London: Policy Research Bureau.

Gill, B., Dunn, M. and Goddard, E. (2002a) *Student Achievement in England*, London: The Stationery Office.

Gill, B., Dunn, M and Goddard, E. (2002b) *Student Achievement in Northern Ireland*, London: The Stationery Office.

Gillborn, D. (2000) *Rationing Education: Policy, practice, reform and equity*, Buckingham: Open University Press.

Gillborn, D., and Mirza, H. S. (2000) *Educational Inequality: Mapping race, class and gender, a synthesis of research evidence* London: Office for Standards in Education.

GLA (2001a) *Homelessness in London, 28*, Greater London Authority Housing and Homelessness Team, www.london.gov.uk.

GLA (2001b) *Homelessness in London, 30*, Greater London Authority Housing and Homelessness Team, www.london.gov.uk.

Glendinning, A., Kloep, M. and Hendry, L. B. (2000) 'Parenting practices and well-being in youth: Family life in rural Scotland and Sweden', in H. Ryan and J. Bull (eds) *Changing Families, Changing Communities: Researching health and well-being among children and young people*, London: Health Development Agency.

Glennester, H. (2001) *United Kingdom education 1997–2001*, CASE paper no 50, London School of Economics, Centre for Analysis of Social Exclusion.

Goddard, E. (1997) *Young Teenagers and Alcohol in 1996*, Volume 1, England, Office for National Statistics, London: The Stationery Office.

Goodman, R., Ford, T. and Meltzer, H. (2002) 'Mental health problems of children in the community: 18 month follow-up', *British Medical Journal*, 324, pp. 1496–7.

Gorin, S. (2004) *Understanding what children say about living with domestic violence, parental substance misuse or parental health problems*, JRF Findings 514 York: Joseph Rowntree Foundation.

Graham, J. and Bowling, B. (1995) *Young People and Crime: Self-reported offending amongst 14–25-year-olds in England and Wales*, Home Office Research Study 145, London: Home Office.

Grainger, S. and Robinson, A. (2004) *Housing and Health in Scotland: Analysis of the 2002 Scottish House Condition*, Edinburgh: Scottish Executive/ Scottish Communities.

Grant, G. (2004) Book review: Aldridge, J. and Becker, S. (2003) *Children Caring for Parents with Mental Illness*, Bristol: The Policy Press, in *Journal of Social Policy* Vol. 33, Part 2, pp. 333–4.

Griffiths, C. and Kirby, L. (2000) 'Geographic variations in conceptions to women aged under 18 in Great Britain during the 1990s', *Population Trends* 102, London: The Stationery Office.

Hague, L. and Campbell, P. (2002) *Analysis of Juveniles Admitted onto Remand in Northern Ireland*, Research and Statistical Bulletin 6/2002, Belfast: Northern Ireland Office.

Hall, S., Powney, J. and Davidson, P. (2000) *The Impact of Homelessness on Families*, Edinburgh: Scottish Council for Research in Education.

Hamilton, C. (2003) *Protecting Children in Employment: A survey of byelaws in England and Wales*, Children's Legal Centre, Commissioned by the TUC.

Hamlyn, B., Brooker, S., Oleinikova, K. and Wands, S. (2002) *Infant Feeding, 2000*, London: Department of Health.

Harrison, L. (ed.) (1996) *Alcohol Problems in the Community*, New York: Routledge.

Hawthorne, J., Jessop, J., Pryor, J. and Richards, M. (2003) *Supporting Children through Family Change: A review of interventions and services for children of divorcing and separating parents*, Joseph Rowntree Foundation, York: York Publishing Services.

Hawton, K., Rodham, K., Evans, E. and Weatherall, R. (2002) 'Deliberate Self-harm in Adolescents: Self-report survey in schools in England', *British Medical Journal*, 325, pp. 1207–11.

Hawton, K., Simkin, S. and Deeks, J. (2003) 'Co-proxamol and Suicide: A study of national mortality statistics and local non-fatal self poisonings', *British Medical Journal*, 326, pp. 1006–8.

Hazel, N., Hagell, A., Liddle, M., Archer, D., Grimshaw, R. and King, J. (2002) *Assessment of the Detention and Training Order and its impact on the secure estate across England and Wales*, London: Youth Justice Board http://www.youth-justice-board.gov.uk.

Health Promotion Agency (2001) *Eating for health? A survey of eating habits among children and young people in Northern Ireland*, HPA

Health Promotion Agency for Northern Ireland (2001) *Design for Living: Research to support young people's mental health and well-being*, Belfast: Health Promotion Agency for Northern Ireland.

Health Protection Agency, Scottish Centre for Infection and Environmental Health and the Institute of Child Health (2004) *AIDS/HIV Quarterly Surveillance Tables: Cumulative UK data to end June 2004*, London: Health Protection Agency.

Health Survey for England (2001) http://www.publications.doh.gov.uk/stats/trends1.htm

Health, J., Jeffries, R. and Lloyd, A. (2003) *Asylum Statistics: United Kingdom 2002*, London: Home Office.

Henry, P. and McArdle, E. (2003) 'Struggling to be Heard: Young deaf people in Northern Ireland', *Youth and Policy*, Winter, pp, 64–81.

Higgins, K. and McElrath, K. (2000) 'The Troubles with Peace: The cease-fires and their impact on drug use among youth in Northern Ireland', *Youth and Society*, 32, 1, pp. 29–59.

Hill, K. (1995) *The Long Sleep: Young people and suicide*, London: Virago Press.

Hill, M. and Jenkins, S. (2001) 'Poverty among British Children: Chronic or transitory?', in B. Bradbury, S. Jenkins and J. Micklewright (eds) *The dynamics of child poverty in industrialised countries*, Cambridge: University Press.

Hillman, M. J., Adams, J. and Whitelegg, J. (1990) *One False Move: A study of children's independent mobility*, London: Policy Studies Institute.

Hillyard, P., Kelly, G., McLaughlin, E., Patsio, D. and Tomlinson, M. (2003) *Bare Necessities: Poverty and social exclusion in Northern Ireland – key findings*, Report No 16, Belfast: Democratic Dialogue.

Himmelweit, S. and Sigala, M. (2004) 'Choice and the Relationship between Identities and Behaviour for Mothers with Pre-School Children: Some implications for policy from a UK study', in *Journal of Social Policy*, 33, 3, pp. 455–78.

HM Treasury (2002a) *Opportunity and Security for All.*

HM Treasury (2002b) *Technical Note for HM Treasury's Public Service Agreement 2003–2006*, London.

HM Treasury (2004a) *Child Poverty Review*, London: The Stationery Office.

HM Treasury (2004b) HC 301 *Prudence for a Purpose: A Britain of stability and strength*, London: The Stationery Office.

HM Treasury (2004c) *Spending Review Stability, Security and Opportunity for All:*

Investing for Britain's long-term future, New Public Spending Plans 2005–2008, London: The Stationery Office.

Hobbs, S. and McKechnie, J. (1997) *Child Employment in Britain: A social and psychological analysis*, Edinburgh: The Stationery Office.

Hobcraft, J. (1998) *Intergenerational and Life-Course Transmission of Social Exclusion: Influences of childhood poverty, family disruption and contact with the police*, CASE Paper 15, London: London School of Economics.

Holeman, T. L. , Barett-Connor, E., Holmen, J. and Bjermer, L. (2000) 'Health problems in teenage daily smokers versus non-smokers in Norway 1995–7, the Nord-Trondelag health study', *American Journal of Epidemiology*, 151, pp. 148–55. Cited in T. Bjarnason, A. G. Davidaviciene, P. Miller, A. Nociar, A. Pavlakis, and E. Stergar (2003) 'Family structure and adolescent cigarette smoking in eleven European Countries', *Addiction*, 98, pp. 815–24.

Holzhausen, E. and Pearlman, V. (2000) *Caring on the breadline. The financial implications of caring*, London: Carers National Association.

Home Office (2003) *Criminal Statistics England and Wales 2002*, London: National Statistics.

Home Office (2001) *Building Cohesive Communities*, The Denham Report, London: The Home Office.

Horton, C. (ed.) (2003) *Working with Children 2004–5*, NCH/Society Guardian.

House of Commons Education and Skills Committee (2003) *Government Response to the Committee's Seventh Report of 2002–3: Secondary Education – Pupil Achievement*, London: The Stationery Office.

House of Commons Work and Pensions Select Committee (2004) *Child Poverty in the UK*, Second Report (Session 2003–04), HC 85-1, London: The Stationery Office.

House of Lords (2003) *The UN Convention on the Rights of the Child, Tenth Report of Session 2002–2003*, House of Commons Joint Committee on Human Rights, HL paper 117, HC 81, London: The Stationery Office.

Housing Statistics in the European Union (2003) available at www.iut.nu.

Howieson, C. (2003) *Destinations of Early Leavers: Evidence from the Scottish School Leavers Survey*, Special CES Briefing No 28, Edinburgh: Centre for Educational Sociology, University of Edinburgh.

http://www.dfes.gov.uk/rsgateway/DB/VOL/v000451/index.shtml

http://www.dhsspsni.gov.uk/publications/2004/Child02_03.pdf

http://www.lgduwales.gov.uk/Documents/Data_Set/PSS/2002-2003

http://www.prisonreformtrust.org.uk

http://www.scotland.gov.uk/stats/bulletins/00072-04.asp

http://www.scotland.gov.uk/stats/bulletins/00072-04.asp

http://www.scotland.gov.uk/stats/bulletins/00287-00.asp

http://www.statistics.gov.uk/downloads/theme_compendia/Regional_Trends_38/RT38_summary.pdf

http://www.the-childrens-society.org.uk/media/pdf/media/Grumpy_Grown_Ups_Summary.pdf

http://www.wales.gov.uk/themessocialdeprivation/content/social-inclusion/37050-index-e.htm

http://www/youth-justice-board.gov.uk

http://www.dfes.gov.uk/rsgateway/DB/SBU/b000424/table4.xls

http://www.scotland.gov.uk/stats/bulletins/00287-00.asp

ISD Scotland (2003) ISD Scotland forms ISD(D)2 and ISD(D)3 (http://www.isdscotland.org/isd).

Jackson, S., Ajayi, S. and Quigley, M. (2003) *By Degrees: The first year, from care to university*, London: The Frank Buttle Trust.

Jamieson, J., McIvor, G. and Murray, C. (1999) *Understanding Offending among Young People*, Edinburgh: The Stationery Office.

Johnson, J. L., Bottorff, J. L., Moffat, B., Ratner, P. A., Shoveller, J. A., Lovato, C. Y. (2003) 'Tobacco Dependence: Adolescents' perspectives on the need to smoke', *Social Science and* Medicine, 56, pp. 1481–1892.

Jones, L. H. and Finkelhor, D. (2003) 'Putting together Evidence on Declining Trends in Sexual Abuse: A complex puzzle', *Child Abuse & Neglect*, 27, pp. 133–5

Jones, A. (2002) 'Child Labour', in J. Bradshaw (ed.) *The Well-being of Children in the UK*, London: Save the Children/The University of York.

Jones, A., Pleace, N. and Quilgars, D. (2002) *An Evaluation of Homeless to Home*, London: Shelter.

Jones, L., Davis, A. and Eyers, T. (2000) 'Young people, transport and risk: comparing access and independent mobility in urban, suburban and rural environments', *Health Education Journal*, Vol. 59, pp. 315–28.

Joseph Rowntree Foundation (1997) *Young People and Drugs*, Social Policy Research 133, York: Joseph Rowntree Foundation.

Joshi, H. (2000) *The Changing Home: Outcomes for children*, ESRC Children 5–16 Research Programme, Briefing No. 6.

Kelly, L., Burton, S. and Regan, L. (1991), *An Exploratory Study of the Prevalence of Sexual Abuse in a Sample of 16–21-year-olds*, PNL: Child Abuse Studies Unit.

Kelly, S. and Bunting, J. (1998) 'Trends in suicide in England and Wales 1982–96', *Population Trends* 92, Summer 1998, London: Office for National Statistics.

Kiernan, K. (1997) *The Legacy of Parental Divorce: Social, economic and family experiences in adulthood*, Social Policy Research 131, Joseph Rowntree Foundation, York: York Publishing Services.

Kiernan, K. and Smith, K. (2003) 'Unmarried Parenthood: New insights from the Millennium Cohort Study', *Population Trends No. 114*, London: Office for National Statistics.

Kirkbride, H. and White, J. (2004) 'Infectious Diseases', in *The Health of Children and Young People*. London: ONS.

Kotch, J. B., Browne, D. C. and Ringwalt, C. L. (1995) 'Risk of Child Abuse or Neglect in a Cohort of Low-Income Children', *Child Abuse & Neglect, Volume 19, Issue 9*, pp. 1115–30.

Kotch, J. B., Browne, D. C., Ringwalt, C. L., Dufort, V. and Ruina, E. (1997) 'Stress, Social Support and Substantiated Maltreatment in the Second and Third Years of Life', *Child Abuse & Neglect*, Volume 21, Issue 11, pp. 1025–37.

Kreitman, N. and Foster, J. (1991) The Construction and Selection of Predictive Scales with a Particular Reference to Parasuicide, *British Journal of Psychiatry*, 159, pp. 185–92.

Kumar, V. (1995) *Poverty and Inequality in the UK: The effects on children*, London: National Children's Bureau.

Lader, D., Singleton, N. and Meltzer, H. (2000) *Psychiatric Morbidity Among Young Offenders in England and Wales*, London: ONS.

Laming, Lord (2003) *The Victoria Climbié Inquiry Report*, London: Stationery Office.

Learning and Skills Council for West Yorkshire, (2002), *Bradford Metropolitan District Area-wide Inspection of all 16–19 Education and Training Provision: Action Plan*. Bradford: LSC.

Lee, E. *et al* (2004) *A Matter of Choice? Explaining national variations in teenage abortion and motherhood*, York: Joseph Rowntree Foundation.

Levene, S. and Bacon, C. J. (2004) 'Sudden unexpected death and covert homicide in infancy', *Archives of Disease in Childhood*, 89, pp. 443–7

Lewis, J. (2003) 'Developing Early Years Childcare in England, 1997–2002: The Choices for (Working) Mothers', in *Social Policy and Administration*, Vol. 37, No. 3, pp. 219–38.

Licence, K. (forthcoming) *Promoting and protecting the health of children and young people. Child: Care, Health and Development* (November 2004).

Livingstone, S. and Bober, M. (2004) *UK Children Go Online*, Project funded by the Economic and Social Research Council under the 'e-Society' Programme, with co-funding from AOL, BSC, Childnet-International, Citizens Online and ITC. http://personal.lse.ac.uk/bober/UKCGOsurveyreport.pdf

Macfarlane, A., Stafford, M. and Moser, K. (2004) 'Social inequalities', in *The Health of Children and Young People*, London: ONS.

Machin, S. and Vignoles, A. (2004) 'Educational Inequality: The Widening Socio-Economic Gap', *Fiscal Studies*. 25, 2. pp 107–128.

Macinko, J. A., Shi, L. and Starfield, B. (2004) 'Wage inequality, the health system, and infant mortality in wealthy industrialized countries, 1970–1996', *Social Science and Medicine*, 58, pp. 279–92.

Mackett, R. L., Lucas, L., Paskins, J. and Turbin, J. (2002) *Children's car use: The implications for health and sustainability*, Proceedings of the European Transport Conference, Cambridge, London: PTRC.

Maclean, M. (2004) *Together and Apart*, Foundations, Joseph Rowntree Foundation, York: York Publishing Services.

Madge, N. (1996) 'Suicide behaviour in children and young people', *Highlight*, No. 144, London: National Children's Bureau and Barnardo's.

Madge, N. and Harvey, J. G. (1999a) *A Life of Our Own: An evaluation of three RHA-funded projects in Merseyside*, Manchester: University of Manchester.

Madge, N. and Harvey, J. G. (1999b) 'Suicide among the young – the size of the problem', *Journal of Adolescence*, 22, 1, pp. 145–55.

Marsh, A., Gordon, D., Pantazis, C. and Heslop, P. (1999) *Home Sweet Home? The Impact of Poor Housing on Health*, Bristol: Policy Press.

Marttunen, M. J., Hillevi, M. and Lonnqvist, J. K. (1992) 'Adolescent suicide: endpoint of long-term difficulties', *Journal of the American Academy of Child and Adolescent Psychiatry*, 31, pp. 649–54.

Matthews, H. (2001) *Children and Community Regeneration: Creating better neighbourhoods*, London: Save the Children.

Matthews, H. and Limb, M. (2000) *Exploring the 'Fourth Environment': Young people's use of place and views on their environment*, ESRC: Children 5–16 Research Briefing. Swindon: Economic and Social Research Council.

Mayall, B. (2000) 'Negotiating Childhoods', *Children 5–16 Research Briefing No. 13*, ESRC.

May-Chahal, C., Hicks, S. and Tomlinson, J. (2004) *The Relationship Between Child Death and Child Maltreatment: A research study on the attribution of cause of death in hospital settings*, NSPCC.

Mayhew, E. and Bradshaw, J. (forthcoming) 'Children's health and development' in Dex, S. and Joshi, H. (eds) (forthcoming) Babies of the New Millennium: Babies of the 21st century, London: Policy Press.

Mayhew, E., Urichard, E., Beresford, B., Ridge, T. and Bradshaw, J. (forthcoming) *UK: Children's Welfare*, Country Report for the COST-Action A19 programme, funded by the European Union.

McCrum, J. (2001) *Homeless Families, Homeless Children*, Belfast: Simon Community, Northern Ireland.

McGlone, F. (2001) 'Youth crime', in J. Bradshaw (ed.) *Poverty: The outcomes for children*, London: Family Policy Studies Centre, pp. 143–52.

McKendrick, J., Bradford, M. and Fielder, A. (2000a) 'Kid Customer? Commercialisation of play space and the commodification of childhood', *Childhood*, Vol. 7(3), pp. 295–314.

McKendrick, J., Fielder, A. and Bradford, M. (2000b) 'Enabling play or sustaining exclusion? Commercial playgrounds and disabled children', *The North West Geographer*, Vol. 3, pp. 32–49.

McKendrick, J., Fielder, A. and Bradford, M. (2000c) 'Privatisation of collective play spaces in the UK', *Built Environment*, Vol. 25(1), pp. 44–57.

McLaughlin, E. and Fahey, T. (1999) 'The family and State in Ireland, North and South', in R. Breen, A. Heath, and C. Whelan (eds) *Ireland, North and South*, London: British Academy.

McQuail, S., Mooney, A., Cameron, C., Candappa, M., Moss, P. and Petrie, P. (2003) *Early Years and Childcare International Evidence Project: Child Outcomes*, London: DfES and DWP.

Melhuish, E. C. (2004a) *A Literature Review of the Impact of Early Years Provision on Young Children, with Emphasis given to Children from Disadvantaged Backgrounds*, London: Institute for the Study of Children, Families & Social Issues, Birkbeck, University of London/NAO.

Melhuish, E. C. (2004b) *Child Benefits – The importance of investing in quality childcare*, Facing the Future Policy Paper, No. 9, Daycare Trust, London: Daycare Trust.

Melhuish, E. C., Sylva, K., Sammons, P., Siraj-Blatchford, I. and Taggart, B. (2001) *The Effective Provision of Pre-school Education Project, Technical Paper*

7: Social/Behavioural and cognitive development at 3–4 years in relation to family background, London: Institute of Education/DfEE.

Meltzer, H. and Gatward, R. with Goodman, R. and Ford, T. (2000) *Mental Health of Children and Adolescents in Great Britain*, London: The Stationery Office.

Meltzer, H., Harrington, R., Goodman, R. and Jenkins, R. (2001) *Children and Adolescents who try to Harm, Hurt or Kill Themselves*, London: Office for National Statistics.

Meltzer, H., Gatward, R., Corbin, T., Goodman, R. and Ford, T. (2003a) *Persistence, Onset, Risk Factors and Outcomes of Childhood Mental Disorders*, London: The Stationery Office.

Meltzer, H., Gatward, R., Corbin, T., Goodman, R. and Ford, T. (2003b) *The Mental Health of Young People Looked After by Local Authorities in England*, London: The Stationery Office.

Meltzer, H., Lader, D., Corbin, T., Goodman, R. and Ford, T. (2004) *The Mental Health of Young People Looked After by Local Authorities in Scotland*, London: The Stationery Office.

Mental Health Foundation (1999a) *Bright Futures*, London, Mental Health Foundation.

Mental Health Foundation (1999b) *The Big Picture, Summary of the Bright Futures Programme*, http://www.mentalhealth.org.uk

Miller, P. and Plant, M. (2001) *Drinking, Smoking and Illicit Drug Use amongst 15 and 16-year-old School Students in Northern Ireland*, Department of Health, Northern Ireland.

Mitchell, J. and Bradbury, J (2004) 'Devolution: Comparative Development and Policy Roles' in *Parliamentary Affairs*, Vol. 57, No. 2, pp. 329–46.

Mittler, P. (2000) *Working Towards Inclusive Education: Social Contexts*, London: David Fulton.

Mondimore, F. (2000) 'Sexual orientation and abuse', in U. McCluskey and C. A. Hooper (eds), *Psychodynamic Perspectives on Abuse*, London: Jessica Kingsley.

Monteith, M. and McLaughlin, E. (2004) *Children and Severe Poverty in Northern Ireland*, Belfast: Save the Children.

Monteith, M., McLaughlin, E., Milner, S., and Hamilton, L. (2002) *'Is Anyone Listening? Childhood disability and public services in Northern Ireland*, Belfast: Barnardo's Northern Ireland.

Mooney, A., Moss, P., Cameron, C., Candappa, M., McQuail, S. and Petrie, P.

(2003) *Early Years and Childcare International Evidence Project: Summary*, London: DfES and DWP.

Mooney, E,. McDowell, P. and Taggart, K. (2004) *Northern Ireland Care Leavers (2002/03)*, http://www.dhsspsni.gov.uk/publications/2004/NI-CareLeavers-A4Pub.pdf.

Market & Opinion Research International (MORI) (2001) *Listening to Parents: Their worries, their solutions, National Family & Parenting Institute Survey*, National Family & Parenting Institute.

Market & Opinion Research International (MORI) (2003) *Youth Survey 2003*, Research Study conducted for the Youth Justice Board by MORI – January to March 2003, London: Youth Justice Board.

Morrison, A., Headrick, D., Wasoff, F. and Morton, S. (2004) *Family Formation and Dissolution: Trends and attitudes among the Scottish population*, Edinburgh: Scottish Executive.

Morrow, V. (2001) *Networks and Neighbourhoods: Children's and young people's perspectives*, London: Health Development Agency.

Motion, C. (2000) *Breaking the Cycle of Homelessness in West Lothian: A study of repeat homelessness*, Dissertation submitted for the Diploma in Housing Studies, Department of Applied Social Science, University of Stirling.

Muldoon, O. T., Trew, K. and Kilpatrick, R. (2000) The legacy of the Troubles on the Young People's Psychological and Social Development and their School Life, *Youth and Society*, 32, 1, pp. 6–28.

Mulvihill, C., Rivers, K. and Aggleton, P. (2000) 'A qualitative study investigating the views of primary-age children and parents on physical activity', *Health Education Journal*, Vol. 59, pp. 166–79.

Mumford, K. (2000) *Talking to Families in East London*, CASE Brief 19, London: London School of Economics.

Mumford, K. and Power, A. (2003) *East Enders: Family and Community in East London*, Bristol: The Policy Press.

Mumtaz, S. (2001) 'Children's enjoyment and perception of computer use in the home and the school', *Computers and Education*, 36, 4, pp. 347–62.

Munn, P., Lloyd, G. and Cullen, M. A. (2000) *Alternatives to Exclusion from School*, London: Paul Chapman Publishing Ltd.

Munro, H., Davis, M. and Hughes, G. (2004) 'Adolescent Sexual Health', in *The Health & Children and Young People*, London: Office for National Statistics.

National Association for the Care and Resettlement of Offenders (NACRO) (2000) *Doing Something Positive*, London: NACRO.

National Association for the Care and Resettlement of Offenders (NACRO) (2003) *Some Facts about Young People who Offend – 2001*, Youth Crime Briefing, London: NACRO.

National Assembly for Wales (2001a) *Social Services Statistics, Wales 2000*, Cardiff: Statistical Directorate.

National Assembly for Wales (2001b) *Welsh House Condition Survey, 1998*, Cardiff: National Assembly for Wales.

National Assembly for Wales (2004a) *Care Standards Inspectorate for Wales Annual Report 2002–2003* www.wales.gov.uk/subisocialpolicycarestandards/content/publications/annual-report-0203-e.pdf

National Assembly for Wales (2004b) *Children Looked After by Local Authorities, 31 March 2003*, http://www.lgduwales.gov.uk/Documents/Data_Set/PSS/2002–2003.

National Audit Office (2004a) *Connexions Service: Advice and Guidance for all Young People*, Report by the Comptroller and Auditor General, HC 484 2003-2004, 31st March 2004.

National Audit Office (2004b) *Early Years: Progress in developing high quality childcare and early education accessible to all*, Report by the Comptroller and Auditor General, HC 268 Session 2003-2004, London: The Stationery Office.

National Statistics (2003) *A Commentary on Northern Ireland Crime Statistics 2001*, Belfast: Northern Ireland Office.

National Statistics (2004) *Crime in England and Wales 2002/03: Supplementary vol. 1: Homicide and gun crime*, London: The Stationery Office.

NCH (2000) *Factfile 2000*, London: National Children's Home.

Nestle UK Ltd (2002) *Make Space for Young People* Nestle Family Monitor, No 15, www.nestlefamilymonitor.co.uk.

Newburn, T. and Shinner, M. (2001) *Teenage Kicks? Young people and alcohol: A review of the literature*, Joseph Rowntree Foundation cited in Alcohol Concern (2004) *Young People's Drinking, Factsheet 1: Summary*, www.alcohol concern.org.uk

Newburn, T. (2002) 'Young people, crime and youth justice', in M. Maguire, R. Morgan and R. Reiner (eds) *The Oxford Handbook of Criminology*, 3rd edition, Oxford: Oxford University Press, pp. 531–78.

Newburn, T., Ward, J. and Pearson, G. (2002) *Drug use among young people in care, Research Briefing, 7*. Swindon: Economic and Social Research Council.

Newman, T. (2002) 'Young carers and disabled parents: Time for a change of direction?', *Disability & Society*, Vol. 17, No. 6, pp. 613–25.

New Policy Institute (2002) *The Value of Children's Play and Play Provision: A systematic review of the literature*, New Policy Institute.

Nichol. A., Ellimna, D. and Begg, N. T. (1989) 'Immunisation: Causes of failure and strategies and tactics for success', *British Medical Journal*, 299, pp. 808–12.

Noble, M. *et al* (2004) *Report for the Select Committee for Work and Pensions on small area child income deprivation in England and Wales in 1999–2001*, The Social Disadvantage Research Centre, Department of Social Policy and Social Work University of Oxford.

Northern Ireland Statistics and Research Agency (NISRA) (2000) *Community Statistics 1 April 1999 – 31 March 2000*, London: National Statistics.

Northern Ireland Statistics and Research Agency (2001) *Report of the Promoting Social Exclusion Working Group on Travellers*, Belfast: New Targeting Social Need Unit.

Northern Ireland Statistics and Research Agency (2002) *Northern Ireland Health and Social Well-being Survey, 2001*, Belfast: Department of Health, Social Services and Public Safety.

Northern Ireland Statistics and Research Agency (2004a) *Continuous Household Survey 2002/2003*. Belfast: Central Survey Unit, NISRA.

Northern Ireland Statistics and Research Agency (2004b) *Equality and Inequalities in Health and Social Care in Northern Ireland: A statistical overview*, Belfast: Northern Ireland Statistics and Research Agency.

Northern Ireland Housing Executive (2003) *Northern Ireland House Condition Survey, 2001*, Belfast: Northern Ireland Housing Executives.

Northern Ireland Housing Executive (2004*) Northern Ireland Housing Statistics 2003–04*, Belfast: Department for Social Development.

Norwich, B. (2001) *LEA Inclusion Trends in England 1997–2001: Statistics on special school placements and pupils with statements in special schools*, Bristol, CSIE.

National Playing Fields Association (2000) *Best Play*, London: National Playing Fields Association, Playlink and the Children's Play Council.

O'Brien, M. (2003) 'Regenerating children's neighbourhoods: What do children want?', in P. Christensen and M. O'Brien, *Children in the City: Home, Neighbourhood and Community*, London: Routledge Falmer.

O'Brien, M., Jones, D., Sloan, D. and Rustin, M. (2000) 'Children's independent spatial mobility in the urban public realm', *Childhood*, 7, 3, pp. 253–77.

O'Connor, T., Heron, J., Golding, J., Beveridge, M. and Glover, V. (2002)

'Maternal antenatal anxiety and children's behavioural/emotional problems at 4 years', *British Journal of Psychiatry*, 180, pp. 502–8.

O'Connor, T. G., Dunn, J., Jenkins, J. M., Pickering, K. and Rasbash, J. (2001) 'Family settings and children's adjustment within and across families', *British Journal of Psychiatry*, 179, pp. 110–15.

O'Mahony, D. and Deazley, R. (2000) *Juvenile Crime and Justice*, Research Report: 17, Belfast: The Stationery Office.

Organisation for Economic Co-operation and Development (2003) *OECD Health Data 2003: A comparative analysis of 30 countries*, OECD.

Office of the Children's Rights Commissioner for London (2001) *The State of London's Children Report.*

Office of the Deputy Prime Minister (ODPM) (2002) *Homelessness Code of Guidance for Local Authorities*, London: ODPM.

Office of the Deputy Prime Minister (2003a) *English House Condition Survey 2001*, London: ODPM.

Office of the Deputy Prime Minister (2003b) *Sustainable Communities: Building for the future*, London: ODPM.

Office of the Deputy Prime Minister (2004) Delivering decent homes – number of non-decent homes reduced by one million, *ODPM News Release*, 5 May, www.odpm.gov.uk

Ofsted (2003) *Registered childcare providers and places in England 30 June 2003.*

Oliver, C. and Kandappa, M. (2003) *Tackling Bullying: Listening to the views of children and young people – summary report*, London: Thomas Coram Research Unit

Office of Law Reform (OLR) (2001) *Physical Punishment in the home – thinking about the issues, looking at the evidence*, Northern Ireland Office of Law Reform.

Office for National Statistics (ONS) (1994) *Social Focus on Children*, London: ONS

ONS (1997) Regional Trends 32: 1997 Edition. London: The Stationery Office.

ONS (1998a) *Key Health Statistics from General Practice 1996*, Series MB6 No. 1, London: Office for National Statistics.

ONS (1998b) Regional Trends 33: 1998 Edition, London: The Stationery Office.

ONS (1999) Regional Trends 34: 1999 Edition, London: The Stationery Office.

ONS (2000a) *Annual Abstract of Statistics: 2000*, London: The Stationery Office.

ONS (2000b) *Mortality Statistics: Childhood, infant and perinatal. Review of the*

Registrar General on deaths in England and Wales, 2002, Series DH3 no. 31, London: ONS.

ONS (2000c) Regional Trends 35: 2000 Edition, London: The Stationery Office.

ONS (2000d) *Social Focus on Young People*, London: ONS.

ONS (2001a) 'Households and Families', *Social Trends 30*, London: ONS.

ONS (2001b) *Mortality Statistics: Childhood, infant and perinatal. Review of the Registrar General on deaths in England and Wales, 2002*, Series DH3 no. 32, London: ONS.

ONS (2001c) Regional Trends 36: 2001 Edition, London: The Stationery Office.

ONS (2002a) *Children's Day care Facilities at 31ˢᵗ March 2002: England*, http://www.dfes.gov.uk/statistics/DB/SFR/

ONS (2002b) *Living in Britain: General Household Survey 2002*. London: ONS.

ONS (2002c) *Mortality Statistics: Childhood, infant and perinatal. Review of the Registrar General on deaths in England and Wales, 2002*, Series DH3 No. 33, London: Office for National Statistics.

ONS (2002d) Regional Trends 37: 2002 Edition, London: The Stationery Office.

ONS (2002e) *UK 2000 Time Use Survey*, Office for National Statistics.

ONS (2003a) *Census 2001: National report for England and Wales*. London: The Stationery Office.

ONS (2003b) 'Households and Families', *Social Trends No. 33*, London: ONS.

ONS (2003c) 'Infant and perinatal mortality by social and biological factors, 2002. *Health Statistics Quarterly*, 20, p. 61.

ONS (2003d) 'Infant and perinatal mortality 2002: Health areas, England and Wales', *Health Statistics Quarterly*, 19, pp. 70–73.

ONS (2003e) 'Investigation into the increase in stillbirth rate in 2002 in England and Wales', *Health Statistics Quarterly*, 19, pp. 66–67.

ONS (2003f) *Mortality Statistics: Childhood, infant and perinatal. Review of the Registrar General on deaths in England and Wales, 2002*. Series DH3 no.34. London: Office for National Statistics.

ONS (2003g) *Population Trends No. 114*, London: Office for National Statistics.

ONS (2003h) *Social Trends, No. 33*. London: The Stationery Office.

ONS (2003i) 'Sudden infant deaths', *Health Statistics Quarterly*, 19, pp. 55–59.

ONS (2003j) *Contraception and Sexual Health 2002*, London: ONS.

ONS (2004a) *Census 2001: National report for England and Wales, Part 2*, London: ONS.

ONS (2004b) Households and Families, *Social Trends No. 34*, London: ONS.

ONS (2004c) *Mortality Statistics: Childhood, infant and perinatal. Review of the*

Registrar General on deaths in England and Wales, 2002. Series DH3 no. 35. London: ONS.

ONS (2004d) *Population Trends No. 117*, London: ONS.

ONS (2004e) Regional Trends 38: 2004 Edition. London: The Stationery Office.

ONS (2004f) *Social Trends, No. 34.* London: The Stationery Office.

ONS (2004g) *The Health of Children and Young People*, London: The Stationery Office.

ONS (2004h) *UK 2000 Time Use Survey*, www.statistics.gov.uk/timeuse/default.asp

Office of Law Reform (OLR) (2004) *UK 2000 Time Use Survey*, www.statistics.gov.uk/timeuse/default.asp.

Osler, A., Watling, R., Busher, H. Cole, T. and White, A. (2001) *DfEE Research Brief No. 244: Reasons for Exclusion from School*, Nottingham: DfEE Publications.

Oxley, H., Dang, T., Forster, M. and Pellizzari, M. (2001) 'Income inequalities and poverty among children and households with children in selected OECD countries', in K. Vleminckz and T. Smeeding (eds) *Child Well-being, Child Poverty and Child Policy in Modern Nations*, Bristol: Policy Press

Palmer, T. (2001) *No Son of Mine! Children abused through prostitution*, London: Barnardo's.

Parke, R. D. and Buriel, R. (1998) 'Socialisation in the family: Ethnic and ecological perspectives', in W. Damon (Series Ed.) and N. Eisenberg (Vol. Ed.), *Handbook of child psychology: Vol. 3: Social, emotional and personality development* (5th edition), pp. 463–552, New York: Wiley.

Parker, H., Bury, C. and Eggington, R. (1998) *New Heroin Outbreak Among Young People in England and Wales*, Police Research Group, Crime Prevention and Detection Series Paper 92, London: HMSO.

Parsons, C. (1999) *Education, Exclusion and Citizenship.* London: Routledge.

Patterson, G. R. (1986) 'The contribution of siblings to training for fighting: A microsocial analysis', in D. Olweus, J. Block, and M. Radke-Yarrow (eds) *Development of Anti-social and Pro-social Behaviour* (pp. 235–61), New York: Academic Press.

Perry, A., Douglas, G., Murch, M., Bader, K. and Borkowski, M. (2000) *How Parents Cope Financially on Marriage Breakdown*, Family Policy Studies Centre, Joseph Rowntree Foundation, York: York Publishing Services.

Public Health Laboratory Service (2002) *Sexual Health in Britain: Recent changes in high risk sexual behaviours and the epidemiology of sexually transmitted infections including HIV*, London: PHLS Communicable Disease Surveillance Centre.

Pinkerton, J. and McCrea, J. (1999) *Meeting the Challenge? Young people leaving care in Northern Ireland*, Aldershot: Ashgate.

Platt, S., Backett, S., and Kreitman, N. (1988) 'Social construction or causal ascription: distinguishing suicide from undetermined deaths', *Sociology Psychiatry and Psychiatric Epidemiology*, 23, pp. 217–21, in K. Hill (1995) *The Long Sleep: Young people and suicide*, London: Virago Press.

Platt, S. D., Martin, C. I., Hunt, S. M. and Lewis, C. W. (1989) 'Damp housing, mould growth and symptomatic health state', *British Medical Journal*, 298, pp. 1673–78.

Polat, F., Kalambouka, A., Boyle, W. F. and Nelson, N. (2001) *Post-16 Transitions of Pupils with Special Educational Needs*, Research Report 315, Department for Education and Employment, London: The Stationery Office.

Ponsonby, A. L., Dwyer, T. and Cochrane, J. (2002) 'Population trends in sudden infant death syndrome', *Seminars in Perinatology*, 26, pp. 296–305.

Post Primary Review Body (2001) *Education for the 21ˢᵗ Century*, Belfast: Department of Education.

Potter, K. (2002) *Consultation with Children and Young People on the Scottish Executive's Plan for Action on Alcohol Misuse*, Central Research Unit, Scottish Executive.

Prescott-Clarke, P. and Primatesta, P. (eds) (1998) *Health Survey for England 1997, The Health of Young People 1995–97*, London: The Stationery Office.

Priestley, M., Rabiee, P. and Harris, J. (2003) 'Young disabled people and the 'new arrangement' for leaving care in England and Wales', *Children and Youth Services Review* 25, 11, pp. 863–90.

Prime Minister's Strategy Unit (2004) *Alcohol Harm Reduction Strategy for England*, Strategy Unit, London.

Prison Reform Trust (2004) *Fact File – July 2004*.

Quilgars, D. (2002) 'The Mental Health of Children', in J. Bradshaw (ed.) *The Well-being of Children in the UK*, London: Save the Children.

Rabiee, P., Priestley, M. and Knowles, J. (2001) *Whatever Next? Young disabled people leaving care*, First Key, Leeds.

Raey, D. (2000) 'Children's Urban Landscapes: Configuration of class and place', in S. Muat (ed.) *Cultural Studies and the Working Class*, London: Cassell.

Raffe, D. (2000) *'Home International' Comparisons of Post-16 Education and Training*, Edinburgh: Centre for Educational Sociology, University of Edinburgh.

Raffe, D. (2003) *'Young People Not in Education, Employment or Training: Evidence from the Scottish School Leavers Survey*, Special CES Briefing No 29. Edinburgh: Centre for Educational Sociology, University of Edinburgh.

Ramsay, M. and Partridge, S. (1999) *Drug Misuse Declared in 1998: Results from the British Crime Survey*, Home Office Research Study 197, London: Home Office.

Ramsay, M., Baker, P., Goulden, C., Sharp, C. and Sondhi, A. (2001) *Drug Misuse Declared in 2000: Results from the British Crime Survey*, London: Home Office, Research Development and Statistics Directorate.

Raws, P. (2001) *Lost Youth: Young runaways in Northern Ireland*, Belfast: The Children's Society.

Reid, D. *et al* (1995) 'Reducing the prevalence of smoking in youth in Western Countries: An international review', *Tobacco Control*, 4, (3), pp. 266–77. Cited in Action on Smoking and Health (ASH) (2004) *Factsheet No 3, Young people and smoking*, www.ash.org.uk/html/factsheets/html/fact03.html

Rendall, M. (2003) 'How important are intergenerational cycles of teenage motherhood in England and Wales? A comparison with France', *Population Trends* 111, spring 2003, pp. 27–33.

Research Development and Statistics Directorate (2003) *Criminal Statistics England and Wales 2002 – Supplementary Tables (Internet only)*, http://www.homeoffice.gov.uk/rds/crimstats02.html (accessed 5 October 2004).

Revell, K. and Leather, P. (2000) *The State of UK Housing*, Bristol and York: York Policy Press and Joseph Rowntree Foundation.

Richardus, J. H., Graafmans, W. C., Verloove-Vanhorick, S. P., Mackenbach, J. P., Euronatal International Audit Panel, Euronatal Working Group (2003) 'Differences in perinatal mortality and suboptimal care between 10 European regions results of an international audit', *BJOG: an International Journal of Obstetrics and Gynaecology*, 110, pp. 97–105.

Rickards, L. (2004) *Living in Britain: Results from the 2002 General Household Survey*, London: The Stationery Office.

Riddell, S., Banks, P., Wilson, A., Kane, J., Baynes, A., Dyson, A. and Millward, A. (2001) *Raising Attainment of Pupils with Special Educational Needs*. Interchange, 67, Edinburgh: Scottish Executive.

Ridge, T. (2002) *Childhood Poverty and Social Exclusion: From a child's perspective*, Bristol: Policy Press.

Rigby, K. (2002) *New Perspectives on Bullying*, London: Jessica Kingsley.

Riggio, H. R. (1999) 'Personality and social skill differences between adults with and without siblings', *Journal of Psychology*, Vol. 133, pp. 514–22.

Ritakallio, V-M. and Bradshaw, J. (2005) *Child Poverty in the European Union*, University of York, SPRU Working Paper.

Rivers, I. and Duncan, N. (2002) 'Understanding homophobic bullying in schools: Building a safe learning environment for all pupils', *Youth & Policy*, no 75, pp. 30–41.

Roberts, C., Kingdon, A., Parry-Langdon, N. and Bunce, J. (2002*) Young people in Wales: Findings from the Health Behaviour in School-aged Children (HBSC) study 1986–2000*, Health Promotion Wales.

Roberts, R., O'Connor, T., Dunn, J., Golding, J. and the ALSPAC Study Team (2004) 'The effects of child sexual abuse in later family life: Mental health, parenting and adjustment of offspring', *Child Abuse & Neglect*, 28, pp. 525–45

Robertson, M. and Walford, R. (2000) 'Views and visions of land use in the UK', *The Geographical Journal*, 166, 3, pp. 239–54.

Rodgers, B. and Pryor, J. (1998) *Divorce and separation: the outcomes for children*, Joseph Rowntree Foundation, York: York Publishing Services.

Rona, R. J., Chinn, S. and Burney, P. G. (1995) 'Trends in the prevalence of asthma in Scottish and English primary school children 1982–1992', *Thorax* 1995: 50, pp. 992–3.

Rowe, J., Hundleby, M. and Garnett, L. (1989) *Child Care Now*, London: British Agencies for Adoption and Fostering.

Royal College of Physicians (1994*) Homelessness and Ill Health*, London: The Royal College of Physicians.

Rutherford, A. (1992) *Growing Out of Crime: The new* era, Winchester: Waterside Press.

Rutter, M. and Smith, D. J. (1995) *Psychosocial Disorders in Young People: Time trends and their causes*, Chichester: John Wiley and Sons.

Rutter, M., Giller, H. and Hagell, A. (1998) *Anti-social Behaviour and Young People*, Cambridge: Cambridge University Press.

Salihu, H. M., Aliyu, M. H., Pierre-Louis, B. J. and Alexander, G. R. (2003) 'Levels of excess infant deaths attributable to maternal smoking during pregnancy in the United States', *Maternal and Child Health*, 7. pp. 219–27.

Sammons, P., Sylva, K., Melhuish, E. Siraj-Blatchford, I., Taggart, B. and Elliot, K. (2002) *Measuring The Impact of Pre-School on Children's Cognitive Progress over the Pre-School Period*, Technical Paper 8a, London: Institute of Education.

Sammons, P., Sylva, K., Melhuish, E. Siraj-Blatchford, I., Taggart, B. and Elliot, K. (2003) *Measuring The Impact of Pre-School on Children's Social/Behavioural*

Development over the Pre-School Period, Technical Paper 8b, London: Institute of Education.

Sawtell, M. (2002) *Lives on hold: Homeless families in temporary accommodation*, London: The Maternity Alliance.

Schools Health Education Unit (2003) *Young People in 2002*, Exeter: SHEU.

Schools Health Education Unit (2004) *Trends – Young People and Emotional Health and Well-being incorporating Bullying, 1983–2003*, Exeter: SHEU.

Scott, J. (1996) *Changing British Households: How are the children?*, Paper presented to the conference on European Societies or European Society?, Social Exclusion and Social Integration in Europe, Blarney: Ireland.

Scottish Executive (2000) *For Scotland's Children Report*, Scottish Executive.

Scottish Executive (2001a) *Children Looked After in the Year to 31 March 2000*.

Scottish Executive (2001b) *Exclusions from schools, 1999/2000*, http://www.scotland.gov.uk/stats/bulletins/ooo55.pdf, August 2001.

Scottish Executive (2002a) *An analysis of calls to ChildLine on the subject of child abuse and neglect*.

Scottish Executive (2002b) *Better Communities in Scotland: Closing the gap*, Edinburgh: Scottish Executive.

Scottish Executive (2002c) *Choose Life: A National Strategy and Action Plan to Prevent Suicide in Scotland*, Edinburgh: Scottish Executive.

Scottish Executive (2002d) *Closing the Opportunity Gap: The Scottish Budget for 2003–2006*, Edinburgh: Scottish Executive, Social Inclusion Division.

Scottish Executive (2002e) *Exclusions from schools 2000/01*, http://www.scotland.gov.uk/stats/bulletins/00144.pdf, July 2004.

Scottish Executive (2002f) *'It's everyone's job to make sure I'm alright': Report of the child protection audit and review*, Edinburgh: HMSO.

Scottish Executive (2002g) *Messages from young people who have experienced child protection proceedings*.

Scottish Executive (2002h) *Operation of the Homeless Persons Legislation in Scotland: Households in temporary accommodation: quarter ending 30 September 2002*, Edinburgh: Scottish Executive.

Scottish Executive (2002i) *Scotland's Action Programme to Reduce Youth Crime*, Edinburgh: Scottish Executive.

Scottish Executive (2002j) *The Plan for Action on Alcohol Problems*, Edinburgh: Scottish Executive.

Scottish Executive (2003a) *Attendance and absence in Scottish schools 2002–03*, July 2004.

Scottish Executive (2003b) *Consultation: Integrated Strategy for the Early Years*, Edinburgh: Scottish Executive.

Scottish Executive (2003c) *Exclusions from schools 2001/02*, http://www.scotland.gov.uk/stats/bulletins/00236.pdf, July 2004.

Scottish Executive (2003d) *Getting our Priorities Right: Good practice guidance for working with children and families affected by substance misuse*, Edinburgh: Scottish Executive.

Scottish Executive (2003e) *National Programme for Improving Mental Health and Well-being, Action Plan 2003–2006*, Edinburgh: Scottish Executive.

Scottish Executive (2003f) *Pupils with a Record of Needs*, September 2002, http://www.scotland.gov.uk/stats/bulletins/00291.pdf, July, 2004.

Scottish Executive (2003g) *Statistical Bulletin on Criminal Proceedings in Scottish Courts 2001*, CrJ/2002/9, http://www.scotland.gov.uk/stats/bulletins/00212-07.asp (accessed 5 October 2004).

Scottish Executive (2003h) *Statistics Publication Notice Education Series, Summary of Results of the 2003 Pre-school and Daycare Census*, http://www.scotland.gov.uk/stats/publist.aspx?theme=37&pillar=people

Scottish Executive (2004a) *A Breath of Fresh Air For Scotland – Improving Scotland's Health: The Challenge Tobacco Control Action Plan*, Edinburgh: Scottish Executive.

Scottish Executive (2004b) *Analysis of Ethnicity in the 2001 Census*, Edinburgh: Scottish Executive. Web: http://www.scotland.gov.uk/library5/social/aescr.pdf.

Scottish Executive (2004c) *Children's Social Work Statistics 2002–03*.

Scottish Executive (2004d) *Education: Factsheets*, Edinburgh: Scottish Executive.

Scottish Executive (2004e) *Exclusions from schools 2002/03*. Downloaded from http://www.scotland.gov.uk/stats/bulletins/00321.xls, June 2004.

Scottish Executive (2004f) *Protecting Children and Young People: The charter*, Edinburgh: Scottish Executive.

Scottish Executive (2004g) *Scottish House Condition Survey, 2002*, Edinburgh: Scottish Executive.

Scottish Executive Central Research Unit (2002a) *The 2000 Scottish Crime Survey Overview Report*, Edinburgh: Scottish Executive.

Scottish Executive Central Research Unit (2002b) *Young People and Crime in Scotland: Findings from the 2000 Scottish Crime Survey*, Edinburgh: The Stationery Office.

Scottish Executive Justice Department (2000) *The Physical Punishment of Children in Scotland: A consultation*, Edinburgh: Scottish Executive.

Searle, B. (2002a) 'Diet and Nutrition', in J. Bradshaw (ed.) *The Well-being of Children in the UK*, London: Save the Children/The University of York.

Searle, B. (2002b) 'Youth Suicide', in J. Bradshaw (ed.) *The Well-being of Children in the UK*, London: Save the Children/The University of York.

Sefton, T. (2003) *A Child's Portion: Public spending on children in Wales*, Cardiff: Save the Children.

Sefton, T. (2004) *A Fair Share of Welfare: Public spending on children in England*, CASE report 25, London: STICERD.

Selwyn, J., Sturgess, W., Quinton, D. and Baxter, C. (2003) *Costs and Outcomes of Non-infant Adoptions*, Report to the Department for Education and Skills, Bristol: University of Bristol.

Shatwell, S. (2003) *We're just like other kids*, Unpublished report by the Homeless Project, Leeds.

Shaw, A., McMinn, A. and Field, J. (ed.) (2000) *Scottish Health Survey, 1998*, Edinburgh: Scottish Executive.

Shepherd, P., Smith, K., Joshi, H. and Dex, S. (2003) *The Millennium Cohort Study First Survey: Guide to the SPSS Data Set*, Centre for Longitudinal Studies, London: Institute of Education, University of London.

Short, G. (2002) 'Faith-based Schools: A threat to social cohesion', *Journal of Philosophy of Education*. 36, 4, pp. 559–72.

Sibert, J. R., Payne, E. H., Kemp, A. M., Barber, M., Rolfe, K., Morgan, R. J. H., Lyons, R. and Butler, I. (2002) 'The incidence of severe physical child abuse in Wales', *Child Abuse & Neglect*, 26, pp. 267–76.

Sidebotham, P., Heron, J., Golding, J. and the ALSPAC Study Team (2002) 'Child maltreatment in the 'children of the nineties': deprivation, class and social networks in a UK sample', *Child Abuse & Neglect*, 26, pp. 1243–59.

Sidebotham, P., Heron, J. and the ALSPAC Study Team (2003) 'Child maltreatment in the 'children of the nineties': the role of the child', *Child Abuse & Neglect*, 27, pp. 337–52.

Simmons, J. and Dodd, T. (eds) (2003) *Crime in England and Wales 2002/2003*, Home Office Statistical Bulletin, London: Home Office.

Sinclair, I., Gibbs, I. and Wilson, K. (2000) *Supporting foster placements, Reports one and two*, York: University of York, Social Work Research & Development Unit.

Sinclair, I. and Gibbs, I. (1998) *Children's Homes: A study in diversity*, Chichester: Wiley.

Sinclair, I., Baker, C., Wilson, K. and Gibbs, I. (forthcoming) *Foster Children: Where they go and how they do*, London: Jessica Kingsley.

Sinclair, I., Gibbs, I. and Wilson, K. (2004) *Foster Carers: Why they stay and why they leave*, London: Jessica Kingsley.

Siraj-Blatchford, I., Sylva, K., Taggart, B., Sammons, P., Melhuish, E. and Elliot, K. (2003) *Intensive Case Studies of Practice Across the Foundation Stage*, Technical Paper 10, London: Institute of Education.

Skinner, C. (2002) 'Childcare Provision', in J. Bradshaw (ed.) *The Well-being of Children in the UK*, London: Save the Children/The University of York.

Sloper, P. and Quilgars, D. (2002) 'Mortality', in J. Bradshaw (ed.) *The Well-being of Children in the UK*, London: Save the Children/The University of York.

Smart, C., Neale, B. and Wade, A. (2001) *The Changing Experience of Childhood: Families and divorce*, Cambridge: Polity Press.

Social Exclusion Unit (1998a) *Rough Sleeping*, London: The Stationery Office.

Social Exclusion Unit (1998b) *Truancy and Exclusion*, Cm 3957, London: The Stationery Office.

Social Exclusion Unit (1999a) *Bridging the Gap: New opportunities for 16–18-year-olds not in Education, Employment or Training*, Cm 4405, London: The Stationery Office.

Social Exclusion Unit (1999b) *Teenage pregnancy*, Cm 4342, London: The Stationery Office.

Social Exclusion Unit (2003) *A Better Education for Children in Care*, London: The Stationery Office.

Social Exclusion Unit (2004) *Jobs and Enterprise in Deprived Areas*, London: Office of the Deputy Prime Minister.

Social Services Inspectorate (1995) *Young Carers: Something to think about*, Report of Four SSI Workshops May – July 1995, London: Social Services Inspectorate, Department of Health.

Soni Raleigh, V. and Balarajan, R. (1995) 'The health of infants and children among ethnic minorities', in B. Botting (ed.) *The Health of our Children, The Registrar General's decennial supplement for England and Wales*, London: HMSO.

Speak, S. (2000) 'Children in urban regeneration: Foundations for sustainable participation', *Community Development Journal*, 35, 1, pp. 31–40.

Sproston, K. and Primatesta, P. (eds) (2003) *Health Survey for England 2002: The health of children and young people*, London: The Stationery Office.

Stack, N. and McKechnie, J. (2002) 'Working Children', in B. Goldson, M.

Lavalette and J. McKechnie (2002) *Children, Welfare and the State*, London: Sage.

Stein, M. (2004) *What Works for Young People Leaving Care?*, Ilford: Barnardo's.

Stein, M., Pinkerton, J. and Kelleher, J. (2000) 'Young people leaving care in England, Northern Ireland, and Ireland', *European Journal of Social Work* 3, 3, pp. 235–46.

Stein, M., Rees, G. and Frost, N. (1994) *Running the Risk: Young people on the streets of Britain today*, London: The Children's Society.

Stewart, J (2004) 'Scottish solutions to Scottish problems? Social welfare in Scotland since devolution', in N. Ellison, L. Bauld and M. Powell (eds) *Social Policy Review 16*, Bristol: Policy Press.

Stocker, C. and Dunn, J. (1990) 'Sibling relationships in childhood: Links with friendships and peer relationships', *British Journal of Developmental Psychology*, Vol. 8, pp. 227–44.

Strachan, D. P. (1988) 'Damp housing and childhood asthma: Validation of reporting of symptoms', *British Medical Journal*, 297, pp. 1223–26.

Strategy Unit Cabinet Office (2002) *Delivering for Children and Families: Inter-Departmental Childcare Review – November 2002*, London: Strategy Unit.

Street, K. *et al* (2004) 'How great is the risk of abuse in infants born to drug-using mothers?', *Child*, 30, pp. 325–30.

Sure Start England (2004) web page: http://www.surestart.gov.uk/ surestartservices/surestartlocalprogrammes/

Sure Start Scotland (2004) web page: http://www.scotland.gov.uk/about/ED/ CnF/00015939/page742971352.aspx

Sutherland, H. (2004) *Poverty in Britain: The impact of government policy since 1997. An update to 204-5 using micro simulation*, Micro simulation Research note No. MU-Rn-44, April 2004.

Sweanor, D. and Martial, L. R. (1994) 'The Smuggling of tobacco products: Lessons from Canada, Non-Smokers Rights Association', Cited in ASH (2004) *Factsheet No 3, Young people and smoking*, www.ash.org.uk/html/ factsheets/html/fact03.html

Sweeting, H. and West, P. (1996) 'The relationships between family life and young people's lifestyles', *Findings*, April.

Sylva, K., Melhuish, E., Sammons, P., Siraj-Blatchford, I., Taggart, B., Elliot, K. (2003) *The Effective Provision of Pre-School Education (EPPE) Project: Findings from the pre-school period*, Research Brief No: RBX 15–03), London: DfES.

Tabberer, S. (2002) 'Teenage pregnancy and teenage motherhood', in J. Bradshaw (ed.) *The Well-being of Children in the UK*, London: Save the Children/The University of York.

The Children's Society (2004) http://www.childsoc.org.uk/media/pdf/media/ Playday_2004_Survey_Summary.pdf

Thoburn, J., Norford L. and Rashid, S. (2000) *Permanent Family Placement for Children of Minority Ethnic Origin*, London: Jessica Kingsley.

Torsheim, T., Valimaa, R. and Danielson, M. (2004) 'Health and well-being', *In Young People's Health in Context. Health Behaviour in School-aged Children (HBSC) study: international report from the 2001/2002 survey*, Denmark: WHO.

Towner, E. (2002) 'The prevention of childhood injury. Background paper prepared for the Accidental Injury Task Force', in Department of Health (2002) *Preventing Accidental Injury: Priorities for action*, Report to the Chief Medical Officer of the Accidental Injury Taskforce, London: Department of Health

Trade Unions Congress (2001) *Class Struggles*, London: Trade Unions Congress.

Tucker, J. S., Ellickson, P. L., and Klein, D. J. (2003) 'Predictors of the Transition to Regular Smoking During Adolescence and Young Adulthood', *Journal of Adolescent Health*, 32, pp. 314–24.

UK Government White Paper (1998) *Smoking Kills – A White Paper on Tobacco*, Cm 4177, London: The Stationery Office.

UNICEF (2000) *A League Table of Child Poverty in Rich Nations*, Innocenti Report Card 1, Florence: UNICEF Innocenti Research Centre.

UNICEF (2001a) *A League Table of Child Deaths by Injury in Rich Nations*, Florence, Italy: Innocenti Research Centre.

UNICEF(2001b) *A League Table of Teenage Births in Rich Nations*, Innocenti Report Card, Issue No. 3. Florence: UNICEF Innocenti Research Centre.

UNICEF (2003) *A League Table of Child Maltreatment Deaths in Rich Nations*, Innocenti Report Card, Issue No. 5, September.

United Nations (1989) *The Convention on the Rights of the Child*, New York: United Nations.

Valentine, G. and Holloway, S. (1997–1998) *'Cyberkids' (Computer file)*, 2nd Edition. Colchester, Essex: UK Data Archive (distributor), 6 October 1999. SN: 4030.

Van der Rijt, G. A. J., Haenenns, L. S. J. and Van Straten, P. (2002) 'Smoking and Other Substance Use as Distinct Features of Teenage Subcultures', *Journal of Adolescent Health*, 31, pp. 433–5.

Vegeris, S. and Perry, J. (2003) *Families and Children 2001: Living standards and children*, Research report No. 190, Leeds: Department for Work and Pensions.

Vogeltanz, N. D., Wilsnack, S. C., Harris, T. R., Wilsnack, R. W., Wonderlich, S. A. and Kristjanson, A. F. (1999) 'Prevalence and risk factors for childhood sexual abuse in women: National survey findings', *Child Abuse & Neglect*, Volume 23, Issue 6, pp. 579–92.

Vostanis, P. and Cumella, S. (1999) *Homeless Children: Problems and needs*, London: Jessica Kingsley.

Vostanis, P. Grattan, E. and Cumella, S. (1998) 'Mental health problems of homeless children and families: A longitudinal study', *British Medical Journal* 316, pp. 899–902.

Vulliamy, G. and Webb, R. (2000) 'Stemming the Tide of Rising School Exclusions: Problems and Possibilities', *British Journal of Educational Studies*, 48 (2), pp. 119–133.

Wade, A. and Smart, C. (2002) *Facing Family Change: Children's circumstances, strategies and resources*, Joseph Rowntree Foundation, York: York Publishing Services.

Wade, H. and Badham, B. (2004) *Hear by Right: Standards for the active involvement of children and young people*, The National Youth Agency and Local Government Association.

Walby, S. and Allen, J. (2004) *Domestic violence, sexual assault and stalking: findings from the British Crime Survey*, Home Office Research Study 276, HORDS.

Walker, M., Hill, M. and Triseliotis, J. (2002) *Testing the Limits of Foster Care: Fostering as an alternative to secure accommodation*, London: British Agencies for Adoption and Fostering.

Ward, J., Henderson, Z. and Pearson, G. (2003) *One Problem Among Many: Drug use among care leavers in transition to independent living*, Research Study 260. London: Home Office.

Wellings, K., Nanchahal, K., MacDowell, S., Erens, B., Mercer, C., Johnson, A., Copas, J., Korovessis, C., Fenton, K. and Field, J. (2001) 'Sexual Behaviour in Britain: Early heterosexual experience', *The Lancet*, 358 (9296), 1843–1850.

Welsh Assembly (2001) *Permanent Exclusions from Schools in Wales*, http://www.wales.gov.uk/keypubstatisticsforwalesheadline/content/education/2001/hdw1002, August 2001.

Welsh Assembly (2002) *National Curriculum Assessments of 7,11 and 14-yr-olds*, Local Education Authorities in Wales, http://www.wales.gov.uk/

keypubstatisticsforwales/content/publication/schools-teach/2002/sdr55-2002.pdf, August 2004.

Welsh Assembly (2003a) *Absenteeism from Secondary Schools in Wales 2002–03*, http://www.wales.gov.uk/keypubstatisticsforwales/content/publication/schools-teach/2003/sdr63-2003/sdr63-2003.pdf, July 2004.

Welsh Assembly (2003b) *Pupils with Statements of Special Educational Needs*, http://www.wales.gov.uk/keypubstatisticsforwales/content/publication/schools-teach/2003/sdr35-2003/sdr35-2003.htm, July, 2004.

Welsh Assembly (2004a) *Assessment and Examination Performance in Wales: Comparison with England and its Regions*, http://www.wales.gov.uk/keypubstatisticsforwales/content/publication/schools-teach/2004/sb33-2004/sb33-2004.pdf, July, 2004.

Welsh Assembly (2004b) *Exclusions from Schools in Wales, 2002/03*, http://www.wales.gov.uk/keypubstatisticsforwales/content/publication/schools-teach/2004/sdr20-2004/sdr20-2004.pdf, July 2004.

Welsh Assembly Government (2003a) *Cymorth: Children and Youth Support Fund – Guidance*, www.wales.gov.uk/subichildren/content/partnership/index.htm

Welsh Assembly Government (2003b) *Early Entitlement: Supporting children and families in Wales*, www.wales.gov.uk/subichildren/content/entitlement/early-entitlement-2004-e.htm

Welsh Assembly Government (2003c) *Third annual Report on Social Inclusion in Wales*.

Welsh Assembly Government (2004a) *Children and Young People: Rights to Action*, Welsh Assembly Government, www.wales.gov.uk/subichildren/toc-e.htm

Welsh Assembly Government (2004b) *National Service Framework for Children, Young People and Maternity Services in Wales*, Consultation Document, Cardiff: Children and Families Directorate, Welsh Assembly Government.

West, P. and Sweeting, H. (2003) 'Fifteen, female and stressed: Changing patterns of psychological distress over time', *Journal of Child Psychology and Psychiatry*, 44, 3, pp. 399–411.

Wheway, R. and Millward, A. (1997) *Child's Play: Facilitating play on housing estates*, London: Chartered Institute of Housing.

Whitehead, B. D. (1997) *Divorce Culture: Rethinking our commitments to marriage and family*, New York: Alfred A. Knopf, Distributed by Random House.

Wilcox, S. (2003) *The UK Housing Review, 2003/04*, Huddersfield: Joseph Rowntree Foundation, Instituted of Chartered Housing, Council of Mortgage Lenders.

Woolley, H., Spencer, C., Dunn, J. and Rowley, G. (1999) 'The Child as Citizen: Experiences of British town and city centres', *Journal of Urban Design*, Vol. 4(3), pp. 255–82.

World Health Organization (2001) *Declaration on Young People and Alcohol*, WHO – www.euro.who.int/aboutwho/policy

World Health Organization (2002a) *Diet, Nutrition and the Prevention of Chronic Diseases*, Joint WHO/FAO expert consultation, Geneva: WHO.

World Health Organization (2002b) *WHO report on violence and health*, Geneva: WHO.

World Health Organization (2004a) *What are the most effective and cost-effective interventions in alcohol control?*, Health Evidence Network Synthesis report, Copenhagen: WHO Europe.

World Health Organization (2004b) *Young People's Health in Context. Health Behaviour in School-aged Children (HBSC) Study: international report from the 2001/2002 survey*, Copenhagen: WHO

Youngblade, L. M. and Dunn, J. (1995) 'Individual differences in young children's pretend play with mother and sibling: Links to relationships and understanding of other people's feelings and beliefs', *Child Development*, Vol. 66, pp. 1472–92.

Youth Justice Board (2003) *Youth Justice – Annual Statistics 2002/03*, London: Youth Justice Board for England and Wales.

Youth Justice Board (2004) *Working with Young Refugees and Asylum Seekers*. http://www.youth-justice-board.gov.uk/PractitionersPortal/Diversity/Refugees

Young Women's Christian Association (YWCA) Briefings (2004) *Pride not prejudice: Young lesbian and bisexual women*. Oxford: YWCA.

Index